THE GREENHAVEN ENCYCLOPEDIA OF

TERRORISM

Other Books in the
Greenhaven Encyclopedia Series

THE GREENHAVEN ENCYCLOPEDIA OF

TERRORISM

by Patricia D. Netzley

Moataz A. Fattah, *Consulting Editor*

GREENHAVEN PRESS
An imprint of Thomson Gale, a part of The Thomson Corporation

THOMSON
━━━✦━━━ ™
GALE

Detroit • New York • San Francisco • New Haven, Conn. • Waterville, Maine • London

Christine Nasso, *Publisher*
Elizabeth Des Chenes, *Managing Editor*

© 2007 Thomson Gale, a part of The Thomson Corporation.

Thomson and Star logo are trademarks and Gale and Greenhaven Press are registered trademarks used herein under license.
For more information, contact:
Greenhaven Press
27500 Drake Rd.
Farmington Hills, MI 48331-3535
Or you can visit our Internet site at http://www.gale.com

Cover photograph reproduced by permission of Ricky Flores/The Journal News/Corbis.

LIBRARY OF CONGRESS CATALOGING-IN-PUBLICATION DATA

Terrorism / Patricia D. Netzley, book editor ; Moataz A. Fattah, consulting editor.
p. cm. (Greenhaven encyclopedia of)
Includes bibliographical references and index.
ISBN-13: 978-0-7377-3235-1 (lib.)
ISBN-10: 0-7377-3235-0 (lib.)
Terrorism--Encyclopedias. I. Netzley, Patricia D. II. Fattah, Moataz A., 1972- III. Title: Terrorism.
HV6431.G735 2007
363.32503--dc22
2007008156

Printed in the United States of America
10 9 8 7 6 5 4 3 2 1

Contents

Dedication

With thanks to Jan Klisz, Andrea Brown, and Raymond, Matthew, Sarah, and Jacob Netzley for their patience during a long and difficult project.

Contents

Contents

The Greenhaven Encyclopedia of Terrorism

Contents

Preface

In recent years, terrorism has become perhaps the central issue in world affairs, with terrorist events mentioned in the media daily. However, scholars, historians, politicians, and others disagree on how to determine what exactly constitutes an act of terrorism. Such acts involve violence, of course, but of what nature and for what reason?

The most common definition of terrorism, of the dozens put forth over the years, is that it involves deliberate attacks on people or property in an attempt to use fear and chaos to force a government to change its policies or a citizenry to bow to the will of the state. But this view ignores the fact that such attacks are sometimes motivated not by a political agenda but out of hatred for a religious or ethnic group, and that even when politics is the reason for an attack, the perpetrators often argue that their motive is connected to a noble purpose. (Thus the old adage: "One man's terrorist is another man's freedom fighter.") And when motives are unclear, it becomes even more difficult to say with any certainty that the actions of a particular organization or person should be categorized as terrorism.

Nonetheless, a survey of literature on the subject shows that certain individuals, groups, places, events, and issues have repeatedly been associated with terrorism, and *The Greenhaven Encyclopedia of Terrorism* has included the most prominent of these. Its more than four hundred entries, then, are not intended to be exhaustive, but they do offer a solid overview for readers who need a starting point for a more thorough examination of terrorism from ancient times to the present. To this end, the work presents information on domestic and international terrorist groups and acts throughout history and throughout the world (although because of the current political climate, slightly more emphasis is placed on terrorism arising from the Middle East) and discusses various types of terrorism, including state terrorism, non-state, or dissident, terrorism, religious terrorism, criminal terrorism, and right-wing versus left-wing terrorism, along with terrorists' methods and motivations. The work also offers biographical information on terrorists and on those people and agencies attempting to prevent terrorism, as well as details about issues and policies related to terrorist acts. After studying this material, the reader should come away with a deeper understanding of terrorism and the difficulties of defining and combating it.

Abu Nidal Organization (ANO)

Originally part of the Palestine Liberation Organization (PLO) and its efforts to further the creation of an independent Palestinian state, the Abu Nidal Organization (ANO) was one of the most prominent terrorist groups of the 1970s and 1980s. Under the leadership of its founder Sabri al-Banna (also known as Abu Nidal)—a Palestinian who in 1948, at the age of eleven, had been forced to flee his homeland when Israel assumed control—the group split from the PLO in 1974 to redirect its efforts toward pan-Arabism, which argues that all Arabs should be united in a single state regardless of national borders. Shortly thereafter ANO began receiving financial support from Iraq, then ruled by Saddam Hussein, in exchange for performing terrorist acts against Iraq's enemies in Syria, but in 1983, after a falling out with Hussein, ANO began working for Syria instead. The group was also receiving money from Libya, and in 1987 it established a headquarters there, with a training center south of Tripoli, while continuing to engage in terrorist activities for a variety of sponsors. This work enabled the group to make business and real-estate investments worth an estimated $400 million in 1988.

Though based at various times in Lebanon, Sudan, Libya, Iraq, and Syria, ANO recruited members from nearly every Arab country. By the mid-1980s it had over five hundred members, organized into four- or five-person cells that conducted operations in over twenty European and Middle Eastern countries under various names, including the Arab Revolutionary Council and the Fatah Revolutionary Council. These activities resulted in the death or injury of over nine hundred people.

There is some evidence that ANO collaborated with al Fatah, Yasir Arafat's faction of the PLO, in the Black September massacre of eleven Israeli athletes at the 1972 Olympic Games in Munich, Germany. However, ANO's leader, al-Banna, also masterminded attacks designed to thwart Arafat's attempts, along with Jordan's king Hussein, to reach an agreement with Israel regarding the fate of Palestinian territories taken by Israel. For example, in 1978, al-Banna ordered the assassination of Sa'id Hammami, the PLO's representative in London, England, because he had been making concessions in his political negotiations with Israel.

ANO's most notorious operation was the November 23, 1985, hijacking of a Boeing 737 aircraft en route from Athens, Greece, to Cairo, Egypt, with ninety-eight passengers and crew members. Three ANO terrorists took over this flight, EgyptAir 648, and forced it to land in Luqa, Malta, where they killed two Israeli and three American passengers—three outright and two when Maltese authorities refused to refuel the plane after twelve hours of negotiation. Shortly thereafter, an Egyptian counterterrorist group, Force 777, used explosives to blast a hole in the plane's roof, intending to drop inside to rescue the hostages. Instead, the explosion killed twenty passengers and triggered a gun battle between terrorists and counterterrorists. This struggle lasted six hours and left fifty-seven passengers dead; witnesses later accused the counterterrorists of shooting passengers who ran from the plane.

Three other notable ANO operations occurred in the mid-1980s. On December 27, 1985, members of the group used hand grenades and firearms to kill seventeen people and injure over one hundred at airport terminals in Rome, Italy, and Vienna, Austria. On September 6, 1986, they killed twenty-two worshippers at a synagogue in Istanbul, Turkey, and that same day murdered another twenty-one people and wounded over one hundred more while firing assault rifles in an attempt to hijack a Pan Am Boeing 747 at the Karachi airport in Pakistan. The two 1986 incidents were, according to ANO, acts of retaliation for Israel's recent attack on a terrorist base in Lebanon.

ANO also assassinated a few dignitaries from Jordan and, in response, the Jordanian government aggressively pursued the group during the late 1980s. Around that same time, ANO's leader, al-Banna, allegedly killed several ANO members whom he suspected of plotting to overthrow him. Whether because of these internal problems or Jordan's counterterrorism efforts, ANO's attacks ended in 1991, though some terrorism experts believe they are ongoing. Its last-known headquarters, as of December 1998, was in Baghdad, Iraq, where in 2002 al-Banna was found dead in his apartment. Iraqi officials announced that al-Banna had committed suicide, even though he had several gunshot wounds; according to rumor, he was killed in a shoot-out with Iraqi security forces.

SEE ALSO: Black September; Hussein, Saddam; Munich Olympics crisis; Palestine Liberation Organization

Abu Sayyaf (Bearer of the Sword)

Comprised of Muslim insurgents and based on the island of Basilan in the southern Philippines, the Abu Sayyaf (Bearer of the Sword) group engaged in kidnapping, extortion, and drug trafficking, both for profit and to support its efforts to create an independent Muslim state within the Philippines (where approximately 5 percent of the population is Muslim), during the early 1990s. Terrorism experts disagree on whether the group originated as a part of another Filipino Muslim group, the Moro Islamic Liberation Front (MILF), or whether it developed independently from a small group of guerrillas. In either case, its founder was Abdurajak Abubakar Janjalania, a Filipino Muslim who had fought in the 1979 *jihad*, or holy war, against Soviets invading Afghanistan. While in Afghanistan, Janjalania apparently met Osama bin Laden, whose terrorist network, al Qaeda, later offered financial support, manpower, and terrorist training to Janjalania's Abu Sayyaf group. (Some terrorism experts believe that other Middle Eastern terrorist groups supported Abu Sayyaf as well.)

But despite this support, when Abu Sayyaf began its terrorist activities, it concentrated on actions that would bring in money, such as raiding villages and kidnapping and ransoming wealthy Filipinos; often the group killed its hostages after being paid to release them. Soon, however, Abu Sayyaf was also conducting assassinations and bombings. During the mid-1990s, the group claimed to have thousands of members, although terrorism experts generally believe there were only two hundred to five hundred followers.

In December 1998, the group's leader, Janjalania, was killed in a gun battle with Philippine police, but despite this loss, Abu Sayyaf conducted its most notorious terrorist actions in 2000 and 2001. In March 2000 it orchestrated a raid on a school, where twenty-seven children and teachers were held hostage until an army attack forced the terrorists to flee with five of the hostages. (Four terrorists were killed during the attack; ten hostages were injured.) In April 2000 on the Malaysian island of Sipidan, the group kidnapped twenty-three people, including foreign tourists and journalists, holding them for ransom for months while negotiating their release. Abu Sayyaf used the ransom money, estimated to be as much as $25 million, to purchase guns and boats, and in May 2001 the group kidnapped another twenty people, again holding them for ransom. The following month, group members beheaded an American hostage after failing to receive their demands. As a result of this act and Abu Sayyaf's known connection with al Qaeda, shortly after the September 11, 2001, terrorist attacks on the United States, the U.S. government provided the Philippine government with $100 million and military training to further its efforts to eliminate Abu Sayyaf. By 2002 hundreds of the group's members had been killed or driven from the country, and terrorism experts disagree on whether it remains a viable organization today.

SEE ALSO: bin laden, Osama; Philippines, the; September 11 attacks on America

Achille Lauro, the

On October 7, 1985, four terrorists from the Palestine Liberation Front (PLF) took over the Italian cruise ship *Achille Lauro* en route from Genoa, Italy, to Ashod, Is-

rael. The terrorists' original plan was to hide on the ship until it reached Israel, then hold any Israeli passengers hostage while demanding the release of fifty Palestinians imprisoned in Israel. However, when a crewman entered the terrorists' cabin and saw them with their weapons, the terrorists then felt compelled to take action. They immediately seized the ship and held its 427 passengers and 80 crew members hostage for two days, separating them by nationality and threatening to blow up the ship. To show that their threats were serious, they killed a wheelchair-bound Jewish American, sixty-nine-year-old Leon Klinghoffer, and threw him overboard.

Terrorism experts believe that the hijacking of the *Achille Lauro* was in retaliation for an Israeli air attack on the Palestine Liberation Organization's (PLO) headquarters in Tunis, Tunisia, on October 1, 1985, which killed at least fifty PLO members. The PLF had strong ties with the PLO, and the PLF's leader, Abu Abbas, served on the PLO executive committee. Consequently when the *Achille Lauro* docked in Cairo, Egypt, and Egyptian officials began negotiating for the hostages' release, Abbas, who was not on board the ship, was involved in the negotiations. Eventually it was agreed that Egypt would supply the terrorists with an airplane that would fly them, and Abbas, to Tunis in exchange for the release of the hostages. Once the terrorists were in the air, however, U.S. fighter planes forced it to land at a NATO (North Atlantic Treaty Organization) air base in Sicily, Italy, even though this action was a violation of international law.

The U.S. government intended for Abbas as well as the four terrorists to be arrested for their roles in the *Achille Lauro* incident, but the Italian government released Abbas, who then fled to Yugoslavia while the four terrorists were tried in Rome, Italy, and sentenced to lengthy prison terms. A subsequent international outcry convinced Italy to sentence Abbas in absentia to life in prison, and an international warrant was issued for his arrest. Nonetheless, he was never taken into custody, although he traveled openly and even appeared in television interviews, and when the warrant expired it was never reissued. Meanwhile, the international community condemned the PLO, believing the organization had been connected to the *Achille Lauro* affair and therefore also to the murder of an innocent, helpless man. In response to this widespread condemnation, in November 1985 Yasir Arafat issued the Cairo Declaration, which stated that the PLO officially opposed any terrorist acts taking place outside of Israel or Israeli-held lands and made it clear that the PLO did not support violence against innocent people. In addition, while insisting that it had not been involved in the *Achille Lauro* affair, the PLO paid an undisclosed sum to Leon Klinghoffer's family in 1997 to compensate them for his death.

SEE ALSO: Arafat, Yasir; hijackings, aircraft; Palestine Liberation Organization

Action Directe (AD)

Also called Direct Action, Action Directe is a French terrorist group, founded in 1979, responsible for at least fifty anti-American and anti-NATO (North Atlantic Treaty Organization) attacks during the 1980s. For example, in 1985 the group planted a bomb at a U.S. air base in Germany, killing two Americans, and subsequently bombed a U.S. missile site. Most of these attacks were intended to show support for the creation of an independent Palestinian state. Moreover the group used the Palestine Liberation Organization (PLO) as a model to try to unite several leftist European terrorist groups under one organization. To this end, from 1985 to 1987 Action Directe worked in cooperation with three other anti-American terrorist groups in Europe: the Red Army Faction of Germany, the Red Brigades of Italy, and the Communist Combat Cells of Belgium. However, Action Directe has not committed any acts of terrorism since the 1990s, and terrorism experts now believe that the group is defunct.

SEE ALSO: Palestine Liberation Organization; Red Army Faction; Red Brigades

Afghanistan, U.S. bombings in

The United States has twice launched bombing attacks on Afghanistan in retaliation for terrorist attacks perpetrated by Afghanistan-based Islamic extremists believed to be part of Osama bin Laden's al Qaeda terrorist network. The first such U.S. attacks, which were in response to terrorist bombings of U.S. embassies in Kenya and Tanzania, took place in August 1998, when American ships in the Arabian Sea and the Red Sea fired missiles at six suspected terrorist bases in Afghanistan near its border with Pakistan. The ships' missiles also intentionally destroyed a pharmaceutical factory in Sudan. Many criticized this act because the target had no clear connection to al Qaeda, though U.S. officials insisted that chemicals from the factory were being produced for al Qaeda operatives to make chemical weapons. The second wave of U.S. bombings in Afghanistan took place in October 2001 as an immediate response to al Qaeda's September 11, 2001, attacks on America. This time the United States acted in cooperation with several other countries, but primarily Great Britain, to bomb Afghanistan and send ground troops into the country. Within two months these forces had captured the cities of Kabul and Kandahar and replaced the religious regime running Afghanistan, the Taliban, with a new, interim government supported by the United States.

SEE ALSO: al Qaeda; September 11 attacks on America; Taliban

Africa, terrorism in postcolonial

In the eighteenth and nineteenth centuries, Europeans from such countries as Great Britain, France, Italy, and Germany established colonies throughout Africa, using brutality to subjugate the native populations in these lands. When colonial rule ended, the former colonies were without clear leadership, and native tribes that had been at odds with one another for decades fought over control of each region. This fighting involved guerrilla warfare, terrorism, and atrocities that included torture, mutilation, and the destruction of entire villages by burning down homes and poisoning water sources. In some areas, the violence became so severe that natives welcomed help from European forces. But even with outside intervention, Africa's problems continued. Civil war and ethnic violence, including genocide, as well as terrorist attacks continue to take place in various parts of the continent. The African continent averaged ten terrorist attacks a year throughout the 1990s, including the bombings of U.S. embassies in Kenya and Tanzania in 1998, the murder of three Spanish workers and the injury of one American worker for the international aid society Doctors of the World in Rwanda in 1997, and the murder of eight American and British tourists visiting a gorilla

preserve along the border of the Congo and Uganda in 1999.

Rwanda. The tourist attack was related to a conflict between two tribes in Rwanda, the Hutu and the Tutsi. Prior to 1994, the Hutu were in control of Rwanda and engaged in the genocide of over five hundred thousand Tutsi in an attempt to prevent them from gaining control of the country. Eventually, however, Tutsi rebels drove the Hutus from power, and the Hutus who had been involved in the genocide fled to neighboring countries. Those in the Congo formed the Army for the Liberation of Rwanda (ALIR), which conducts terrorist operations from camps along the Congo-Rwanda border. It was this group that killed the tourists at the gorilla preserve in 1999, after demanding that the United States and Great Britain stop supporting the Rwandan government.

Uganda. During the late 1990s, Rwandan terrorists also attacked tourists as well as civilians in Uganda, striking at them from bases in the Congo. In 1999, for example, Rwandan terrorists kidnapped fourteen Western tourists in the Bwindi National Forest, killing eight before releasing the remainder. In the 1970s Uganda endured domestic terrorism under dictator Idi Amin, who was responsible for anywhere from one hundred thousand to five hundred thousand deaths during a brutal regime that included mass executions of political opponents and members of rival tribes.

Angola, Nigeria, and Sierra Leone. Foreign tourists have also been attacked in Angola, Nigeria, and Sierra Leone. In Angola, guerrillas from a group called the National Union for the Total Independence of Angola (UNITA) have primarily targeted aid workers, while the Cabinda Liberation Front-Cabinda Armed Forces (FLEC-FAC) has most often attacked corporate workers. In Nigeria oil workers are common targets of the many groups struggling to control the country's natural resources, although the groups target one another as well. In Sierra Leone in 1999 the Revolutionary United Front (RUF) kidnapped several missionaries, while also committing terrorist acts against civilians that they perceived as supporting government policies.

Somalia. Foreigners were also targets in Somalia in the 1990s, when a prolonged drought caused severe famine across much of the country. To alleviate this crisis, the United Nations (UN) sent aid workers, food, and supplies into the region guarded by UN and U.S. troops. Various clans immediately began fighting over control of these resources, and the situation deteriorated into guerrilla warfare. In 1993 guerrillas killed twenty-four UN soldiers and, in a separate incident, fifteen U.S. soldiers, which resulted in the pullout of U.S. forces in 1994. In 1999 twenty guerrillas kidnapped UN and European aid workers in the village of Elayo, releasing them unharmed shortly thereafter. Today rival clans continue to fight over control of resources in the country, which is now called the Republic of Somaliland.

However, warfare has been a part of life in Somalia ever since the country achieved its independence from Great Britain, France, and Italy in 1960. At that time, a nomadic tribe of Somalis living in northeastern Ethiopia demanded that their land, the Ogaden, be included in the new Somali Republic. When the Ethiopians refused to allow this, the Somali Republic funded a guerrilla force, the Western Somalia Liberation Front (WSLF), which engaged in terrorist attacks against Ethiopians in the Ogaden. By May 1977 a full-scale war had developed between the Ethiopian army and the WSLF, the latter of which was soon joined by Somali army forces. Before the year's end, the Ogaden was under the control of Somalia. However, the Soviets, who had been supporting Somalia in this conflict, suddenly decided to support Ethiopia instead, after Ethiopians ousted their pro-U.S. government in favor of an anti-U.S. one. As a result, the Soviets stopped supplying Somalia with military aid, and the Ethiopians, with help from Soviet and Cuban forces, were able to regain control of the Ogaden in March 1978. In 1982 Ethiopian guerrillas began engaging in terrorist attacks against the Somali government, and in 1988 they invaded northern Somalia. The resulting yearlong civil war killed over ten thousand people, and violence continued to plague the region even after the Somali government drove the Ethiopians from the country.

Ethiopia. In addition to its war with Somalia over control of the Ogaden, Ethiopia fought a civil war against rebels fighting for the independence of Eritrea, a land of approximately 4 million people that was annexed by Ethiopia's ruler, Haile Selassie, in 1962. (Prior to this, beginning in the nineteenth century, Eritrea had been under Italian colonial rule, though the United Nations granted it limited autonomy in 1952.) Shortly before the annexation, a largely Muslim guerrilla group called the Eritrean Liberation Front (ELF) established itself in a remote mountain area of Eritrea. During the 1960s the group set up terrorist bases in numerous rural villages from which it could launch attacks on Ethiopian forces and government officials. In response, the government destroyed villages in those areas where the ELF was active, sometimes killing the people living there. This violence brought many Christians into the Eritrean independence movement, and when they had difficulty fitting into ELF, some formed another guerrilla group: the Eritrean People's Liberation Front (EPLF). Though ELF and EPLF were sometimes at odds, they were able to work together to fight the Ethiopian army, which grew even more committed to holding on to Eritrea after Selassie's regime fell in 1974 and a revolutionary council, the Dergue, took over. By 1985, however, the Dergue had nearly destroyed both groups. Then EPLF created an army, the Eritrean People's Liberation Army (EPLA), and began recruiting and training soldiers, over one-third of them women. For supplies, the group raided or captured Ethiopian army weaponry, equipment, and provisions, and it focused on destroying communications systems and any equipment it could not capture. Meanwhile, it continued its recruitment efforts, and eventually comprised more than one hundred thousand members from all nine of Eritrea's ethnic groups. These forces, combined with a growing amount of weaponry, enabled the EPLA to advance across the landscape, establishing bases as it went. Finally in 1983 the EPLA abandoned guerrilla warfare for open warfare with Ethiopian forces. After several EPLA victories, the Dergue became short of manpower, and it began conscripting both men and boys into its army. These untrained, unwilling soldiers were no match for the well-trained EPLA soldiers who had volunteered to fight for their freedom, and in 1991 the EPLA won the war and Eritrea's independence.

South Africa. In South Africa, a different type of struggle was taking place. From 1948 until the early 1990s, an all-white government ruled the country, even though most of the population was black

or of mixed race. This all-white government—comprised primarily of Afrikaners (the descendants of the Dutch who colonized the country in the seventeenth century) and the ancestors of British colonists—established a collection of laws and policies that enforced racial segregation under a system known as apartheid. One of these laws was that every black person was required to carry an identification card, which the police could demand to see at any time and for no reason. In March 1960 a crowd led by members of two groups dedicated to fighting for racial equality in South Africa, the nonviolent African National Congress (ANC) and the violent Pan-Africanist Congress, publicly protested this law, and the police fired at them, killing sixty-seven blacks and injuring over two hundred. Angered at this brutality, thousands of black South Africans rioted and marched in the streets, and the government responded by arresting as many ANC and Pan-Africanist Congress members as it could find, including ANC leader Nelson Mandela. Although the Pan-Africanist Congress did not recover from this assault, the ANC created a military branch, known as the Umkhonto we Sizwe (Spear of the Nation), whose purpose was to strike back at the government through terrorism directed primarily at property. This group was largely ineffective.

During the early 1970s another force, the Black Consciousness movement, attempted to influence South African politics through nonviolent political demonstrations. This effort was also ineffective, because it only resulted in more police brutality. In June 1976 a Black Consciousness–led protest—this time against the government's decision to force black schoolchildren to learn Afrikaans, the language of the Dutch white minority—

sparked rioting throughout South Africa, and hundreds of blacks were killed. Afterward, the ANC and the Umkhonto we Sizwe gained many new members and established bases outside of South Africa, where it trained guerrillas and planned terrorist attacks, but these forces still were no match for the South African police. In most cases, terrorist attacks ended with the terrorists either arrested or dead.

Nonetheless, in 1984 the ANC led several protests against the government, and in October their efforts incited riots in the Vaal Triangle, a region encompassing the cities of Johannesburg and Pretoria, and over forty thousand mine workers there went on strike. Violence broke out when police tried to force them back to work, and the South African government sent the military into the region. Thousands of troops were deployed, but the violence quickly spread to other areas. In 1985 it reached the Cape Province, where police interpreted a funeral procession as a protest and shot at its participants, killing twenty innocent blacks. The military subsequently fired on other gatherings of blacks in the Cape, killing more than a thousand within the next three months. The ANC retaliated with terrorist bombings, often leaving bombs in trash cans around tourist areas. Meanwhile black workers continued to protest and to stage strikes, and police brutality escalated. Arrests also increased; during 1986 over thirty thousand blacks, including children, had been jailed. The country would have continued on this course had it not been for political leader F.W. de Klerk, who took over the government of South Africa in 1989. He ended apartheid and partnered with Nelson Mandela, after releasing him from prison, to establish a political system shared by blacks and whites. In 1994 blacks were finally allowed to vote, and Mandela and de Klerk were elected president and vice president, respectively.

SEE ALSO: Amin, Idi; apartheid; Rwandan genocide; Somalian terrorism and the Mogadishu incident

agricultural terrorism

Also called agroterrorism, agricultural terrorism involves attacks on crops, livestock, farm equipment, and farms. Ecoterrorists have engaged in such attacks to protest the use of pesticides, while animal-rights activists have employed agricultural terrorism to fight against large-scale housing projects and the slaughtering of farm animals. However, the damage that these individuals have caused has been minor and localized, whereas more militant terrorists have attempted to use agricultural terrorism to disrupt food production, distribution, and trade on a wider scale. For example, in Israel in 1978 Palestinian terrorists injected oranges with cyanide, hoping to destroy the Israeli fruit-exporting trade. Governments have employed similar tactics; for example, during World War I, Germany sent livestock intentionally infected with a disease known as anthrax to enemy countries, and several nations, including the United States, have engaged in research projects designed to detect whether biological agents, such as fungi that attack rice, could be used as an agricultural weapon in wartime. Experts in terrorism have warned that countries throughout the world are extremely vulnerable to agricultural terrorism, because there is no way to make a nation's food supply tamper-proof. But such experts have also noted that given government policies regarding quarantining contaminated foods and diseased livestock, such an attack would probably be contained before causing serious damage. Indeed, this has been the case with natural outbreaks of hoof-and-mouth disease among livestock in the United States and Great Britain, where government authorities have acted quickly to prevent livestock from affected areas from being transported outside those areas.

SEE ALSO: animal-rights movement; ecoterrorism

Air India Flight 182

While en route from Toronto, Canada, to London, England, on June 23, 1985, Air India Flight 182, which originated in Vancouver, Canada, and was ultimately destined for New Delhi, India, exploded at an altitude of 31,000 feet (9.4m) over the Atlantic Ocean. That same day, another bomb exploded in the baggage area of Tokyo's Narita Airport, killing two people and wounding four, after the luggage had been unloaded from an Air India flight arriving from Vancouver. An investigation subsequently revealed that the same man had booked passage on both flights in Vancouver, putting a suitcase on each plane but not boarding either flight himself. Terrorism experts generally believe that this man was Talwinder Singh Paramar, a member of a Sikh extremist group known as the Babbar Khalsa Society, and that the bombings were in response to a 1984 attack by the Indian government on a Sikh shrine, a militant stronghold called the Golden Temple, in Amritsar, India. But although the Canadian government arrested Paramar for the crime, they could not build a case against him and eventually he was released. They were, however, ultimately able to convict one of Paramar's associates, Inderjet Singh Reyat, for constructing the bombs.

SEE ALSO: hijackings, aircraft; Sikh extremists

airport security measures

Airports throughout the world have long taken various precautions to prevent people from carrying weapons onto domestic and international flights. However, after the September 11, 2001, terrorist attacks on America, in which airplanes were hijacked and flown into buildings, the precautions increased in both number and severity, especially in the United States. For example, airport security personnel refused to allow people without a ticket for an upcoming flight into the airport terminal on any given day, which meant that passengers could not be accompanied by others at departure or arrival gates. Also, tickets had to be purchased in person rather than electronically, and airports implemented strict security procedures while checking in both passengers and baggage. Before entering boarding areas, passengers had to subject themselves and their luggage to searches for weapons or bombs; both people and bags were scanned with metal detectors and other devices and, in some cases, hand searched as well. Passengers also had to present their shoes for inspection, because shortly after September 11, terrorist Richard Reid tried to smuggle explosives on board a plane in the heel of his shoe (an act which earned him the nickname "the Shoe Bomber"). Initially, airport personnel confiscated any item that could be used as a weapon, including such seemingly innocuous objects as bamboo knitting needles, but as more time passed following September 11, airports began loosening some of their restrictions. For example, knitting needles were once again allowed on most flights and tickets could once again be purchased

After the terrorist attacks on September 11, 2001, airport security tightened to prevent further hijack attempts. MARY ANN CHASTAIN. © AP IMAGES

electronically. However, these changes were not instituted uniformly, and today there is no common consensus on which security measures should be followed and to what degree. In most European airports, for example, nonticketed companions are still not allowed to accompany passengers to their departure gates, whereas in the United States most airports allow this practice (primarily because restricted access hurt sales at shops and restaurants). Regardless of how many security precautions an airport takes, investigative journalists and security testers have still managed to get weapons past airport screeners, particularly in the United States. Because of this, some people believe that the U.S. government, rather than airport managers, should take control of securing the nation's airports, while others argue that no one can prevent a determined terrorist from finding a way to thwart security measures.

SEE ALSO: Reid, Richard; September 11 attacks on America

al-Zarqawi, Abu Musab (1966–)

One of the most prominent leaders of the terrorist group al Qaeda, Jordanian Islamic terrorist Abu Musab al-Zarqawi has been credited with killing at least seven hundred people in Iraq during its occupation by U.S. forces, using bombs to target Iraqi and American soldiers, American civilians working in Iraq, and large groups of Iraqi civilians. Terrorism experts believe that al-Zarqawi masterminded the bombing of the United Nations (UN) headquarters in Iraq in August 2003, and in May 2004, a voice suspected to be al-Zarqawi's was heard on a videotape showing the execution of an American hostage, Nicholas Berg, taken in Iraq. In September 2004 al-Zarqawi declared war on all Muslims in Iraq because of their willingness to accept American occupation without a struggle, and in October 2004 he acknowledged his connection to al Qaeda, though continuing to serve as the leader of his own terrorist group, Jama'at al-Tawhid wal Jihad (Unification and Holy War Group). Al-Zarqawi formed this group, which was once a rival to al Qaeda, sometime in the mid-1990s. It was originally dedicated to turning the country of Jordan into an Islamic state, and its early actions were attacks on Jordanian targets. For example, Jordanian authorities believed that al-Zarqawi was responsible for the bombing of a Radisson hotel in Amman, Jordan, in 1991, and they sentenced him to death in absentia for this crime, as well as for funding the assassination of U.S. diplomat Laurence Foley in Jordan in 2002. After al Qaeda's September 11, 2001, attacks on the United States, al-Zarqawi briefly moved his base of operations to Afghanistan before establishing it in Iraq. Throughout 2005 there were rumors that al-Zarqawi had been seriously injured or perhaps killed in an attack by U.S. forces there, but in January 2006 he released a videotape proving he was still alive. U.S. officials do not know where he is currently located.

SEE ALSO: al Qaeda; September 11 attacks on America

al-Zawahiri, Dr. Ayman (1951–)

One of the leaders of the terrorist group al Qaeda, physician Ayman al-Zawahiri became involved with this organization after first being a member of another terrorist group, the radical Egyptian Islamic Jihad, which he joined in 1979. Al-Zawahiri was one of the leaders of this group as well, helping to plan its attacks on the government of Egypt and recruiting many new members. Consequently he was arrested as a suspect in the 1981 assassination of Egyptian president Anwar Sadat. Though he could not be connected to this act, he was sentenced to three years in prison for

having illegal weapons; he subsequently traveled to Afghanistan, where he worked as a physician for Arabs fighting a Soviet invasion. In 1989, after this conflict was over, al-Zawahiri returned to Egypt, where he again became an aggressive recruiter for Islamic Jihad. Soon, though, he feared another arrest, so in 1992 he left Egypt permanently, first traveling to Sudan and then to Afghanistan, where he joined with the founder of al Qaeda, Osama bin Laden, to create another terrorist group, the World Islamic Front for Jihad Against Jews and Crusaders. In 1997 al-Zawahiri was involved in planning a terrorist attack in Luxor, Egypt, in which fifty-eight tourists were killed. Two years later the Egyptian government convicted him in absentia of this crime and several other acts of terrorism Because of his connection to al Qaeda, al-Zawahiri is wanted by the U.S. government as well.

SEE ALSO: al Qaeda; bin laden, Osama; Sadat, Anwar

al Aqsa Martyrs Brigade

Founded in 2000 by at least seven men in a Palestinian refugee camp, the al Aqsa Martyrs Brigade has committed dozens of suicide bombings, car bombings, and sniper attacks against Israeli civilians in the West Bank from 2000 to 2002. The group's formation was triggered by an event in September 2000: Israeli prime minister Ariel Sharon, accompanied by over a thousand security officers, made a symbolic visit to Jerusalem's al Aqsa Mosque, which was located on a site considered holy by Jews as well as Muslims. Palestinians regarded this act to be a violation, and they immediately began an *Intifadeh* (shaking off), or uprising, against Israeli occupation of their land. As a result, the al Aqsa Martyrs Brigade was able to recruit martyrs—that is, people willing to commit suicide bombings—from other Palestinian terrorist groups, and it allied itself with one of the most powerful of these groups, al Fatah. The group's last-known terrorist act was a suicide bombing on March 30, 2002, committed by a sixteen-year-old girl named Ayat A-Akhras, that killed three (including the bomber) and wounded twenty-two in a Jerusalem supermarket.

SEE ALSO: al Fatah; martyrs

al Fatah

Founded in 1959 by Yasir Arafat, who later became the leader of the Palestine Liberation Organization (PLO), al Fatah (Victory) is both a terrorist group and a political party in Palestine. The terrorist group began as a loose network of Palestinian terrorists advocating the destruction of Israel. During the 1960s the group became well organized, increased its membership through the publication of a magazine, *Our Palestine: The Call to Life*, and gained the support of Syria, though it insisted that all of its members be Palestinian. (This position ran contrary to the prevailing notion in the Muslim world at the time that all Arabs, regardless of country, should work together for Arab causes.) Al Fatah also established training camps in Jordan and Lebanon, from which it launched attacks on Israel. These attacks intensified after 1967, when Israel took over the West Bank, the Gaza Strip, and other areas that had previously belonged to Palestine. However, during the 1970s, having joined the PLO in 1969, al Fatah was expelled from Jordan because of a political dispute between that country's leaders and the PLO. Al Fatah also had to abandon its Lebanese training camps when Israel invaded Lebanon in 1982. The group's relationship with Syria then strengthened, while its relationship with Arafat grew strained. In fact, in the 1980s al Fatah tried unsuccessfully to wrestle control of the PLO from Arafat, with support from Syria. Nonetheless the group remained a part of the PLO.

In the late 1980s moderate members of al Fatah formed a political party that quickly became the leading force in the PLO. Under Yasir Arafat's leadership, it remained the most powerful entity in Palestinian politics for more than forty years, but it was also extremely corrupt. Consequently in 2006, after Israel relinquished control of the Gaza Strip to the Palestinians, the al Fatah party failed in an election to establish the first Palestinian Parliament, putting the newly created government, the Palestinian Authority, under the control of the radical terrorist group Hamas. By this time, al Fatah had renounced violence and its leader, Mahmoud Abbas, had been elected president of the Palestinian Authority with the support of the Western world. (Abbas took control of the Fatah party after Arafat died in 2004.) However, after the announcement of the results of this election, in which Hamas received seventy-six seats in Parliament to al Fatah's forty-three, al Fatah threatened to end its participation in the coalition government rather than work with Hamas, even though Abbas agreed to remain president.

In February 2007, leaders of both sides struck an agreement to work together to establish a Palestinian provisional government. A cease-fire was declared, but just days later a battle broke out in the Gaza Strip between members of the two factions, using grenade launchers, assault rifles, and rockets. Dozens of people were killed or injured, two universities were damaged by fire, and a radio station was blown up.

SEE ALSO: Arafat, Yasir; Hamas; Palestine Liberation Organization

al Jihad

Also called Egyptian Islamic Jihad or the Jihad Group, al Jihad has been in close partnership with another terrorist group, al Qaeda, since 1998, and many terrorism experts believe that it was involved in al Qaeda's September 11, 2001 attacks on America. Al Jihad was definitely behind the assassination of Egyptian president Anwar Sadat in 1981, and it attempted to assassinate Egypt's prime minister Atef Sedky and interior minister Hassan al Alfi in 1993. Since its inception in the 1970s, al Jihad has advocated violence against secular officials in Egypt, hoping that the country will eventually fall under the control of Islamic fundamentalists. In response, during the 1990s the Egyptian government tracked down and tortured many members of al Jihad, but instead of destroying the group, this tactic drove al Jihad to partner with al Qaeda and to choose targets outside of Egypt, particularly Egyptian embassies. For example, in 1995 al Jihad bombed an Egyptian embassy in Pakistan. By some estimates, al Jihad currently has nearly a thousand members, divided into two factions. The most radical of the two is led by Ayman al Zawahiri, a close confidant of al Qaeda leader Osama bin Laden.

SEE ALSO: al Qaeda; bin laden, Osama; Egypt, terrorism in; Sadat, Anwar

al Qaeda

al Qaeda (The Base) is perhaps the most notorious terrorist network in the world today, having gained fame for its involve-ment in the September 11, 2001, terrorist attacks on the World Trade Center in New York. It is a loose collection of terrorist cells, located throughout the world, each operating independently though with a shared purpose: to unite all Muslims in a holy war against Westerners, particularly Americans. Terrorism experts disagree on just how many al Qaeda members there are, but the prevailing view is that there are no more than fifty thousand. Experts also disagree on how many cells there are; how large each cell is; how they are organized, both individually and within the hierarchy of the network; how closely each cell remains in contact with al Qaeda's governing council; and what the nature of that council is. Terrorist experts know, however, that the idea of the terrorist network originated with Saudi Arabian terrorist Osama bin Laden and Palestinian terrorist Abdullah Azzam. In 1984 the two men, both Islamic fundamentalists, began financing and training terrorists to fight against the Soviets occupying Afghanistan, establishing training camps in Pakistan. (As the son of a millionaire, bin laden had ample funds for these efforts.) In 1989, after the Soviets left Afghanistan and Azzam was killed by a car bomb, bin laden directed his terrorists to defend Muslims and fight the infidels elsewhere in the world, choosing targets as they saw fit.

Shortly thereafter, bin laden left Afghanistan for his native Saudi Arabia, where he became an outspoken critic of the Saudi government because he believed that its rulers had strayed too far from the tenets of Islam. He also condemned the Saudi royal family for associating closely with the American government. Eventually his verbal attacks, some of which were broadcast publicly, so angered the Saudi royals that bin laden feared for his family's

Members of al Qaeda pose during a military training exercise. © AFP/CORBIS

safety, and in April 1991 he relocated, along with his many wives and children, to Sudan, where he established several al Qaeda terrorist training camps. Over the next five years, these camps trained thousands of terrorists and inspired the creation of several other Muslim terrorist groups.

In 1993 the Saudi government took steps to prevent bin laden from accessing his personal fortune there, but this did not stop al Qaeda from operating. In fact, throughout the 1990s al Qaeda continued to attract and train new recruits who subsequently established terrorist cells in countries throughout the world, where they conducted various acts of terrorism. In 1993, for example, terrorists trained by al Qaeda were linked to the deaths of eighteen U.S. soldiers in Somalia (shot down

over the city of Mogadishu) and six people in a World Trade Center bombing that injured over a thousand. After several more terrorist attacks had been linked to al Qaeda, the Sudanese government decided that its association with the terrorist group was politically unwise, and in 1997 it expelled bin laden from the country. He then established a new base of operations in Afghanistan, where most experts in terrorism believe he remains today.

From Afghanistan, bin laden has directed members of his network to kill Americans whenever and wherever possible. In 1998 al Qaeda was responsible for the bombings of two U.S. embassies in East Africa, and afterward the United States bombed al Qaeda training camps in Afghanistan, as well as a site the U.S. government believed to be an al Qaeda chemical-weapons factory in Sudan. This did not deter al Qaeda, which plotted (but did not successfully carry out) several millenium bombings (i.e., bombings that would take place on the stroke of midnight on New Year's Eve 1999) and used suicide bombers to attack an American battleship, the USS *Cole*, in Yemen in October 2000. The following year, on September 11, al Qaeda carried out its infamous attacks on the World Trade Center in New York and the Pentagon in Washington, D.C. In response, the United States again bombed Afghanistan, this time with much more force, and by October 7 it had taken control of the country. Nonetheless bin laden escaped capture, and the al Qaeda network remains intact, though probably weakened.

SEE ALSO: Afghanistan, U.S. bombings in; bin laden, Osama; cells, terrorist; *Cole*, USS; September 11 attacks on America

Alcohol, Tobacco, and Firearms (ATF), U.S. Bureau of

A federal agency, the U.S. Bureau of Alcohol, Tobacco, and Firearms (ATF) enforces laws related to firearms and explosives, as well as to the sale of alcohol and tobacco, which means that it is involved in efforts to apprehend terrorists. To this end, it tracks the sale of bombs and investigates bomb sites. For example, ATF agents were involved in tracking down the terrorists who bombed the World Trade Center in 1993 and the Alfred P. Murrah Federal Building in Oklahoma City, Oklahoma, in 1995, and in 2001 ATF agents were among the first investigators to visit the sites of the al Qaeda attacks of September 11. However, the ATF has also been severely criticized for some of its actions, most notably a fifty-one-day standoff with the members of a religious cult, the Branch

Davidians, in Waco, Texas, in 1993. The standoff began when ATF agents arrived to search the Branch Davidian compound for a stockpile of illegal weapons; when it ended, more than eighty people, including four ATF agents, were dead.

SEE ALSO: Branch Davidians; Oklahoma City bombing; September 11 attacks on America

Algeria and Islamic fundamentalist terrorism

During the 1950s and '60s, Algeria experienced a war of independence that pitted Muslim nationalists against the French who controlled the country. After the nationalists took control of Algeria in 1962, anti-European sentiment remained strong among Muslims, and this provided an opportunity for Islamic fundamentalism to develop there. The fundamentalists, however, were in opposition to the group that ran the government—the National Liberation Front (FLN), which had been the driving force in the fight for independence. In the decades after the war, the FLN had become increasingly corrupt and oppressive, using violence to quell civil unrest and to ensure that no other group would be able to seize control of Algeria. However, in the fall of 1988, after Algerian authorities killed hundreds while trying to end a workers' strike and student protests, the public turned against the government so severely that the FLN, attempting to prevent widespread rebellion, announced it would allow the creation of political parties and hold the first multiparty elections, beginning with a vote at the municipal level in which voters would decide who would be in charge of Algeria's forty-eight regional departments. The municipal elections took place on June 12, 1990; to the dismay of the FLN, the winner of thirty-two of the departmental positions was the Islamic Salvation Front (Front Islamique de Salut, or FIS), an Islamic fundamentalist party. As the national elections approached—they would take place in two stages, on December 26, 1991, and January 16, 1992—tensions between the FIS and the FLN mounted. When the FIS held antigovernment demonstrations and workers' strikes, riots broke out, and when the government sent in military troops to restore order, several people were killed. The government announced that there would be no elections as long as the country remained in a state of unrest, and perhaps for this reason, the riots soon stopped. The elections were back on.

By this time, the FIS was calling for Algeria to become an Islamic state, which meant that the people of Algeria would have to follow the Sharia, or holy law of Islam. This would require many changes in Algerian society; for example, women would no longer be allowed to work or to participate in physical education, and boys and girls could not attend school together. Moreover, elections would be eliminated—which meant that if the FIS won the elections, there would be no subsequent votes to remove them from power. Consequently, when the FIS overwhelmingly won the first stage of the elections, the FLN invalidated the votes and cancelled the second stage of elections in order to maintain its group's control of the national government. An outraged FIS then incited more riots, and Algeria was once again roiled with violence. This time, the FIS relied heavily on bombing to strike out at the government, planting bombs at police stations, military bases, and government-run buildings, killing or injuring hundreds. In response, the government declared it illegal to belong to the FIS or to any other political party that promoted a particular religious ideology. This only served to drive the Islamic fundamentalist militants underground, and they created several terrorist groups dedicated to opposing the Algerian government. Two of the most violent groups were the Armed Islamic Movement (Mouvement Islamique Armé, or MIA) and the Armed Islamic Group (Groupe Islamique Armé, or GIA), which murdered foreigners, particularly Christians, as well as secular academics, teachers, doctors, and journalists and brutalized and killed rural villagers indiscriminately. Meanwhile Algerian troops massacred hundreds of Islamic fundamentalists and arrested thousands more. By some estimates, between 1992 and 1997, 120,000 people died in Algeria as a result of the conflict between the government and Islamic militants. In 1999—four years after a national election that resulted in the FLN retaining power—the Algerian government offered all Islamic fundamentalists amnesty if they surrendered and promised to abandon terrorism; over five thousand militants accepted this offer. Nonetheless Islamic fundamentalism still exists in Algeria, and the potential for conflict between religious and secular elements of the country is still present.

SEE ALSO: Algerian war of independence

Algerian war of independence

Between 1954 and 1964, Muslim nationalists in Algeria engaged in a war of independence against the French colonial government that controlled the country. The nationalists used terrorism to instigate this war and in response the French became just as brutal. By the end of the conflict, according to some estimates, over a million people had died, many after being tortured. The war was triggered by a built-up resentment by Muslim Algerians toward

European settlers who held all the power in Algeria but made up only about 10 percent of the population. In 1945 the tension between these two groups led to violence. At a parade in the town of Sétif celebrating the end of World War II, Muslims killed 20 French policemen and 103 other Europeans in the streets, many of whom had been tortured and mutilated. In response, French authorities and settlers murdered thousands of Muslims, which ended the Muslim attacks but not the feelings that prompted the violence. Consequently, in the early 1950s a group of Algerian nationalists established the National Liberation Front (FLN), and in 1954 it initiated the war against the French and engaged in terrorism against European settlers, often savaging victims before killing them. The first major FLN attack on civilians, known as the Philippeville Massacre, took place in April 1955 in the town of Philippeville, where nationalists rioted and brutally murdered 37 men, women, and children. In 1956 the FLN detonated bombs at various locations and murdered a French political leader, Amédée Froger. This murder, combined with a 1957 labor strike by Muslims throughout the country, led French authorities to take drastic measures to eliminate nationalism, even as French settlers began abandoning the country in massive numbers. (In 1954 there were nearly a million settlers in Algeria; by 1962 there were less than thirty thousand.) French soldiers arrested and tortured hundreds of Muslims, including an influential FLN leader, Ben M'Hidi. After M'Hidi died in prison (authorities claimed he had committed suicide), other Muslims began to fear being arrested, and many abandoned the nationalist cause; some abandoned Algeria as well, moving to other countries to escape the violence.

Ironically, by this time politicians in France had begun to question whether Algeria should remain under French control, given the degree of effort it took to maintain order there. In the fall of 1959, French president Charles de Gaulle announced that Algerians would be allowed to govern themselves, though Algeria would remain a French colony. This meant that Muslims, as the majority, would become a powerful political force in Algeria—against the wishes of the Europeans who lived there. Consequently in 1960, before de Gaulle could implement his plan, some of them tried to regain control of Algeria. The French military thwarted this effort, but four generals unhappy with the idea of a Muslim-controlled Algeria attempted their own takeover of the government in 1961. They too failed. Meanwhile, an anti-Muslim terrorist group called the Secret Army Organization (OAS) detonated bombs in places where Muslims were likely to congregate, killing over one thousand people between 1961 and 1962. After Algerian independence was achieved in 1962 and the FLN took control of the government, Muslims who had been loyal to the nationalist cause sought to punish not only any anti-Muslim Europeans still in the country but Muslims who had failed to take up the nationalist cause, had sided with the French, or had left the country while it was in turmoil only to return to reap the rewards of independence. Consequently the war between Muslims and Europeans did not end for two more years after the onset of Algerian independence.

SEE ALSO: Algeria and Islamic fundamentalist terrorism

American Indian massacres

During the nineteenth century in the western United States, American Indians massacred nonnative people while U.S. soldiers massacred Indians. Conflict between these two groups was responsible for thousands of deaths and the destruction of the traditional Native American way of life. Friction between native and nonnative Americans was present from the first contact between these two peoples due to their diverse cultures. However, for the most part there was little trouble until 1830, when the U.S. government enacted the Indian Removal Act. This law allowed the U.S. military to use force to relocate any Indian who would not sell his land to the government. As a result, over the next ten years at least one hundred thousand Indians were pushed west of the Mississippi River against their will. Still, there were relatively few deaths until 1849, when thousands of American settlers headed to California after hearing that gold had been discovered there the year before. As they traveled, these settlers killed game that the Indians needed to survive, and in response certain tribes of Indians massacred entire wagon trains of pioneers (though they sometimes took the women, girls, and young boys captive before killing everyone else). To protect its citizens, the U.S. government sent troops to fight the Indians, and during the 1850s, '60s, and '70s there were many violent confrontations between soldiers and Indians throughout the western Plains. Among these were massacres of Indians in the 1860s by forces led by U.S. general George Armstrong Custer, who in turn was massacred along with his more than two hundred men by Cheyenne and Sioux Indians in 1876. By 1887 most of the Indians had been killed or confined to reservations. On the northern Plains, however, a new religion, the Ghost Dance, developed among the Indians that inspired them to believe their old way of life would

soon return. When many of these believers left their reservation to gather at Wounded Knee Creek, South Dakota, in December 1890, the government arrested the leaders of the group. One of these leaders, Sitting Bull, was killed during the arrest, and two weeks later the U.S. Seventh Cavalry attacked the remaining Indians at Wounded Knee, massacring over two hundred men, women, and children who had already agreed to return to their reservation. This was the last such massacre; afterward the Indians remained on their allotted lands.

SEE ALSO: American Indian Movement

American Indian Movement (AIM)

During the 1970s, the American Indian Movement (AIM) was a militant group dedicated to achieving civil rights for Native Americans. The group argued that Native Americans should be allowed to resume their traditional way of life, should have autonomy over their own tribal affairs, and should be afforded the legal rights of all American citizens, which included the right to control the natural resources on their lands. AIM also demanded that the U.S. government return any ancestral lands it had stolen from the Indians and honor its treaties by returning lands given to the Indians but later taken away. Founded in Minnesota in 1968, AIM publicized its views primarily through public protests. These included an occupation of Alcatraz Island off the coast of San Francisco, California, in 1969–71, a march on Washington, D.C., and the occupation of the Washington office of the Bureau of Indian Affairs in 1972, and a protest in 1973 at Wounded Knee, South Dakota, where in 1890 the U.S. military massacred over two hundred Native Americans without good cause. By 1978 so many of the group's leaders had been jailed for their actions that AIM could no longer function at the national level. Nonetheless for the next few years the group continued to stage protests at the local level. The last major activity in this regard was a 1981 occupation in the Black Hills of South Dakota, which had once been taken from the Indians by the U.S. government.

SEE ALSO: American Indian massacres

Amin, Idi (Idi Amin Dada Oumee)
(1923 or 1925–2003)

African dictator Idi Amin (Idi Amin Dada Oumee) was responsible for anywhere from one hundred thousand to five hundred thousand deaths during a brutal regime that included mass executions of political opponents and members of rival tribes. A convert to Islam, he was a member of the King's African Rifles, a regiment of the British colonial army, in Uganda as a young man, fighting against the Mau Mau in Kenya in 1952, and in 1961 he was the first native Ugandan to become a commissioned officer for the British. The following year he was nearly court-martialed when, under his command, his troops tortured and murdered tribesmen suspected of stealing cattle, an incident known as the Turkana Massacre. The British overlooked this incident because Uganda was on the brink of gaining its independence from Britain. After this occurred in October 1962, Amin became a military commander in the Ugandan army and was sent to Israel to train as a paratrooper. On his return he continued his rise in the military, but was also involved in various illegal activities. In 1971, suspecting that he was about to be arrested for stealing millions of dollars from the military, Amin took over the government, while its prime minister was out of the country. In doing so, he had support not only from a majority of Ugandans, who were unhappy with the way the government had been run, but from Great Britain and Israel, who supplied him with arms.

Amin started his presidency by holding mass executions to rid himself of anyone loyal to the former government. In 1972 he ordered anyone who was not black to leave his country within ninety days, then gave their property and possessions to blacks loyal to him. Shortly thereafter, Britain and Israel withdrew their support. Amin responded by allying himself with Libya and the Soviet Union, while expelling Britons from his country and seizing their property. In addition, he supported efforts by Palestinians to attack Israeli targets. In his own country, he established military squads that killed thousands of people who were not of Amin's tribe or did not agree with his policies.

Another round of executions occurred in 1976 after Amin became involved in a Palestinian terrorist act involving an Air France passenger plane. Known as the Entebbe raid, this incident began when Palestinian terrorists hijacked the plane, whose passengers were primarily Israelis, and forced it to fly to Uganda. While it was on the ground there and the terrorists were making their demands, Israeli commandos seized the plane and rescued the hostages. Afterward they accused Amin of sneaking reinforcements and supplies to the terrorists while participating in negotiations with them. This accusation convinced Amin that more people in his government had turned against him, and he ordered the deaths of over two hundred of his soldiers and officials. In 1977 he killed one of his archbishops and two cabinet ministers after accusing them of plotting against him. By this time, Great Britain and the United States had cut all ties with Uganda, and soon Libya withdrew its aid to the country as well. Consequently, Uganda's economy started to fail and rebellions broke out. In 1979 Amin was forced to flee to Libya, but he was not welcome there. He then went to Iraq, followed by Saudi Arabia, where he remained until his death from health problems in 2003.

SEE ALSO: Entebbe raid

Amritsar massacre, the

Committed on April 13, 1919, by British soldiers in colonial India, the Amritsar massacre was one of the most vicious suppressions of public protest in history. Earlier in the year, the native people of India had begun to rebel against British rule, and on March 30 and April 6 some participated in a labor strike led by Mohandas Gandhi (also known as the mahatma, or wise man). After the colonial police arrested some of the strikers, other Indians rioted in the city of Amritsar within the state of Punjab, killing three innocent Europeans. Consequently the British military sent troops there to quell the riots, under the command of Brigadier-General R.H. Dyer. Dyer was intentionally harsh in reestablishing order. For example, he decreed that all Indians had to crawl, rather than walk, past a spot where a white woman had been attacked during the unrest; anyone who refused was flogged. He also forbade Indians from gathering in groups of more than four and established a curfew that kept them confined to their homes after 8 PM. Nonetheless on the afternoon of April 13, approximately 20,000 Indians men, women, and children gathered near a temple to hold a peaceful meeting. Dyer responded by ordering ninety soldiers to fire into the crowd without warnings. As

the unarmed people tried to run away, the troops kept firing for nearly ten minutes. In the end, 380 Indians were killed and 1,200 seriously wounded, and later Dyer admitted that he had intentionally slaughtered as many Indians as possible in order to instill terror in any who might think of rioting in the future.

Indeed the Amritsar massacre did put an end to riots in the region, and the Europeans living in Punjab hailed Dyer as a hero. In Great Britain, however, news of the massacre led to a public outcry, and politicians in Parliament ordered an investigation into what had happened. They concluded that Dyer had been wrong in ordering his troops to fire without first giving the crowd a chance to disperse, and that he had used more force than was necessary to combat an unlawful but peaceful assembly as opposed to a rebellion. They stripped Dyer of his command and ordered him back to India. Meanwhile Indians who were outraged over the massacre began to organize themselves into a resistance effort that eventually ended British colonial rule in India.

SEE ALSO: colonialism

anarchism

Arising in the nineteenth century, anarchism is a philosophy based on the tenet that people do not need, and are indeed better off without, any form of central authority or government. People who support anarchism, known as anarchists, generally believe that all governments are evil and that all political leaders are corrupt. They further believe that in the absence of government, human beings will voluntarily work together to solve their problems using shame, shunning, and other psychological forms of manipulation rather than physical force to ensure that everyone in the community behaves well and contributes to the group as a whole. Because anarchists view governmental power as a corrupting agent, they do not agree with socialists, such as the followers of Karl Marx (Marxists), who argue that the best way to destroy a government is to take it over. (Socialist movements are typically attempts of the working class to supplant the capitalist class.) Instead anarchists argue that it is best to let governments collapse, then work to create a new society.

During the late nineteenth and early twentieth centuries, some anarchists attempted to hasten this collapse by committing violent acts against government leaders, institutions, and organizations as well as in public places to create havoc and fear, much the way modern terrorists do today. For example, in France anarchists exploded a bomb in a music hall in 1882, in a government hall in 1893, and in a café in 1894. Anarchists were also responsible for the assassinations of France's president Said Carnot in 1894, Austria's empress Elizabeth in 1898, Italy's king Umberto in 1900, America's president William McKinley in 1901, and Spain's prime minister Canalejas y Mendez in 1912.

Some of the most violent anarchists were part of a movement known as collective anarchism, also known as collectivism. Their leader, Russian anarchist Mikhail Bakunin, is sometimes called the grandfather of terrorism, primarily for two reasons. First, he promoted the idea that all acts of violence against the government are worth committing, no matter how many people get killed or injured in the process, because in any fight of good against evil, individual lives are expendable. Second, he argued that the only way for any revolutionary group to avoid corruption is to shun a large organizational

structure in favor of a loose connection of small groups with safeguards in place to ensure that if authorities captured one of these groups, its members would not be able to provide the location of the others. This structure—known as a network of cells—is used by many modern terrorist groups.

Bakunin also promoted the idea that labor strikes could be used to destroy governments, and he was associated with efforts to establish labor organizations in Latin countries, such as Italy and Spain. This use of labor strikes was promoted more aggressively in the late 1880s by another anarchist movement, anarcho-syndicalism, or syndicalism. However, as workers banded together in order to gain more power, some anarchists argued that labor organizations were much like the government and therefore evil.

Meanwhile, governments took harsh measures to suppress anarchism. In the United States, for example, after McKinley's assassination, Congress passed a law stating that immigrants who were anarchists would not be allowed to live in America, and by 1917 over 240 anarchists had been deported. Indeed most American anarchists during this period were European immigrants who shared their views through anarchist newspapers published in German, French, Italian, Czechoslovakian, and Yiddish. Today there are few anarchists, and anarchism as a movement no longer exists. However, radical activists who use violence to protest government policies sometimes call themselves anarchists.

But despite the longtime association of violence and anarchism, anarchism originated out of a desire to create a more peaceful society. In 1793 *An Enquiry Concerning Political Justice* by William Godwin first put forth the idea that society would thrive without a government, and in 1840 *Qu'est ce que la propriéte?* (*What Is Property?*) by French anarchist Pierre-Joseph Proudhon suggested that if the concept of personal property was eliminated, people would share all resources with their community and therefore lead a more harmonious life. Proudhon rejected the use of violence in creating a better society, arguing that people should be encouraged to change rather than forced to change. Nonetheless some of the anarchists inspired by Proudhon's work did turn to violence, usually after trying and failing to sway people through political propaganda. For example, in Russia in 1873, anarchists distributed pamphlets in an attempt to convince the rural masses to reject the regime of Russia's ruler, or czar. When the Russian peasants failed to respond, the anarchists formed a group called Narodnaya Volya, or the People's Will, whose purpose was to engage in acts of terrorism against the regime. Members of the People's Will generally believed that if they assassinated government leaders, the peasants would see how weak and vulnerable such leaders were and reject them. But when the Russian anarchists succeeded in assassinating Alexander II on March 1, 1881, the result was not as they intended: People throughout Russia expressed outrage at what the anarchists had done.

SEE ALSO: Archduke Franz Ferdinand, assassination of; assassination, political; Bakunin, Mikhail; Marx, Karl

Angolan guerrilla groups

A country in southern Africa, Angola was a colony of Portugal for over five hundred years, but during the 1960s native Angolans became increasingly unhappy with Portuguese rule. Consequently three guerrilla groups—the Front for the Liberation of Angola (FNLA), the National Union for the Total Independence of Angola (UNITA), and the Movement for the Liberation of Angola (MPLA)—developed to force the Portuguese out using terrorist attacks. The brutality of these attacks in northern Angola was so severe that in 1975 the Portuguese abandoned the country. This did not end the violence, however. The three groups attacked each other in an attempt to gain sole control of Angola, with the help of several other countries. (The United States, for example, supported both the FNLA and the UNITA, while Russia and Cuba sided with the MPLA.) Eventually the MPLA succeeded in taking charge of the government of Angola, but the UNITA continually attempted to overthrow it until its leader, Jonas Savimbi, died in 2002. But although this event reduced the power of UNITA, its guerrillas continue to attack foreign tourists, aid workers, and corporate workers in the country, as do other Angolan guerrillas, in hopes of disrupting the economy and the government.

SEE ALSO: Africa, terrorism in post-colonial

animal-rights movement

The modern animal-rights movement, which began in England and the United States in the late 1960s, has spawned several groups dedicated to protecting animals, and in many cases these groups employ illegal and dramatic tactics in order to attract media attention. Consequently animal-rights activists are sometimes called terrorists, though few actually resort to the kind of violence that can be considered terrorism.

Among those who do use violence, the most prominent is the Animal Liberation Front (ALF), which was established in

1971 in England and in 1979 in the United States. This group has not only broken into research labs, pet stores, and other facilities to release caged animals, but also has severely damaged such facilities, sometimes committing arson in the process. In addition the ALF has assaulted people during at least two attacks in England in October 1984, one at a dog kennel and the other at the home of the director of a medical research center. After the U.S. branch of ALF set fire to a university research facility in California in 1987 (killing the animals there in the process, which ALF members later said was necessary to save future animal victims at the site), the Federal Bureau of Investigation (FBI) classified the group as a terrorist threat. Nonetheless the group continued to engage in violent activities, particularly against aspects of the fur industry. For example, in 1997 it released minks at a fur farm in Oregon and then blew up the facility.

Other violent animal-rights groups include the Animal Rights Militia (ARM) and the Justice Department. Both of these groups, the first in Canada and the second in Great Britain, use fear to intimidate people into abandoning practices that might directly or indirectly harm animals. For example, during the 1990s ARM sabotaged products on store shelves then warned the public about its actions. ARM's goal was to encourage consumers to stop buying these products because the manufacturers employed product testing procedures that harmed animals in the process. Also during the 1990s, the Justice Department mailed envelopes contaminated with various poisons or tainted materials to people involved in industries that harmed animals.

Another animal-rights group often accused of engaging in terrorism is the People for the Ethical Treatment of Animals (PETA), because members of this group have attacked individuals who appear to disregard the well-being of animals. For example, PETA members have thrown red paint, symbolizing blood, on people wearing fur coats, and they have disrupted fox hunts by scaring horses in attempts to unseat riders. However, these attacks, though upsetting to the victims, are essentially nonviolent, and PETA does not promote violence, preferring to create change through political activism and media campaigns that influence public opinion. Consequently, though its tactics might be shocking, it is no more a terrorist group than the first animal-rights organizations, the Royal Society for the Prevention of Cruelty to Animals (RSPCA), founded in England in 1824, and the American Society for the Prevention of Cruelty to Animals (ASPCA), founded in the United States in 1867. These two organizations, and others like them, have fought for improved treatment of animals and have been responsible for many animal-protection laws and policies.

SEE ALSO: Animal Liberation Front; People for the Ethical Treatment of Animals; single-issue terrorist groups

Animal Liberation Front (ALF)

Established in England in 1971 by British animal-rights activist Ronnie Lee, the Animal Liberation Front (ALF) is a radical animal-rights group operating in England, the United States, and Canada that employs violence in its attempts to "liberate" animals from human captivity. This violence is primarily against property; ALF members break into such places as medical research facilities, pet stores, and mink farms, release all the animals, and then damage or completely destroy the cages and buildings that confined the animals, in the hopes that replacing the structures would not be cost effective to the owners. Lee had engaged in these activities even before establishing ALF, and in fact had spent time in prison from 1975 to 1976 after setting a pharmaceutical plant on fire. With ALF, however, his attacks escalated. In January 1981 the group broke into and damaged the homes of several scientists in Oxford, England, who engaged in animal research. In March 1984 ALF put bleach in random bottles of shampoo on store shelves in London, Leeds, and Southhampton, England, then warned the public about the existence of the bottles; the group's intent was to economically damage the company that had manufactured the shampoo because the product had been tested on animals. In October 1984 the British branch of ALF assaulted three people during an attack on a dog kennel and one person during an attack at the home of a medical research director and it seriously damaged two research facilities; three years later, it firebombed several fur stores.

The first ALF action in the United States occurred in 1979, when American ALF members freed animals housed at the New York Medical Center. In 1980 there were several more such actions in both the United States and Canada. For example, in 1982 the group freed 35 cats at Howard University Medical School in Washington, D.C.; in 1984 it freed 115 animals at the City of Hope National Research Center in California; and in 1985 the group freed a rhesus monkey at a research lab of the University of Western Ontario, Canada, and hundreds of animals at the life sciences building of the University of California, Riverside, which it then bombed. In April 1987 ALF members set fire to the Animal Diagnostics Lab at the University of California, Davis. The attack on the Riverside university caused hundreds of thousands of dollars in damage, and the damage to the Davis lab was over $3.5 million. In addition, the Davis attack led the Federal Bureau of Investigation (FBI) to classify ALF as a terrorist threat, but this did not deter ALF's members. In May 1997 they freed hundreds of mink from the Arritola Mink Farm in Mount Angel, Oregon, then planted bombs at the farm; the bombs exploded the next morning, causing over a million dollars in damages. The group attacked other U.S. fur-trade facilities in the 1990s as well, primarily in the Pacific Northwest, in addition to research labs in various states. ALF also attacked fast-food restaurants, especially those serving chicken from birds once housed in conditions that the group considers inhumane. Today ALF continues to attack places that cage animals or that support the caging of animals, such as pet stores and butcher shops. However, such activities have lessened in recent years because the government has become more aggressive in dealing with radical animal-rights activists, thanks to new laws enacted to punish them more severely.

SEE ALSO: animal-rights movement

anthrax

Used by terrorists as a biological weapon, anthrax is a sometimes fatal infectious disease caused by the *Bacillus anthracis* bacteria. Spores of these bacteria can enter the body through a cut in the skin, breathing anthrax-contaminated air, or eating contaminated meat or plants, after which the disease develops within six weeks. Both people and livestock can develop anthrax; in humans, naturally occurring cases of the disease are typically the result of eat-

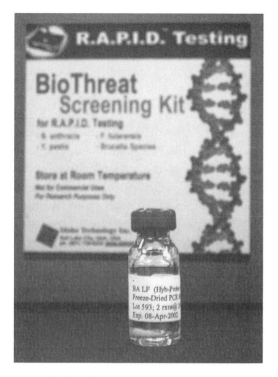

A vial of a freeze-dried reagent, which is enough for two testings, is displayed at the Idaho Technology, Inc. DOUGLAS C. PIZAC. © AP IMAGES

ing or touching infected animals. Terrorists, however, try to pass the spores through inhalation, usually via an aerosol spray or a fine powder or soil, with varying results.

For example, in the early 1990s, members of a Japanese religious cult, Aum Shinrikyō (Supreme Truth), used an aerosol device to release anthrax spores into the air in various parts of Tokyo, Japan, hoping to make one of its doomsday prophecies come true, but no one contracted the disease. In 2001 twenty-two people developed anthrax, five of them fatally, after coming into contact with anthrax-contaminated powder sent through the U.S. Postal Service. There were only four envelopes containing this powder, sent from Trenton, New Jersey, by an unknown terrorist to U.S. senators Patrick

Leahy and Tom Daschle in Washington, D.C., and to NBC newsman Tom Brokaw and the *New York Post* offices in New York City, but these envelopes contaminated mail, mailrooms, and offices en route to their recipients. Consequently although Leahy, Daschle, and Brokaw did not become ill, people in Florida, Connecticut, and New Jersey, as well as New York, died because of the incident. The resulting media attention inspired several anthrax hoaxes, whereby uncontaminated powder was sent through the mail with notes claiming the person opening the letter had just been exposed to anthrax. However, genuine anthrax letters were subsequently found in other countries, including Pakistan and Germany, though no one became ill from handling the minimally contaminated powder they contained.

Governments have also attempted to use anthrax as a biological weapon. For example, Japan in 1937 and Great Britain in 1942 conducted anthrax-related tests, with Britain's detonation of an anthrax bomb resulting in the contamination of an entire island, Guinard, off the coast of Scotland. In 1979 a Russian military base accidentally exploded anthrax into the air, killing perhaps as many as a thousand people in the Ural Mountains. In 1995 Iraq admitted to testing anthrax's potential as a biological weapon as well.

SEE ALSO: bioterrorism

antiabortion movement

The antiabortion movement, which began in the United States in the 1970s, has spawned several groups dedicated to preventing abortions and reversing the legal decision that allows them (*Roe v. Wade*, decided in 1973). Most of these groups do not endorse violence, though they do promote the harassment of abortion providers and their prospective patients. However, a few groups, most notably the Army of God (which first surfaced in 1982), advocate the kind of violence that can be classified as terrorism, with the rationale that it is justified in order to save an innocent life. However, antiabortion violence is typically a single act by a lone individual, rather than a group effort. For example, the first antiabortion attacks, which took place in 1977 through 1979, involved activists who walked alone into abortion clinics and attempted to set abortion providers or their assistants on fire. The first murder connected to antiabortion activism occurred in March 1993 when activist Michael Griffin shot abortion provider Dr. David Gunn outside of his Florida clinic while an antiabortion protest was taking place there. Similarly, in July 1994 activist Paul Hill, who had been a vocal supporter of Griffin's attack on Gunn, shot and killed abortion provider Dr. John Bayard Britton in Florida; in December 1994 John Salvi III killed two people who worked in the office of an abortion clinic in Massachusetts; and in October 1998 a sniper—later identified as James Kopp—shot abortion provider Dr. Barnett Slepian at his Amherst, New York, home.

Also during the 1990s, antiabortionists bombed, set fire to, or otherwise damaged roughly half of the abortion clinics in the United States. These attacks include several January 1998 bombings in Georgia and Alabama, which authorities believe were committed by Eric Rudolph even though a letter sent by the bomber to local media was signed "Army of God." This signature also appeared on threatening letters sent to abortion providers in October 2001; authorities later identified the sender of the letters as antiabortion activist Clayton Lee Waagner. In both cases, the letter writers might not have belonged to the Army of God, but instead might have used the name because the group had produced a guide to violent antiabortion tactic *The Army of God Manual*, that was well-known among antiabortionists.

Other antiabortion groups have produced or distributed guides on how to shut down abortion clinics by harassing patients and physicians or otherwise disrupting clinic operations; such groups include the National Right to Life Committee (NRLC), founded by Joseph Scheidler in 1980, and Operation Rescue, founded by Randall Terry in 1986. In addition Neal Horsley of the American Coalition for Life Activists established a Web site in January 1997 that published a list of home addresses of abortion providers and their assistants. The list encouraged activists to confront abortion providers at their homes in order to circumvent the Freedom of Access to Clinic Entrances Act established by the U.S. government in May 1994 to prevent activists from interfering with physicians outside their clinics. (This Web site was apparently the means by which Kopp found Slepian's house.)

SEE ALSO: Army of God; Griffin, Michael; Hill, Paul; Rudolph, Eric

anti-Semitism

Anti-Semitism, which is the hostile discrimination against Jews because of their race or their religion or both, has been the basis of many terrorist acts over the centuries. The word "anti-Semitism" was first used in 1879 in reference to anti-Jewish campaigns in Europe, but such discrimination has existed since the times of ancient Greece and Rome, and it worsened after the advent of Christianity. During the Middle Ages in many European towns,

Jews were segregated from the rest of the populace in ghettos, forbidden to hold certain jobs, and denied certain rights. When Jews managed to succeed economically despite these restrictions, jealousy over this success led to violence against Jews on both an individual and a group level. In some places, Jews were massacred in large numbers, and several countries forcibly expelled Jews from part or all of their territories, including England in 1290, France in the fourteenth century, Germany in the 1350s, Spain in 1492, and Portugal in 1498. (Though in some places, Jews who converted to Christianity were not expelled.)

Jews continued to be persecuted until the eighteenth century, when they enjoyed a brief period of respite from violence first in France after the French Revolution and then in the rest of western Europe. In the nineteenth century, however, anti-Semitism again became the norm in Europe, though now it was based more on race than on religion, and spread to Russia, where Jews were attacked during anti-Jewish riots in the late 1870s and early 1880s. This violence increased in the late 1890s after the publication of a book entitled *The Protocols of the Learned Elders of Zion*. It was supposedly the proceedings of a meeting of Jews plotting to take over the world, in association with a group called the Freemasons, but it was actually written in approximately 1895 by the secret police of Russia's czar Nicholas II, who hoped to justify their anti-Jewish policies. The Russian public accepted the book as true, as did Europeans who heard about it. As a result, violence against Jews increased in Russia and both western and eastern Europe, where governments engaged in organized, violent anti-Jewish campaigns known as pogroms. By the advent of World War II, anti-Semitic groups in France, Hungary, England, and the United States were routinely attacking innocent Jews.

Nothing could compare, however, to the violence perpetrated against the Jews in Nazi Germany from 1933 to 1945 under the rule of Adolf Hitler. The German government took away their lands and possessions and then, during World War II, decided to exterminate them as a people by sending them to death camps, where roughly 6 million were killed. In promoting his persecution of the Jews, Hitler routinely mentioned *The Protocols* and the Jewish plot to take over the world—an idea supported, in some people's minds, by the fact that several leaders of the Russian Revolution had been Jewish. Many Germans also supported the extermination of the Jews under the asumption that Jews were genetically inferior to Aryans and therefore needed to die in order to keep the "master race" pure. After World War II, however, most Germans repudiated this belief, and anti-Semitism weakened in Europe, Great Britain, and the United States. It remains weak in these places today, but is on the rise elsewhere in the world, especially the Islamic Middle East, where anti-Semitism has existed since ancient times even though Arabs, like Jews, are Semites. Because both groups share a common ancestry, Arab opposition to Jews is not based on race, but on religion, and since 1948 (when the state of Israel was established) on territory disputes as well. Centuries ago, anti-Jewish sentiment among Muslims was expressed through laws that forced Jews to live apart from others. In modern times, however, it has triggered terrorist acts against Jews and, in 2006, warfare between Israel and Palestine.

SEE ALSO: Holocaust, the; Middle East, terrorism in the; Nazi terrorism

antiterrorism

The term "antiterrorism" refers to measures, policies, and directives that are enacted in order to deter or prevent terrorist acts. In other words, antiterrorism is a defensive response to terrorism, as opposed to "counterterrorism," which involves proactive attempts to eliminate terrorists and terrorist groups. Antiterrorism, then, includes actions that tighten security at airports and at government buildings and other structures that are likely terrorist targets—a practice known as "target hardening." Sometimes a target is hardened merely by adding security guards to the site (perhaps along with surveillance cameras) and searching people who visit it, while other times more permanent measures are taken. For example, governments might erect walls or other barricades to prevent people from driving up to or parking near government buildings, such as the White House in Washington, D.C. Walls are also erected along borders to prevent terrorists from moving in and out of countries or disputed territories, such as the West Bank, with ease.

SEE ALSO: counterterrorism

Antonescu, Ion
(1882–1946)

As the leader of Romania, Ion Antonescu was responsible for the death of at least 110,000 Romanian Jews (and possibly double that amount) during World War II. Prior to the war, as General Antonescu, he joined with the paramilitary branch of a Romanian fascist, anti-Semitic terrorist group known as the Iron Guard, which committed numerous assassinations during the 1930s in an attempt to overthrow the government. The Guard's victims included a prime minister, a former prime minister, a major political leader, and the premier of Romania. With the Guard's support, Antonescu was able to force Romania's monarch, King Carol II, to turn the throne over to his son, Prince Michael, in September 1940, after which Antonescu established a new government, the National Legionary Government. For the next few months, Antonescu shared power with the Iron Guard, which conducted a reign of terror against Jews and anyone who had once supported King Carol II. However, in January 1941 the Guard turned on Antonescu, trying to take sole control of the government. Antonescu not only overcame this effort but, after crushing the Guard, increased his powers to the level of a dictatorship.

By this time Antonescu was a staunch ally of Adolf Hitler's Nazi regime in Germany, and he decided to support Hitler's efforts to eradicate the Jews. In June 1941 Antonescu ordered thousands of Jews to relocate from their village homes to concentration camps and urban ghettos, brutally killing all who resisted and some who did not. Many died en route to these destinations or from diseases contracted at the crowded, unsanitary relocation sites. Meanwhile Russia's Red Army managed to plant activists in Odessa, a Ukrainian city taken over by Romanian soldiers, to act as partisans in attacking the Romanian military from within. In October 1941 these partisans, or perhaps other Russian agents, bombed an Odessa military headquarters. In retaliation, Antonescu burned the city, killing 25,000 Jews in the process. He also went after partisans elsewhere, attempting to kill as many as possible. Antonescu's brutal grip on his territories continued until August 1944, when Russian forces invaded them. These forces helped Romania's King Michael retake the government and imprison Antonescu, after which Romania allied itself with Russia and declared war on Germany. In 1946 Antonescu was put on trial as a war criminal, found guilty, and executed.

SEE ALSO: anti-Semitism; fascism; assassination, political; Romanian terrorism in World War II

apartheid

Apartheid was a system of racial segregation established in South Africa in 1948 by its political leaders, the Afrikaners, who were white supremacists of Dutch descent. (The majority of South Africans were black.) The system was dismantled in 1989 after a long period of antiapartheid civil unrest and terrorist attacks, led by members of a political group called the African National Congress (ANC). The ANC was initially nonviolent, and its insistence on nonviolence so aggravated some of its members that they broke away in 1959 to form another group, the Pan-Africanist Congress, that in 1960 engaged in a confrontation with police that triggered violent riots in Cape Town, South Africa. During this confrontation, police killed sixty-seven blacks and injured hundreds more, and afterward the government banned both the Pan-Africanist Congress and the ANC, arresting any members it could find. Consequently the ANC decided to launch a terrorist campaign against the government, an action that resulted in the arrest of many of its leaders. Nonetheless the ANC, and the Pan-Africanist Congress as well, continued to engage in violent protests and guerrilla attacks, as did other blacks in the country, and in 1984 riots spread throughout South Africa. Over the next few years, the ANC and others bombed buildings associated with the government and Afrikaner businesses. They also engaged in strikes, demonstrations, protests, and boycotts in an attempt to disrupt order throughout South Africa, and attacked civilians who supported apartheid, even if those supporters were black.

During the last years of apartheid, the government established death squads called Askaris that tracked down and killed ANC members, not only within South Africa but elsewhere as well. The government also encouraged black-against-black violence by supporting a group of Zulu tribespeople, the Inkatha Freedom Party, who were violently opposed to the ANC because the ANC was comprised of people from various ethnicities. As a result of these and other government policies and practices, by some estimates South African forces killed over eleven thousand anti-apartheid activists and their supporters between 1990 and 1994.

SEE ALSO: Africa, terrorism in postcolonial

apocalypticism

A collection of beliefs related to what will happen when the world ends, apocalypticism (derived from the Greek word *apokalupsis*, or "revelation") has influenced the behavior of some of the radical terrorists who adhere to the Christian, Judaic, or Islamic faiths. Apocalypticism developed among these faiths after first arising in sixth-century Iran within a religion known as Zoroastrianism. Then and now, believers think that some sort of cataclysm will destroy the world as we know it, that at the end of the world God will pass judgment on each and every human being, and that those who are judged worthy will be richly rewarded in the aftermath of the end-time, when God will create a new heaven and earth. (In Christianity, these beliefs are expressed in the Bible's Book of Revelations.) Inspired by apocalypticism, some people have committed terrorist acts in an attempt to trigger the cataclysm that will bring about the end-time, while others have engaged in terrorism thinking that their actions will lead God—whom they believe supports their cause—to judge them favorably.

Arab-Israeli wars

There have been many conflicts between Arabs and Israelis, but six have been considered major enough to qualify as Arab-Israeli wars; these occurred in 1948–49, 1956, 1967, 1973, 1982, and 2006. The first conflict was a response to the May 1948 creation of the state of Israel, which divided Palestine into Jewish and Arab regions. Months earlier, Arab guerrillas in four organizations—the Arab Army of Liberation, the Arab Army of Salvation, the al-Futuwwah (Young Chivalry), and the al-Najjadah (the Helpers)—had begun attacking Jewish forces in an attempt to prevent Palestine's division, and once it occurred the guerrillas were joined by soldiers from Egypt, Jordan, Syria, Lebanon, and Iraq. From the parts of southern and eastern Palestine that had not been given to the Jews, these fighters launched a successful attack on a Jewish section of Jerusalem, but the Israelis were able to ward off other attacks. The second Arab-Israeli war was sparked by Israel's 1956 capture of the Sinai Peninsula, where Egypt had military bases. The Israelis felt that this attack was justified because Egypt had recently taken control of the Suez Canal, then owned by European interests, but the British and French governments insisted that Israel leave the peninsula in March 1957. The third Arab-Israeli war, also known as the Six-Day War, occurred in June 1967, when Syria bombed Israeli villages and Israel

shot down Syrian planes. Egypt quickly joined the fray, but Israel destroyed its air force, then recaptured the Jewish section of Jerusalem taken by the Arabs in 1948, as well as the Sinai, the Gaza Strip, the West Bank (then belonging to Jordan), and the Golan Heights on the Israeli-Syrian border. The fourth Arab-Israeli war, in 1973, was the Arabs' attempt to regain these lands; both Egypt and Syria attacked Israel, but Israel was still able to fight back the invasion and actually gain territory, taking parts of Syria and the Suez Canal. Peace negotiations throughout the mid- and late 1970s, among them the Camp David Accords of March 1979, ended the conflict; the accords also brought two major concessions: Israel gave the Sinai Peninsula to Egypt and Egypt conceded that Israel had a right to exist. But in June 1982, shortly after the last Israeli forces left the Sinai Peninsula, the fifth Arab-Israeli war broke out. This conflict was triggered by Israel's decision to bomb and then invade parts of Lebanon in order to destroy bases of the Palestine Liberation Organization (PLO), which was dedicated to establishing an independent Palestinian state using violence if necessary. Though the Israelis insisted their actions were justified as a way to fight terrorism, this invasion caused international outrage, and amid pressure from multinational forces, Israel pulled its forces out of Lebanon. The sixth Arab-Israeli war, which occurred in 2006, was a similar conflict; Israel bombed Palestine in an attempt to wipe out terrorist bases there, but this time it was the terrorists who forced the attack to come to an end, by launching rocket bombs at Israel until peace was declared.

SEE ALSO: Arab Muslim terrorism, origins of; Palestine; Palestine Liberation Organization

Arab Muslim terrorism, origins of

Terrorism in the Arab world has its origins in the conquest and occupation of Muslim lands by Christians. These foreign incursions have, at various times in history, inspired anticolonialism, Pan-Arab nationalism, secular leftist radicalism, and Islamic extremism among Arabs.

The first Christian attacks on Muslim lands were the Crusades, which were eleventh-, twelfth-, and thirteenth-century military expeditions whose goal was to seize the holy places mentioned in the Bible. The main target of the Crusades was the city of Jerusalem, which is considered holy not only in the Christian faith but also in the Muslim and Jewish faiths. Christians began making pilgrimages to this city in ancient times, and after 326 they began building shrines there, followed by churches, monasteries, and hospices. Many of these structures were destroyed when Persians invaded the city and killed its inhabitants in 614. However, after a series of Muslim caliphs took control of the city, beginning in 638, Christian and Jewish pilgrims were allowed to visit it, and by the eleventh century pilgrimages to Jerusalem had become extremely popular among Europeans. Consequently when in 1071 the Seljuk Turks took control of the Holy Land and cut off all pilgrimage routes into the region, Christians became outraged. In 1095 European noblemen, encouraged by Pope Urban II, began sending soldiers (knights) into the Middle East, and in 1099 the crusaders conquered Jerusalem, slaughtered the Muslims and Jews living there, banned any other Muslims and Jews from entering the city, and converted all Muslim religious sites to Christian ones. All of these actions were reversed after Muslims retook the city in 1187, though Christians again held Jerusa-lem from 1229 to 1239 and from 1240 to 1244. When the crusades ended in 1270, Europeans still did not control Jerusalem (then in Egyptian hands), but they had increased anti-Christian sentiments in the region, through their actions not only in Jerusalem but elsewhere in the Middle East, because throughout the region, the crusaders had engaged in terrorism against non-Christians, and sometimes against Orthodox Christians as well.

Nonetheless, beginning in the eighteenth century, the French and the British conquered various parts of the Middle East and established colonial governments there. Wherever this occurred, Muslims chaffed under foreign rule and, in some cases, rebelled against their occupiers. For example, after the French and the British divided the Middle East between themselves at the end of World War I, the Arabs of Syria, Lebanon, and Iraq, who had allied with Britain and France against Germany with the promise that their countries would become independent, were infuriated by the decision to make them colonies, and in the 1920s Arabs in Palestine attacked Jewish settlements that the British had allowed to be established there. Just prior to and during World War II, when thousands of Jews entered Palestine to escape the persecution of Adolf Hitler's regime in Germany, Palestinian Arabs established terrorist bands to attack Jews, and Jews responded in kind.

By this time, anticolonialism was turning to nationalism, as Arabs sought to establish their independence. Leftists encouraged this nationalist movement by advocating violence against foreign governments during the postwar years, and during the 1950s and '60s Arab nationalist groups, some of them with Marxist leanings, engaged in numerous acts of terrorism against Westerners while advocating Arab unity. After the Cold War, however, the appeal of secular leftist extremism gave way to Islamist extremism in most of the Arab world; by this time, many Muslims believed not only that Christians were their enemies, but that life in Western nations is immoral and therefore an affront to God. Religious fervor quickly accomplished what radical secular resistance to Westerners did not; membership in Arab Muslim terrorist groups increased dramatically, as did terrorist attacks against Western targets. Moreover, whenever secular Arab governments—particularly those with ties to the West—tried to quell Islamic extremism, they became the targets of domestic terrorism. This situation continues today, as more and more Arab Muslims embrace the most radical interpretations of Islam.

SEE ALSO: Arab-Israeli wars; Islamic extremists; Palestine

Arafat, Yasir
(1929–2004)

As the leader of the Palestine Liberation Organization (PLO), Yasir Arafat was considered a terrorist by some but a freedom fighter by others. Both of his parents were Palestinian, though he was born in Cairo, Egypt (despite his later claim to have been born in Jerusalem), and in 1959 he founded al Fatah (Victory), a group dedicated to destroying Israel while creating an independent Palestinian state. Under Arafat's leadership, al Fatah attempted to blow up an Israeli water station in 1965 and fought in a skirmish with Israeli soldiers in 1968. Shortly thereafter, al Fatah became the dominant member of an organization of militant anti-Israeli groups, the Palestine Liberation Organization, and Arafat was named head of the PLO's forces. In 1973 he became head of the po-

litical branch of the PLO as well. By this time, the PLO had tried to establish operations in Jordan but, after a battle with Jordanian troops, had been expelled from the country and relocated in Lebanon. From there it launched several attacks on Israel, and in September 1972 one PLO group, Black September, killed eleven Israeli athletes at the Olympic Games in Munich, Germany. Worldwide public outrage over this incident led Arafat to decree that in the future the PLO would only commit acts of violence in lands held by Israelis.

In November 1974 Arafat went to the United Nations (UN) General Assembly in New York to ask that the PLO be given diplomatic recognition, and within three years the UN granted the PLO observer status. Nonetheless Israel was determined to destroy the PLO and, to this end, invaded Lebanon in 1982. Arafat and many other members of the PLO fled the country, leaving the Palestinian refugees there unprotected; Israeli forces then slaughtered hundreds of innocent Palestinians, including women and children. Al Fatah denounced Arafat for abandoning these people and began attacking PLO members, who had taken refuge in various Middle Eastern countries. Arafat fled to Tunis, Tunisia, where he continued to direct PLO operations. At the same time, however, he began to lay the groundwork for peace negotiations. In the late 1980s he acknowledged that Israel had a right to exist, and during the early 1990s he secretly met with Israeli diplomats to work out a peace agreement. In September 1993 Arafat signed a peace declaration between the PLO and Israel, appearing at the White House in Washington, D.C., beside the prime minister of Israel, Yitzhak Rabin. The following year, both men were awarded the Nobel Peace Prize. Afterward Arafat moved back to Palestine, first to the Gaza Strip and then to the West Bank, and in January 1996 he was elected president of the governing body of Palestinian lands, the Palestinian Authority.

Arafat continued to negotiate peace agreements during the late 1990s, gradually putting more land under Palestinian control. In 2000, however, he broke off negotiations for a new agreement with Israeli prime minister Ehud Barak, and after that, conditions between Palestine and Israel deteriorated. In fact, several terrorist acts, including suicide bombings, were committed against Israel, which held Arafat responsible for them. In December 2001 Israeli military forces attacked the Palestinian city of Ramallah on the West Bank, where Arafat had established his headquarters, and trapped Arafat within his compound until May 2002, when the United States and Great Britain helped negotiate his release. Two months later, U.S. president George W. Bush called for Arafat to step down as leader of the Palestinian Authority, but Arafat ignored this.

In 2003 Arafat's finance ministry launched an investigation into his bank accounts, suspecting that he had stolen money from the Palestinian Authority. Meanwhile the European Union (EU) investigated the financial records of the Palestinian Authority to see whether its money had been used to fund terrorism. These investigations failed to prove corruption or show any connection to terrorism, but the EU and the finance minister, Salam Fayyad, successfully demanded that Arafat turn over some of his investment holdings to the Palestinian Authority. The following year, in October 2004, Arafat became ill, and a month later he fell into a coma and died.

SEE ALSO: al Fatah; Bush, U.S. president George W.; Rabin, Yitzhak; Palestine Liberation Organization

Archduke Franz Ferdinand, assassination of

On June 28, 1914, a group of seven Serbian national terrorists assassinated Franz Ferdinand, the archduke of Austria, and his wife, the Countess Sophie Chotek, while they were visiting Sarajevo, Bosnia. Led by Gavrilo Princip, the assassins were associated with a terrorist group, the Serbian Black Hand Society, which had planned the attack, trained the assassins, and smuggled them into Bosnia, where they shot the archduke and his wife as the two were traveling along a parade route in an open car. At the time, Ferdinand was the heir to the Hapsburg throne and therefore the eventual ruler of the Austro-Hungarian Empire. Consequently after the Austrian government tracked down all seven assassins and connected them to Serbia, Austria declared war on Serbia, an act that directly led to World War I.

SEE ALSO: assassination, political; Black Hand, the (Serbian)

Argentina, terrorism in

Since the 1990s, Argentina has had to deal with terrorist attacks launched primarily from neighboring Paraguay, where the city of Ciudad del Este has become the center of a smuggling business that supports numerous terrorist groups. For example, in 1992 the Israeli embassy in Argentina was bombed by a Hezbollah cell operating from Ciudad del Este. However, Argentina's greatest difficulties with terrorism occurred during the 1970s, after an economic downturn led to deplorable living conditions throughout the country.

The first act of rebellion took place in May 1969, when workers in the city of Córdoba protested against the policies of the military government then ruling the country. Shortly thereafter several terrorist groups sprang up to fight for the establishment of a socialist government; the most significant among them are the Montoneros and the People's Revolutionary Army (ERP), the latter of which was an offshoot of a labor-supported political party, the Workers' Revolutionary Party (PRT). In 1970 these groups attacked the government via bombings, arson, kidnappings, and the assassination of key military officials and businessmen.

Three years later the former president of Argentina, Juan Domingo Perón, who had been forced into exile by the military in 1955, returned to power, but even with a new government the violence continued, as the right-wing and left-wing elements of Perón's political party began to fight with one another. In June 1973 right-wingers opened fire on a gathering of left-wingers, killing more than a dozen people, and in response the left-wing Montoneros assassinated one of the leaders of a right-wing group, the General Confederation of Workers (CGT). Meanwhile the ERP engaged in kidnappings and other terrorist attacks, particularly against military forces and structures, in an attempt to force Perón to embrace the left wing of his party and reject the right wing.

Nonetheless, when Perón died in 1974, his successor—his widow, Isabel—allied herself with a right-wing group, the Argentine Anti-Communist Alliance (AAA), which then used death squads to track down and kill left-wing terrorists. In response, the Montoneros assassinated members of the AAA and struck out at military and police targets. Then in 1976 the military ousted Isabel Perón, took over the government, and began a ruthless campaign against left-wing terrorists. Known as the dirty war, this campaign employed the AAA death squads to round up not only members of the Montoneros and the ERP, but anyone who had spoken out against the government. These people were imprisoned, sometimes tortured, and often killed; by some estimates, nearly thirty thousand people died at the hands of AAA and government forces. In addition, by the end of 1979 both the ERP and the Montoneros had been destroyed. However, many of those who had been involved in the dirty war, whether in the AAA or the military, were put on trial for their actions after Argentina became a democracy in 1983; those who were convicted and imprisoned were pardoned by President Carlos Menem in December 1990.

SEE ALSO: Hezbollah; Paraguay, Ciudad del Este

Armed Islamic Front

Like the Armed Islamic Group, the Armed Islamic Front is dedicated to overthrowing the secular government of Algiers and replacing it with an Islamic state. To this end, the Front has killed thousands of people, often through bombings and shootings, targeting not only government officials but prominent journalists and other secular civilians as well. In 1997 the leader of the Front, Abdelkadur Seddouki, was murdered by agents of the Algerian government, but the group continued its efforts, though in 1999 many of its members left the Front in response to an amnesty offer by Algerian president Abdelaziz Bouteflika.

SEE ALSO: Armed Islamic Group; Islamic extremists

Armed Islamic Group (GIA)

The Armed Islamic Group (Group Islamique Armée, or GIA) is an extremely violent Islamic terrorist group dedicated to establishing an Islamic state in Algiers. The group was formed in 1991 after the secular Algerian government refused to recognize an election that gave control of the legislature to the Islamic Salvation Front (FIS), an Islamic political party. (A second election was scheduled for 1992, but was cancelled when it became clear that the FIS would win once again.) Since then GIA has slaughtered hundreds of innocent people in Algeria, including visiting tourists and journalists, through mass shootings, individual murders, and bombings. The group has also conducted bombings in France, because of that country's longstanding ties with Algeria, and in 1994 it hijacked an Air France flight en route to Algeria from France. Some terrorist experts consider the Armed Islamic Group to be more radical than a similar Algerian terrorist group, the Armed Islamic Front, while others think both groups are roughly the same. In either case, in 1999 many members of both groups abandoned terrorism as part of an amnesty offer by Algerian president Abdelaziz Bouteflika.

SEE ALSO: Armed Islamic Front; Islamic extremists

Armenian massacres, the

Located in Asia Minor near the Black Sea, Armenia was the site of massacres during the late nineteenth century, when the country was divided between Russia and the Ottoman Empire (now Turkey). The latter was ruled by the Turks, and these Muslim people persecuted the Armenians, who were Christian. In fact, the Turks so hated the Armenians that they encouraged the Kurds, another Muslim people who lived in the same region as the Armenians, to commit violent acts against them in an effort to drive the Armenians from the empire. In addition, the Turks forced the Armenians to pay exorbitant taxes and killed any who did not comply. Consequently, during the 1890s hundreds of thousands of Armenians died at the hands of either Kurds or Turkish troops, while others were tortured, raped, or otherwise brutalized. In 1896 the Armenians who had not fled to Russia began to strike back at their tormentors, killing government officials and attacking buildings associated with the government. Of these attacks, the most significant was the seizure of the Ottoman Bank by Armenian rebels in 1896, because afterward the Turks killed over fifty thousand Armenians in retribution. When a group of Turkish revolutionaries took over the Ottoman Empire in 1909, such violence eased for a time, but in 1915 the new government again began attacking Armenians. Now, though, the Turks' intent was to exterminate all Armenians in the entire empire (not just those in Armenia) rather than just drive them from their territories. With this in mind, Turkish troops rounded up thousands of Armenians and forced them to march hundreds of miles to concentration camps, where conditions were so poor that the Armenians were sure to die. Those who escaped this fate were killed outright or deported in forced marches across the desert, which would likely lead to death. By the end of 1916, the Turks had killed over 1.5 million Armenians and deported over 1,750,000.

SEE ALSO: genocide; Kurds, the; Turkey

Armenian Secret Army for the Liberation of Armenia (ASALA)

Created in 1975 by Armenian terrorist Hagop Hagopian, the Armenian Secret Army for the Liberation of Armenia is dedicated to publicizing the 1915 genocide of thousands of Armenian Christians in Turkey; it does this primarily by assassinating Turkish political figures and bombing targets connected to Turkey. Its first attack, however, was against the World Council of Churches in Beirut, Lebanon, in 1975. Hagopian was born in Lebanon, and his group's headquarters were in Beirut until 1982, when Israel took over Lebanon. The following year, ASALA bombed the Turkish Airlines check-in counter at the Orly, France, airport, killing or wounding dozens of people. This act caused dissention in the group, with members arguing over whether it was right to kill innocent bystanders, and ASALA split into two factions. Afterward its membership, which numbered at least a hundred prior to the split, declined dramatically, particularly after Hagopian was murdered in Greece in 1988. (Most terrorist experts suspect that the Turkish government was behind the murder.) ASALA's last known attacks were in the mid-1990s.

SEE ALSO: genocide

Army for the Liberation of Rwanda (ALIR)

The guerrilla force of the political group known as the Party for the Liberation of Rwanda (PALIR), the Army for the Liberation of Rwanda (ALIR) is dedicated to destroying the current government of Rwanda, led by the Tutsi people, and replacing it with a government run by the Hutu. Prior to 1994 the Hutu were in control of Rwanda and engaged in the genocide of over five hundred thousand Tutsi in an attempt to stop them from gaining control of the country. Eventually, however, Tutsi rebels drove the Hutus from power, and the Hutus who had been in-

volved in the genocide fled to neighboring countries. ALIR was formed by members in the Congo, where the group is still based, conducting its operations from camps along the Congo-Rwanda border. In 1999, after demanding that the United States and Great Britain stop supporting the Rwandan government, ALIR retaliated by killing eight American and British tourists who were visiting a game park, known for its mountain gorillas, along the Congo-Uganda border.

SEE ALSO: genocide

Army of God

The Army of God has claimed responsibility for several abortion-clinic bombings in the United States, kidnappings of and attacks on physicians associated with such clinics, and attacks on gays and lesbians. Terrorism experts disagree on whether it is an organized group or a network of anti-abortion terrorists working individually. In either case, the Army of God associates itself with Protestant fundamentalism and white supremacy, and its Web site combines biblical quotations with graphic abortion-related photographs. In addition, *The Army of God Manual* (author unknown) provides information on how to attack abortion clinics.

The Army of God's first-known violent actions occurred in 1982, when anti-abortion terrorists professing to belong to the group bombed a Florida abortion clinic and kidnapped an Illinois physician. Authorities arrested several people connected to these crimes, including a man they suspect had founded the Army of God, religious fanatic Don Benny Anderson. However, his absence did not stop the group from bombing clinics in Virginia and Maryland in 1984; in Atlanta, Georgia, in 1997; and in Birmingham, Alabama, in 1998. An apparent member of the Army of God, Eric Robert Rudolph, later pleaded guilty to committing some of these bombings, as well as a bombing at the Centennial Olympic Park in Atlanta, Georgia, during the 1996 Summer Olympic Games. In 2005 he was sentenced to five consecutive life sentences for his crimes. In 2001 another apparent member of the group, Clayton Lee Waagner, sent hundreds of letters that were signed only "the Army of God" to abortion clinics across the country, falsely claiming that the envelopes held deadly anthrax.

See Also: anthrax; antiabortion terrorism

Aryan Nations (AN)

Also called the Church of Jesus Christ Christians, the Aryan Nations (AN) is a radical Christian group with ties to the neo-Nazi movement. It came to the attention of the American public in the 1980s, when some of its members, calling themselves the Order, joined with members of the Ku Klux Klan and a neo-Nazi group called National Alliance to commit several bank robberies that brought in over $4 million. Their aim was to finance certain political terrorist acts that they had read about in a 1978 novel entitled *The Turner Diaries* by National Alliance leader William Pierce. However, in 1985 they were caught and imprisoned before they could commit any of those acts. These and other AN members already in prison, who called themselves the Aryan Brotherhood, worked with those on the outside to create a newsletter called *The Way*, promoting their beliefs. They particularly encouraged neo-Nazis, skinheads, and white supremacists to join with them, and thanks to these efforts their membership grew dramatically during the 1990s. Then in 1998 an incident occurred that dealt a serious blow to the group. When a woman named Victoria Keenan and her son Jason happened past the AN headquarters—a twenty-acre compound in Hayden Lake, Idaho—several security guards there brutally attacked them out of paranoia. The two later sued AN, and in 2000 a jury awarded them over $6 million, a settlement that included taking possession of the Hayden Lake compound. Consequently, although the group still exists, it has few assets and few members.

See Also: neo-Nazis; skinheads; white supremacists

Asahara, Shoko
(1955–)

As the leader of a Japanese cult known as Aum Shinrikyō, Shoko Asahara was responsible for a 1994 terrorist attack on a Japanese neighborhood and a 1995 attack on the Tokyo subway system, both of which involved the use of poisonous gas. The first attack was intended to murder three judges who were deliberating a case against Aum Shinrikyō; all three were injured and, seven people in the neighborhood were killed. The second attack was intended to disrupt the Japanese transit system, thereby striking a blow at the government. This attack killed twelve, injured thousands, and instilled fear in mass-transit passengers throughout the world. Moreover it caused governments to issue guidelines for how to deal with future gas attacks.

Nearly blind in one eye, Asahara nonetheless was a childhood bully, but in the early 1980s he became extremely religious and studied a variety of faiths. In 1984 he started teaching seminars on religion in Tokyo, Japan, and in 1987, after visiting India, he claimed that he had attained the highest level of spirituality known to Buddhists: Enlightenment. (Only Buddha himself had attained this.) At another time he claimed to be a reincarnated Hindu god, Shiva. In addition, Asahara embraced the Christian concept of Armageddon, a battle between the forces of good and evil at the end of the world. He told the attendees of his seminars that he could show them how to save people from this battle and how to levitate and teleport themselves using mind power, if they submitted themselves completely to his leadership. In this way, he created the cult Aum Shinrikyō (Supreme Truth), which at its peak had over nine thousand members. This group had harsh rules and punishments, including beatings for those who tried to leave the cult. It also required members to engage in strange rituals accompanied by drug use and to give all of their money to the cult. Eventually the group expanded beyond Japan into such countries as Russia, the United States, Australia, and Sri Lanka.

In 1990 Asahara, along with several of his followers, ran for political office, expecting to become a member of the Japanese Parliament (known as the Diet). When he lost the election, he became angry at humanity and decided that rather than save people from Armageddon, members of Aum Shinrikyō had a duty to create their own Armageddon, by battling evil people in the hope of bringing about the end of the world. He therefore began amassing weapons, including biological and chemical ones, and by 1993 he was planning attacks on various targets. In 1995 Asahara was arrested for his gas attacks and other crimes, and during his trial his attorneys tried unsuccessfully to prove that he was mentally insane. In February 2004 Asahara was sentenced to death by hanging; however, given Japan's lengthy appeals process, it might take as long as ten years before he is executed or has his sentence reversed.

SEE ALSO: Aum Shinrikyō

Asia, terrorism in

Most terrorism in Asia stems either from criminal activities related to the drug trade or from ethno-nationalism, the latter of which occurs when ethnic groups fight out of a belief that they must defend their cultural identity and traditions, religious or otherwise. Asian ethno-nationalist terrorism has its roots in the postcolonial period after World War II, when European powers were forced to give up their colonies in the region. In most cases, the postcolonial states had a ruling majority that remained tied politically, economically, and militarily with the foreigners who had once controlled their lands, along with one or more ethnic minority that had been shut out of the political process for years. When these minority groups continued to be shut out despite increasing demands for a political voice, they often called for the creation of their own independent state, and the resulting nationalist movement typically inspired terrorism. Leftist extremists fueled the violence, as Marxists continually encouraged peasants to fight against foreign influences. Marxist-based terrorism is less common in Asia today, but it does still exist, particularly in Nepal.

One of the most prominent examples of ideology-inspired terrorism in Asia is the case of Cambodia, where nationalist Communists have triggered much of the violence since World War II. Prior to the war, this country was held by the French; together with Laos and Vietnam it comprised French Indochina. Vietnamese nationalist rebels began fighting against the colonial government in 1944, and Cambodians soon joined in the rebellion. In 1954 the French abandoned French Indochina, whereupon Cambodia became a monarchy. The establishment of this postcolonial government angered Cambodian Communists, among them a Marxist revolutionary named Pol Pot who had been involved in the fight against the French. In the mid-1960s he established a guerrilla insurgency known as the Khmer Rouge (Red Khmers; "red" refers to the Communist Party, "Khmers" to the ethnicity of most of the participants). From jungle bases, in 1967 the Khmer Rouge began launching attacks on the forces of the government, then ruled by Prince Norodom Sihanouk. Though the attacks were unsuccessful, in 1970 the prince was overthrown by members of his own government, and in an attempt to regain his throne he turned to the Khmer Rouge for help. With the prince's support, the insurgency quickly grew in strength. Its membership increased dramatically after the United States attacked Cambodia in 1970, because Cambodians believed that the Khmer Rouge would be more effective than the government at fighting the foreigners. Consequently in 1975 the Khmer Rouge had enough forces to take control of the capital city of Phnom Penh, and thus the government. The insurgents then renamed Cambodia "Democratic Kampuchea" and forced hundreds of thousands of people in Phnom Penh to move into the countryside and work on building and agricultural projects. Those who refused to work were executed, while others died of starvation, disease, or exhaustion; the bodies (by some estimates, nearly 2 million) were dumped in an area later called the killing fields. For the next four years, until the Khmer Rouge lost power, the state engaged in these and other acts of domestic terrorism in an attempt to create their version of a Communist society in Cambodia.

The Republic of the Philippines is another example of Asian terrorism caused by a nationalist movement, and it too has Marxist elements, but in this case religion is more at issue than ethnicity. The country is over 90 percent Christian, with Muslims and Buddhists in the minority. During the 1990s, Islamic militants called for the creation of a Muslim state in the southern Philippines. One militant group, Abu Sayyaf, has committed numerous terrorist acts in the furtherance of this cause. In 2001 in order to call attention to its cause, Abu Sayyaf kidnapped twenty people from a resort in Malaysia and shortly thereafter beheaded one of the American hostages.

Radical Islamic movements have also appeared in Indonesia, Pakistan, Malaysia, and Afghanistan. Religious and ethno-nationalist terrorist groups operate in many other parts of Asia as well, largely because it is comprised of so many different ethnic, religious, and cultural groups. In the Punjab region of India, for example, Sikh nationalists (believers in the religion of Sikhism) commit terrorist acts against non-Sikhs, while in Jammu and Kashmir regions controlled by India, Muslim terrorists strike out at non-Muslims. Chechnya and Sri Lanka have also experienced terrorism; in fact, Sri Lanka was the birthplace of one of the most vicious terrorist groups in the world, the Liberation Tigers of Tamil Eelam (LTTE, also known as the Tamil Tigers). This group was responsible for assassinating several political and military leaders, including Premier Rajiv Gandhi of India in 1991 and President Ranasinghe Premadasa of Sri Lanka in 1993.

The Tamil Tigers are funded primarily through the drug trade, and many other

Asian terrorist groups, including Abu Sayyaf, traffic in drugs as well. This is understandable, since most of the world's opium and heroin are manufactured in southwest and Southeast Asia and then sent to central Asia for transport to other countries. Various groups, not only in Asia but elsewhere, have fought with one another over who will control this industry. For example, Islamic extremists in Afghanistan have tried to take control of the heroin and opium trade in order to promote *jihad* (a holy war against those who do not support Islam), whereas groups in Myanmar (Burma) have sought the same control out of a desire to fund a nationalist movement.

SEE ALSO: Abu Sayyaf; Cambodian killing fields; Khmer Rouge; Philippines, the; Sikh extremists; Sri Lanka; Tamil Tigers, the

assassination, political

Political assassination—the killing of someone for political reasons—has been employed against hundreds of heads of state and other government officials, as well as against representatives of political organizations, the military, law enforcement, and corporations. Writers, filmmakers, teachers, and other public figures have also been assassinated, or threatened with assassination, for sharing their political views. Regardless of the target, most assassinations are committed by terrorists, anarchists, revolutionaries and other individuals who believe that their actions are justified because they serve a greater good.

Anarchists in particular believe that assassination is a necessary component of the revolutionary violence that will enact political and therefore social change. Consequently in the late nineteenth and early twentieth centuries, anarchists assassinated

the Russian czar Alexander II, the Austro-Hungarian empress Elizabeth, the Italian king Umberto I, the French president Carnot, and U.S. president William McKinley, hoping that the elimination of these leaders would decentralize political power, thereby destroying capitalism and state socialism and allowing individualism and atheism to flourish. Although this did not come to pass, the assassinations significantly influenced the political climate of their time, and other assassinations of world leaders have done the same. For example, the assassination of the archduke of Austria, Franz Ferdinand, by a Serbian terrorist group led to World War I, and the assassination of U.S. president Abraham Lincoln by John Wilkes Booth led to changes in how the Union dealt with the Confederacy after the Civil War.

Some assassinations, however, are based more on religion than on politics. This has been the case with Jewish and Muslim terrorists in the Middle East, who typically view their conflicts as being part of a struggle between the faithful and the unbelievers. In fact, radical Jews and Muslims will sometimes attack members of their own religion whom they perceive as having lost their faith. For example, on November 4, 1995, a Jewish extremist, Yigal Amir, assassinated Israeli prime minister Yitzhak Rabin because Amir felt that Rabin's political decisions (which included making peace with Muslims) had made him an enemy of the Jews. Amir later said that God had guided his actions.

But not just individuals and terrorist groups employ assassination; the state also uses it to destroy its enemies, targeting either a single person or a specific group of people. For example, in September 1976, the former Chilean foreign minister, Orlando Letelier, and his assistant were killed in Washington, D.C., by a bomb that was planted by agents of Chile's secret police. When such actions are taken against terrorist leaders and their supporters, it is known as counterterrorist assassination. Israel has engaged in this practice extensively; its most common targets have been Palestinian nationalists. For example, Israeli agents tried unsuccessfully to assassinate two members of the Palestine Liberation Organization (PLO) in Beirut, Lebanon, in July 1970 and a Hamas leader in Amman, Jordan, in September 1997. They were successful, however, in the July 2002 assassination of a leader of Hamas, Sheik Salah Shehadeh, his wife, and three children. In 1972 and 1973 covert Israeli agents also assassinated at least twenty Palestinian terrorists connected to a massacre of eleven Israeli athletes during the 1972 Munich Olympics, tracking the terrorists down one by one in Europe and the Middle East as an act of revenge. In the United States, however, such assassinations have been illegal since December 1981, when President Ronald Reagan signed an executive order prohibiting all government employees from engaging in the practice or from hiring anyone as an assassin. (By this time, the government had—officially, at least, since the end of the Vietnam War—stopped engaging in the practice of assassinating its political enemies, and Reagan's predecessor, President Gerald Ford, had signed his own executive order restricting its use.) Many other nations also insist that they do not engage in state-sponsored assassinations, even as a counterterrorist tool. However, there is no way to know whether this is actually the case, or whether covert assassination operations are in place.

SEE ALSO: anarchism; counterterrorism; Black September; Hamas; McKinley, William; Munich Olympics crisis; Rabin, Yitzhak

Assassins Sect, the

Also called the Brotherhood of Assassins, the Assassins Sect was a Muslim cult that committed terrorist acts in the Middle East from the eleventh to the thirteen centuries. The cult arose out of a dispute within the Fatimid Dynasty (AD 909 to 1171), a political and religious empire, adhering to the Ismaili sect of the Shiite branch of the Islamic religion, that controlled North Africa and Egypt as well as the Middle East. In 1094 its ruler, al-Mustansir, died after nominating the elder of his two sons, Nizar, as his successor. However, the leader of the Fatimid military, al-Afdal, supported al-Mustansir's younger son, Ahmad, because Ahmad was married to al-Afdal's sister. In the resulting conflict, Ahmad—who changed his name to al-Mustali—emerged victorious, ruling the empire from Cairo, Egypt, until 1101. However, in what is now Iran, Iraq, Syria, and central Asia, many people refused to accept al-Mustali's right to the throne; among them was Hasan-e Sabah, the leader of an Ismaili mission in Iran. Sabah created a group, the Nizari Ismailis, dedicated to assassinating people who supported the new ruler. Their first target was a Turkish minister, Nizam al-Mulk, in 1092, followed shortly thereafter by one of Nizam's sons, Fakhri. In 1130 they succeeded in killing al-Mustali's son, al-Amir, who had assumed the throne in 1101. The group also targeted people who did not adhere to their form of Islam, believing that it was their divine purpose to spread Ismaili Islam throughout the Muslim world.

Because they struck without warning, the Nizari Ismailis generated fear throughout much of the Middle East, where they were commonly known as *hashishin* because their members were rumored to use the drug hashish before committing murder. (Most historians believe that these rumors were untrue.) Christian Crusaders heard this word as "assassin," and when they returned to Europe they referred to the Nizari Ismailis as the Assassin Sect. Soon Europeans were using the word "assassin" to refer to individuals who killed in the same manner as members of the Sect; typically, an individual member of the Sect—usually disguised as a cleric, a beggar, or some other harmless person—would catch the victim alone and stab him with a dagger, without any concern over whether subsequent escape was possible. Indeed, most of the Sect's assassins were caught and killed immediately after carrying out their mission.

SEE ALSO: assassination, political

Atlanta's Centennial Park bombing

In Atlanta, Georgia, on July 27, 1996, a cluster of three pipe bombs hidden inside a backpack exploded in Centennial Park, one of the sites staging the 1996 Olympic Games, and wounded over a hundred people, two of whom died (one from injuries sustained in the blast and the other from a heart attack). Most of the injuries were caused by flying debris, because the pipe bombs contained screws and nails in addition to gunpowder.

Roughly twenty minutes before the bombing, a man called 9-1-1 and said that an explosion would happen in the park in thirty minutes; authorities later suspected that the phone call was intended to make sure that police would be in the park when the bomb went off. By the time of the call, however, the bombs had already been found by a security guard, Richard Jewell,

employed by the communications company AT&T to protect its towers in the park. Jewell alerted authorities, who then started evacuating the area; nonetheless, three days later, authorities decided that Jewell must have planted the bomb. For months thereafter, investigators struggled to gather evidence that would prove Jewell was the bomber, and media reports of the investigation severely damaged his reputation. He was cleared, however, after additional bombings took place in Atlanta and Birmingham, Alabama, that were similar to the Centennial Park bombing. In late 1997 these bombings led police to suspect that an antiabortion activist, Eric Robert Rudolph, had committed all of the bombings, including the one in Centennial Park. In October 1998 Rudolph was charged with the Centennial Park bombing, though he could not be located at the time; he remained at large until 2005, and after he was captured he pleaded guilty in exchange for receiving five consecutive life sentences rather than the death penalty. Rudolph revealed that he planted the bomb in Centennial Park in an attempt to stop the Olympics, so that the hosting country, the United States, would be lessened in the eyes of the world, which Rudolph believed it deserved given its stance on abortion. Nonetheless the Olympic Games continued as planned.

SEE ALSO: Olympic Games as terrorist targets; Rudolph, Eric

Atta, Mohamed (1968–2001)

Egyptian terrorist Mohamed Atta was one of the masterminds of the September 11, 2001, terrorist attacks on America, leading the hijacking of one of the planes that crashed into New York's World Trade Center. As a young man, he studied engineering and architecture at the Cairo University in Egypt, and urban planning at the Technical University in Hamburg, Germany. While in Hamburg, he became involved with the al Qaeda terrorist group, though terrorism experts disagree on how this came about. After graduating from the Technical University in 1999, he went to the United States and, in 2000, enrolled in flight school in Florida, occasionally interrupting his studies—which involved numerous practice flights—to travel to other cities, both in the United States and abroad, to meet with suspected terrorists. On September 11, 2001, he and another man, Abdul Alomari, boarded American Airlines Flight 11 in Boston, Massachusetts, having flown there from Portland, Maine, the day before. Also on board were three other terrorists who, along with Atta and Alomari, took over the plane shortly after takeoff and flew it into the north tower of the World Trade Center.

SEE ALSO: al Qaeda; September 11 attacks on America

Aum Shinrikyō

Founded by religious extremist Shoko Asahara in 1985, Aum Shinrikyō (Supreme Truth) is a Japanese religious cult responsible for several terrorist attacks using poisonous gas. In 1993 the group sprayed first botulism and then anthrax into the air at two locations in Tokyo, hoping these biological weapons would kill thousands. Instead, they failed to make even one person sick, so they turned to sarin gas, a deadly chemical weapon, and on June 17, 1994, they released it into a residential neighborhood where three judges whom they considered their enemies were living. (The judges were about to rule on a property dispute case against the cult, probably with a guilty verdict.) This time the gas worked,

but because of a shift in the wind it killed 7 people instead of the judges and injured 150 more. On March 20, 1995, the cult struck again after learning that the police were about to raid a compound where most cult members lived. This time, 5 cult members released sarin gas at five separate locations along Tokyo's subway line, killing 12 and injuring several thousand.

Aum Shinrikyō turned to terrorism after its founder decided that it was the mission of his cult to hasten the coming of Armageddon, a battle between good and evil at the end of the world. Asahara attracted members to his cult by conducting religious seminars in a Tokyo storefront, where he also taught yoga. He told attendees that only by purifying themselves would they be able to enter the spiritual world that would emerge after Armageddon destroyed the physical world. His cult, he said, offered the necessary purification methods. Asahara also said that he could teach cult members how to levitate and teleport themselves, and he claimed at various times to be a reincarnated Hindu god, Shiva, or an Enlightened being like Buddha. He made his followers drink his blood, take drugs, and give him all of their money, and he beat them when they wouldn't cooperate or tried to run away. He also ordered the murder of a lawyer who tried to help the families of his cult members escape from Asahara's grasp.

Asahara invested the money he earned through the cult in a variety of businesses, and these earned him still more money. By some estimates, during the 1990s Aum Shinrikyō had assets of over a million dollars and over 9,000 members, primarily in Tokyo but also in the United States, Russia, Australia, and Sri Lanka. The group also had its own manufacturing plants for conventional weapons, biological weapons, and chemical weapons. After the Tokyo subway attacks, several of the cult's members were jailed, including Asahara, though some are still being sought by police.

In February 2004 Asahara was sentenced to death by hanging. However, the group is still active and renamed Aleph (The Beginning). Terrorism experts estimate that it has approximately 1,650 members in Japan and 300 in Russia, the majority contributing their income to the group. In addition, Aum Shinrikyō owns several businesses, primarily in the computer software field, and offers yoga classes and religious seminars through which it recruits new members.

SEE ALSO: Asahara, Shoko

Ayyash, Yahya
(1966–1996)

Yahya Ayyash orchestrated dozens of suicide attacks against Israel as one of the leaders of the Palestinian terrorism group Hamas. Born in Palestine's West Bank, he studied engineering and chemistry at a university in Saudi Arabia, and when he returned to Palestine he immediately began using this knowledge to build bombs. His work made him a hero to Palestinians, who called him "the Engineer," while Israel targeted him for assassination. In 1996, someone—probably an Israeli agent—rigged Ayyash's cell phone to detonate when he answered it, and the resulting explosion decapitated him.

SEE ALSO: bombers, suicide; Palestine

Bakunin, Mikhail (1814–1876)

One of the first anarchists and among the most violent, Russian radical Mikhail Bakunin is sometimes called the grandfather of terrorism, primarily for two reasons. First, he promoted the idea that all acts of violence against a corrupt government are worth committing, no matter how many people are killed or injured in the process. Second, he argued that the only way for a revolutionary group to avoid corruption is to shun a large organizational structure in favor of a loose connection of small groups with safeguards in place to ensure that if authorities captured one of these groups, its members would not be able to disclose the location of the others. This structure—known as a network of cells—is used by many terrorist groups today.

Biographers of Bakunin have speculated that he developed his hatred of government, and therefore of authority, while attending a strict military school as a boy. After graduating, he spent only six months as a soldier before leaving the Russian Army to meet up with radicals in Moscow and elsewhere in Europe, and give speeches advocating his anarchist beliefs. While he was outside of Russia, the Russian government charged him with treason, put him on trial in absentia, and sentenced him to exile in Siberia. Consequently Bakunin did not return to Russia, but instead took part in various revolutions in Europe in 1848 and 1849. Arrested, tried, convicted, and sentenced to death in both France and Austria for his activities, he escaped execution only because the Russian czar officially requested that he be returned to Moscow, and after several years of imprisonment there, in 1857 Bakunin was sent to Siberia. Four years later, however, he escaped Siberia and made his way back to Europe, where he again engaged in revolutionary activities.

As the leader of a movement known as collective anarchism or collectivism, Bakunin also promoted the idea that labor strikes be used to destroy governments and engaged in efforts to establish labor organizations in Latin countries, such as Italy and Spain. During this period, he and fellow Russian revolutionary Sergey Nechayev authored a pamphlet called *Catechism of a Revolutionist* (1869), which included the notion that a revolutionary had to devote himself wholeheartedly to his cause, without concern for family or friends—an idea embraced by modern terrorists.

SEE ALSO: anarchism

Basque Homeland and Liberty (Euskadi ta Askatasuna, or ETA)

Formed in 1959, the terrorist group known as Basque Homeland and Liberty ("Euskadi ta Askatasuna" in the Basque language of Euskara), commonly called ETA, has used bombings, assassinations, kidnappings, and other attacks and assaults to promote its cause: liberating the Spanish Basque region from Spain. This region is in the Pyrenees Mountains between

Spain and France, as is the French Basque region. Both regions were an independent land until approximately 1800, when Spain and France each took control of half of this land. But even then the Basques continued to have a unique culture and language and were allowed to manage their own affairs. Under Spain's dictator Francisco Franco, however, in the 1930s the Basques were denied their traditional autonomy; in fact, they were ordered to speak Spanish instead of their own language. As a result, a Basque separatist movement developed in Spain during the 1940s–1960s. By the 1970s the idea of Basque nationalism had many supporters, not only in Spain but in France, and the ETA was able to establish a network in France from which it could plan attacks on Spanish targets. The group killed several officials in the Spanish government. Among the most prominent was the prime minister, Admiral Carrero Blanco, whose assassination in 1973 was accomplished by planting a bomb beneath the road he would travel; the resulting explosion blew his car over a five-story building.

In 1975, after Franco died, the ETA increased its activities, hoping that the change in Spain's government would lead to the Basque separatism it sought, and indeed, the new government did give the Basques back some of their autonomy, providing them with civil liberties and allowing them to elect their own parliament and form their own labor organizations. This was enough for many members of ETA, and the group's numbers seriously declined, particularly after the Spanish government legalized the Basque separatist political party, the Basque Nationalist Party (PNV), and established a program during the mid-1980s that forgave ETA members for past terrorist acts providing

they renounced the ETA. Nonetheless remaining members continued to fight for full separatism; in fact more than 90 percent of the approximately eight hundred deaths attributable to the ETA occurred after Franco's death. Moreover several factions of the ETA formed, some of which cooperated with a similar group in the French Basque region, the Enbata. This cooperation proved troublesome for ETA, because the Enbata's attacks on French soil led the French government to partner with Spain in eliminating Basque terrorism. To this end, the French ended political asylum for Spanish nationals, making it possible for authorities to send members of ETA's network in France back to Spain. By 1992 this network had largely been dismantled; however, in 2000 two Basque separatist youth groups, Jarrai in Spain and Gasteriak in France, joined to create a new group, Haika, that is allied with the ETA and engages in terrorist activities in France.

The ETA continues to be active in Spain as well, despite government efforts in the 1980s and '90s to convince members that their terrorist activities were no longer necessary given increased autonomy among the Basques. One of the ETA's most notable attacks occurred in 1987, when the group killed twenty-one people during a supermarket bombing in Barcelona. In 2001 eight ETA members were arrested while planning a car bombing that was intended to target tourists and therefore disrupt Spain's tourism industry. Others wanted by the police fled to Cuba, which, according to a U.S. Department of State report issued in 2001, continues to offer a safe haven to any ETA terrorists escaping the law. Also in 2001 the ETA participated in the Basque election, hoping to gain a majority of the seats in Parliament, but came in second to the PNV. Terrorism experts interpreted this to mean that although many Spanish Basques want full separation from Spain, they are unwilling to support violence in order to achieve this aim.

SEE ALSO: Basque separatists

Basque separatists

Basque separatists are people from the Basque regions in Spain and France, located in the Pyrenees Mountains between the two countries, who believe that their homeland should become a separate nation. The Spanish Basque region and the French Basque region were an independent land until approximately 1800, when Spain and France divided it up between them, but even then the Basques maintained a unique culture and language and were allowed to manage their own affairs. Under Spain's dictator Francisco Franco, however, in the 1930s the Basques were denied their traditional autonomy and ordered to speak Spanish instead of their native language of Euskara. As a result, a Basque separatist movement developed in Spain and eventually spread to France as well. Out of this movement came a political party, the Basque Nationalist Party (PNV), as well as terrorist groups dedicated to promoting Basque separatism; the most prominent and most violent of these terrorist groups is ETA (Euskadi ta Askatasuna, which means "Basque Homeland and Liberty" in Euskara). In the late 1970s, after Franco's death, Basque separatists in Spain managed to gain some independence when the Spanish government allowed the Basque to elect their own parliament and provided them with other rights. Nonetheless, members of the PNV, the ETA, and other pro-separatism groups continue to work for full autonomy. In 2001 both the PNV and the ETA vied for control of the Basque Parliament, the former advocating a peaceful approach to the fight for separatism. The PNV won the majority of seats in the election.

SEE ALSO: Basque Homeland and Liberty

Bataan death march

An example of Japanese terrorism toward prisoners during World War II, and one of the worst war crimes of the twentieth century, the Bataan death march occurred on the Bataan Peninsula in the Philippines. In April 1942 over seventy thousand American and Filipino soldiers surrendered to the Japanese in the Philippines. The Japanese then forced them to march 55 miles (88-km) through jungles, from the southern end of the peninsula to the town of San Fernando. Once there they boarded a train to another town, Capas, from which they had to march 8 miles (13-km) to reach their prisoner-of-war camp, Camp O'Donnell. During their 63-mile (101-km) march, those who walked too slowly were brutally beaten, and those who dropped to the ground were either killed or buried alive; others died of starvation, dysentery, or disease. As a result, approximately ten thousand prisoners died before reaching camp, while at least fourteen thousand more escaped into the jungle. After Japan lost the war, its commander in the Philippines, Lieutenant General Homma Masaharu, was found guilty in a U.S. military court for his role in the Bataan death march and was executed on April 3, 1946.

SEE ALSO: Japan; Philippines, the

Begin, Menachem

As the prime minister of Israel, Menachem Begin launched a 1982 attack on Lebanon that was intended to destroy the bases of the Palestine Liberation Organization (PLO) but resulted in the deaths of thousands of innocent Palestinians in refugee camps. Long before becoming prime minister in 1977, however, Begin was known for his careless use of violence. In the 1940s he led the Irgun Zvai, a terrorist group dedicated to the establishment of an independent Israeli state, in blowing up the King David Hotel in Jerusalem; this act was an attack on British officials staying at the hotel, but it also killed or injured dozens of innocent tourists and hotel workers. Nonetheless in 1979 Begin entered into a peace treaty with Egyptian president Anwar Sadat, and in 1978 both men were awarded the Nobel Peace Prize. Begin ended his service as prime minister in 1983 and never again held public office.

SEE ALSO: King David Hotel bombing; Sadat, Anwar

Beirut bombings (1983)

In 1983 terrorists struck out at the United States via two suicide bombings in Beirut, Lebanon. During the first attack, which occurred in April, the bomber rammed a pickup truck filled with explosives into the U.S. embassy, killing 17 Americans and 46 Lebanese and injuring 120 others. During the second attack, in October, the bomber entered a U.S. Marine base, which was also a French military headquarters, killing 241 American marines and 58 French paratroopers. The terrorist group Hezbollah took credit for both bombings. Its goal was to drive out the multinational peacekeeping force that had entered Lebanon the previous year, and eventually it succeeded; in early 1984 American, French, British, and Italian troops pulled out of the region.

SEE ALSO: Hezbollah; Lebanon

Osama bin Laden is the leader of the terrorist group al Qaeda, and suspected to be behind the terrorist attacks on September 11, 2001. AP IMAGES

bin laden, Osama

Saudi Arabian terrorist Osama bin Laden is the leader of the terrorist group al Qaeda and believed to be responsible for the September 11, 2001, attacks on the World Trade Center and the Pentagon. Among the most radical of the Islamic fundamentalists, bin laden abhors secular governments and wants to create a new world order in which Islam dominates, there are no borders between Muslim countries, and the state of Israel no longer exists. In the short term, he wants to drive the United States out of the Middle East and overthrow the governments of Saudi Arabia, Egypt, and other Middle Eastern countries with ties to the United States. Because of such views, bin laden is estranged from his family, which owns a construction company, the bin laden Group, that has done business with the Saudi and U.S. governments.

bin laden was an extremely religious Muslim even as a young man, but it was during his college years at the King Abd al-Aziz University in Jeddah, Saudi Arabia, that he embraced radical Islamic fundamentalism, having been influenced in his thinking by some of the professors there. In December 1979, at the age of twenty-two, he decided to fight in what Islamic clerics call a *jihad*, or holy war, in Afghanistan, where Muslims were defending their lands against Russian invaders. Once in Afghanistan, he began using money that he had inherited when his father died to finance this war and to establish training camps for the Muslims who traveled there to become soldiers. (bin laden's father was killed in a helicopter crash in 1968, leaving behind an inheritance worth billions of dollars to be divided among fifty-one children.) In 1984 bin laden and a Palestinian Muslim, Abdullah Azzam, created a recruitment office, the Maktab al-Khidamat, to encourage more Muslims to join the fight; after Azzam was killed in a car bombing in 1989, bin laden continued his recruitment efforts alone, even after Russia retreated from Afghanistan. With this war over, bin laden's fighters spread out throughout the Middle East, creating the terrorist cells that would form al Qaeda.

Meanwhile, bin laden went to Saudi Arabia, where he spoke out publicly against that country's government and its relationship with the United States. Many of these speeches, which became even more anti-American after the United States stationed troops in Saudi Arabia in early 1991 as part of its Operation Desert Shield mili-

tary campaign, were recorded and then disseminated in Saudi Arabia and elsewhere in the Middle East, where they acted as recruitment tools for al Qaeda. In April 1991 bin laden decided to abandon Saudi Arabia for Sudan, largely because Sudan's government was radical Islamic. There he started three new military camps that trained Muslim guerrillas from many different countries, as well as a political group, the Advice and Reform Council, whose aim was to work toward the overthrow of the Saudi government. He also established a construction company and other businesses that both enhanced Sudan's infrastructure and funded al Qaeda operations.

In 1993 al Qaeda began attacking American troops, at first by planting bombs in hotels in Yemen where soldiers were to be housed en route to Somalia. The intended victims were not there, however, so the bombs killed tourists instead. That same year al Qaeda members killed eighteen American soldiers in Mogadishu, Somalia, and were possibly responsible for a bombing of the World Trade Center in New York. Several other bombings occurred from 1994 to 1996, when bin laden relocated to Afghanistan. At that time, the country was under the control of radical Islamic fundamentalists called the Taliban, with whom bin laden quickly established ties. He also continued to access a large financial network and to distribute funds to terrorists all over the world, despite the fact that in 1993 the Saudi government froze his assets in an attempt to stop his terrorist activities.

These activities escalated once bin laden was in Afghanistan. In 1996 he called for all faithful Muslims to join in a *jihad* against Americans and Jews in the Middle East, and in 1998—the same year that U.S.

president Bill Clinton authorized the use of force, deadly if necessary, to capture bin laden—he issued a *fatwa*, or religious decree, that compelled Muslims to kill all Americans everywhere, even innocent civilians. As a result, there were several more al Qaeda bombings, culminating in the September 11, 2001, attacks on American soil. By this time, the Taliban had asked bin laden to stop his campaign against the United States, fearing retribution against Afghanistan; nonetheless the Taliban refused to surrender bin laden to the United States after the attacks, saying there was no evidence that bin laden was behind the September 11 terrorism. Angered over this refusal, U.S. president George W. Bush ordered air strikes against Afghanistan, bombing the country under a military operation known as Operation Enduring Freedom, which resulted in the ouster of the Taliban; the new Afghan government was essentially a puppet of the United States, but bin laden still had supporters in the country, and he was able to avoid capture in a mountainous region of eastern Afghanistan. In the early 2000s, apparently while still in hiding there, he made several videotapes in which he called for Muslims to attack Americans. Today his whereabouts are unknown, though many people believe he is still in Afghanistan, where the Taliban is again gaining power. The United States has offered a $25 million reward for his capture.

SEE ALSO: al Qaeda; September 11 attacks on America; Taliban

bioterrorism

Also known as biological terrorism, bioterrorism employs biological agents that poison or induce disease in humans via organisms or pathogens, the latter of which include toxic plants, bacteria, and viruses.

Victims of bioterrorism might be exposed to these biological agents through skin contact or exposure to contaminated air, food, or water. In committing bioterrorism, terrorists' aim is generally to kill a large number of people at a time; however, it is difficult to produce and distribute enough biological agents to create this type of widespread destruction.

Biological agents were first used as weapons in ancient times, when warriors laying siege to a city might intentionally contaminate the city's food and water sources with rotting carcasses or the bodies of people known to have died of a disease. Since then, many governments have turned to biological weapons in times of war. For example, during the French and Indian Wars of the eighteenth century, the British tried to wipe out Native American populations by giving the tribes blankets that had been contaminated with the smallpox disease; in World War II, the Japanese attempted to decimate the Chinese by delivering plague-ridden fleas to Chinese towns via air drops of flea-ridden wheat; during the Cold War both the United States and Russia manufactured large amounts of the deadly anthrax disease; and in the Persian Gulf War, Iraq manufactured a variety of biological weapons.

But although world leaders have sometimes authorized the manufacture of biological weapons, they have also feared becoming victims of bioterrorism. In 1925 this fear led several nations to sign a treaty, the Geneva Conventions, that included a pledge not to use biological weapons. In 1972 these nations and others signed another treaty, the Biological and Toxin Weapons Convention, that banned not only the use of biological weapons but their development, manufacture, and storage. However, there is no way to verify whether any particular nation at any particular time is honoring this treaty, and in fact, there is evidence to suggest that as many as thirty to forty nations have secret facilities that manufacture biological weapons. For example, after the Gulf War, stockpiles of anthrax and other biological agents, as well as chemical agents, were found at a laboratory in Iraq, and after the fall of the Soviet Union (now Russia), U.S. intelligence officers learned that the Soviets had accidentally released anthrax spores into the air around a secret bacteriological warfare facility in the Ural Mountains in April 1979; several people died as a result of this incident.

Anthrax was also used in the first instance of widespread bioterrorism in the United States, which occurred shortly after the September 11, 2001, terrorist attacks on American soil. A disease affecting both livestock and humans, anthrax is caused by a bacterium called *Bacillus anthracis*; when grazing animals ingest anthrax spores in soil, the spores germinate into bacteria inside their intestinal systems and are later released in great numbers, via blood and body fluids, back into the soil, where the bacteria again form spores. These spores are extremely hardy, and they are the only way that anthrax can spread. In other words, a person sick with anthrax cannot infect another person with the disease. Instead, people contract anthrax when spores enter the body in one of three ways: through a skin cut or lesion, in which case the victim has cutaneous anthrax; by breathing in spores, in which case the victim has inhalation anthrax; or by eating spore-contaminated meat. In the 2001 case, someone sent letters contaminated with anthrax spores through the mail to government and media offices in

the eastern United States; the five people who died as a result of opening the envelopes had breathed in the spores and suffered inhalation anthrax, which is the most deadly form of the disease.

In addition to anthrax, three other deadly biological agents have been identified by terrorism experts as those most likely to be used by terrorists: smallpox, botulism, and bubonic plague. Smallpox has been eliminated in nature, but some research laboratories still have samples of this highly contagious disease, and terrorism experts fear that terrorists will steal this material and use it to infect others. Botulism is a common bacterium that can occur naturally in food that has been improperly packaged (indeed in October 2006 one brand of organic carrot juice was pulled from grocery-store shelves after it caused some people to contract botulism), but it can be highly deadly in certain forms and concentrations; some terrorism experts believe that if delivered in an aerosol spray under ideal weather conditions, this toxin could kill the inhabitants of a small city. As for the bubonic plague, this bacterium is spread via the bite of a plaque-infected flea and is almost always deadly.

Another potential biological weapon is the E. coli bacterium, which like botulism is a common bacterium that causes food poisoning. However, E. coli is much less likely than botulism to be deadly, so its purpose as a terrorist weapon would be to cause widespread fear rather than widespread death, and to negatively impact the economy of a nation whose food system has been compromised. This was the case in October 2006, when several cases of E. coli occurred in the United States as a result of tainted fresh spinach. When word spread that contaminated spinach had caused numerous illnesses and the death of a few children and elderly people, sales of not only spinach but other salad greens plummeted, and some Americans speculated that terrorists might have been behind the contamination. (Instead the contamination was more likely caused by E. coli-laced cattle waste unintentionally tracked in to the spinach fields by wild pigs.)

In the 1990s there were several cases of terrorists' trying to acquire biological agents to use as weapons of mass destruction. For example, a member of the white-supremacist group Aryan Nations in the United States tried to buy bubonic plague bacteria to be shipped through the mail, and members of the Japanese terrorist group Aum Shinrikyō tried to purchase the Ebola virus, which is both deadly and highly contagious. (Aum Shinrikyō also successfully received sarin gas, which it used in chemical attacks in 1995.) Terrorism experts remain extremely concerned about such activities, noting that there is no way to know how many biological agents have been manufactured over the years, where they might be stockpiled, or who might be able to access them.

SEE ALSO: anthrax; Aum Shinrikyō; chemical weapons; weapons of mass destruction; weapons, types of terrorist

Birmingham, Alabama, bombings

Several bombings in Birmingham, Alabama, have been classified as acts of terrorism. One of them was inspired by the antiabortion movement, while the rest were racially motivated. The racially motivated bombings took place between 1947 and 1965, when a white-supremacist group called the Ku Klux Klan targeted Birmingham's African American population. In all, members of this group bombed over fifty houses and other buildings.

The Klan attack on September 15, 1963 was particularly notorious because the target was place of worship on a Sunday morning, and four girls wre killed in the explosion: eleven-year-old Denise McNair and three fourteen-year-olds, Carole Robertson, Cynthia Wesley, and Addie Mae Collins. The bomb had been planted in the basement of the Sixteenth Street Baptist Church, where the girls were getting ready for Sunday school; twenty more people gathering in the church upstairs were injured during the blast. Immediately afterward, the African American community reacted with violence against whites, rioting in the streets, setting fires, and throwing rocks and bricks at white-owned cars and houses. The next day, order had been restored in Birmingham, but throughout the country the American public was expressing outrage over the death of the girls and the violation of the sanctity of a church on a day of worship. In fact, this event so moved the nation that it ultimately triggered the passage of the Civil Rights Act of 1964. Nonetheless, Birmingham law-enforcement authorities continued to insist that blacks, not whites, had bombed the church, intentionally ignoring the fact that the Ku Klux Klan had been threatening the attack for months because the church had served as a meeting place for civil rights activists. The police also failed to charge an obvious suspect in the case, Robert Chambliss, a well-known member of the Ku Klux Klan who was caught with illegal dynamite right after the bombing. Consequently the FBI (Federal Bureau of Investigation) stepped in to take over the investigation and soon determined that Chambliss and three other men—Herman Cash, Thomas Blanton Jr., and Bobby Cherry—planned the bombing, but the head of the FBI, Herbert

Hoover, refused to let his agents prosecute the men. (At the time, Hoover said that his decision was based on the fact that there was not enough evidence to win a conviction against them, but years later an investigation into Hoover's activities suggested that he had concealed the existence of such evidence.) In 1971, however, the Alabama attorney general, Bill Baxley, decided he could build a case against Chambliss, and five years later Chambliss was tried. Witnesses revealed much about the activities of the Klan in general and Chambliss in particular at the time of the bombing, and he was swiftly convicted of murder. Chambliss died in jail in 1985, while Cash died elsewhere in 1994. In 2001 Blanton was finally put on trial for the crime, and he too was convicted of murder, as was Cherry in 2002.

The Birmingham antiabortion bombing occurred on January 29, 1998, at the New Woman All Woman Health Center. It was the first antiabortion bombing in the United States to cause a fatality; a security guard was killed in the explosion that also injured a nurse. Witnesses had noticed a 1989 Nissan pickup truck at the scene, and this information led police to determine that antiabortionist Eric Rudolph had committed the crime. They charged him with this crime and other bombings and issued a warrant for his arrest, but could not find him until 2005. After his arrest, Rudolph pleaded guilty in exchange for receiving five consecutive life sentences rather than the death penalty.

SEE ALSO: bombs, types of; Ku Klux Klan; Rudolph, Eric

Black and Tans, the

Named for the color of their uniforms, the Black and Tans were a group of eight hundred disbanded soldiers that the British government sent into Ireland on March 26, 1920, to oppose terrorist attacks there. The attacks were being conducted by the Irish Republican Army (IRA) and the Sinn Féin (Ourselves Alone) political party as part of a drive to form an Irish Republic independent from Great Britain. However, in responding to the violence the Black and Tans often attacked innocent Irish civilians. Moreover the presence of the Black and Tans did not dissuade the terrorists; in fact it increased the violence. The terrorists burned or bombed buildings, including over a hundred police stations, and murdered police, soldiers, and public officials, while encouraging riots in the streets. Eventually British authorities decided to replace the Black and Tans with conventional troops, and by December 1920 there were over forty-three thousand soldiers there, attempting to keep order under martial law.

SEE ALSO: Irish Republican Army; Sinn Féin

Black Hand, the (Serbian)

Also called Union or Death ("Ujedinjenje Ili Smrt" in Serbo-Croatian), the Black Hand (Crna Ruka) was a secret society formed in 1911 to liberate Serbs living in Bosnia, which was annexed by Austria in 1908. The first members of the Black Hand were Serbian army officers and government officials unhappy that the Serbian prime minister, Nikola Pasic, refused to press Serbia's legitimate claim to the annexed land. They felt that the best way to drive the Austrians from Bosnia was through terrorist attacks in the region, and to this end the Black Hand supported terrorist groups in Bosnia and Macedonia and launched attacks on Austrian targets in Bosnia, including government buildings and officials. The leader of the Black Hand,

Colonel Dragutin Dimitrijevic (also known as Colonel Apis), was once the head of the Serbian intelligence agency, a position he obtained after the 1903 assassination of Serbia's King Alexander. Dimitrijevic was one of the leaders of the assassination plot, and in 1913 he led the Black Hand in plotting the assassination of Archduke Franz Ferdinand, who as heir to the Hapsburg throne would eventually rule the Austro-Hungarian Empire. Under Dimitrijevic's guidance, the Black Hand trained seven assassins and smuggled them into Bosnia, where the archduke was planning to visit Sarajevo, the capital city of Bosnia-Herzegovina. There one of the assassins shot and killed the archduke and his wife while they were driving along a parade route in an open car on June 28, 1914. Afterward, the Austrian government tracked down all seven assassins, and eventually they connected the men to Serbia. War broke out between Serbia and the Austro-Hungarian Empire, which resulted in World War I as other countries joined the fray. Meanwhile the Black Hand continued to terrorize politicians in Serbia until 1917, when Serbian military officials tried and executed Dimitrijevic and arrested more than two hundred of his associates, thereby effectively destroying the group.

SEE ALSO: Archduke Franz Ferdinand, assassination of

Black Hand, the (Sicilian)

Also called La Mano Negra, the Black Hand was an organized-crime society of the early twentieth century that engaged in terrorism for profit, threatening violence in order to extort money. The name "Black Hand" was inspired by the fact that in making demands for payment, the group left a menacing note that was "signed" only with a black handprint. The Black Hand originated in Sicily, Italy, in approximately 1750 as part of the Italian Mafia crime syndicate; when one of its members, Don Vito Cascioferro, immigrated to New York in approximately 1900, he established an American version of the Black Hand. More ruthless than its Italian counterpart, this Black Hand terrorized Italian-Sicilian immigrants in New York, Chicago, New Orleans, and other major U.S. cities, demanding that businessmen and shopkeepers make weekly payments in exchange for protection from violence. Anyone who refused to pay this protection money risked being killed or seeing his loved ones tortured or killed, and many had their businesses destroyed. For example, in Chicago from 1900 and 1918, the Black Hand detonated over eight hundred bombs and gunned down dozens of men.

The most notorious Black Hand murderer was Ignazio Saietta, also known as Lupo the Wolf. Police officials knew of his activities and tried unsuccessfully to bring him to justice, but he repeatedly avoided conviction, largely due to the fact that witnesses were afraid to testify against him. Nonetheless New York police lieutenant Joseph Petrosino, also an Italian immigrant, managed to build cases against dozens of other Black Hand members, working to break up the group until he was gunned down by Cascioferro and his henchmen in 1909. Subsequent attempts to eliminate the Black Hand were also unsuccessful. The group continued into the 1920s, when its members became involved with other societies of organized crime.

SEE ALSO: Mafia, the

Black November, Cyprus

In Cyprus, the phrase "Black November" refers to November 1956, when 416 terrorist attacks resulted in over thirty-five deaths in one month. These attacks were conducted by a terrorist group known as the EOKA, or National Organization of Cypriot Fighters, which sought to end British rule on the Mediterranean island. Many of the Greeks on the island wanted Cyprus to become part of Greece, and to this end throughout 1954 they held political demonstrations and asked the United Nations to take up their cause. When these peaceful efforts failed, some turned to violence, forming the EOKA with the intent of using terrorism to drive the British away. Dozens of attacks ensued. For example, on May 24, 1955, the EOKA attempted to kill Cyprus governor Sir Robert Armitage, blowing up a movie theater where he had been just moments before; on November 26, 1955, the group bombed a hotel ballroom filled with Scottish and British partygoers, killing four; and on March 3, 1956, the EOKA blew up a plane that was just about to board passengers. Shortly thereafter, the British government expelled a prominent Greek nationalist, Archbishop Makarios III, from the island, believing him to be tied to the EOKA. This resulted in even more violence, not only against any British living on the island but against the Turks living there as well, because the Turkish Cypriots (who made up roughly one-fifth of the civilian population, which was four-fifths Greek) generally opposed unification with Greece. In addition, in March 1956 the EOKA once again attempted to kill the governor, now Sir John Harding, but the bomb planted in his home failed to explode. Subsequent bombings and shootings, however, were more successful, particularly during Black November—but the violence did not end at that time. Instead, the deaths continued for another two years, until the British

government agreed to allow Cyprus to become an independent republic. At the end of 1958, after this decision was made, the EOKA disbanded, and a year later, on December 14, 1959, the formerly exiled Archbishop Makarios became the president of Cyprus.

SEE ALSO: Greece, terrorism in

Black Panthers

Also called the Black Panther Party for Self-Defense, the militant black-activist group Black Panthers formed in 1966 in Oakland, California, as a violent response to white oppression. Its founders, Huey Newton and Bobby Seale, were angry about the brutality with which Oakland's white police officers treated black suspects at crime scenes. Consequently the Black Panthers acquired devices that allowed them to listen to police radio transmissions, and whenever they heard that police were heading to a crime scene, they sent members of the group there too, armed with guns to ensure that the police did not abuse their power. (It was then legal in California for citizens to carry guns without special permits.) Newton and Seale borrowed the idea for this tactic from another group, the Community Alert Patrol, that had been formed in Los Angeles, California, in 1965 as a response to police brutality during a riot in the Watts area of the city (an event known as the Watts Riots). However, the Black Panthers—who took their name from the symbol of another African American organization, the Lowndes County Freedom Organization of Alabama—took the tactic further by brandishing weaponry and waving law books in front of police while warning them to behave. Otherwise, however, the Panthers did not interfere in any way with police business at the scene. California law-enforcement authorities still complained about the Panthers, and the federal government sent undercover agents to infiltrate the group with the intent of destroying it from within.

Meanwhile the Panthers developed a public face and a private one: In public, they worked politically to achieve better health care and legal representation for blacks and published a newspaper, *The Black Panther*, that helped them grow into a national organization; in private, they trained an underground army and engaged in various illegal activities. Because of these activities, by the early 1970s the group had over forty chapters and more than 2,000 members, but was also considered by the FBI to be a serious threat to public safety. Law-enforcement officials began raiding Panther offices and arresting members, and as a result, over 130 Black Panthers were convicted of serious crimes. The group was also assaulted from within, as fights among its leaders divided it into several factions. In the early 1980s, this infighting led to an end of the Black Panthers in its original form.

SEE ALSO: Black Power movement

Black Power movement

During the 1960s in America, several black nationalist groups formed as part of the Black Power movement, which was a response to white oppression. This movement emphasized political empowerment, self-interest, and black pride, promoting the idea that African Americans need to rediscover their cultural identity while banding together to help and protect themselves. Protection was a key issue, because Black Power emerged as a direct response to violence against African Americans; the spark that created the movement was an attack on civil rights leader James

Meredith, who suffered a gunshot wound while demonstrating that it was safe for blacks to register to vote. Afterward another activist, Stokely Carmichael, spoke in favor of meeting such violence with violence; at his rallies, he encouraged crowds to shout "Black power!" and raise their fists as a sign of solidarity against white oppression. The clenched fist quickly became the symbol of the Black Power movement.

Some members of the Black Power movement advocated nationalism, suggesting that blacks separate themselves from whites physically, socially, and economically. As this idea took hold, certain Black Power groups turned to radicalism and militarism, taking up arms against symbols of white authority. These groups, the most notable of which was the Black Panther Party for Self-Defense, or Black Panthers, engaged in confrontations with white police officers as well as public demonstrations and encouraged all African Americans to arm themselves in self-defense. By the early 1980s, however, this group and others like it had largely disintegrated.

SEE ALSO: Black Panthers

Black September

On September 5, 1972, eight terrorists stormed into the rooms of Israeli athletes at the Olympic Village in Munich, Germany, where the 1972 Olympic Games were being held, wounding a coach, killing one athlete, and taking nine others hostage; when asked to identify themselves, the terrorists said that they were members of a Palestinian terrorist organization called Black September. It is unclear, however, whether such a group actually existed, or whether Black September was the name of the operation. Some terrorism experts believe that the real terrorist group behind the event, which itself became known as Black September, was the Abu Nidal Organization (ANO), which was originally part of the Palestine Liberation Organization (PLO), and that the ANO collaborated with a faction of the PLO, al Fatah, to plan and execute Black September. Other experts believe that al Fatah was solely responsible for the attack. Indeed, in 1999, a member of the Palestine National Council, Mohammed Daoud Machmoud Auda, in his autobiography *Palestine: From Jerusalem to Munich* written under the name Abu Daoud, said that Black September and al Fatah were one and the same.

But regardless of which terrorist organization was responsible for the incident, the hostage-taking did not end as the terrorists intended. They demanded the release of two hundred Arabs from Israeli prisons in exchange for the hostages, but Israel refused to negotiate. Germany then decided to allow the terrorists to leave the country, on a plane to Tunisia, if the hostages were released. But after the terrorists, with their hostages in tow, left the building and began to board helicopters that would take them to a military air base where the plane was waiting, German sharpshooters opened fire. In the resulting confusion, all eleven Israeli athletes were killed, some by the Germans and some by the terrorists; five of the terrorists were also killed, while the other three were captured. Afterward, in 1972 and 1973, covert Israeli agents assassinated at least twenty more Palestinian terrorists connected with Black September, tracking them down one by one in Europe and the Middle East as revenge for the Olympics massacre.

SEE ALSO: Abu Nidal Organization; al Fatah; Munich Olympics crisis

Blackshirt Militia, the (Armata Milizia)

Also known as the Armata Milizia, the Blackshirt militia was a fascist group established by Benito Mussolini in Italy in 1919–1921. Its members, who dressed entirely in black, were out-of-work ex-soldiers unhappy with the socialists and Communists then in power in the Italian government. In order to defeat their political opponents, the Blackshirts used terrorist tactics, including torture, kidnapping, and murder, to force Italians throughout the country to vote for fascist candidates. In 1922 Mussolini led one hundred thousand Blackshirts into Rome in order to take over the buildings of the government, the media, and law enforcement, thereby becoming the leader of Italy and establishing a dictatorship. For years afterward, the Blackshirts continued to use terrorism to keep Mussolini in power, kidnapping or murdering anyone whom he deemed his enemy. They also fought in Africa, Spain, and Russia under Mussolini's orders, as he sought to spread his influence to foreign countries. However, after Mussolini was killed by Italian partisans on April 29, 1945, and Italy was taken over by Allied forces, the Blackshirts destroyed their uniforms and pretended that they had never supported the dictatorship.

SEE ALSO: Mussolini, Benito

Blitz, the

A period of sustained bombing from September 7, 1940, to May 16, 1941, the Blitz ("the lightning," in reference to lightning-strike attacks) was Nazi Germany's attempt to convince the British to back out of World War II by terrorizing the people of London, England, and weakening the country's infrastructure. In fact Germany's ruler, Adolf Hitler, was certain that his air strikes would eventually turn the working-class British against their upper-class leaders and bring about a revolution in England. He also hoped that his bombs would destroy England's defenses, paving the way for a German invasion.

The first air strike on September 7, during which 600 German fighter planes escorted 300 bombers, targeted the Port of London and was followed immediately with a second strike using 180 bombers. As a result, over 430 people were killed in the London area, and over 1,500 were injured. The attacks continued in London every night through the middle of November, using an average of 200 bombers each night, whereupon the Germans began targeting not just London neighborhoods but industrial and port cities throughout England. British attempts to ward off these air assaults with antiaircraft guns and fighter planes were largely unsuccessful; only 75 German planes were downed between November 1940 and February 1941.

Despite the bombings, however, by February the Germans had decided that an invasion of England was unfeasible, so they concentrated on the terror aspect of their air campaign. To this end, they increasingly chose targets based on whether they would kill or at least demoralize innocent civilians as opposed to destroying important military sites. For example, in May 1941 they bombed the British Museum, as well as the Houses of Parliament and St. James's Palace. Numerous churches were also bombed during the Blitz, as well as the London Library, Buckingham Palace, the Café de Paris, the Central Telegraph Office, and many other public buildings. In all, approximately 43,000 civilians died during the Blitz, more than 140,000 were injured, and at least a million homes were demolished. Nonetheless the Ger-

mans failed to turn the British people against one another; instead, the British remained united in their resistance to the Germans.

Bolsheviks, the

The Bolsheviks ("those of the majority," as opposed to their political rivals, the Mensheviks, or "those of the minority") were members of a socialist political group, the Russian Social Democratic Workers' Party, that seized control of Russia in 1917 and, after renaming itself the Communist Party, used terrorism from 1917 to 1921 to destroy their opponents and maintain control of the Russian people. As part of this terrorism, known as the Red Terror, the Bolsheviks conducted mass arrests and took hostages, sending their prisoners to concentration camps or executing them without first putting them on trial. Led by Vladimir Ilyich Lenin, the Russian Social Democratic Workers' Party developed in 1903, when it was restricted to people willing to devote all of their time to revolutionary activities. The Bolsheviks joined with other revolutionaries during the failed Russian Revolution of 1905–1907, but afterward they decided to end ties with other socialist organizations, and they gradually became popular among urban workers and soldiers. In 1917, after the Bolsheviks seized control of Russia (an event called the October Revolution), their Communist Party became the dominant political power in the country, and its political platform became known as Bolshevism. The subsequent terrorism conducted by the Bolsheviks, much of it carried out by a Party organization called the Extraordinary Commission for the Struggle with Counterrevolution and Sabotage (or Cheka), isolated the Communists from socialists elsewhere in the world, who condemned this approach to governance. In

The first explosions of atomic bombs in the 1940s later gave rise to the fear that terrorists would someday use such weapons to wipe out entire populations worldwide. THE LIBRARY OF CONGRESS

the United States the name "Bolshevik" eventually came to be used as a pejorative for anyone with extreme left-wing views. The word has also been used to refer to any supporter of a Marxist-Leninist party or ideology.

SEE ALSO: communism; Lenin, Vladimir

bomb, atom

Also called an atomic bomb, an A-bomb, or a fission bomb, an atom bomb is an explosive weapon whose force comes from the sudden release of energy during a nuclear reaction (specifically, a fission—or splitting—of the nuclei within atoms of heavy elements such as uranium or plutonium). Another type of reaction, fusion, occurs when the nuclei of atoms are pressed together instead of split apart; this process can create a fusion bomb, also called a thermonuclear bomb or hydrogen bomb. Fusion bombs use hydrogen in their reaction, whereas atom bombs use either uranium or plutonium; together these two types of bombs are called nuclear weapons.

Fusion bombs are far more destructive than atom bombs, but also more difficult to work with; they must be combined with a fission bomb for detonation. Consequently, except for small fusion bombs called neutron bombs (which produce only a small amount of blast and heat but release massive amounts of lethal radiation to kill large numbers of people without damaging buildings), most efforts to produce nuclear weapons have concentrated on atom bombs, which are also highly destructive. Using an atom bomb, less than 33 pounds (15-kg) of nuclear material can cause an explosion big enough to destroy a town, with the explosion generating a fireball and a shock wave. Fission also produces neutron and gamma radiation, both of which can be deadly to human beings, which means that atomic explosions release radioactive dust or gas into the air. Given the right wind conditions, this material can spread for miles, coming down to earth as radioactive fallout.

Experts in terrorism fear that terrorists will someday get their hands on an atom bomb. Such a weapon is not easy to manufacture; the process requires special equipment and ingredients, and the steps to produce the bomb are highly complex. Nonetheless, several nations have developed nuclear weapons, and not all of them have kept a close watch on their stockpiles of this material. In fact, experts believe that the Union of Soviet Socialist Republics (USSR), also known as the Soviet Union, lost some of its weapons when it dissolved at the end of 1991.

The USSR tested its first atomic bomb in 1949, Great Britain in 1952, France in 1960, China in 1964, and Pakistan in 1998. Israel had the bomb by 1967, India by 1974, and South Africa by 1982 (though this country has since destroyed such weapons). North Korea is currently developing its nuclear program, and in the fall of 2006 it launched several missiles in order to test its capacity to deliver its bombs to their intended targets. In 1980 Iran acquired non-weapons-grade uranium intended for use in atomic power plants, but with the right technology the country's scientists could easily enrich this uranium for use in bombs. Indeed, in recent years, investigations into the nuclear industry revealed that Pakistan sold secrets on how to make the centrifuge equipment necessary to enrich uranium to Iran, as well as to Libya and North Korea. The person responsible for these sales, Abdul Qadeer Khan, visited at least eighteen other countries during the period that he was marketing nuclear secrets, including Saudi Arabia, Syria, Egypt, Niger, Nigeria, and Sudan. In addition, Argentina and Australia have developed plans to begin enriching uranium.

As a result of such activities, representatives of the International Atomic Energy Agency, which monitors and regulates nuclear proliferation, have stated that as of September 2006 as many as forty-nine nations had the ability to make nuclear weapons. Consequently at that time the organization began discussing ways to tighten restrictions on who can produce nuclear fuel. Some of the participants in

these discussions want all nuclear fuel to go into a fuel bank that nations could access, with full awareness of other nations, only for non-weapons purposes. However, Iran and some other developing nations have insisted that it is their right to have their own nuclear materials, just as the United States does.

The United States is the only country so far to have used the atom bomb as a weapon against another country. Eager to end World War II, it tested its first atom bomb on July 16, 1945, in a desert near Los Alamos, New Mexico, then dropped an atom bomb on Hiroshima, Japan, the following month (on August 6), killing or injuring over 140,000 people. Three days later it dropped an even more powerful atom bomb on Nagasaki, Japan, killing thousands more. The project that developed the atom bomb for the United States, known as the Manhattan Project, involved teams of scientists working at various secret locations, and even they were concerned about what would happen once their weapon was used in the world. The first talks to limit the testing of nuclear weapons occurred in the mid-1950, and in 1963 the first Nuclear Test-Ban Treaty was established between the United States, the Soviet Union, and the United Kingdom; there have been several subsequent agreements restricting nuclear proliferation.

SEE ALSO: bombs, types of; nuclear weapons

bombers, suicide
Suicide bombers are terrorists who blow themselves up in order to kill others and instill fear in the general population. Most suicide bombers kill by strapping explosives, sometimes combined with shrapnel to maximize damage, to their bodies, usually hidden under their clothes, and then

walking into a heavily populated area before triggering the explosion with a detonating device. Others, however, fill a car with explosives, drive it to their intended target, and detonate it. Airplanes have also been used to deliver an explosion. For example, the September 11, 2001, terrorist attacks on the United States, during which terrorists flew airplanes into buildings, have been called suicide bombings, because although the airplanes were not filled with explosives prior to takeoff, the terrorists knew that the jet fuel within the plane would cause a tremendous explosion upon impact.

As in the September 11 attacks, many suicide bombers target ordinary civilians. When this is the case, they typically blow themselves up in a crowded location in order to maximize casualties. For example, in March 2002 a twenty-two-year-old Arab man blew himself up in a restaurant in Haifa, Israel, killing fifteen people. Other suicide bombers, however, target a specific type of person, such as military personnel, diplomatic personnel, government leaders, or foreign workers and tourists. For example, in the 1940s suicide bombers belonging to a group called the League for the Independence of Vietnam (Viet-Nam Doc-Lap Dong-Minh, or the Vietminh) targeted French and Japanese forces in French Indochina in an attempt to force them out of Vietnam, and in recent years, suicide bombers belonging to the radical Islamic group al Qaeda have killed dozens of U.S. soldiers in Iraq. In other instances, the suicide bomber targets a very specific person. For example, in May 1991 a woman who belonged to a Sri Lankan terrorist group called the Tamil Tigers blew herself up in order to assassinate former Indian prime minister Rajiv Gandhi, who was standing next to her. In September

2001, two Afghan al Qaeda operatives assassinated Ahmad Shah Massoud, an Afghani commander who fought against the Taliban movement in Afghanistan, by blowing themselves up while pretending to interview Massoud on film. A suicide bomber might also choose when to explode himself or herself based on the significance of a location rather than on how many people are nearby. For example, al Qaeda suicide bombers attacked several American embassies in 1998 and the USS *Cole*, an American destroyer, in 2000, while Japanese suicide pilots called *kamikaze* intentionally flew their planes, which had been filled with explosives, into U.S. warships during World War II.

Most suicide bombers are religious or ethno-national terrorists, and of these the majority are Arab Muslims, whose Islamic faith teaches them that they will be rewarded in the afterlife for committing such an attack. (In fact, after their deaths, they are considered martyrs among others of their faith.) According to some terrorism experts, the first terrorists to become suicide bombers were members of a radical Islamic splinter group of Hezbollah known as the Islamic Jihad or of Hezbollah itself. These groups, which had backing from Iran and Syria, both took credit for a series of suicide bombings that occurred from 1983 to 1985 in Lebanon, which was then occupied by American and French peacekeeping troops. During this period in the city of Beirut, the bombers killed 241 U.S. Marines and 58 French paratroopers, after which both the United States and France pulled their forces out of the region. This success inspired another terrorist group, Hamas, to embark on a suicide bombing campaign against Israeli civilians in retaliation for a February 1994 attack on Muslim worshippers by an Israeli. The

Hamas campaign killed dozens of people, which led Hamas, the Palestine Liberation Organization (PLO), and the al Aqsa Martyrs Brigade to launch a new suicide-bombing campaign whose intent was to make it difficult for Israelis to go about their daily lives. Consequently they targeted marketplaces, commuter stations, buses, and similar sites throughout 2001 and 2002. During this campaign, roughly two hundred people were killed for every thirteen suicide bombers. In other instances as well, one suicide bomber can do a great deal of damage. For example, in May 2002 just one suicide bomber killed fourteen people standing outside a hotel in Karachi, Pakistan. Consequently governments do as much as possible to screen people for explosives before allowing them access to places that would be likely targets for suicide bombers.

SEE ALSO: al Aqsa Martyrs Brigade; al Qaeda; bombs, types of; *Cole*, USS: Hamas; Hezbollah; Palestine Liberation Organization; Tamil Tigers; Vietminh

bombs, types of

Terrorists use many types of bombs and explosives. Most of their bombs are handmade, rather than purchased from suppliers of military weapons, with the most common types being gasoline bombs, pipe bombs, car and truck bombs, and suicide bombs. Gasoline bombs are made by putting gasoline in a bottle and stuffing a rag in the bottle's opening; the rag is then lit and the bottle thrown. Pipe bombs are made by filling a metal pipe with explosives, then sealing both ends of the pipe. In many cases, small metal objects, like bolts and nails, are put inside the pipe or taped along its outside, so that the explosion will be accompanied by dangerous flying shrapnel. The same is true for car

and truck bombs, which have been responsible for some of the most devastating terrorist attacks. For example, in April 1995 American right-wing terrorist Timothy McVeigh parked a truck bomb next to the Alfred P. Murrah Federal Building in Oklahoma City, Oklahoma, and the resulting explosion killed 68 people, 19 of them children who had been attending a day-care center on the ground floor. Similarly, in August 1998 a terrorist group called the Real Irish Republican Army exploded a car bomb in Omagh, Northern Ireland, that killed 29 people and injured 220. Suicide bombs can also be very deadly, depending on where the suicide bomber—a person with a bomb strapped to his or her body—triggers the explosion.

The most common explosive materials used in terrorists' bombs are dynamite, plastic explosives, and ammonium nitrate-fuel oil (ANFO) explosives. Dynamite is a commercial explosive primarily comprised of nitroglycerin, while plastic explosives are compounds that can be shaped like sculpting clay, and ANFO explosives are made from ammonium nitrate fertilizer. Since a lot of fertilizer is needed to make a large explosion, ANFO explosions are most commonly delivered via car and truck bombs. To trigger explosions, terrorists use timers of various types, fuses, pressure triggers (whereby the bomb goes off when someone steps on a device, for example, or when the air pressure around the device changes), remote-control devices, radio signals, motion detectors, or triggers that react to heat or light.

Bombs might also be dropped from planes or delivered via rocket-propelled missiles (also called rockets) which have explosive materials in their nose cones. The rockets used by terrorists typically have an extremely short range; this has been the case, for example, with the rockets that the terrorist group Hezbollah has lobbed at Israel from Lebanon in recent years. (The rocket attacks began in 2001 and are ongoing.) Long-range missiles are used to deliver nuclear bombs, and although no terrorist has yet used such a weapon, experts in terrorism fear that this will someday occur. Experts also fear that terrorists will gain the ability to use "dirty bombs," which would employ conventional explosives to release radioactive elements such as uranium or plutonium into the air, which can be lethal to anyone who inhales or ingests the material or absorbs it through the skin.

SEE ALSO: bomb, atom; bombers, suicide; weapons, types of terrorist

Bosnian genocide

The Bosnian genocide was a period of ethnic cleansing that occurred in Bosnia, Srebrenica, and Herzegovina from 1992 to 1995, when three ethnic groups in the region were at war with one another. (The phrase "ethnic cleansing," which means to purge a region of one particular ethnic group by systematically killing or violently driving away all members of this group, was first coined in reference to this conflict, the Bosnian War.) The trigger for the war was the breakup of Yugoslavia in the early 1990s. When one part of the former Yugoslavian federation, Bosnia, declared its independence, the Serbs (who were of the Orthodox Christian faith), the Muslims (members of the Islamic faith), and the Croatians (Roman Catholics) in Bosnia began fighting. Soon the Serbs decided to eliminate the Muslims via genocide—that is, to commit violence against not only soldiers but innocent civilians, including women and children. To this end, Bosnian Serb soldiers and paramilitaries

massacred thousands of Bosnian Muslims, often engaging in systematic rape and torture as well.

In one such slaughter, the Srebrenica massacre, approximately eight thousand Muslim men and boys were systematically killed after being separated from sisters, wives, and daughters, then buried in a mass grave. The murders took place on July 11, 1995, immediately after Serb forces captured Srebrenica, violating a United Nations declaration that the region was to be a "safe zone" in the war. Later, Serbs dug up the bodies and relocated them, hoping to hide their crimes, and today many Serbs deny that the massacre ever took place, or argue that the number of the dead has been grossly inflated or that the deaths were not acts of genocide but merely ordinary casualties of war. Nonetheless the International Criminal Tribunal for the former Yugoslavia (ICTY) declared the massacre an act of genocide, and in 1997 Germany convicted a Serb soldier, Nikola Jorgic, to life imprisonment for participating in the massacre.

The International Court of Justice is currently investigating other incidents of genocide in the region, and there is evidence that the Serbs established roughly five hundred concentration camps in Bosnia and Herzegovina that were dedicated to ethnic cleansing. In all, Serbian forces in Bosnia-Herzegovina killed approximately two hundred thousand people, raped or tortured tens of thousands more, and drove at least 2 million people from their homes. In many cases, the Serbs pretended to be relocating Bosnian Muslims before massacring them without warning. However, as the war progressed, Bosnian Muslims and Croatians also engaged in ethnic cleansing against the Serbs, sometimes after creating Serb-only districts in their territories. In these activities, the Bosnian Muslims were aided by Arabs from elsewhere in the Middle East, who had traveled to Bosnia to help their fellow Muslims after learning of the Serbs' atrocities.

SEE ALSO: ethnic cleansing; Yugoslavia

Boston Tea Party

The American Revolution (1775–1783) is not typically associated with terrorism; however, terrorism experts have noted that one of the key events leading up to the conflict, the Boston Tea Party, would now be classified as a terrorist act under the guidelines of the Federal Bureau of Investigation (FBI). In fact, some experts have said that whereas the men who participated in the Boston Tea Party are commonly called patriots, if they committed such an act today they would be called terrorists.

The Boston Tea Party took place in Boston, Massachusetts, on the night of December 16, 1773, when approximately sixty American colonists disguised as Mohawk Indians boarded three ships, the *Dartmouth, Eleanor,* and *Beaver,* at Griffin's wharf and dumped some of their cargo, 342 chests of tea belonging to the British East India Company, into the harbor. The men were protesting the fact that Great Britain, then in control of the American colonies, had granted the East India Company a monopoly on the tea trade and, more importantly, established a tax on tea without colonial approval (a situation known as taxation without representation). Though this act failed to change government policy (a failure that ultimately led to war), because it involved the destruction of property with the intent of influencing political policy the FBI would consider it a terrorist act.

SEE ALSO: Federal Bureau of Investigation; revolutionary terrorism

Branch Davidians

Involved in a 1993 shoot-out with Federal Bureau of Investigation (FBI) agents after stockpiling weapons at its religious compound, the Branch Davidians are members of a religious sect that believes Jesus Christ will soon be returning to earth. They have also been called a cult and are considered a part of the right-wing, anti-government Patriot movement, out of which has arisen several violent acts against government forces.

The Branch Davidian sect arose from a split within a religious group called the Shepherd's Rod, which itself was created as part of a split within the Seventh-Day Adventist Church. The original conflict took place in 1935, when Bulgarian immigrant Victor Houteff told the members of his Adventist church near Waco, Texas, that he had received a new holy book from God, *The Shepherd's Rod.* When they would not accept this, he became highly critical of their religious teachings, and in response the leaders of his church excommunicated him. Houteff then established the Shepherd's Rod sect, which in 1942 he renamed the Davidian Seventh-Day Adventists after the kingdom he believed Jesus would restore on earth (the Davidic Kingdom). In 1955 disagreements within this group led to the establishment of the Branch Davidian sect, with "Branch" referring to the name that Jesus would take upon his return. The leader of this new sect was Benjamin Roden; his wife, Lois, who took over the sect when he died in 1978, insisted that God told her that the Holy Spirit was feminine, and this too caused disagreements within the group, as did a failed attempt by Lois's son, George, to supplant her. There was also conflict between George and another member, Vernon Wayne Howell, whom Lois allowed to teach his own interpretation of scripture at Branch Davidian worship services. Eventually all of this discord split the sect into several factions, one of them led by Howell. In 1990 he renamed himself David Koresh.

By this time, Koresh had established a compound called Mount Carmel near Waco, Texas, on land belonging to the Branch Davidian sect as a whole. There he taught his followers that the Apocalypse was close at hand, and in preparation for this event he stockpiled a variety of weapons. However, he also practiced polygamy and abused children, and when some of his members abandoned his sect and went to U.S. authorities with this information and their knowledge of Koresh's extensive weaponry, the federal government decided to investigate the group. On February 28, 1993, agents from the Bureau of Alcohol, Tobacco, and Firearms (ATF) tried to execute a search warrant at the compound, whereupon the Branch Davidians opened fire on them. Four federal agents were killed in the shoot-out. Afterward the ATF and the FBI surrounded the building housing Koresh and his followers and, after a siege of fifty-one days, used heavy equipment to break through its walls. Because of the weapons inside, this invasion ignited a fire so fierce that it killed seventy-six Davidians, including Koresh and twenty-seven children. Those Davidians who survived were arrested and charged with the death of the federal agents; all were found innocent of murder, though a few were convicted of voluntary manslaughter. There was also a lawsuit regarding the Mount Carmel property, with various Branch Davidian leaders fighting over

ownership of the land. In 1994 a court ruled that Mount Carmel belonged to the entire Branch Davidian Seventh-Day Adventist Church, whereupon the Davidians began fighting over who would act as trustees of the property. Today Mount Carmel is controlled by the leader of one of the oldest factions of the group, Charles Pace, a Canadian who had been opposed to Lois Roden's taking over her husband's ministry. Before taking control in 2006, Pace lived on the property, as did a few other members, and argued with those who had established a memorial to David Koresh and the other Davidians who had died in the standoff with FBI and ATF agents. After the other members moved away, Pace destroyed the memorial, saying that only pagans gathered at such sites. This act reignited disputes over who should make decisions regarding Mount Carmel; these disputes are ongoing.

SEE ALSO: Alcohol, Tobacco, and Firearms, U.S. Bureau of; apocalypticism; Federal Bureau of Investigation; right-wing terrorists, U.S.

Brazil, terrorism in

In recent years, the Brazilian government has been criticized for using the public's fear of terrorism to manipulate the masses in order to gain control over them and to enact measures that curtail personal freedom. No instances of international terrorism have occurred in the country, though the region where the borders of Brazil, Argentina, and Paraguay meet has become a haven for Islamic extremists. Domestic terrorism, however, has been an ongoing threat, particularly in the city of Rio de Janeiro, and drug trafficking has become such a serious problem throughout the country that in 2004 the Brazilian government stated its intent to shoot down the planes of any drug traffickers in its airspace, saying that such illegal activities fund terrorism. Brazil's announcement was immediately condemned by the United States, which has a policy not to support governments that shoot down civil aircraft without first determining exactly who and what are aboard and receiving approval for the shoot-down from the head of state. (This policy was enacted after Peru shot down a plane that it believed was carrying drug traffickers, only to discover later that it held a missionary and her child.) Consequently Brazil held off on enacting its shoot-down policy.

Domestic terrorism in Brazil peaked during the late 1960s and 1970s, when two guerrilla groups, the Popular Revolutionary Vanguard (VPR) and the Action for National Liberation (ALN), challenged Brazil's oppressive government. Prior to the formation of these groups in the late 1960s, rural guerrillas had created a variety of small groups, some inspired by Cuban revolutionary Che Guevara, but they were not strong enough to confront Brazil's military forces. Still the VPR was able to launch a series of successful terrorist attacks in 1968–1969; however, it was nearly wiped out by police in early 1969, and when its leader, Carlos Lamarca, was shot by police in September 1971, the group disbanded.

By this time, several other similar groups had developed, but none was as effective as ALN. Founded by dissidents within the Brazilian Communist Party (PCB), it was led by Brazilian revolutionary Carlos Marighella, who authored a guide to guerrilla warfare in cities, the *Minimanual of the Urban Guerrilla* (1969).

Marighella not only advocated the use of terrorism against his country's dictatorship but said that terrorism was an honorable and necessary response to oppression. His work was read on Brazilian radio in 1969 after the ALN and another group, the MR-8, kidnapped the American ambassador to Brazil, Charles Burke, and then bargained his release in exchange for the radio broadcast of their antigovernment statements and the release of fifteen imprisoned ALN members. In 1970 the ALN kidnapped the West German ambassador, after killing one of his guards and wounding two more, and released him in exchange for seventy imprisoned members; later that same year, the group kidnapped the Swiss ambassador, Giovanni Bucher, and exchanged him for seventy prisoners.

Marighella's vision of ALN was to use it to start an urban guerrilla movement, because he believed that the urban arena would be more significant in terms of influencing public policy, and hopefully a mass uprising as well. (Previously, Brazilian guerrilla warfare had taken place primarily in rural areas, with little success.) Instead, the public so feared an escalation of terrorism that it supported the military government, which aggressively tracked down and committed violence against ALN members. As a result, by the end of 1970 the group had effectively been destroyed. Since then, Brazilian police have prevented urban terrorism by engaging in social cleansing, which occurs when authorities intimidate, abuse, drive away, or even kill members of their society that they consider to be undesirable, such as drug users, homeless people, or political dissidents.

SEE ALSO: Marighella, Carlos; South America, terrorism in

The forty-third president of the United States, George W. Bush, declared a "War on Terror" after the 9/11 attacks on the World Trade Center and the Pentagon. KENNETH LAMBERT. © AP IMAGES

Bush, U.S. president George W. (1946–)

The forty-third president of the United States, George W. Bush declared a "War on Terror" after the September 11, 2001, terrorist attacks on American soil and has since promoted various controversial policies, measures, and military actions in the name of combating terrorism. For example, to give law enforcement more power to jail suspected terrorists, Bush suspended the writ of habeas corpus, by which people cannot be held indefinitely without being charged with a crime; as a result, some Muslims have been imprisoned for five years without being charged with any crimes. He also created the USA Patriot Act, which established new crimes related to domestic and international terrorism and allows law enforcement and intelligence officials greater authority in regard to intercepting formerly private communications and records. For example, the Patriot Act expanded wiretapping and made it possible for the government to access such information as what books library patrons check out. Such activities have led some people to criticize Bush for ignoring civil liberties, free speech, and privacy rights, while others have defended his actions as being necessary in a time of growing terrorist threats.

Bush has also been criticized for declaring war on Iraq as a preemptive strike against terrorism, rather than because that country was involved in the September 11 attacks. At the time of those attacks, the leader of Iraq, Saddam Hussein, was actually an enemy of the terrorist group responsible for September 11, al Qaeda, because he considered its leader, Osama bin Laden, to be a threat to his despotic regime. Nonetheless Bush told the American people that Hussein had weapons of mass destruction (a claim later proved false, though it is unclear whether or not Bush knew this when he made the claim) and suggested that there was a link between Iraq and the September 11 terrorists, even though these men were Saudi Arabians like bin laden. In March 2003 Bush told Hussein that if he did not step down as the ruler of Iraq, his country would face invasion by the United States and its ally in the conflict, Great Britain. (Other U.S. allies were opposed to Bush's position, as were Russia, China, and many other nations.) Hussein refused to leave office, and on March 19 U.S. and British forces began their attack. Within a month, the United States controlled most of Iraq, and Hussein had gone into hiding. (He was not found for several months.) Nonetheless the country was wracked with sectarian and anti-U.S, violence, and it remains a violent, unstable place today even though it is still occupied by U.S. forces.

Bush had taken a similar approach with Afghanistan in the aftermath of September 11, demanding that its leaders, the Taliban, turn over Osama bin Laden and, when they refused, launching an attack on that country. After massive air and ground raids, he succeeded in taking over Afghanistan, but failed to capture bin laden or destroy al Qaeda. In fact, bin laden remains at large, al Qaeda remains strong, and despite the installation of a new Afghan government with ties to the United States, the Taliban is regaining its power. Moreover, because of Bush's attacks in the Middle East, anti-U.S, sentiment is at an all-time high in the region, and several nations throughout the world consider the United States to be a threat to their security. In fact, two of these nations, Iran and North Korea, have been developing nuclear weapons in order to defend themselves from U.S. attacks, largely because Bush equated Iran and North Korea with Iraq. (Prior to his attack on Iraq, he said that all three countries formed an "axis of evil.")

Bush has also had to deal with threats from within the United States, in the form of domestic terrorism. In late 2001, for example, someone mailed envelopes contaminated with anthrax spores, which can be lethal to humans, to U.S. government and media offices. Since then, there have been several other threats related to bioterrorism, and other forms of terrorism as well, though U.S. agencies have been able to deal with them fairly effectively. To combat domestic terrorism, Bush established the Department of Homeland Security as part of the U.S. cabinet in November 2002. (This department has always faced criticism for its handling of various events, with the most severe criticisms following its failure to act quickly to help victims of Hurricane Katrina in August 2005.) Nonetheless people remain afraid that terrorists are going to strike again in the United States, whether through violent attacks like bombings or through more subtle means, such as contaminating food sources. (In October 2006 some people initially suspected that cases of bacteria-contaminated spinach, lettuce, meat, and carrot juice were due to bioterrorism, when in fact they were due to unsanitary practices at some point between the time the food was produced and the time it was packaged.) Though Bush had to deal with many other issues besides terrorism in the years following the September 11 attacks, his other accomplishments have been overshadowed by his war on terrorism and his military actions in Iraq. However, when Bush took office in January 2001, terrorism was not a major political issue, and most Americans had never heard of al Qaeda. In fact, in the days prior to the presidential election, the media's main concern was Bush's recent admission that he had once been an alcoholic. Nonetheless he won the election based on the vote of the electoral college. (He lost the popular vote, receiving 49,820,518 votes as opposed to 50,158,094 votes received by his opponent, Al Gore.) In 2004 he won a second term amid accusations that voting machines in certain states, particularly Ohio, had been tampered with. Bush also served as the governor of Texas, beginning in 1994 and ending with his run for president. Prior to his political career, he worked as an executive in the oil and gas industry (1975–86) and a managing partner of the Texas Rangers baseball team (1989–94). As a young man he received an undergraduate degree from Yale University and an M.B.A. from Harvard, and he trained as a pilot in the Texas National Guard. His father, George H.W. Bush, was the forty-first president of the United States.

SEE ALSO: al Qaeda; anthrax; bin laden, Osama; bioterrorism; Hussein, Saddam; Iraq

Caesar, Julius, assassination of

The assassination of Roman dictator Julius Caesar in 44 B.C. is one of the most famous political assassinations in history. Led by Gaius Cassius Longinus and Marcus Junius Brutus, the assassins were a group of conspirators from the Roman senate. These men, who were all nobles, were unhappy with various political and social reforms that Caesar was in the process of launching at the time of his death, which took place in the Senate House on March 15, a day known in ancient Rome as the Ides of March.

SEE ALSO: assassination, political

Cambodian killing fields

The phrase "Cambodian killing fields" refers to areas in the countryside of Cambodia where the country's rulers, radical Communists known as the Khmer Rouge (the Party of Democratic Kampuchea), killed over 2 million Cambodians via torture, execution, or starvation. Khmer Rouge guerrillas took control of Cambodia's capital, Phnom Penh, on April 17, 1975, whereupon its leader, Pol Pot, ordered all people living in the city to march to labor camps in the countryside, including over twenty thousand hospital patients. There the laborers—including women and children—had to work twelve to fourteen hours a day, every day, to create Pol Pot's vision of a Communist agricultural society, and anyone who could not work hard enough was executed, as were babies, the elderly, and people perceived as

being too intellectual for agricultural work (including teachers, professors, writers, engineers, and physicians). Also executed were people who spoke out against their ill treatment or otherwise displeased their guards. Those who were allowed to live received only one meal a day, a soup made of water and a little rice, and many died from malnutrition. The bodies of the dead were thrown in mass graves, which were discovered after Vietnam drove out the Khmer Rouge in the 1980s. In 1991 the United Nations established a peacekeeping force in Cambodia to help its people recover from their treatment at the hands of the Pol Pot regime.

SEE ALSO: Khmer Rouge

Capone, Al
(1899–1947)

The crime boss of Chicago, Illinois, from 1925 to 1931, Al (Alphonse) Capone, nicknamed Scarface because of a scar across his left cheek, controlled his criminal empire through terrorism, threatening anyone who did not cooperate with him and gunning down serious rivals. In one such attack, on February 14, 1929, his henchmen trapped members of a rival gang in a garage and machine-gunned them to death, an incident that became known as the Saint Valentine's Day Massacre. Capone became the crime boss of Chicago in 1925, after the previous boss, his employer Johnny Torrio, retired and left him in control of his illegal business ventures: gam-

Carlos the Jackal
(1949–)

Born Ilyich Ramirez Sanchez, Carlos the Jackal was one of the most notorious terrorists of the twentieth century, operating in Europe and the Middle East though he grew up in Venezuela. He took the name Carlos after becoming a terrorist, but the press dubbed him "the Jackal" because of his ruthlessness. His father, however, had named him Ilyich after Russian revolutionary, Vladimir Ilyich Lenin, and in 1966 sent his son to a guerrilla-training school in Cuba. Four years later, Carlos entered a terrorist training camp in Amman, Jordan, that was run by the Popular Front for the Liberation of Palestine (PFLP), whose leader at the time, George Habash, is said to have trained Carlos personally in guerrilla tactics. During the early 1970s the Jackal worked for the PFLP, primarily in London, England, participating in assassination attempts and bombings. He quickly became one of the heads of the PFLP, and on December 21, 1975 he led a terrorist attack on the headquarters of the Organization of Petroleum Exporting Countries (OPEC), where a conference of the world's oil-industry leaders was taking place. During this attack, the Jackal and six of his men took more than sixty people hostage, demanded a plane, and took off with forty-two of the hostages, freeing thirty in Algiers, Algeria, a few more in Tripoli, Libya, and the remainder back in Algiers after receiving a payment of $50 million and a promise of asylum in order to release them. Afterward the Jackal traveled to Libya and disappeared. In 1976 he was arrested in Yugoslavia but released to Baghdad, where he again disappeared, though there is evidence that he led bombings in the Middle East and France during the 1980s. In 1994 he was arrested in

The notorious crime boss of the 1920s, Al Capone, became a leader of his own terrorist empire by threatening and murdering people who would not cooperate with his leadership and authority. THE LIBRARY OF CONGRESS

bling, prostitution, and bootlegging (transporting and selling alcohol during Prohibition, when such activities were illegal). Capone far exceeded the success of his predecessor, however; just two years after taking over, his empire was worth nearly $100 million. In 1931 Capone was convicted of income-tax evasion and sentenced to eleven years in prison, but after serving only eight years he was released to a hospital because of ill health. He subsequently settled on his estate in Palm Island, Florida, still in poor health, and remained there until his death in 1947.

SEE ALSO: criminal terrorism

Sudan and sent to France, where he was wanted for several murders committed in the 1970s. On December 24, 1997, the Jackal was convicted of these crimes and sentenced to life in prison.

SEE ALSO: Habash, George; hostages; Popular Front for the Liberation of Palestine

Carnot, Sadi
(1837–1894)

As president of the Third Republic of France, Marie-Francois-Sadi Carnot was assassinated by an Italian anarchist, Sante Caserio, in 1894. Carnot was elected to the presidency in 1887, after serving as minister of commerce and finance, and was generally well liked by the people of France, retaining his position through the formation of ten different governments over seven years. The public also admired his father, Hippolyte Carnot, who had been a vocal leftist opponent of the monarchy, and grandfather, Lazare Carnot, who had been dubbed the "Organizer of Victory" of the French Revolution. Nonetheless Sadi Carnot was targeted by members of the anarchist movement, simply because he represented the French government. He was shot while giving a speech at an exposition in Lyon, France, and died of his wounds a short time later.

SEE ALSO: anarchism; assassination, political; France, terrorism in

Castro (Ruz), Fidel
(1926–)

Fidel Castro (Ruz) was a Cuban revolutionary who took control of Cuba in 1959 as part of a Communist revolution in Latin America. He embraced violence as a student at the University of Havana in the

Fidel Castro, dictator of Cuba since 1959, is best known for being a violent revolutionist in Latin America. AP IMAGES

1940s, where he became the leader of a student gang and was charged unsuccessfully with murdering another leader. In 1953 in the city of Santiago de Cuba, he led a failed revolution against a military barracks and, while on trial for his actions, spoke out against the government; his words were later published as *La Historia Me Absolverá* (History Will Absolve Me). He was sent to prison until 1955, when he traveled to Mexico and planned another Cuban revolution. The following year he led a group to the Oriente province in Cuba and engaged in guerrilla warfare there against government forces. Thanks to these and other efforts by Cuban revolutionaries, the Fulgencio Batista government fell in December 1958, whereupon

Castro became the commander in chief of Cuba's armed forces. A year later he was prime minister, and in 1976 president of the State Council of the Cuban National Assembly and secretary-general of the Communist Party of Cuba. Still leader of the Cuban government and military today, Castro controls all mass media and does not allow political dissent, though he has supported violent revolutions in South America, Central America, Angola, and elsewhere.

SEE ALSO: Cuba

cells, terrorist

Prior to the late twentieth century, most terrorist organizations were organized in much the same way as a military organization, with a command structure in which superior officers oversaw the activities of the inferiors below them. During the 1990s this "vertical" command structure began to be replaced by a "horizontal" one, in which small groups, called cells, operate independently within a network, with each cell having equal power and none being under the direct control of the superiors in the terrorist organization to which they belong. The advantage of this type of structure is that if the members of a cell are captured, they know so little about the other cells in their network or about their organization as a whole, that they are unable to lead authorities to their fellow terrorists. Moreover a terrorist cell can have as few or as many members as are necessary to accomplish a particular task, and once that task is finished, members are free to splinter off to form other cells. Indeed some cells have only one member, called a "lone wolf." The concept of the cell was first introduced by nineteenth-century Russian anarchist

Mikhail Bakunin, who is sometimes called the grandfather of terrorism.

SEE ALSO: Bakunin, Mikhail

Central Intelligence Agency (CIA), U.S.

The U.S. Central Intelligence Agency (CIA) contributes to the American war on terrorism by providing the president with intelligence related to national security issues. The agency was established in 1947 by President Harry Truman; mindful of Japan's sneak attack on Pearl Harbor in Hawaii six years earlier, he wanted to make sure that the United States would have advance knowledge of any foreign plots against it. In its early years, the CIA only provided foreign intelligence gathered in other countries. Today it gathers intelligence within the United States as well, in cooperation with the U.S. Department of Homeland Security. At one time the agency also supported assassination attempts on foreign leaders, but in 1976 President Gerald Ford signed an order forbidding such actions.

SEE ALSO: assassination, political; Homeland Security, U.S. Department of

Chechen separatists

A Muslim people, the Chechens are the predominant group in Chechnya, a republic in southwestern Russia, alongside the Ingush and the Russians; Chechen separatists are those Chechens who want their lands to become independent from Russia. To this aim, during the 1990s the Chechen separatists engaged in guerrilla warfare in an attempt to oust the Russians from Chechnya, and in return the Russian government engaged in state terrorism against the Chechens. Some terrorism experts believe that the Chechen separatists, who planted bombs in Moscow and other cities, were funded in part by foreign Muslim extremists, such as Osama bin Laden.

The Chechens have a long history of resisting Russian control. During the nineteenth century, they fought Russian invaders on numerous occasions, and even after becoming a Russian province in 1920, they managed to retain autonomy. In 1934, when the Chechen province was combined with the Ingush province, these groups were still autonomous. During World War II, however, the Chechens and Ingush, who are also Muslim, were accused of aiding the Germans, and as punishment the Russian government eliminated the Chechen-Ingush province and exiled its Chechen and Ingush people to central Asia. They returned to their native lands after Russia became the Soviet Union; consequently in 1957 the Soviets established the Chechen-Ingush republic, and in 1991 the republic declared its sovereignty and divided into two separate republics. Shortly thereafter, the Chechen separatist movement developed and the violence in the region began.

chemical weapons

Chemical weapons are weapons that employ potentially lethal chemical agents in solid, liquid, or gas form, such as chlorine gas, which can destroy the respiratory system; sarin gas, which can destroy the nervous system; and pesticides, which can cause a variety of illnesses. Aerosols, bombs that disperse chemicals upon explosion, and bullets, shells, and cylinders that have chemical agents within their casings have all been used to disseminate these agents. Such weapons can be relatively easy for terrorists to obtain; certain kinds can be manufactured at home using instructions found on the Internet, while others can be purchased from willing na-

tions that have stockpiles of chemical weapons or from people who have stolen the materials from poorly secured chemical plants. However, in order to kill large numbers of people with chemical weapons, terrorists would need large quantities of chemical agents, and such quantities would require a lot of effort to produce and transport.

For this reason, terrorist attacks using chemical weapons have usually been small-scale operations. This was the case with a sarin-gas attack on the Tokyo, Japan, subway system by members of the Aum Shinrikyō religious cult in March 1995. These terrorists were well funded (by some estimates, they spent $30 million developing their attack and employed well-trained chemists), but even then, they could not produce more than a small quantity of sarin gas, and they failed to develop a sophisticated way to disseminate the gas. Instead, then, they relied on a simple method: Each of five cult members carried a package of sarin gas onto a subway train, then punctured the package as the train was coming into the station, tossed it on a seat, and left the train. Twelve people died as a result of this attack and thousands more were injured.

But while terrorist groups have been unsuccessful in causing widespread death via chemical weapons, governments have managed to kill thousands in this manner. For example, during World War I over one hundred thousand people died as a result of gas attacks. The Germans were the first to employ such a weapon, releasing chlorine gas into the air when the wind was blowing toward French troops. Shortly thereafter, the British and the French began using mustard gas, which causes choking and skin burns and blisters. Victims suffered so terribly that after the war several world leaders formally agreed not to use chemical weapons anymore. However, this agreement—the Geneva Conventions of 1925—did not address the issue whether nations could manufacture and stockpile the weapons, and many continued to do so until 1995, when a new agreement, the Convention of the Prohibition of the Development, Production, Stockpiling and Use of Chemical Weapons (CWC), required nations not only to stop manufacturing and stockpiling chemical weapons but to destroy existing stockpiles as well. Most nations have signed this agreement.

Still, chemical plants continue to produce chemical agents for industrial purposes, and some terrorism experts have expressed the concern that terrorists will sabotage such places in order to release toxic materials into the surrounding atmosphere. Terrorists might also wreak havoc by derailing trains or overturning trucks that are transporting chemical agents, or use chemical agents to contaminate food and water sources. The toxic effects of such activities would be localized; nonetheless terrorists would find them an effective way to instill fear in the general public and disrupt society.

SEE ALSO: Aum Shinrikyō; sarin gas; weapons, types of terrorist

Chile, terrorism in

The South American country of Chile has been experiencing a significant amount of terrorism since the 1960s, when a group called the Movement of the Revolutionary Left (MIR)—which was comprised primarily of university students—began attacking Chile's democratic rulers in an attempt to establish a Marxist regime. Led by Miguel Enriquez and supported in part by the Cuban government (a dictatorship under Fidel Castro), the group engaged in political assassinations and various acts of violence as well as bank robberies and other illegal activities. Nonetheless when a Marxist was elected president (Dr. Salvador Allende Gossens), he met with the MIR to elicit their support, which the group gave but only minimally. Meanwhile the MIR gained political and military support in the countryside, where the group curried favor with peasants by helping them to seize farmland from people who had previously taken the land from the peasants. By 1972 roughly 75 percent of Chilean land suitable for farming was in the hands of the peasants or the MIR, which used some of the land to establish training camps for terrorists.

As the MIR grew in power, it also became increasingly dissatisfied with the Marxist government, which it believed did not go far enough to spread Marxism throughout the country. Thus its attacks on the government resumed, although the group was careful not to hurt any civilians in the process. Other groups attacked the government as well, but typically because they opposed Marxism altogether. One group, Fatherland and Liberty Nationalist Front, was formed by people wanting to attack the MIR; instead, its most notable action was an assassination attempt on a cabinet minister, General Carlos Prats González, after which the government's aggressive attempts to capture its members forced the group into inactivity.

The government still was not safe, though. In 1973, after the MIR tried unsuccessfully to take it over via a paramilitary action, the government fell to a military coup, during which the president was killed in a bomb attack. The new government, headed by General Augusto Pinochet (Ugarte), then began arresting, torturing, and killing civilians suspected of supporting terrorism. The MIR joined with other guerrilla groups to fight this police state, but government forces were too strong and many members of the MIR were killed, as were many of Chile's peasants. In the early 1980s the few remnants of the MIR managed to assassinate some government officials and to engage in bomb attacks that targeted not only the government but big business.

Meanwhile another guerrilla group, the Manuel Rodriguez Patriotic Front (FPMR), started engaging in bomb attacks as well. Formed in 1983, this group struck power plants and government buildings, and in 1986 it nearly assassinated Pinochet himself. Three years later, an election replaced Pinochet's military government with a civilian one, but the FPMR continued to engage in terrorist attacks. Chilean forces pursued their attackers and captured most of the members of the FPMR, but not until the end of the 1990s. Today the remnants of this group are believed to be in Cuba, where they might be planning future attacks.

Christian Identity movement (CIM)

Dudng the eighteenth century in Britain, a racist Englishman named Richard Brothers argued that whites were God's chosen people and therefore destined to rule over all human beings. He further said that whites were descended from Adam and Eve (who, according to the Old Testament of the Bible, were the first human beings), that the Jews were descended from Satan, and that all other minorities were descended from beasts with no souls. His ideas soon spread to the United States, where Americans expanding on his views inspired the Christian Identity movement.

There are two basic branches of this movement, the One-Seedline branch and the Two-Seedline branch. Adherents of the One-Seedline Christian Identity movement believe that all human beings are descended from Adam and Eve but only whites are blessed by God. Adherents of the Two-Seedline Christian Identity movement believe that only whites are descended from Adam and Eve, because only one of Eve's two children, Abel, was Adam's son; they say that the other son, Cain, was fathered by the devil, and after he was cast out of the Garden of Eden, he joined with the soulless, inhuman beasts who lived there—the ancestors of all nonwhites—to father the Jews. Thus the Two-Seedline Christian Identity adherents believe that nonwhites are inhuman while Jews are evil; most further believe that the Jews are plotting to destroy the whites. During the 1940s both branches of the Christian Identity movement in the United States increased in popularity, particularly among members of the Ku Klux Klan, and by the 1980s there were several white-supremacist and neo-Nazi groups, including Aryan Nations in Idaho and the Covenant, the Sword, and the Arm of the Lord in Arkansas, dedicated to the movement.

SEE ALSO: Aryan Nations; Covenant, the Sword, and the Arm of the Lord, the; Ku Klux Klan; neo-Nazis; white supremacists

Christian Patriots (CP)

Members of the Christian Patriots (CP) are Americans who believe that the U.S. Constitution and the Bill of Rights were inspired by God and are therefore holy. They further believe that any amendments, including those that freed the slaves and gave blacks and women the right to vote, or nonliteral interpretations of these documents are evil. Typical of members of militia groups, most Christian Patriots refuse to pay taxes, and many adhere to the racist beliefs of the Christian Identity movement. Among the most prominent Christian Patriots are Illinois millionaire John Harrell, founder of the Christian Patriots Defense League (a Christian Identity group operating in Illinois and Missouri); James Nichols, whose brother Terry was convicted of participating in the Oklahoma City, Oklahoma, bombing; and the Montana Freemen, who were involved in the Ruby Ridge standoff with federal agents.

SEE ALSO: Christian Identity movement; Montana Freemen; Oklahoma City bombing; Ruby Ridge

Cole, USS

An American destroyer more than 500 feet (152m) long, the USS *Cole* was attacked by two suicide bombers (Ibrahim al-Thawr and Abdullah al-Misawa) in October 2000 while in port at Aden, Yemen. The bombers rowed a rubber raft filled with explosives alongside the *Cole* while it was refueling, but because of U.S. military policy the sailors on board the *Cole* were not allowed to shoot at the men. (The rules of engagement policy prevented the guards on board from firing without prior approval from a commanding officer.) Consequently the bombers were able to detonate their explosives without interference, not only blowing themselves up but putting a 40 x 60-foot (12mx18m) hole in the side of the destroyer. As a result of this damage, seventeen of the men on board were killed and thirty-nine more were injured, and damage to the ship amounted to $250 million.

Meanwhile the U.S. government launched an investigation (with almost no cooperation from officials in Yemen) to try to determine which terrorist group was behind the suicide bombing. This investigation led nowhere, though the U.S. Federal Bureau of Investigation (FBI) strongly suspected that a radical Islamic group was responsible, specifically the group al Qaeda, whose leader, Osama bin Laden, subsequently praised the attack. However, the Yemeni government did arrest several people for taking part in planning the attack, without connecting them to bin laden.

In 2006 former U.S. president Bill Clinton, who was in office during the *Cole* bombing, was criticized by Republicans for not having responded to the attack the way U.S. president George W. Bush did after the September 11, 2001, terrorist attacks on the United States—that is, by trying to kill bin laden. Clinton responded to this criticism by pointing out that he had already authorized the capture or killing of bin laden prior to the *Cole* incident. Other Democrats have noted as well that the United States had no hard evidence of bin laden's involvement in the *Cole* bombing when Clinton left office. (Tensions with Yemeni officials and anonymous death threats had forced the investigators to leave Yemen.) In fact, at the time, the Central Intelligence Agency (CIA) and FBI disagreed on whether bin laden was responsible.

The investigation is still incomplete and bin laden has not officially been connected to the bombing. However, his terrorist group, al Qaeda, has been linked to a failed bombing attempt that was nearly identical to the circumstances of the *Cole* bombing. In 2000 suicide bombers in a boat filled with explosives tried to maneuver alongside the USS *The Sullivans*, which was at a port in the Persian Gulf, but their boat sank from the weight of its load. Consequently most terrorism experts now believe that when al Qaeda failed to bomb *The Sullivans*, Osama bin Laden went after the *Cole*.

SEE ALSO: bin laden, Osama; counterterrorism; bombers, suicide

Colombia, terrorism in

The Latin American country of Colombia has experienced a great deal of terrorism over the years. It is home to several left-wing guerrilla groups, most notably the Revolutionary Armed Forces of Colombia (FARC), the National Liberation Army (ELN), and the April 19 Movement (M-19); together these groups have engaged in hundreds of kidnappings in order to raise money via ransoms. (In 1990 alone an average of four kidnappings a day took place in Colombia.) The groups also attack foreign businesses in the country and extort "protection money" from these businesses in order to fund their operations, which aim to eliminate Colombia's right-wing government. Guerrilla attacks on security forces have resulted in hundreds of deaths; for example, in just two months of 1996, the FARC killed over fifty soldiers.

The beginnings of guerrilla warfare in Colombia grew out of an extremely violent period of civil war known as "the Violence," which lasted from 1948 to 1962. This period, which resulted in over two hundred thousand deaths (at least half of them peasants), began with the assassination of a left-wing politician who opposed the country's corrupt right-wing government. In 1964 the first and most successful of the left-wing guerrilla groups, the FARC, formed to challenge this government, promoting a revolutionary movement among peasants who had suffered great poverty and other hardships due to unfavorable government policies. However, the FARC also killed peasants who did not

support the revolution, and it engaged in illegal activities, particularly drug-related, to finance its activities. In the early 1970s the FARC raised additional funds by kidnapping and ransoming off several foreign and Colombian businessmen, the Dutch consul and a volunteer with the U.S. Peace Corps, and it extorted money from businesses as well. In the late 1970s and early 1980s, the group bombed the facilities of U.S. companies in Colombia.

Today the FARC continues to kidnap and ransom foreigners and to attack American businesses. The group also kidnaps and kills political candidates and office-holders and plants bombs at various sites associated with government security forces and businesses friendly to the government. In 2000 the group attacked the facilities of a U.S. coal company, Drummond Inc., in Colombia, because it refused to pay the FARC extortion money.

That same year, the ELN attacked a major crude-oil pipeline in Colombia over 150 times because it was run by a foreign company, Occidental Petroleum. Formed in 1958 and second in size and power to FARC, the ELN is the most active terrorist group in the country, engaging in the same activities as the FARC but on a broader scale. It is also distinct in that several of its members are Catholic priests and that it is willing to engage in extreme violence to keep its members in line. During the late 1960s, the group executed nearly sixty of its members because they openly disagreed with its policies. In addition to the attack on the Occidental Petroleum pipeline in 2000, the ELN has attacked other pipelines as well, and it is estimated that from 1987 to 1991, these activities caused losses of over $634 million to the oil companies. As a result, several oil companies have been paying the Colombian military to protect their pipelines.

The M-19 has also raised money by kidnapping people, primarily targeting diplomats and other political figures. Formed in 1973 in response to a corrupt election, the group engaged in mortar attacks on the presidential palace between 1979 and 1982, and during this same period it cut into the signal of a Colombian television station in order to broadcast political statements. In 1985 the group stormed the Palace of Justice in Bogotá, Colombia, and took its occupants captive; the military responded by bombarding the building with gunfire and cannon fire. Over one hundred innocent people were killed during this attack. Another one hundred were killed the following year, when three hundred M-19 guerrillas attacked the city of Cali, Colombia. Once again a shoot-out with military forces ended the incident, but this time more than half of the dead were M-19 members, and by 1990 the group was largely extinct.

There are other terrorist groups in Colombia as well, largely because the drug trade is so predominant in the country. Assassins within various Colombian drug cartels kill anyone who threatens their trade, including politicians, police officers, and police informants. Both the FARC and the ELN are heavily involved in the drug trade as well. In addition, the country is home to several right-wing paramilitary groups that have sprung up in opposition to the FARC and ELN, particularly in areas where coca is grown. (Coca leaves are used to make the drug cocaine.) Right-wing terrorists kidnapped seven congressional representatives in 2000, releasing them in exchange for money and concessions from the government.

Meanwhile, the Colombian government and its businessmen have responded harshly to terrorist threats. In 1981 landowners who feared being kidnapped by guerrillas established a paramilitary group, Death to Kidnappers (MAS), and by 1988 there were over three hundred similar groups; some of these created death squads to kill citizens suspected of being guerrillas or supporting guerrilla activity. By 1990 there were over 140 active death squads, some of them allied with a Colombian drug cartel, the Medellin. At the same time, the Colombian government turned to state-sponsored terrorism to counter guerrilla terrorism. As a result, between 1986 and 1993 over twenty thousand Colombians died from terrorist violence, and of these deaths, more than two-thirds were the result of either government forces or paramilitary groups. Today, however, the government is trying to lessen the violence in the country, and there are ongoing peace talks between public officials, the FARC, and the ELN.

See Also: National Liberation Army; Revolutionary Armed Forces of Colombia

colonialism

Colonialism is a system of policies and actions by which nations keep and expand their control over foreign, usually distant lands; nations that maintain such control are called colonial powers, and their foreign dependencies are called colonies. Natives of such lands who want to expel a colonial power are called nationalists, and they often resort to violence in their struggles for independence, which are called decolonization campaigns. Because these campaigns can be extremely violent—particularly when a colonial power does not want to relinquish control of its colonies—colonialism has been responsible for a great deal of terrorism throughout the world.

SEE ALSO: decolonization campaigns

Committee of Public Safety

From 1793 to 1794 in France, during a period known as the Reign of Terror, the twelve-member Committee of Public Safety oversaw state-sponsored terrorism intended to quell revolution among the French people. This committee established courts to examine the guilt of people accused of being revolutionaries, and in just two months, June and July 1794, these courts convicted over fifteen hundred people, many of them innocent. Those convicted were then sent to the guillotine for execution. While awaiting trial, suspected revolutionaries were imprisoned under deplorable conditions and subjected to torture. Meanwhile, local authorities shot hundreds of revolutionaries, either in the heat of civil unrest or after they had been taken prisoner, believing their actions would be sanctioned by the Committee. One official, a representative of the city of Nantes named Jean Baptiste Carrier, drowned thousands of prisoners in the Loire River in 1794 rather than bother with trials. However, the Committee decided that such extreme actions would only fuel the revolution and ordered them stopped. Nonetheless the Committee was forced to give up most of its powers after a political coup in mid-1794.

SEE ALSO: France, terrorism in; Montagnards, the

communism

Communism is a political system in which communities, rather than individuals, own all property, with citizens sharing in the benefits of society according to need. In other words, in an ideal Communist society, people would work together to create wealth, whether in the form of money or of goods, that would be distributed fairly and evenly, so that there would be no social classes, no rich or poor. People who believe this system should be the norm throughout the world are called Communists, and in order to see their vision realized, many have resorted to violent revolution. In fact, so common is violence among Communists that the word communism has come to mean any revolutionary movement fueled by Communist principles.

These principles were developed primarily by Karl Marx and Vladimir Lenin in the nineteenth century, though the concept of communism—that is, a classless society—existed long before their time. In 1848 Marx, with his friend Friederich Engels, published *The Communist Manifesto* in which he suggested that communism would develop out of a struggle between capitalist rulers and the people they exploited for personal gain. Marx believed that industrialism would trigger such a struggle, because it concentrated wealth and power in the hands of a few while leaving the working classes poor and starving. He further believed that in order to have the complete equality of communism, a society first had to embrace socialism, in which the workers, or proletariat, governed.

Marx thought that the workers would rise up on their own, but Lenin believed that they needed professional revolutionaries to guide them. To this end, in 1917 Lenin led the Communist Party (which Marx had founded in 1847 as the Communist League) in a revolution that took control of Russia. The Communists immediately outlawed all other political parties and enacted other strict policies to maintain control. In addition, Lenin developed various economic principles based on socialism that, together with his other views on governance, became known as Leninism.

After World War II, Russia's Communist government supported the development of communism in other Eastern countries, such as Czechoslovakia, Hungary, and Poland, and communism spread elsewhere on its own. In 1949 China was taken over by a Communist, Mao Tse-tung through revolution, guerrilla warfare, and civil war. His form of communism was less elite than Russia's, with a greater emphasis on the power of the peasantry. In the 1950s a few other Asian countries, including North Vietnam and Cambodia, followed his lead in embracing communism. Today China remains Communist, but by the early 1990s communism fell throughout Russia and Eastern Europe.

SEE ALSO: Lenin, Vladimir; Marx, Karl

Contras

A group of guerrilla rebels in Nicaragua, the Nicaraguan Democratic Force (FDN), more commonly known as the Contras, was opposed to the 1979 formation of a government led by a group known as the Sandinistas. The Sandinistas took their name from their support of General Augusto Sandino, a guerrilla who had fought against U.S. forces in Nicaragua in the 1920s and 30s, because like Sandino they hated the United States. In fact, in December 1974, five years before they took power, the Sandinistas seized the U.S. embassy and held its occupants hostage until the Nicaraguan government released Sandinista political prisoners. Consequently the U.S. government did not want the Sandinistas in power, so in 1981 U.S. president

Ronald Reagan secretly authorized the U.S. Central Intelligence Agency (CIA) to work with Nicaraguan guerrillas to create the Contras. With U.S. military training, assistance, and financing of approximately $20 million a year, the group was able to attack a variety of targets designed to disrupt the Nicaraguan economy, including oil facilities and ports. In 1984 mines (bombs) planted by the Contras in one port severely damaged foreign vessels, and the United Nations drafted a resolution condemning the act, but the United States refused to sign it.

In 1986 Reagan secretly authorized another $100 million in Contras funding, though in public he pretended that he was opposed to the support of revolutionaries. This money had come from an illegal sale of weapons to Iran, and when information about the transaction was leaked to the press, the result was widespread condemnation of what became known as the Iran-Contra scandal. Afterward the United States stopped funding the Contras, who continued to operate but with much fewer forces, arms, and effectiveness. Former Contras also formed their own guerrilla groups, and some of them struck at U.S. targets within Nicaragua. For example, in 1996 one such group kidnapped a member of a U.S. aid organization, USAID, who had gone to Nicaragua to help with elections there. She was only held one day, however, because of international pressure for her release.

SEE ALSO: Nicaragua

counterterrorism

Whereas antiterrorism involves security measures and other steps taken to defend against terrorist attacks, counterterrorism involves actions designed to seek out and destroy terrorist groups or to destabilize governments and situations that support terrorism. Consequently, counterterrorism often involves force, and in many cases its actions are covert, which means they are performed in secret. These actions might include assassination; domestic or international military, paramilitary, law enforcement, or intelligence operations; the infiltration of terrorist groups or disinformation campaigns; economic sanctions or computer investigations designed to prevent the transfer of money to terrorist groups; or diplomacy. The United States and several other nations have special units devoted to counterterrorism activities and training.

Assassination. In the United States, government-sanctioned assassinations have been illegal since December 1981, when President Ronald Reagan signed an executive order prohibiting all government employees from engaging in the practice or from hiring anyone as an assassin. Since the end of the Vietnam War, the government had officially stopped engaging in the practice of assassinating its political enemies, and Reagan's predecessor, President Gerald Ford, had signed his own executive order restricting its use. These orders did not specifically address counterterrorist assassination, which only targets terrorist leaders and their supporters, but until the September 11, 2001, terrorist attacks on America, few people made a distinction between political assassination and counterterrorist assassination. Afterward, however, many began to suggest that the United States employ assassins to kill terrorists, under the argument that terrorists fall into a different category than political enemies. In fact when U.S. president George W. Bush declared a war on terror, some of his supporters said that this act made terrorists like Osama bin

Laden military enemies, and therefore it was a soldier's duty to kill them. (Using similar reasoning, in August 1998 U.S. president Bill Clinton, in authorizing the capture of bin laden, declared that U.S. forces could use deadly force if necessary, shooting down bin laden's plane or shooting missiles at his bases if they could be found.) Nonetheless, as of November 2006, bin laden still had not been captured or killed, and no similar authorizations have been made.

Other nations, however, have had no such qualms about engaging in counterterrorist assassinations. Israel, for example, has engaged in this practice extensively, particularly against Palestinian nationalists. In 1970 Israeli agents tried unsuccessfully to assassinate two members of the Palestine Liberation Organization (PLO) in Beirut, Lebanon, and in 1997 they attempted to kill a Hamas leader in Amman, Jordan. In 2002 they successfully assassinated a leader of Hamas, Sheik Salah Shehadeh, along with his wife and three children. In 1972 and 1973 covert Israeli agents also assassinated at least twenty Palestinian terrorists connected to a massacre of eleven Israeli athletes during the 1972 Munich Olympics, tracking the terrorists down one by one in Europe and the Middle East as an act of revenge.

Military and paramilitary operations. Military operations might be a short-term attack designed to punish terrorists for an action they have taken (punitive strike) or prevent them from taking a particular action (a preemptive strike), or a long-term operation intended to eliminate terrorists, their bases, and their support systems. As an example of the former, in 1998 the United States engaged in a military strike on terrorist bases in Afghanistan and Sudan in retaliation for attacks on U.S.

embassies in Tanzania and Kenya. As an example of the latter, U.S. president George W. Bush launched Operation Enduring Freedom in 2001 as a long-term military campaign against terrorists.

Paramilitary operations are actions in which a group of civilians, organized in a military fashion, engages in military operations with or without support from the military. For example, when the Colombian government was unable to prevent terrorists' kidnappings of wealthy business and landowners, these people supported the formation of paramilitary units dedicated to protecting them; in 2002 one of these paramilitary groups, the United Self-Defense Forces of Colombia (AUC), joined with the Colombian army to fight a battle against terrorists from the Revolutionary Armed Forces of Colombia (FARC).

Law-enforcement operations. In the United States, law-enforcement operations against terrorists involve the Department of Homeland Security, which was formed after the September 11, 2001, terrorist attacks, with cooperation from the Federal Bureau of Investigation (FBI) and Central Intelligence Agency (CIA). (Prior to the creation of Homeland Security, these two entities worked with the State Department to capture terrorists.) In combating terrorism, all U.S. law-enforcement personnel have for years afforded terrorists, even foreign ones, all of the rights and protections of American law. During the administration of George W. Bush, however, some of these rights and protections were eliminated; for example, in 2006 Bush eliminated the right of habeas corpus, which had made it necessary for anyone who had been arrested to be charged with a crime and put on trial within a reasonable amount of time. Consequently, some terrorists have languished in prison for years

without any charges being made. Under legislation known as the Patriot Act, the Bush administration also made it easier to wiretap and otherwise spy on people's activities in order to capture terrorists, and to torture terrorists in order to get information that might prevent future terrorist acts. Many other countries have long had no qualms about using such tactics or about holding people prisoner for years without trial, but the Bush administration was severely criticized for resorting to this behavior. Bush's defenders have correctly pointed out that at times in the past, terrorists have escaped arrest by relying on the protection of U.S. laws. However, in the 1990s, under the administration of President Bill Clinton, traditional law-enforcement approaches to terrorism investigations were successful in bringing to justice many of the people responsible for the 1993 bombing of the World Trade Center, the 1995 bombing of the Alfred P. Murrah Federal Building in Oklahoma City, Oklahoma, and the 1998 bombings of U.S. embassies in Tanzania and Kenya, and of preventing a 1993 Islamic terrorist bombing plot involving several sites in New York City. In 1996 Clinton also signed the Anti-Terrorism and Effective Death Penalty Act, which established stiffer penalties for anyone engaging in or funding terrorism. This act also provided funding for counterterrorism activities.

Other countries have also curtailed some legal rights in order to make it easier to capture terrorists. For example, the Northern Ireland Act of 1993 suspended civil liberties in Northern Ireland so that the British military could search homes and arrest suspects without any warrants in order to combat terrorism conducted by the Irish Republican Army (IRA); and in the 1990s the country of Algeria established counterterrorism courts dedicated to prosecuting Islamic terrorists as quickly as possible, without necessarily giving them enough time to mount a defense.

Some countries have also used their police forces in ways that fail to respect human rights. For example, Colombian police have abused or even killed suspected terrorists rather than bring them in for questioning. Police have also manufactured evidence in order to convict a suspected terrorist, as was the case in Birmingham, England, in 1974 involving a series of pub bombings. (After police misconduct was uncovered in 1991, the six men convicted of the bombing, which had killed twenty-one people, were released from prison.) Each country has its own laws and policies regarding how to deal with terrorism, but most also cooperate with an international law-enforcement organization known as Interpol (International Criminal Police Organization), which is involved in both counterterrorist and criminal investigations.

Intelligence operations. Intelligence operations are operations designed to collect and analyze information. In recent years, the bulk of intelligence operations requires the use of technology—for example, to intercept cell phone signals, e-mails, or computer records of banking transactions. However, intelligence agencies still engage in traditional spying, whereby agents make contact with people willing to share information meant to be kept secret or at least kept from law-enforcement or government personnel, and document analysis, whereby linguists, decoders, and other experts pore over written materials to look for hidden meanings. Most countries have at least one intelligence agency. Great Britain and Germany have two; the British rely on MI-5 for domestic intelligence and the MI-6 for international intelligence, whereas the Germans rely on the Bureau for the Protection of the Constitution and the Military Intelligence Service. In the United States, four agencies engage in intelligence operations, the CIA (international intelligence), the FBI (domestic intelligence), the Defense Intelligence Agency (military intelligence), and the National Security Agency (technological intelligence). All of these are supposed to share information with each other as needed, though in many cases this does not occur, and with the Department of Homeland Security, which is in charge of protecting America from terrorist attacks. Some of these agencies also have counterintelligence units dedicated to addressing specific issues and problems. For example, in 1996 the CIA established a division within its Counterterrorism Center devoted exclusively to the capture of Osama bin Laden.

Infiltration and disinformation. Counterintelligence also involves the use of infiltration and disinformation. The former occurs when government agents or others who support government counterterrorist activities infiltrate, or join, terrorist groups pretending to be terrorists themselves. Disinformation occurs when false information is provided to terrorists who believe the information to be true; disinformation campaigns are also used to convince the supporters of terrorist groups that these groups are not what they purport to be.

Economic efforts. As previously mentioned, counterterrorists use technology to intercept computer bank records, money transfers and other transactions so that terrorists cannot get the money they need to buy weapons or fund recruitment campaigns. Another way to prevent terrorists from getting money is through economic sanctions (trade restrictions) against governments that engage in or otherwise support terrorism. For economic sanctions to work, however, the international community must stand together in preventing money from flowing into the sanctioned country via trade deals. Still another way to prevent terrorists from getting funds is the establishment of policies that forbid the payment of ransom in exchange for hostages.

Diplomacy. Diplomatic approaches to counterterrorism include negotiations that lessen or end the conflict in a terrorism-ridden area and social reforms that so improve life for people living in such areas that their desire for violence disappears. As an example of the latter, when Peru improved living conditions for its peasants in the early 1990s and increased their political rights, most stopped supporting the actions of a previously popular terrorist group known as the Shining Path. Peace negotiations have brought similar successes, but some countries refuse to negotiate with terrorists (as opposed to government officials). For example, the United States generally will not engage in hostage negotiations, fearing that if terrorists are rewarded for kidnapping people, they will commit even more kidnappings in the future.

Counterterrorism training. Several countries now have special operations forces dedicated to counterterrorism, employing well-trained military or police personnel who know how to deal with domestic and international terrorism crises. Many of these were formed in response to specific terrorist situations. For example, the United States began devoting extensive resources to counterterrorism training after the U.S. embassy in Beirut, Lebanon, was bombed in 1983 and 1984, and in Germany the Grenzschutzgruppe 9 (GSG-9)

counterterrorism police unit was formed after terrorists killed Israeli athletes at the 1972 Munich Olympics. Other counterterrorist units include the Special Air Service (SAS) of the United Kingdom and the French Navy Special Assault Units, which are both military units, and the GEO (Grupo Especial de Operaciones) of Spain, which is a police unit.

SEE ALSO: hostages; Interpol; Munich Olympics crisis; Patriot Act, the U.S.

Covenant, the Sword, and the Arm of the Lord (CSA), the

Established in 1971 by Christian fundamentalist James Ellison, the Covenant, the Sword, and the Arm of the Lord (CSA) was a racist paramilitary group, operating on the Missouri-Arkansas border, that engaged in terrorist activities during the 1980s. Its members adhered to Christian Identity beliefs, which means that they considered Jews and nonwhites to be descended, respectively, from Satan and soulless beasts. Members of CSA published hate literature and armed themselves against the government, which they thought was coming under the control of the Jews and therefore Satan. In 1983 the group declared war on the government and began plotting to kill various public officials. Its members also attempted to burn down a Jewish center and a liberal church and to destroy a natural-gas pipeline. By this time, the CSA had established a compound on 224 acres in Arkansas, where it invited other paramilitary, white-supremacist, and Christian Identity groups to train for the upcoming war against the government. In April 1985, a member of one of these other groups, the Order, caused trouble for the CSA after he gunned down a Missouri state trooper and fled. Police thought that the shooter, David

Tate, was hiding in the CSA compound and surrounded the place, but after a tense four-day standoff with armed CSA members they discovered he was not there. Nonetheless, federal authorities shut down the compound, after arresting several people there, including CSA leader Ellison, for having illegal firearms, explosives, and other weapons. Ellison and the others were sent to prison for their crimes; another CSA member, Richard Snell, was executed on April 19, 1995 for the 1983 murder of a businessman he thought was Jewish. Some terrorism experts believe it is no coincidence that the Oklahoma City, Oklahoma, bombing at the Alfred P. Murrah Federal Building occurred on the day of Snell's execution. Snell and the CSA had once plotted to blow up the same building (though they abandoned their plan as unworkable), and the man who did commit the crime, Timothy McVeigh, shared the same antigovernment and white-supremacist beliefs as Snell, though he was neither a member of CSA nor apparently involved in the Christian Identity movement.

SEE ALSO: Christian Identity movement; McVeigh, Timothy; Oklahoma City bombing

criminal terrorism

Criminal terrorism is terrorism that is committed purely for profit. Some terrorists engage in criminal terrorism as a means to an end—that is, in order to make enough money to support a political or religious agenda. Other terrorists, however, engage wholly in criminal terrorism; this is the case, for example, with members of organized crime groups such as the Mafia and the Chinese Triads, and with drug cartels, particularly those in Colombia and other parts of Latin America. In fact, the drug trade is the major enterprise of all people involved in criminal terrorism. (This type of criminal terrorism is sometimes called narco-terrorism, with "narco" being short for narcotics, or drugs.) Politically motivated terrorist groups that are heavily involved in the drug trade include the Taliban, the Tamil Tigers, Abu Sayyaf, the Revolutionary Armed Forces of Colombia (FARC), and Shining Path. These groups use their drug profits primarily to buy weapons.

SEE ALSO: Abu Sayyaf; Colombia, terrorism in; drugs and terrorists; Mafia, the; Revolutionary Armed Forces of Colombia; Shining Path, the; Taliban; Tamil Tigers, the

Cuba

Under the control of Fidel Castro, the island republic of Cuba has supported terrorist activities in other parts of the world and has provided shelter to terrorists escaping arrest in their own countries. For example, Cuba has provided a safe haven for members of two Colombian terrorist groups, the Revolutionary Armed Forces of Colombia (FARC) and the National Liberation Army (ELN), as well as to a Spanish group called Basque Homeland and Liberty. Moreover, experts in terrorism believe that the Cuban revolution, which put Castro in power in 1958, has acted as an inspiration for other revolutionary movements throughout the world by people who share Castro's anti-U.S, sentiments. The Cuban revolution occurred after a long period of guerrilla warfare against a Cuban dictatorship with business ties to the United States. A Communist, Castro immediately abolished capitalism upon taking control of Cuba and established close ties with the Soviet Union, which was also a Communist country. He sent forces to Angola and Ethiopia, then associated with the Soviets as well, and established terrorist training camps in Cuba. When the Soviet Union dissolved in the early 1990s, however, Cuba lost a great deal of economic support and could no longer afford to operate terrorist training camps. Nonetheless in 1999 it was able to orchestrate meetings between Colombian terrorists and Colombian government officials. Castro has been seriously ill in recent years, and it is unclear what the fate of his country will be after his death.

See Also: Basque Homeland and Liberty; communism; guerrilla warfare; National Liberation Army; Revolutionary Armed Forces of Colombia

cyberterrorism

Cyberterrorism is terrorism involving cyberspace attacks, with cyberspace being the information systems of the Internet. Some of these attacks are fairly benign, as when cyberterrorists hack (force their way) into a computer system simply to make a political statement. For example, in 1999 members of an antiwar group hacked into computers at a nuclear weapons research center in India in order to send an antiwar message. In most cases, however, cyberattacks involve the spreading of computer viruses after the hacking of computer systems in order to commit crimes such as financial or identity theft or to harm people, institutions, or governments. As an example of the latter, a cyberterrorist might hack into a computer in order to disrupt the electrical power in a particular city, thereby hurting people whose lives depend on electrical equipment, or in order to disrupt the air-traffic control system of a particular airport, thereby causing a plane crash. Cyberterrorists can also send "e-mail bombs"—that is, electronic

messages that are sent over and over in order to overload a computer's mailbox. For example, animal-liberation activists sent one such bomb to a Swedish company, Smittskydinstitute, in 1998 because the group believed that company was engaging in medical research that hurt monkeys. As a result, the company's computer system received over five thousand e-mails in two days and crashed (shut down), wiping out its database of medical research information.

Whereas e-mail bombs work from without, viruses work from within the computer, as programs that install themselves on the computer and subsequently damage it in some way. In most cases, the damage comes in the form of a crash. For example, a 1999 virus called "Melissa" that spread from computer to computer caused approximately $80 million in losses from crashes. Most other types of cyberattacks are also economic, intended either to financially enrich the cyberterrorist or to damage the financial health of a company, government, or institution. In fact experts in terrorism fear that cyberterrorists will someday hack into computers related to the American stock market to cause a financial disaster.

The first person to use the term *cyberterrorism*—an expert in computer security, Barry Collin of the Institute for Security and Intelligence in California, in the 1980s—has expressed great concerns about the risk that cyberterrorism poses to people's economic well-being and physical safety. In the late 1980s, most people ignored his warnings, but gradually business and government officials became aware of the threat. In 1998 U.S. president Bill Clinton created the National Infrastructure Protection Center, which was charged with protecting the computer systems of government offices, power companies, tele-communications companies, and other public institutions. Still, cyberterrorism experts believe that not enough has been done to protect the nation's most vital computer systems.

death camps

The phrase "death camps" typically refers to the concentration camps in Germany and nations occupied by Germany where the Nazis, under Adolf Hitler, sent Jews to be executed via poison gas, hanging, shooting, torture, and other means. This state-sponsored campaign of genocide, known as the Holocaust or Hitler's Final Solution, resulted in the death of most of Germany's Jewish population over a period of twelve years; by some estimates the number of deaths was between 10 and 12 million.

SEE ALSO: Holocaust, the; Nazi terrorism

decolonization campaigns

Decolonization campaigns are struggles for independence in which natives whose lands have been occupied by a colonial power try to expel all foreigners. Some of these campaigns can be extremely violent; the most brutal acts of decolonization-

A concentration camp during World War II, where Jews were sent by German Nazis under the leadership of Adolf Hitler to be executed. AP IMAGES

driven terrorism have occurred in Africa, India, Southeast Asia, Greece, and Cyprus. (There was also a violent struggle for independence in North America, where the Revolutionary War against the British resulted in the formation of the United States, but this struggle pitted colonists rather than the native inhabitants against the colonial power.) This terrorism was committed not only by those wanting independence (nationalists) but also by colonial governments and foreign settlers wanting to maintain the status quo.

Africa. During the nineteenth century, several European nations established colonial powers in various parts of Africa, and by the early twentieth century the nationalists in these places were determined to get rid of the ruling Europeans. Some of the worst terrorism during this period occurred in French Algeria, Kenya, Zimbabwe (Rhodesia), Namibia, and Portuguese Africa, places where the colonial powers did not give up control of their dependencies easily. (In other parts of Africa, the violence did not escalate until after decolonization had taken place, as postcolonial governments led by whites tried to oppress black majorities.)

Algeria experienced its first significant anticolonial terrorism immediately after World War II, led by Muslim nationalists who wanted the French colonists and other Europeans out of their county. At first this violence was spontaneous; for example, at a war-victory parade in the town of Sétif in May 1945, the Arabs in the crowd began attacking French police officers and then all Europeans. The Arabs also committed atrocities against their victims, including torture and rape; most of the 130 Europeans and twenty police officers died violently. In response, colonial forces killed thousands of Arabs in the region, not all of them guilty, and the colonists killed hundreds more, usually by hanging. Nonetheless the violence continued, particularly after nationalists formed the National Liberation Front (FLN), which launched a war of independence against the French in 1954. This group tortured and hacked off the body parts of anyone who sided with the French, and in April 1955 they brutally massacred Europeans—men, women, and children—in the town of Philippeville after starting a riot there. (Afterward, the Europeans responded in kind against Muslims.) In 1956, the FLN planted bombs at various locations in the city of Algiers, Algeria, including near the cemetery plot where a politician whom they had assassinated, Amédée Froger, was about to be buried. (The bomb was discovered before it detonated.) By the end of 1957, though, there were few attacks on colonial forces in Algiers, thanks to aggressive efforts by French troops to capture or kill Muslim nationalists. This did not mean, however, that the terrorism had ended, because French troops engaged in horribly violent practices against Muslims, brutally torturing them to get information on nationalist plots. These actions, however, made the French in France uncomfortable, and by 1958 several politicians there were calling for France to grant Algeria its independence. In 1959, with the inauguration of Charles de Gaulle as France's president, Algeria was given the right to decide how it should be governed, whereupon French generals in the country—backed by the colonists—tried to seize control of Algeria via a military coup. When this failed, some colonists started a bombing campaign against Muslim targets, while others left the country. (Approximately 870,000 colonists had left by mid-1962.) In March 1962 France declared that Algeria would be given its independence, but the Muslims and the French in Algeria continued to savage one another long after decolonization was complete.

In Kenya, the nationalists were a tribal people known as the Kikuyu, and their terrorist campaign was against the British. Kikuyu nationalism was fueled by the British decision in 1950 to ban an ancient Kikuyu society called the Mau Mau because it practiced violent tribal rituals and swore its members to strict obedience. After the ban, the Mau Mau created a guerrilla army approximately twelve thousand strong and began attacking colonists, particularly farmers. An additional thirty thousand or more Mau Mau supporters kept the group well stocked with food and supplies. To combat this force, in October 1952 the British declared a state of emergency and started sending more troops into Kenya. Meanwhile the ranks of the Mau Mau grew by at least another three thousand. A British military campaign against the Mau Mau, however, was largely unsuccessful, because the Mau Mau were able to escape deep into the forests, where they continued to launch brutal attacks on helpless colonists. Finally in 1954 the British decided to take its battle against the Mau Mau into the forests, and in 1955 it successfully drove the Mau Mau out of the trees and into Kikuyu villages. By this time British troops had searched these villages for Mau Mau supporters and arrested them, with the help of information gathered during the aggressive interrogation of thousands of Kikuyu rounded up at random. The Mau Mau now found it difficult to find a safe haven outside of their forests. They were also attacked by bands of natives whom the British had convinced to turn against the Mau Mau. Consequently by the end of 1956 the British had

eliminated the Mau Mau threat, but in 1963 it granted the country its independence.

In the 1960s the British colony of Rhodesia experienced similar violence, with two all-black terrorist groups—the Zimbabwe People's Revolutionary Army (ZIPRA) and the Zimbabwe African National Liberation Army (ZANLA)—engaging in guerrilla attacks on British forces and white settlers. Both groups were supported by foreigners who wanted British powers out of Africa; China supplied weapons to ZIPRA and Russia gave them to ZANLA. The group's terrorist activities started after the blacks in Rhodesia, who constitute 95 percent of the population, declared in November 1965 that they were going to take control of their own country, and British authorities announced that this would never happen. From 1966 until 1979, when Britain finally allowed elections to take place in Rhodesia (whereupon ZANLA leader Robert Mugabe became president and the country was renamed Zimbabwe), the violence continued. ZANLA and ZIPRA terrorists burned down villages, kidnapped boys to train as soldiers, and killed and mutilated white farmers and any blacks who supported white rule, as well as blacks who were members of rival nationalist groups. They also stole supplies and livestock from both whites and blacks, and they destroyed roads and railroads. To try to prevent such violence, Rhodesian troops used helicopters to locate spots where nationalist guerrillas had been sighted, trained dogs to track down guerrilla hideouts, and planted mines to protect villages from invasion. Meanwhile white settlers formed their own groups to defend themselves against attack. The violence continued to escalate until Great Britain decided that the colony was no longer worth maintaining.

Three other African countries to experience a violent decolonization campaign were Namibia, colonized by the Germans; Portuguese Africa, colonized by the Spanish; and South Africa, colonized by the Dutch and British. In Namibia, this campaign began after allied forces from South Africa drove out the Germans during World War I. Afterward, the South Africans refused to let Namibia become independent, even after the United Nations asked them to do so. For years the South Africans kept control and enforced a system of racial discrimination known as apartheid which kept black Namibians from having any say in the governance of their country. In 1971 the International Court of Justice declared that the South Africans had seized control of Namibia illegally, and again they refused to leave. By this time, a group known as the South West Africa People's Organization (SWAPO) was engaging in terrorism throughout the country. Formed in 1960 by Namibian tribesmen, the group attacked white farmers and other civilians, and in the mid-1970s, when the government attacked SWAPO bases, its members established terrorist training camps in neighboring Angola, which in 1975 had achieved independence from Portuguese colonial powers. There SWAPO continued to plan attacks, including a 1988 bombing of a bank in Oshakati, Namibia, that killed twenty-one people. Eventually, however, the United States and the Soviet Union stepped in to stop the violence, negotiating an agreement by which Namibia could gain independence; after the country's first election, SWAPO gained control of the government.

Portuguese Africa. Angola was one of three colonies established by the Portuguese, along with Portuguese Guinea and Mozambique. The Portuguese had been in the region since the fifteenth century, and since then they had exploited the natives as farm laborers. In 1961 Angolan militants rose up against the Portuguese who owned cotton plantations, slaughtering hundreds of farmers and their wives and children. At the same time, various tribes of native Angolans attacked one another. The Portuguese army responded by launching air attacks on the tribes, killing at least fifty thousand, and afterward the government made certain concessions to native workers, hoping to end their rebellion. For example, whereas for years the Portuguese had tried to eliminate the natives' traditional tribal rituals, they now allowed the natives to practice their beliefs as they saw fit. In addition, the Portuguese eliminated forced labor. Nonetheless, the rebellion not only continued but spread to Portuguese Guinea and Mozambique, both of which were involved in their own rebellions by 1964. In Guinea the military took two approaches to quelling the violence: increasing the number of troops in the country and improving the lives of the natives by building new homes, schools, hospitals and other facilities. Meanwhile, Mozambique took the strictly military approach, slaughtering hundreds of Africans in an attempt to maintain control. As a result, the militants in Mozambique were particularly violent, bombing numerous civilian and military targets. By the early 1970s, Portugal had decided it no longer wanted to deal with such problems, and by the end of 1975 all three colonies had been given their independence.

India. In India revolutionary violence against the colonial power, Great Britain, began in the early 1900s in the Bengal region, where nationalists calling for revolution claimed that the fight for independence was a religious duty. Bengali terrorists formed secret societies, or *samitis*, that engaged in terrorist attacks against British police and government officials and any Indians who worked for them; in addition, they started riots that swept others into their rebellion and published antigovernment materials encouraging terrorist activities like bombing. The British countered this activity with increased forces, the establishment of secret-police units dedicated to capturing members of the *samitis*, bans on secret societies and the publication of anti-government materials, and a policy of imprisoning revolutionaries without necessarily bothering with a trial. Nonetheless, in December 1912 some revolutionaries nearly assassinated the British viceroy, Lord Hardinge, in Delhi, India, and afterward the terrorism continued even though the British captured several *samitis* leaders. In addition, after World War I, a nonviolent movement formed to protest British rule, and soon the British were dealing with widespread civil disobedience. Both nonviolent and violent resistance occurred throughout the early 1920s; in response to the riots, attacks on police and other public officials, assassinations, and bombings, the government changed its laws to allow for the immediate imprisonment of terrorist leaders. By 1925 this had largely ended the violence, but two years later, as the terrorist leaders were released from prison, the terrorist attacks resumed. In 1930 a terrorist group called the Indian Republican Army struck the city of Chittagong, killing several soldiers, stealing dozens of weapons, destroying its communications facilities and railroad tracks, and slaughtering the members of British men's club. Once again the British responded by rounding up sus-

pected terrorists and their supporters, allowing police broad powers to search and seize people on the street. This dramatically reduced terrorism, and this time when the terrorists were released from prison in 1937–1938, most did not resume their violent activities. However, they did become involved in the nonviolent movement to free India from British rule, and after Great Britain decided to grant India's independence in 1947, they started attacking one another over which sect of Hindus or Muslims would be in control of the country.

Southeast Asia. In Southeast Asia two regions saw the most anticolonial terrorism, Indochina (now Vietnam, Cambodia, and Laos) and Malaya; Indochina was colonized by the French in the 1880s, who during World War II were temporarily supplanted in most parts of the region by the Japanese, while Malaya was colonized by the British. Nationalists in Indochina began fighting against the French in the 1930s and also against the Japanese during World War II. Most of the terrorism took place in what is now Vietnam. In 1945 Communists and other nationalists, led by Ho Chi Minh, declared Vietnam's independence, and when the French-controlled government refused to accept this, Ho Chi Minh began leading a guerrilla war against French forces. His group, the Vietminh, engaged in numerous terrorist activities, such as bombings, suicide bombings, and sniper attacks, not only against the French but its enemies among the native Vietnamese. Seven years later, the group had driven out the French, and in 1954 the country was divided into North Vietnam and South Vietnam, with the former controlled by Communists and the latter supported by the United States.

In Malaya, another group of Communists, the Malayan Communist Party (MCP), engaged in guerrilla warfare similar to that of the Vietminh. This guerrilla group was organized to fight the Japanese in World War II, during which it was supported by the British. After the war, however, the Communists turned against the British in an attempt to oust the colonial government. After renaming itself the Malayan Races' Liberation Army (MRLA), the guerrilla group began attacking both civilian and military targets, destroying transportation systems, communications systems, mining operations, rubber plantations and police posts and killing thousands of people. (By some estimates, over eleven thousand were killed by the guerrillas, of which there were roughly ten thousand in 1948.) Over time, the MRLA became more organized and did an increasing amount of damage. In response, the British tried to cut off their support systems by moving the Malaysian people into new villages far from guerrilla activity, but in 1950, the MRLA started machine-gunning them. Still, without support among the populace, the group weakened, and its numbers dropped. Nonetheless in 1951 it managed to assassinate the British high commissioner, Sir Henry Gurney, to murder some British women in roadside shootings, and to derail a train. The terrorist attacks continued even after Britain gave Malaya its independence in 1957, as various groups fought for control of the new government.

Greece and Cyprus. An island country in the Mediterranean Sea, Cyprus had a British colonial government when, in 1955, a group called the National Organization of Cypriot Fighters (EOKA) began engaging in terrorism designed to force the British to allow Cyprus to join with Greece. This group bombed government offices, planes, and places where people from Great Britain gathered (such as restaurants and a ballroom where a party was taking place), tried to kill government and military officials and their wives, and shot at innocent civilians walking down streets. At the same time, Greek Cypriots fought with Turkish Cypriots, who did not want the island to unite with Greece. As the country approached civil war, the British decided to make Cyprus independent, without a tie to Greece, at the end of 1958, whereupon the EOKA stopped its terrorism.

Greece experienced its own terrorism during the 1940s, when the Greek Communist Party (KKE) tried to end German colonial power. To this end, KKE supported the establishment of several terrorist and guerrilla groups, all of whom attacked government and military targets, took hostages for use in subsequent negotiations, and tortured and executed Greeks who supported the Germans or did not support communism. This violence continued after the Germans abandoned Greece in 1944, with Communists and anti-Communists fighting over control of the country.

SEE ALSO: Africa, terrorism in post-colonial; Greek Communist Party; Malayan Races Liberation Army; Mau Mau; National Organization of Cypriot Fighters; Vietminh, the

dehumanization

Dehumanization occurs when one person views another person as less than human—that is, like an object rather than a human being. Such a view is often encouraged among terrorists in order to make it easier for them to kill people. Instead of viewing their victims as being just like their sisters, brothers, mothers, fathers, children, or other loved ones, terrorists typically see them as being nothing more than a means to an end: the way for them to realize their political, religious, or personal agendas.

SEE ALSO: terrorism, motivations for

Delta Force

Established in 1977, the First Special Forces Operational Detachment-Delta, or Delta Force, is a U.S. Army military unit whose main focus is counterterrorism. Though average citizens commonly believe that the force draws its members from all branches of the armed forces, in actuality its members are recruited from within the U.S. Army. The public has been provided with almost no information about the force or its activities. However, Delta Force is known to be headquartered at Fort Bragg, North Carolina, where it has extensive training facilities and no more than twenty-five hundred personnel. When performing their duties, members of Delta Force typically do not wear uniforms, in order to keep their participation in the force a secret. Journalists have attempted to uncover details about Delta Force missions, but cannot agree on exactly what these missions might be or to what extent the Delta Force, as opposed to other branches of the military, might have been involved in them. Most believe, however, that Delta Force participated in Operation Eagle Claw in 1980, during which military forces attempted to rescue people taken hostage by terrorists at the U.S. embassy in Tehran, Iran. The operation failed when some helicopters malfunctioned, and afterward the U.S. military established a Special Operations Aviation Regiment (SOAR) dedicated to using and maintaining air transport vehicles. Delta Force was also apparently involved in the invasion of Grenada in 1983, the Gulf War in 1990–1991, and the attacks on Taliban and al Qaeda members in Afghanistan in 2002.

SEE ALSO: al Qaeda; Operation Eagle Claw; Taliban

Department of Justice, U.S.

A federal law-enforcement agency operation headed by the U.S. attorney general and supervising the Federal Bureau of Investigation (FBI), the U.S. Department of Justice (DOJ) is charged with investigating and prosecuting cases of domestic terrorism, in cooperation with the Department of Homeland Security. The DOJ has therefore been involved in numerous high-profile terrorist cases, including the attacks on the World Trade Center in 1993 and 2001. After the 2001 attack, U.S. attorney general John Ashcroft decided that the DOJ should spend as much time preventing terrorist attacks as prosecuting them. To this end the agency embarked on a campaign to jail suspected terrorists for minor violations of U.S. law in order to keep them from committing greater crimes. This approach to combating terrorism continues today, as do DOJ prosecutions of domestic terrorists.

SEE ALSO: Homeland Security, U.S. Department of; Federal Bureau of Investigation

Dirty War, the

The Dirty War, or *la guerra sucia*, is the name commonly used to refer to a government campaign against guerrillas in Argentina, which began after the military seized control of the country in 1976. At that time, the new regime decided that the only way to hold on to its control was to eliminate all left-wing opposition. It therefore launched a program known as the Process of National Reorganization, more commonly called the Process, whereby all revolutionary thought was eradicated through terrorist tactics. Initially the military regime conducted book-burnings, destroyed "subversive" art, and arrested and tortured known guerrillas and any university students and teachers, artists, and politicians who had expressed ideas contrary to those sponsored by the state. But as the Dirty War progressed, the regime established quotas that led military forces to arrest innocent citizens en masse, often during nighttime raids. Many of these citizens were never seen again; they became known as "the Disappeared." The regime also killed people outright, and often when the miltary's death squads, provided by a right-wing, government-allied group called the Argentine Anti-Communist Alliance (AAA), murdered a mother or father it also killed the victim's children, under the theory that they would grow up to avenge their parent's death. By some estimates, over thirty thousand people died during the Dirty War, including over four thousand members of a left-wing revolutionary group known as the Montoneros and most of the leadership of another terrorist group, the People's Revolutionary Army (ERP), both of which had previously struck out against the AAA by assassinating important figures connected to the organization. Consequently many people were afraid to speak out against the AAA or the military regimen, but in 1977 some relatives of the Disappeared bravely formed a group called the Mothers of the Plaza de Mayo and held a demonstration that brought international attention to the government-sponsored terrorism. As a result, some of the group's leaders were arrested, as were some of the foreign journalists who came to Argentina to report on the demonstration. (The journalists were eventually released, but the others joined the numbers of the Disappeared.) Nonetheless the Mothers of the Plaza de Mayo continued its public protests of the regime until the latter collapsed in 1983. By this time, the government had covered up much of the evidence related to its criminal actions, and it justified the rest by saying that such actions were a necessary response to guerrilla terrorism. During the 1990s the new government supported this view, pardoning many of those who had enforced the Process while ignoring witnesses who came forward to tell of the atrocities committed as part of the Dirty War.

Douhet, Giulio
(1869–1930)

Italian military aviation expert Giulio Douhet was the first person to propose that air bombing be used as a form of terrorism. He presented this concept, known as terror bombing, in his 1921 book, *The Command of the Air*. In it, Douhet argued that daily air attacks by fleets of bombers could be the most important weapon during wartime, not just because of the destruction such attacks would cause but because of the terror they would instill in civilians. Moreover he believed that urban bombing would make any war shorter, because such terrorism would lead the people of the attacked country to demand that their government surrender as quickly as possible. This idea influenced America's decision to use the atomic bomb against Japan during World War II. However, in World War I, when Douhet tried to convince Italian military officers and government officials to use five hundred bombers to drop 125 tons of bombs a day on its enemies, they dismissed his suggestion as ridiculous. Then commander of the first Italian military aviation unit, Douhet responded by writing highly critical letters about his superiors, and as a result of his outspokenness he was court-martialed and served a year in jail. After the war his court-martial was overturned, but he soon abandoned the military for a career as a writer and aviation expert, briefly serving as the commissioner of aviation in the government of Benito Mussolini.

SEE ALSO: bombs, types of; wartime terrorism

drugs and terrorists

The drug trade is a major source of revenue for terrorist organizations, which often ally themselves with drug lords who themselves use terrorist tactics to maintain their businesses. Any terrorism associated with the drug trade, whether committed by drug lords or terrorists, is called narcoterrorism, a word first coined in the 1980s. At that time, police in the country of Colombia uncovered an alliance between a terrorist group called the Revolutionary Armed Forces of Colombia (FARC) and a group of drug barons near the capital city of Bogotá. Upon further investigation, authorities learned that the FARC and another terrorist group, the April 19 Move-

ment (M-I9), had struck a deal with the drug lords in 1981: The terrorists would use their arms to protect the drug lords and their drug smugglers and drug-traffickers particularly against interference from government officials in exchange for a 10 percent tax levied against all growers of coca, which is used to make cocaine. At first this amounted to roughly $3.3 million a month, but by 1984 the two terrorist groups together earned $150 million, which they spent on weapons and recruitment efforts. The Colombian terrorists also paid money to Cuba for its help in the drug trade and the sale and procurement of weapons. Sometime in the mid-1980s, the terrorists began laundering drug money in Florida, adding, by some experts' estimates, $15 billion to the U.S. economy. It is unclear whether the Colombian connection between drug lords and terrorists was the first of its kind, or whether it was only the first to be uncovered; however, in the years since the Colombian police found evidence of the connection, many similar relationships have been revealed, particularly in Latin America and Asia.

SEE ALSO: Colombia, terrorism in; criminal terrorism; Revolutionary Armed Forces of Colombia

Earth First!

Founded in 1980, Earth First! is a radical environmental group that practiced ecoterrorism in the United States during the 1980s. Its targets were businesses it determined were harmful to the environment, particularly those involving logging. To prevent logging, the group used such tactics as log roadblocks, human blockades, equipment sabotage, and tree-

Firefighters and police pull an Earth First! protestor to safety during a demonstration in Missoula, MT, on June 19, 2002. TOM BAUER. © AP IMAGES

spiking, whereby metal spikes were hammered deep into trees in order to destroy saws. The founder of Earth First!, David Foreman, created the group after becoming dissatisfied with his job as a lobbyist for the mainstream environmental group the Wilderness Society. Foreman believed that mainstream environmentalists were getting nowhere in trying to promote environmentalism through political channels; his ideas regarding the practices of Earth First! were taken from a 1975 novel, *The Monkey Wrench Gang* by Edward Abbey, in which radical environmentalists destroy dams, bulldozers, and other equipment responsible for the destruction of the landscape. The first act of Earth First!, in 1981, was to unfurl a banner across Arizona's Glen Canyon Dam that made it appear as though the dam had developed a 300-foot-long (91m) crack. In 1985 Foreman wrote *Ecodefense: A Field Guide to Monkeywrenching* in which he gave instructions on how to damage various kinds of equipment used for earth-moving, logging, surveying, and similar activities related to land development. By the mid-1980s, however, Earth First! began to move away from such radical tactics, and in 1987 Foreman left the group to form another, the Evan Mecham Eco-Terrorist International Conspiracy (EMETIC), that would be as radical as Earth First! once was. By this time, Earth First! had chapters in Great Britain and Australia as well as North America, and some of its British members also decided to leave Earth First!

to form another, more radical group, the Earth Liberation Front (ELF). But despite these defections, Earth First! continues to be an active, though fairly moderate, environmental group.

SEE ALSO: Earth Liberation Front; ecoterrorism; Evan Mecham Eco-Terrorist International Conspiracy

Earth Liberation Front (ELF)

Established in 1992 in England but operating in the United States as well, the Earth Liberation Front (ELF) conducts ecoterrorism, attacking businesses and institutions that the group believes are harmful to the environment. Among the creators of ELF were members of another environmental group, Earth First!, who had become dissatisfied with that group's decision to curtail its illegal activities, which were initially similar to those employed by ELF. In conducting its activities, ELF takes precautions to ensure that no humans or animals are killed or injured, concentrating instead on destroying property in order to hurt its targets' profits. For example, the group has damaged logging machinery in various parts of the United States, and in 1998 it set fire to ski lifts at a Colorado ski resort planning to develop an adjacent wilderness area. On May 26, 2001, the group claimed responsibility for a firebombing that took place five days earlier at the University of Washington. The resulting blaze destroyed the university's Center for Urban Horticulture, where scientists had been developing hybrid poplar trees for the logging industry that are faster-growing than normal; ELF issued a statement that hybrid poplars are a threat to the environment because they would quickly overrun native trees in any forest where they were planted. In October 2006 two ELF members, Jennifer Kolar of Se-

attle, Washington, and Lacey Phillabaum of Spokane, Washington, pleaded guilty to committing the firebombing as an act of ecoterrorism. Kolar also pleaded guilty to attempting to firebomb the offices of a gun club in Wray, Colorado, in 1998, when club members were organizing a turkey shoot.

SEE ALSO: Earth First!; ecoterrorism

Easter Rising, the

The Easter Rising was a one-week rebellion in Ireland in 1916. Two years earlier, right before the start of World War I, the British Parliament was considering a piece of legislation, the Home Rule Bill, that would have given the Irish more control over their own country. With the outbreak of war, however, this legislation was set aside, an action that angered Irish nationalists. Their resentment of the British simmered until finally, on Easter Monday, April 24, 1916, an Irish nationalist group called the Irish Volunteers took over government buildings in the Irish city of Dublin and declared that Ireland was now a republic. The British responded by sending a large number of troops into the city, where gun battles broke out and the rebellion was quelled within a week. Nearly eight hundred civilians and over five hundred military personnel were killed during this period, and afterward the British executed sixteen of the rebellion's leaders. Among the Irish these people were considered martyrs.

SEE ALSO: Irish Republican Army

ecoterrorism

Also known as ecotage, ecoterrorism involves the sabotaging of property belonging to businesses whose practices harm the environment or people's enjoyment of the environment. As an example, in the late 1980s, an ecoterrorist group called the Evan Mecham Eco-Terrorist International Conspiracy (EMETIC) tried to destroy ski lifts and other structures at a resort that was planning to develop land considered sacred by two Indian tribes, the Navajo and the Hopi; it attacked a uranium mine on sacred land as well and planned to damage nuclear power plants in Arizona, California, and Colorado. (The plan was thwarted by law-enforcement authorities.)

As with EMETIC, the terrorist groups that engage in ecoterrorism are typically left-wing, single-issue groups, which means that their politics are usually liberal and they do not engage in other types of terrorism. In addition, most ecoterrorists, who are by definition also environmentalists, try not to hurt human beings during their operations; for example, they set fires after-hours, so that buildings are empty when they ignite. The most radical environmentalists, however, do not think about whether or not their actions will hurt human beings, whom they blame as a whole for all cruelties perpetrated against animals and nature. For example, some radical ecoterrorists have injected poison into candy bars of a particular brand, then publicized their actions in an attempt to get people to stop buying the products of that company. Others have hidden metal spikes in tree trunks so that loggers cutting down the trees will damage the machinery, without caring that the spikes might fly up and injure the loggers.

Among the most prominent groups to have engaged in ecoterrorism are Earth First!, the Animal Liberation Front (ALF), the Earth Liberation Front (ELF), and the Sea Shepherd Conservation Society. The latter was formed in the mid-1970s by a member of Greenpeace, an environmental organization that gained notoriety by sabotaging whaling operations beginning in the late 1960s. In conducting these operations, Greenpeace members in small, highly maneuverable boats would place themselves in between whales and whalers' harpoons, making it impossible in many cases for the whalers to shoot without causing an international incident. The Sea Shepherd Society did this as well, but also sank whaling ships in Iceland while damaging a whaling station there. The ALF has planted mail and car bombs, contaminated products on store shelves, physically attacked researchers who use animals as test subjects, and broken into research laboratories, pet stores, kennels, and similar places at night to liberate captive animals. Earth First! has damaged logging and construction equipment and during the 1980s one of its founders, Dave Foreman, encouraged others to take up ecoterrorism via the publication of a book called *Ecodefense: A Field Guide to Monkeywrenching*, which provides information on how to spike trees and damage logging and construction equipment. ELF has also damaged logging machinery in various parts of the United States, and in 1998 it set fire to ski lifts at a Colorado ski resort planning to develop an adjacent wilderness area. In 2001 the group firebombed the Center for Urban Horticulture at the University of Washington, where scientists had been developing hybrid poplar trees for the logging industry that some environmentalists believe will damage native tree species.

Individual environmentalists have also engaged in ecoterrorism. For example, in recent years radical environmentalists, acting alone, have spray-painted or otherwise damaged vehicles that use an excessive amount of gasoline, such as Hummers and sport utility vehicles (SUVs). Prior to the terrorist attacks in America on September 11, 2001, law-enforcement authorities tended to treat this type of small-scale property damage more like an act of mischief than terrorism, but now these types of crimes are dealt with very seriously, with the perpetrators receiving substantial jail sentences and fines.

SEE ALSO: Animal Liberation Front; Earth First!; Earth Liberation Front; Evan Mecham Eco-Terrorist International Conspiracy

Egypt, terrorism in

The country of Egypt has suffered a great deal of domestic terrorism perpetrated largely by Islamic extremists unhappy with Egypt's secular government. One Egyptian terrorist group in particular, the Gama'a al-Islamiyya, engages in terrorist attacks, which include shootings and bombings, specifically because it wants to destabilize the Egyptian government and overthrow it so that a religious authority (an Islamic theocracy) can govern in its place. This group, which remains active today, primarily targets tourists with the intent of harming the Egyptian tourism industry and therefore the country's economy as a whole. To this end, it attacks tour buses, cruise ships, and crowded tourist sites. For example, in November 1997 the group machine-gunned fifty-eight tourists and their Egyptian guides at an ancient temple in the Valley of the Kings of Luxor, Egypt. Two years earlier, the group attempted to assassinate the president of Egypt, Hosni Mubarak, while he was visiting Ethiopia. This attempt was apparently backed by Saudi Arabian terrorist Osama bin Laden and his radical Islamic group, al Qaeda, which is understandable given that bin laden is an outspoken opponent of secular Arab governments and that one of al

Qaeda's highest-ranking members is a former Egyptian police officer, Muhammad Atef, opposed to Egypt's policies. Another Egyptian Islamic extremist group with ties to bin laden, al Jihad, assassinated the president of Egypt, Anwar Sadat, in 1981, masquerading as soldiers in order to get close enough to shoot him at a public event. Al Jihad attacked other members of the Egyptian government in the 1980s and '90s, nearly killing the interior minister and the prime minister in 1993, and bombed an Egyptian embassy in Pakistan in 1995 (another attack linked to support from al Qaeda).

After the assassination of Anwar Sadat, the Egyptian government became much more aggressive in rooting out terrorists. It began by expelling from the country three notorious Sunni Muslim terrorists whose militant Islamic group, Palestinian Islamic Jihad (PIJ), had been operating out of Egypt: Dr. Fathi Shaqaqi, Abdul Aziz Odeh, and Bashir Moussa, all originally from Pakistan. Later it drove most of the members of al Jihad from the country by rounding up people suspected of supporting the group and then torturing them for information about the terrorists. The Egyptian government went after Gama'a al-Islamiyya in a similar fashion after the group's 1997 murder of tourists in the Valley of the Kings, arresting several members of the group and sentencing them to death.

Egypt's struggles with Islamic militancy have existed since 1928, when the militant group Muslim Brotherhood (Ikhwan al-Muslimun) formed in opposition to Great Britain's influence over Egyptian politics. The Muslim Brotherhood wanted to end all Western secular influence in the country, and to this end it engaged in so many terrorist attacks on the Egyptian government that the government banned its existence. Nonetheless the group continued its efforts and advocated the complete destruction of the Egyptian regime under the argument that by maintaining ties with secular governments, Egypt's leaders were going against the teachings of their holy scripture, the Quran. This belief that the Islamic faith mandates the destruction of secular governments still exists among Islamic militants today, not just in Egypt but elsewhere in the world.

SEE ALSO: al Jihad; al Qaeda; bin laden, Osama; Gama'a al-Islamiyya; Sadat, Anwar

El Rukns (Blackstone Rangers)

Also known as the Blackstone Rangers, El Rukns is a Chicago, Illinois, gang of black Muslims that was involved in a terrorist plot in 1985. (The name "El Rukns" is Arabic for "The Foundation," a reference to the foundation stone of an Islamic temple in Mecca.) When the group's leader, Jeff Fort, heard that the Libyan government was paying black Muslims to commit terrorist acts in the United States, he went to Libya to sell the services of El Rukns for $2.5 million. Shortly thereafter, another El Rukns member, Melvin Mayes, fell into a trap set by the Federal Bureau of Investigation (FBI) by buying a rocket launcher, fitted with a hidden tracking device, from undercover federal agents. This device led agents to a house that held other weapons as well. In August 1985 they arrested several members of El Rukns, including Fort, and by November 1987 they had all been convicted and sent to prison, though Mayes was not captured until March 1995. The El Rukns gang still exists, primarily among the prison population.

SEE ALSO: Libya

El Salvador, death squads in

The right-wing government of El Salvador has engaged in violence for over seventy years in order to suppress peasant uprisings. During the 1970s, however, a new source of right-wing violence arose in the private sector: death squads that murdered anyone with left-wing political beliefs, including students, teachers, and workers who supported unionization. The first of these death squads was created by a paramilitary group, ORDEN ("Order"), established in the late 1960s by an army general named José Alberto Medrano with help from the Guardia Nacional (National Guard) and funding from wealthy landowners and businessmen who wanted protection from peasant revolt. During the 1980s, when Marxist revolutionaries from the Farabundo Martí Front for National Liberation (FMLN) started a guerrilla war in an attempt to overthrow the El Salvadoran government (then backed by the United States), the death squads of ORDEN and another right-wing paramilitary group, the White Hand, became extremely active, murdering thousands of people throughout the country. Anyone who spoke out against the right-wing government was at risk; for example, in 1980 a death squad killed a Catholic archbishop performing mass. Between 1979 and 1991, when the war finally ended, over eighty thousand people were killed, roughly thirty thousand of them by death squads.

SEE ALSO: Farabundo Martí Front for National Liberation

Ellerman, Josh (Douglas Joshua Ellerman)
(1979–)

A member of the Animal Liberation Front (ALF), Josh Ellerman faced one of the first, severe prison sentences for terrorism related to animal-rights activism. On March 11, 1997, when he was only eighteen years old, he and other ALF members planted bombs at the Fur Breeders Agricultural Co-Op in Sandy, Utah, which housed live minks intended to be slaughtered for the fur trade. No lives were lost during the explosions and subsequent fire; ALF members made sure that the building was empty and released the minks from their cages before detonating the bombs. Nonetheless when Ellerman was arrested for the crime he faced a sentence of at least thirty-five years in prison. Consequently he made a deal with authorities, helping them arrest other ALF members in exchange for a lesser sentence: seven years in prison, beginning in 1998, and $750,000 in restitution to the mink breeders.

SEE ALSO: Animal Liberation Front; animal-rights movement

embassy bombings

Because terrorists generally view embassies, their diplomats, and their staffs as symbols of the nations they serve, embassy buildings are prime targets for terrorist bombings and kidnappings, particularly since an attack on an embassy draws the media to the site and therefore calls public attention to the terrorists' cause. As a result there have been several attacks on embassies since the late 1960s, the most notable (in chronological order) being:

- a 1973 takeover of the Japanese embassy in Singapore by a Japanese terrorist group called Japanese Red Army (JRA), during which the JRA exchanged hostages for certain concessions from the Japanese government.

- a 1974 attack on the French embassy in The Hague, Netherlands, in which the JRA joined with another group, the Popular Front for the Liberation of Palestine (PFLP), to take the French ambassador and ten others hostage in order to gain ransom money and the release of several Red Army members then in prison in France; the following year, the JRA took over the U.S. and Swedish embassies in Kuala Lumpur, Malaysia, for similar reasons, exchanging over fifty hostages for money and the release of imprisoned JRA, and in June 1987 they attacked the U.S. and British embassies in Rome, Italy, using car bombs and mortars.

- the November 1979 attack on the U.S. embassy in Tehran, Iran, which resulted in sixty-six Americans being taken hostage; fifty-three of them were held for 444 days, until January 1981; this incident is perhaps best known for a failed U.S. attempt to rescue the hostages, Operation Eagle Claw.

- the May 1980 attack on the Iranian embassy in London, England, during which Britain's Special Air Service Regiment almost immediately rescued nineteen hostages.

- two 1981 attacks on Israeli embassies in Athens, Greece, and Vienna, Austria, by a Palestinian terrorist group called 15 May Organization, which at that time operated out of Iraq.

- the 1983 suicide bombing of the U.S. embassy in Beirut, Lebanon, by Islamic terrorists associated with Hezbollah, during which sixty-three people died.

- an April 1992 coordinated attack, by members of the Marxist Islamic group Mujahedin-e-Khalq Organization (MEK), on thirteen Iranian embassies throughout the world, as a strike against the government then in place in Iran.

- a 1992 bombing of the Israeli embassy in Buenos Aires, Argentina, by Islamic terrorists associated with the group Hezbollah, during which nearly thirty people were killed.
- a 1995 bombing of an Egyptian embassy in Islamabad, Pakistan, by the al Jihad terrorist group, which killed seventeen people; in 1998, the group tried but failed to bomb the U.S. embassy in Albania.
- a February 1996 rocket attack on the U.S. embassy in Athens, Greece.
- a 1996 attack by Peru's Tupac Amaru Revolutionary Movement (MRTA) on the Japanese embassy in Lima, Peru; after blowing a hole in an embassy wall to gain entrance during a party, fourteen MRTA members took over six hundred people hostage, including over thirty ambassadors, and held some of them for four months before the Peruvian military stormed the embassy, released the hostages, and killed all of the terrorists.
- the August 1998 coordinated bombing attacks on U.S. embassies in Nairobi, Kenya, and Dar es Salaam, Tanzania, by Islamic terrorists with ties to Osama bin Laden's group al Qaeda; the explosives, which were in trucks (one for each embassy), were detonated near embassy entrances at a time when Muslims would be away at prayer, which meant that none of the 224 people killed in the attack were faithful to Islam.
- an October 2000 attack on the British embassy in Aden, Yemen, the day

after suicide bombers struck the USS *Cole* in port there; the embassy bombing, which only damaged some windows, was later credited to a terrorist group called Aden-Abyan Islamic Army.

To combat such attacks, during the 1970s the leaders of various countries worked together to establish tough punishments for anyone who intentionally harmed diplomats or their staff members, and in the years since then, security measures have been taken to try to protect embassies from attack, with limited success.

SEE ALSO: al Jihad; al Qaeda; bin laden, Osama; *Cole*, USS; Hezbollah; Japanese Red Army; Operation Eagle Claw; Tupac Amaru Revolutionary Movement

Engels, Friederich
(1820–1895)

German socialist philosopher Friederich Engels helped found modern communism with associate Karl Marx and, while doing so, severely criticized German socialists who rejected the idea that revolution was necessary to change society. However, in advocating revolution, Engels and Marx rejected the use of terrorism as a way to spark social change, arguing that such change would be achieved once the working class became fully aware of the ways in which it was being repressed by the upper class and the state. Beginning in the 1840s, the two men wrote several articles together to promote the socialist movement. They also coauthored a statement of Communist principles, the *Manifest der kommunistischen Partei* (commonly called the *Communist Manifesto*), for a secret socialist society, the Communist League, presenting it at the group's second Communist Congress in London, England, in 1848. That same year, Engels and Marx participated in a failed attempt, known as the Revolution of 1848, to overthrow the established political system in Germany. Afterward Engels became a businessman in England, though he continued to write about his beliefs and sent a substantial amount of his income to Marx in support of the Communist movement.

SEE ALSO: Marx, Karl

Entebbe raid

The Entebbe raid was a military operation conducted by Israel in an attempt to rescue hostages from terrorists at the Entebbe Airport in Uganda. The hostage crisis began when seven terrorists—five Palestinians and two Germans—hijacked an Air France Airbus shortly after it took off from Athens, Greece. (The flight originated in Tel Aviv, Israel, and was en route to Paris, France.) The hijackers, most of whom were members of a terrorist organization called the Popular Front for the Liberation of Palestine (PFLP), forced the plane to land at Entebbe. Once on the ground, the terrorists released 142 of its 248 passengers and crew; those hostages who remained were Jews, most from Israel. The terrorists said they would release these captives only if Israel released fifty-three men held as terrorists in Israeli prisons. Instead, Israeli military commandos secretly invaded Uganda (which supported the terrorists), raided the airport—killing some Ugandan soldiers who fired on them—and rescued all but three of the hostages. These three were accidentally shot during the rescue, when the Israelis gunned down all of the terrorists.

SEE ALSO: Israel; Popular Front for the Liberation of Palestine

ethnic cleansing

Also known as genocide, ethnic cleansing is the elimination of an entire ethnic group, typically through murder but also through forced removal, from a particular geographical region. The phrase was first used by Serb nationalists in reference to genocide against Serbs by non-Serbs during the 1990s in Bosnia in the former Yugoslavia. However, the practice has been around at least since biblical times. In the twentieth century, the most notable example of ethnic cleansing was the Holocaust (1939–1945), during which Germans tried to exterminate Jews and Gypsies. More recently, in the 1990s, members of the Hutu tribe in Rwanda and Burundi tried to exterminate those of the Tutsi tribe, killing at least five hundred thousand in the process.

SEE ALSO: Bosnian genocide; Holocaust, the

ethno-nationalist terrorism

A component of some movements toward national independence or a cohesive national identity, ethno-nationalist terrorism occurs when people of one ethnicity are in violent conflict with those of another ethnicity. This type of terrorism is very focused, because enemies are clearly defined; most ethno-nationalist terrorists operate only in their own country, though some might strike international targets with a symbolic connection to their struggle. Africa by far has experienced the most ethno-nationalist conflicts, among various tribal and ethnic groups in most parts of the continent, but there has also been ethno-terrorism in south and central Asia (most notably in Chechnya, Sri Lanka, and Afghanistan), in Latin America (primarily in Guatemala, where roughly two hundred thousand Indians died during a thirty-five-year period of genocide that ended in the 1990s), and in the Basque region of Spain. In Europe and the Middle East, ethnonationalist terrorism is often coupled with religious terrorism, because the ethnic groups there typically derive their cultural unity from shared religious beliefs. Examples of places where ethno-nationalist terrorism has been influenced by religion include Bosnia in the former Yugoslavia, Israel, and Iraq.

In the United States, ethno-nationalist terrorism is not a problem because America has no nationalist movement— that is, members of one particular ethnic group do not expect to break away from the United States to carve their own independent state out of U.S. lands—though the country does have racism-based terrorism, particularly within the white-supremacist movement. However, within Puerto Rico, which is a commonwealth of the United States, a nationalist movement does exist, with members of the movement arguing that the United States should give Puerto Rico its independence. To force this issue into the limelight, in the 1970s and 1980s members of a Puerto Rican terrorist group called Armed Forces for National Liberation (Fuerzas Armadas de Liberación Nacional, or FALN) perpetrated bombings and other terrorist attacks in the United States, particularly in Chicago and New York.

SEE ALSO: Bosnian genocide; ethnic cleansing; racism; white supremacists

Evan Mecham Eco-Terrorist International Conspiracy (EMETIC)

Established in 1987, the Evan Mecham Eco-Terrorist International Conspiracy

(EMETIC) engaged in ecoterrorism in Arizona under the direction of its founder, David Foreman, who had previously created the radical environmental group Earth First! EMETIC's name was a jab at Evan Mecham, a conservative Republican and antienvironmentalist who was then governor of Arizona. The first actions of the group, in 1987 and 1988, were attacks on ski lifts and other structures at a resort that was planning to develop land considered sacred by two Indian tribes, the Navajo and the Hopi. EMETIC targeted a uranium mine on sacred land as well, cutting its power lines. Also in 1988 the federal government planted an undercover agent in the group, who discovered that EMETIC intended to damage nuclear power plants in Arizona, California, and Colorado. The following year, federal agents began arresting members of the group, including Foreman. In 1991 he pleaded guilty to sabotaging nuclear power plants; after four other top members of EMETIC were convicted as well, the group was effectively dissolved.

SEE ALSO: Earth First!; ecoterrorism

Extraordinary Commission for Combating Counterrevolution and Sabotage (Cheka)

The Extraordinary Commission for Combating Counterrevolution and Sabotage, more commonly known as the Cheka, was a terrorist organization created in December 1917 by the Bolsheviks who took over Russia as a result of the Russian Revolution. As part of a Bolshevik directive known as Red Terror, the Cheka was charged with using terrorism to destroy the Bolsheviks' enemies, killing anyone believed to be an enemy of the Soviet state. The organization was so effective that it became Soviet Russia's security police agency. Its leader was Polish revolutionary and fanatic Communist Feliks Dzerzhinskii, who participated in the Russian revolution, was elected to the Bolshevik Party's Central Committee in July 1917, and subsequently established Russia's first concentration camps. Under his command, from 1917 to 1921, the Cheka used fear to prevent rural peasants and urban working-class citizens from rebelling against the Bolsheviks, intimidating or torturing anyone who spoke out against the status quo, and crushing any signs of disorder or unrest.

extremism, right-wing versus left-wing

Regarding terrorism, experts typically classify terrorists' ideologies as being either right-wing or left-wing. In general, right-wing extremism is an attempt to maintain a particular social system or to go back to an earlier time when that system existed in a form that was, the extremists believe, close to perfect. In contrast, left-wing extremism concerns itself with the future rather than the past or present, as it attempts to end the status quo, usually through revolution, in order to create a new social system. In wanting to keep or return to their preferred social system, right-wing extremists emphasize the importance of upholding certain values and traditions and of defending a particular race, ethnicity, or religion, while left-wing extremists wish to replace government oppression and corruption with a classless society in which all people are treated fairly and justly. Both types of extremists often employ partisan political maneuvers in an attempt to get what they want, often

followed by violence when these political maneuvers fail to work.

Within each type of ideology, left-wing and right-wing, are various degrees of extremism. In the center between the two groups is centrism, or the moderate center, in which people do not hold extreme views one way or another. Then, moving to the left, comes liberalism, the far left, and the fringe left; moving to the right of center are conservatism, the far right, and the fringe right. Liberalism has been defined in various ways throughout history and throughout the world, but generally its adherents support the individual (particularly the downtrodden masses) more than or instead of the government and promote various personal freedoms while advocating slow-paced reform to create a fair society in which all people are treated well; the ideal government, to a liberal, would be one that helps people and upholds their rights without oppressing them. The far left and the fringe left have historically been expressions of Marxism, with the latter interpreting Marxism in more extreme ways than the former. Conservatism, just like its left-wing counterpart liberalism, has been defined in many ways, but generally its adherents support entities that maintain order (military, police, paramilitary, etc.), oppose programs such as welfare that devote government resources to the masses, and prefer that the government leave businesses and the wealthy to their own devices; the ideal government, to a conservative, would be one that upholds traditional values and protects the status quo without regulating the marketplace or redistributing money from the wealthy to the poor. The far right and the fringe right often take the concept of class divisions still further, saying that their ethnic, racial, or religious group is superior to all others; the fringe right is said to dehumanize members of other groups and when its adherents engage in terrorist attacks, they typically kill far more innocent people than do members of the fringe left.

SEE ALSO: left-wing terrorists, U.S.; right-wing terrorists, U.S.

Fanon, Frantz (Omar) (1925–1961)

West Indian philosopher and psychoanalyst Frantz Fanon spoke out against racism and urged native people under colonial rule to rise up against their country's occupying European governments, using violence if necessary to free themselves from oppression. His writings include *Peau noire, masques blancs* (*Black Skin, White Masks*; 1952) and *Les Damnés de la terre* (*The Wretched of the Earth*; 1961).

SEE ALSO: colonialism

Farabundo Martí Front for National Liberation (FMLN)

The Farabundo Martí Front for National Liberation (FMLN) was formed in El Salvador in 1979 when five leftist guerrilla groups joined together to fight against their country's military dictatorship, which had been in power for fifty years. During this time the government had killed tens of thousands of people, including the man for whom FMLN was named, Farabundo Martí, who was executed in 1932 for leading a failed peasant rebellion. Consequently El Salvador's guerrillas believed that the only way to defeat the military regime was to combine their forces, which numbered approximately ten thousand men. Between 1979 and 1991, these men participated in a civil war against the military regime, during which over eighty thousand people were killed, and although they did not topple the dictatorship, their

attacks were effective enough to bring about a peace agreement in January 1992. FMLN then became a political party in a new, more democratic El Salvadoran government.

SEE ALSO: El Salvador, death squads in; guerrilla warfare

fascism

A right-wing ideology, fascism is an extreme form of nationalism whose adherents, known as fascists, believe in absolute obedience to the state and its laws and practices. Fascists typically argue that the conservative social and religious traditions of their culture—particularly those traditions connected, however tenuously, to ancient times—are superior to all others and that anyone who is not of their nationality or ethnicity is an inferior human being. Fascism as a political movement arose in Russia in the early twentieth century in opposition to Marxism and anarchism, spread throughout Europe and, during the Great Depression of the 1930s, developed in the United States as well. The first fascist state was created in Italy in the 1920s by dictator Benito Mussolini; Mussolini subsequently influenced Adolf Hitler, who developed his own fascist regime in Germany in the early 1930s. Both Italy and Germany then provided military assistance to Francisco Franco, who established a fascist regime in Spain in the late 1930s. In addition to having a strong leader, all three of these regimes promoted nationalism, opposed both democracy and communism, and suppressed artistic and intellectual expression; fascists in Italy and Germany claimed that their actions were bringing back the glories of the past. (Mussolini was said to be creating a new Roman Empire, while Hitler's Nazism was said to be a movement toward the racial purity of ancient Teutonic tribes.) Italy and Germany also shared an aggressive expansionism, seeking to spread their ideologies and control to other countries, whereas Spain rejected expansionism and therefore refused to participate in World War II.

By the start of this war, fascist regimes had developed in three other countries: Hungary, Romania, and Bulgaria. By the end of the war, all of these regimes, as well as those of Italy and Germany, had fallen. However, this did not mark the end of fascism. Many modern dictatorships, particularly in Latin and South America, have embraced aspects of fascist ideology, as have some right-wing terrorist groups, including those allied with the neo-Nazi movement in the United States.

SEE ALSO: Hitler, Adolf; Mussolini, Benito; Nazi terrorism; neo-Nazis

fatwa

Issued by Islamic clerics, a *fatwa* is a ruling or decree that orders Muslims in how to behave if they want to stay true to their religion. In most cases, the *fatwa* deals with fairly mundane matters, such as clothing and dietary restrictions. Occasionally, though, a cleric issues a *fatwa* that calls on all faithful Muslims to try to murder a person who, in the cleric's opinion, has offended God by insulting any aspect of Islam. For example, in 1989 an Islamic cleric known as the Ayatollah Ruhollah Khomeini, who was then the ruler of Iran, issued a *fatwa* calling for the execution of

Salman Rushdie, the author of the book *The Satanic Verses*, and anyone associated with the book's publication, translation, or distribution who had full knowledge of its contents. *The Satanic Verses* had several passages that were offensive to Muslims, but in case this did not provide enough motivation for followers to carry out the *fatwa*, a group of Iranians offered a monetary reward for Rushdie's death; eventually this reward reached $2.5 million. Rushdie escaped death by spending a decade in hiding. Others, however, were not so fortunate. In the early 1990s, two translators of the book—one Italian and the other Japanese—were shot, as was the publisher of the Norwegian edition. Only the Japanese translator died from his injuries, but in all cases the attackers were never caught. Various clerics in addition to Khomeini have also called for the widespread murder of Americans. For example, in 1998 Osama bin Laden, who later masterminded the September 11, 2001, terrorist attacks on American soil, helped to encourage a group called the International Front for the Jihad Against Jews and Crusaders to issue a *fatwa* against all Americans throughout the world.

SEE ALSO: bin laden, Osama; September 11 attacks on America

fedayeen

The *fedayeen*, or "self-sacrificers," were Egyptians who established bases in the Gaza Strip from which they attacked Israeli settlers in the nearby Negev region in the 1950s. As a result of these attacks, in 1956 Israel invaded the Gaza Strip and quickly destroyed the *fedayeen* bases. Nonetheless in May 1970 several *fedayeen* in Lebanon crossed into Israel and shot three bazooka rockets into a school bus there, seriously injuring twenty-two children and killing eight.

See Also: Israel

Federal Bureau of Investigation (FBI)

An agency of the United States government, the Federal Bureau of Investigation (FBI) investigates crimes against the federal government, including terrorism. Its first investigations related to terrorism were of anarchist bombings in 1919. During the early 1920s the FBI began monitoring groups, such as the Ku Klux Klan, that were suspected of engaging in terrorism or other violent acts. This monitoring continues today and includes groups involved in ecoterrorism, antiabortion activities, the animal-rights movement, and the white-supremacy movement as well as domestic and international terrorism. In addition, the FBI uses a mobile crime laboratory to investigate sites of terrorist attacks, such as the 1993 bombing at the World Trade Center and the September 11, 2001, terrorist attacks in New York and Washington, D.C. The FBI is also currently engaged in counterterrorism activities related to both domestic and international terrorism; these activities began in the 1980s, and in 1996 the FBI established a Counterterrorism Center. Two years later it established a center dedicated to combating terrorist acts against the Internet (cyberterrorism) as well. By this time the FBI had been given the power to deport suspected terrorists and to act on foreign soil to combat terrorism related to U.S. interests abroad. After the September 11, 2001, terrorist attacks on America, President George W. Bush broadened the powers of the agency in regard to secret surveillance, allowing FBI agents to spy on suspected terrorists without first obtaining legal permission to do so.

See Also: antiabortion terrorism; animal-rights movement; counterterrorism; Ku Klux Klan; September 11 attacks on America; white supremacists

Federal Emergency Management Agency (FEMA)

Established in 1979, the Federal Emergency Management Agency (FEMA) is charged with responding to both natural and manmade disasters on American soil, offering aid to victims not only during such disasters but afterward as they struggle to rebuild their lives. To this end, the agency, which has a staff of nearly three thousand but also relies on thousands of federal, state, and local emergency workers and volunteers during times of crisis, provides medical care, food, temporary housing, financial aid, and other services to people who have been through hurricanes, terrorist bombings, and other major catastrophes, including the September 11, 2001, terrorist attacks on the World Trade Center in New York. However, FEMA performed so poorly in the aftermath of Hurricane Katrina, which struck New Orleans and other Gulf Coast cities in 2005, that in May 2006 several members of Congress called for its elimination, arguing that its responsibilities, which include creating emergency plans and training federal, state, and local emergency personnel in anticipation of various disasters, be given instead to another federal agency, such as the Homeland Security Agency.

See Also: September 11 attacks on America

Final Solution, the

The "Final Solution" was what Nazi leaders called their deliberate attempt in 1941 and 1942 to exterminate all Jews in Germany. The Nazis believed that Aryans—people of German and Nordic descent—were superior to people of other races, that the Jewish race was inferior to all others, and that inferior human beings did not deserve to live. Consequently in 1941 they began rounding up Jews and other people they classified as "inferiors," such as Gypsies, homosexuals, and the mentally and physically handicapped, and sending them by train to extermination camps. (The conditions on these trains were so brutal—the passengers were packed, standing, into cars with no food and little water—that roughly 20 percent died en route.) By 1943 there were six such camps, all with large gas chambers and ovens in which the dead could be cremated. At nearby labor camps the most able-bodied Jews were forced to perform manual labor until they grew weak or ill (which was likely given how little food they were given and how hard they were worked), whereupon they were gassed. There were also concentration camps in Germany where Jews might be executed, though not on as large a scale as in the extermination camps. Nazis killed Jews on sight as well, particularly during the German invasion of Russia in 1941; in some cases, Russian Jews had to dig their own graves before being shot and dumped into them. Estimates vary regarding how many Jews died as a result of the Final Solution; most historians, however, believe the number is approximately 6 million.

SEE ALSO: anti-Semitism; Holocaust, the; Nazi terrorism

Finnish Civil War, terrorism in the

In January 1918, after receiving its independence from Russia, Finland fell into civil war when a violent left-wing workers' militia, the Red Guards, seized control of the country's capital, Helsinki. Over the next four months, the Red Guards killed over 1,600 people, often in brutal ways; meanwhile the opposition forces of the Finnish government, the White Guards, brutally executed any Red Guards members they caught, as well as any workers or Russians suspected of supporting them. In one case, the White Guards massacred 350 villagers thought to be on the side of the Reds, and in another case they machine-gunned a group of 50 workers thought to be allied with the left-wing. Soon the White Guards were committing more terrorism than the Reds; by the end of April (the last month of the war), the Whites had killed over 8,000 people at times other than in the heat of battle. Nonetheless, in the aftermath of the war, the victorious Whites government convicted 67,000 of its enemies of terrorist acts, executing nearly 300.

First of October Antifascist Resistance Group (GRAPO)

A Communist paramilitary group established in Spain in 1975, the First of October Antifascist Resistance Group (GRAPO) has engaged in terrorist acts, including bombings and assassinations, against targets associated with the fascist Spanish government. The group has also attacked U.S. military bases, believing that without American support the Spanish government would be severely weakened. By 2000, GRAPO was responsible for the death or injury of nearly three hundred people.

SEE ALSO: Spain

foquismo

After the Cuban Revolution, revolutionary Ernesto "Che" Guevara developed the theory of *foquismo*, or "armed struggle," which states that by sparking an armed struggle in one place, dedicated revolutionaries could create a fire of revolution that would burn quickly through an entire continent. This idea ran counter to the prevailing notion that revolutions developed slowly and that the political climate in one place had no effect on the climate in another. Nonetheless, Guevara hoped that a revolution in South America would affect Latin America; in 1967 he was killed in Bolivia, South America, while trying to trigger a revolution there.

SEE ALSO: Guevara, Che

Force 17

From 1970 to 1994 Force 17 was an elite paramilitary unit serving al Fatah, a faction of the Palestine Liberation Organization (PLO). The unit was established as a personal security force for then head of the PLO, Yasir Arafat, and it is suspected of having assassinated his political opponents as well. During the 1980s Force 17 was also involved in terrorist attacks and paramilitary operations against Israel in the fight for Palestinian liberation. For example, in 1985 the unit took responsibility for the murder of three Israeli intelligence agents in Cyprus. In 1994 Force 17 was dissolved and its forces absorbed into the Presidential Security Force, or al-Amn al-Ri'asah, after a peace agreement was reached between Israel and Palestine.

SEE ALSO: Arafat, Yasir; Palestine Liberation Organization

France, terrorism in

From the French Revolution of the eighteenth century to the present day, France has experienced a great deal of terrorism, except for a period of relative quiet in the 1970s. Some of this terrorism has been sponsored by the state, some of it has been committed by French activists and revolutionaries, and some has come from foreigners with anti-French sentiments. France also produced a terrorism group, Action Directe, that was active outside of France during the 1980s. Founded in France in 1979, this group was responsible for at least fifty anti-American, anti-NATO (North Atlantic Treaty Organization) attacks, including a 1985 bombing at a U.S. air base in Germany that killed two Americans.

The worst period of terrorism in France was the French Revolution. Indeed the words "terrorism" and "terrorists" were first used in their modern sense in reference to the violence of this time, by eighteenth-century philosopher Edmund Burke in condemning the *régime de la terreur*, or Reign of Terror, of June 1793 to July 1794. In the Reign of Terror, the government executed thousands of its enemies (by some estimates, over forty thousand), usually by guillotine. Another revolution in 1848 destroyed the French monarchy, but it saw nowhere near the violence of the Reign of Terror.

France was also the birthplace of the word "anarchist" (first used by the French philosopher Pierre-Joseph Proudhon in 1840) to describe a certain type of left-wing revolutionary, and during the late nineteenth century the country suffered through several anarchist attacks. In 1882 an anarchist planted a bomb in a music hall in the city of Lyon, in 1886 another fired bullets into a crowd at the stock exchange in Paris, in 1893 still another blew up the city's Chamber of Deputies, and in 1894 one anarchist blew up a Paris café. There were several other bombings in Paris as well, especially in 1892.

Left-wing activists have also plagued France in recent times. During the late 1960s, radical university students staged protests and demonstrations on various campuses and throughout the city of Paris; some of these actions turned into violent riots. Of these, the most notable were several student revolts that took place at the Sorbonne University in May 1968. At the first of these revolts, the police responded to a peaceful demonstration with aggressive tactics, arresting students and, when some of the protestors taunted the police, by firing tear gas into the crowd. At the next two demonstrations, the police again attacked the protesteors, violently beating some of them. The French public became outraged at this police brutality, and factory workers went out on strike and seized factories in support of the students. This revolt put tremendous stress on the government, but eventually its president, Charles de Gaulle, brought calm and order back to France, and the factories started running again. In recent years, however, France has once again been plagued by violent student protests of the government's political, economic, and social policies, with several riots taking place in 2006.

France has also experienced terrorist attacks perpetrated by groups unhappy with French policies abroad. For example, from the late 1970s to the present, members of the National Liberation Front of Corsica (FLNC) have struck a number of French targets in protest of its refusal to grant the island of Corsica, a colony of France, its independence. Similarly, in 1995, an Islamic extremist group called the Armed Islamic Group (GIA), which was fighting for an independent Algeria, conducted several bombings in France, including an attack on the French metro rail system, after hijacking an Air France plane the previous year. In the early 2000s several terrorist attacks in France were attributed to Haika, a faction of the Basque terrorist group Basque Homeland and Liberty (ETA), which wants the Basque region, part of which lies in Spain and the other in France, to become an independent state.

France has worked with Spain to track down ETA members and thwart ETA plans for future attacks. It has also helped other countries locate Islamic terrorists within France. This was not always the case, however. In the early 1980s the French government was a safe haven for certain Islamic terrorists, most notably members of the Palestine Liberation Organization (PLO), who had fled to France to avoid capture elsewhere. In addition, the French Intelligence Agency has engaged in covert terrorist activities in order to further certain political aims; for example, in the 1960s it hired an assassin to kill a Moroccan politician, and in 1985 it bombed the ship of an environmental group opposed to French policies.

SEE ALSO: anarchism; Action Directe; Armed Islamic Group; Basque Homeland and Liberty; decolonization campaigns; National Liberation Front of Corsica; Palestine Liberation Organization; Reign of Terror

freedom fighters

Individuals who engage in terrorist acts in order to free their people from an oppressive government typically call themselves "freedom fighters," which casts their cause and their actions in a positive light. Those opposed to the actions of these freedom fighters call them "terrorists" instead—a word with highly negative connotations. Most experts in terrorism, however, have a more objective definition of what consti-

Mujahideen Islamic Resistance fighters defend their land in Kunar Province, Afghanistan, against Soviet military occupation. AP IMAGES

tutes a freedom fighter versus a terrorist: A freedom fighter strikes out at carefully selected government or military targets, whereas a terrorist strikes out wantonly at innocent civilians. This difference reflects the fact that terrorists believe that the way to achieve their goal is to instill terror in the civilian population, which will then rise up against the oppressive government in order to end the terrorism, whereas freedom fighters believe in directly attacking the government they are trying to destroy.

SEE ALSO: terrorism, definitions of

Front du Libération du Québec (FLQ)

Active in Quebec, Canada, from the late 1960s to 1970, the Front du Libération du Québec (FLQ) was a terrorist group dedicated to fighting for Quebec's independence from Canada. The idea of Quebec secession began in the nineteenth century among French-Canadians angry over the fact that French culture was being supplanted by British culture in the province. However, no violence was associated with this issue until the FLQ began its terrorist attacks, which included the kidnappings of two Quebec politicians, British trade commissioner James Cross and labor minister Pierre Laporte, in 1970. (Cross was later released, but Laporte was killed.) The prime minister of Canada, Pierre Trudeau, responded to this violence by sending military troops into the Quebec city of Montreal, where the FLQ was based, and suspending civil rights so that citizens and buildings could be stopped and searched without cause. As a result of these and other tactics, those responsible for the terrorist attacks were apprehended and the FLQ effectively destroyed.

Fuerzas Armadas de Liberación Nacional (FALN)

Established in the late 1960s and most active in the 1970s, the Fuerzas Armadas de Liberación Nacional (FALN) is a terrorist group dedicated to ending U.S. control of Puerto Rico. To this end, the group has detonated bombs in banks, restaurants, business offices, military recruitment offices, government buildings, and other public places in New York, Chicago, and other U.S. cities. In October 1979 it coordinated a series of bombing attacks in Chicago and New York with similar attacks in Puerto Rico by another Puerto Rican nationalist group, the Macheteros. In 1980, to bring more attention to their cause among the American public, nearly a dozen armed FALN members briefly occupied both the Democratic and the Republican presidential campaign offices, an event that eventually led to their arrest. Within a year they had all been convicted of various charges, as were other FALN members arrested in the United States in 1980. More arrests and convictions followed in 1981, 1982, and 1983, seriously reducing the strength of the organization. By 1985, when the FBI raided several FALN hideouts in Puerto Rico, the membership had been reduced to less than a hundred and its terrorist activities had ceased, though the group still exists.

SEE ALSO: Puerto Rico, anti-U.S. sentiments in

funding terrorism

Modern terrorism is funded by a fast-growing international economic system that relies on a variety of legal and illegal activities to generate money. Controlled by terrorist organizations and Islamic states, with input from the heads of organized crime syndicates, drug lords, and other criminal elements, this system is supported by several profit-generating illegal activities, including the drug trade, money laundering, bank robbery, kidnapping for ransom, and arms and oil smuggling.

The diamond and oil trades, whether conducted illegally or legally, also generate a lot of money for terrorism, as do many other legitimate businesses. For example, in the mid-1980s, the Palestine Liberation Organization (PLO) began operating textile factories, fruit plantations, and construction companies in the country of Jordan, and noted terrorist Osama bin Laden owns a network of honey shops in the Middle East, where honey is a valuable commodity. In fact in the late 1990s these shops generated so much money for bin laden's terrorist group, al Qaeda, that in November 2001 the United States convinced the government of Yemen to freeze the bank accounts of several honey sellers there with ties to al Qaeda.

Islamic charities are another major source of terrorist income. Donations to such organizations, which are in the billions of dollars, often end up in terrorists' hands, with or without the knowledge of the donors. Banks can also act as knowing or unknowing contributors to terrorism, whether through loans or through helping to launder terrorist money. By some estimates, Western financial institutions recycle roughly $1.5 trillion in illegal money a year, much of it connected to terrorism, and foreign banks like the Arab Bank, which is a favorite of the PLO, often manage terrorists' loans and financial investments. Arabs also engage in private lending via a credit system, the *hawaala*, that has been in place in the Middle East for centuries.

Still another way that terrorists acquire funds is via predatory wars, which are wars staged by governments or terrorists in order to steal money, goods, and property from others (though the stated reason for the war might be political). In such wars, attackers loot the villages of fleeing citizens and confiscate their lands or other property, either before or after declaring victory. Wars also aid terrorism by bringing more money, weapons, and ammunition into a region as various allies seek to help those involved in the conflict. For example, in the 1980s the United States spent more than $2 billion on weapons and supplies that it then sent to a group of Afghanis, the Mujahideen, who wanted to drive Russian forces from Afghanistan; among these weapons were several missiles that were later sold by terrorists for ten times

their original price of twenty-three thousand dollars each. (One of these missiles was purchased by Iran, which in 1983 fired it at U.S. forces in the Persian Gulf.)

In general, Islamic extremists are the wealthiest of the terrorists; others must often struggle to keep their groups afloat. For example, during the 1970s the Red Brigades of Italy were so strapped for cash that its members were required to maintain careful records of their expenditures, turning over all receipts to group leaders, in order to support activities that, by some estimates, cost $10 million a year. Terrorists' expenses can include rent and food for all members, plane tickets or gasoline to travel to sites of terrorist activities, special training (such as flight school for terrorists intending to hijack airplanes), weapons, ammunition, computers, and other equipment.

SEE ALSO: al Qaeda; bin laden, Osama; criminal terrorism; drugs and terrorists; Palestine Liberation Organization; Red Brigades

Gama'a al-Islamiyya (IG)

Active in Egypt since the 1970s, the Gama'a al-Islamiyya, or "Islamic Group" (IG), is an Islamic extremist group of thousands dedicated to creating an Islamic state in Egypt. To this end, IG has attacked representatives of the Egyptian government as well as anyone viewed as an enemy of Islam, including Christians, and in the 1990s it attacked groups of foreigners visiting popular tourist attractions, particularly in Cairo and Luxor. IG also claimed responsibility for an attempt to assassinate Egypt's president, Hosni Mubarak, while he was visiting Ethiopia in 1995.

SEE ALSO: Egypt, terrorism in

Genghis Khan
(1155-, 1162-, 1167–1227)

After uniting the nomadic tribes of Mongolia under his rule, Mongolian warrior Genghis Khan (originally named Temüjin) conquered China and parts of the Middle East and Europe in battles known for the savagery of the Mongols. When Khan's soldiers took over a city, they tortured and raped its citizens and typically forced its able-bodied men to serve in Khan's army, executing those who refused to comply—though in at least one case, Khan decided it was better to slaughter everyone in the town than to deal with new recruits. Khan also used massacres as a way to instill terror in those he intended to conquer; as his reputation for violence spread, towns were ready to surrender to him even before his forces advanced upon them. However, in 1223 he left the conquests to his generals, preferring to remain at home in the Mongolian steppes until a final campaign in China in 1226–27.

genocide

Genocide (from the Greek word *genos*, or race or tribe, and the Latin word *cide*, or killing) usually refers to the planned, deliberate, mass extermination of one par-

Mongolian warrior and leader Genghis Khan conquered lands in China, the Middle East, and Europe during the 12th century, using terrorist methods of torture, rape, and murder to proclaim power and authority. AP IMAGES

ticular racial, ethnic, religious, or political group. It can also refer to the deliberate physical or mental harm of members of such a group or the enactment of measures whose intent is to make the group die out, whether physically or culturally. For example, the group's persecutors might rape its women, so that any babies born will not be of the same race or tribe, or they might ban the group's religious and social practices so that the group's cultural identity is destroyed. Some cases of genocide take place over a few months, but most take several years. This was the case, for example, in the United States, where the government attempted to exterminate certain tribes of Native Americans during the nineteenth century.

The word genocide was first used in 1943 by Dr. Raphael Lemkin (who was also the first to use it in print, in his 1944 book *Axis Rule in Occupied Europe*) in reference to the systematic killing of thousands of Jews by Nazi Germans (an event known as the Holocaust), though genocide had already existed for centuries by this time. Genocide was officially declared a crime in 1946 during an assembly of the United Nations (UN), out of which came a document called the Convention on the Prevention and Punishment of the Crime of Genocide. Enacted in 1951, this convention stated, among other things, that genocide is a crime regardless of whether it takes place during war or during peace, that it is a matter of international concern rather than a domestic issue, and that the UN would step in to prevent or end acts of genocide when such acts are called to its attention.

Nonetheless, there have been several acts of genocide since the convention was created. In most cases, these are instances of genocidal state terrorism, which is geno-

cide conducted by a country in order to eliminate (physically or culturally) a particular group deemed undesirable by its leaders. In Iraq, for example, in the 1980s dictator Saddam Hussein killed approximately 180,000 members of a minority ethnic group, the Kurds, and was later put on trial for genocide, and in Rwanda in the early 1990s, the Hutu tribe that controlled the government killed over 500,000 members of another tribe, the Tutsi. In Bosnia during the 1990s, the Serbs, who were of the Orthodox Christian faith, massacred, raped, and tortured thousands of Bosnian Muslims in a campaign of genocide that Serb nationalists dubbed "ethnic cleansing."

SEE ALSO: Africa, terrorism in postcolonial; Bosnian genocide; ethnic cleansing; Iraq

Germany, terrorism in

In terms of domestic terrorism, Germany is best known for the atrocities that the Nazis (members of the ruling party, the National Socialist German Workers' Party, from whose name comes the abbreviation "Nazi") committed from 1933 to 1945 when their regime tried to exterminate the country's Jews and Gypsies. These atrocities were associated with state-sponsored anti-Semitism, racism, and white supremacy, all promoted by the Nazis' leader, Adolf Hitler. In modern times, neo-Nazis—right-wing extremists, some of whom are known as "skinheads"—have also embraced these concepts, both in Germany and elsewhere in the world.

The German state has also been the target of terrorists, most notably those from a domestic left-wing terrorist group known as the Baader-Meinhof Gang. This group was founded in 1967 by militant university students as an immediate response to the death of another student,

Benno Ohnesorg, during a student demonstration against the Shah of Iran's visit to West Germany. While the Shah's motorcade was traveling through the city of Berlin, the students threw various objects at his car, and the police responded with violence, firing into the crowd and killing Ohnesorg. Only twenty-six years old, married, and about to become a father, this student was a sympathetic figure whose murder fired up antipolice sentiments among many militant groups, spawning a decade of domestic terrorism in Germany.

The Baader-Meinhof Gang began operating in April 1968, when it firebombed a department store and then taunted police in a phone call threatening more violence. Four members of the gang, Andreas Baader, Gudrun Ensslin, Thorwald Proll, and Horst Sohnlein, were quickly arrested for the crime, put on trial, convicted, and sentenced to three years in prison, but they were released in June 1969 while awaiting an appeal. They then went into hiding to evade the law. During this period, leftwing newspaper columnist Ulrike Meinhof, who had praised the group's firebombing in her radical paper *Konkret*, became coleader of the gang along with Baader. When Baader was caught by police in 1970, Meinhof led an operation to break him out of prison. Afterward the group went through guerrilla training offered by members of the Palestinian terrorist group Popular Front for the Liberation of Palestine (PFLP), then engaged in several bank robberies in Germany in order to finance its plans to spark a revolution through terrorism. Members put some of this money into recruitment, and by 1971 the gang had over 150 adherents.

Throughout 1971 the group continued its bank robberies and, during one such operation, killed a police officer. Group members also broke into police arsenals to get weapons and committed several bombings. One of the bombings destroyed sixty cars at the State Criminal Investigations Office in Munich, Germany, while another seriously injured the wife of a judge who had been involved in previous legal actions against group members. The Baader-Meinhof Gang terrorized others as well, making assassination threats by phone against various German officials and businessmen. The violence continued even after some of the members, including Baader, were captured in a bomb factory in June 1972. In November 1974 the group murdered a German supreme court judge on his own doorstep, and shortly thereafter it kidnapped the Christian Democrat Party candidate for the office of mayor of Berlin, Peter Lorenz. After the government paid a ransom for Lorenz's release, the terrorists were emboldened to invade the West German embassy in Stockholm, Sweden, in April 1975, and hold the ambassador and several others hostage. This time, though, their demands were refused, even after they killed a few of their hostages, and eventually they surrendered. After this, Meinhof committed suicide—an example that other group members would subsequently follow whenever a Gang terrorist operation failed. By the late 1970s, despite a few successful operations, the bulk of the Gang's members were dead or imprisoned, and its reign of terror in Germany had come to an end.

Among the last of the Gang's terrorist operations was the hijacking of an airplane in cooperation with the PFLP; after landing in Mogadishu, Somalia, the plane was stormed by the forces of Germany's counterterrorism unit, Grenzschutzgruppe 9 (GSG-9), which successfully rescued all of

In Warsaw, Poland, in 1940, a group of Jews walk with Nazi soldiers, known as the Gestapo, toward a concentration camp for execution. © BETTMANN/CORBIS

the plane's passengers and killed most of the terrorists. An elite unit whose members are well-trained police commandos, the GSG-9 is particularly known for its skill at rescuing hostages. Today this state agency continues to be highly successful in combating domestic and international terrorism.

SEE ALSO: Gestapo, the; Grenzschutzgruppe 9; hijackings, aircraft; Holocaust, the; Waffen SS, the

Gestapo, the

From 1933 until the end of World War II, the German Geheime Staatspolizei (Secret State Police), or Gestapo, was a Nazi-controlled police force that had a variety of duties but, in terms of terrorism, is best known for rounding up thousands of Jews and sending them to death camps for extermination. The Gestapo also arrested left-wing activists, intellectuals, and any-

one else who spoke out against the current political situation, along with other people that the Nazis considered undesirable elements of the population, such as homosexuals. Like the Jews, these people were sent to camps, many of whom were never seen again. Gestapo death squads also accompanied German soldiers on their military campaigns into Poland and Russia, slaughtering people there, as well. The Nazis placed no restrictions on how the Gestapo could operate; it was allowed to arrest anyone it wanted, regardless of whether that person had done anything wrong, under the guise of preventing future illegal acts or political unrest. Because of various reorganizations within the Nazi government, the Gestapo's duties sometimes overlapped with other Nazi forces; these included the Waffen SS, a military entity that was even more brutal than the Gestapo.

SEE ALSO: Germany, terrorism in; Holocaust, the; Waffen SS

golden age myths

The phrase "golden age myths" refers to an idealism that makes certain people think that one earlier time or another was a golden age when everything was perfect, or at least as close to being perfect as possible. This idealism is closely associated with far-right extremism, whose adherents typically oppose change and are willing to fight to maintain the traditional values, beliefs, and practices that they believe are superior to all others. In the United States, some right-wing religious groups think that the golden age is in the future rather than the past; they believe that an apocalypse will someday destroy the world and create a new, perfect one.

SEE ALSO: apocalypticism; extremism, right-wing versus left-wing

Greece, terrorism in

Since ancient times, political enemies in Greece have tried to assassinate one another, but widespread terrorism against civilians did not begin in the country until 1941. At that time, a guerrilla organization called the People's National Army of Liberation (ELAS) tortured or executed Greeks in rural communities who offered aid to German occupying forces. By 1944, when the Germans were preparing to withdraw from the country, Communists formed three other terrorist organizations in the city of Athens: the Organization for the Protection of the People's Struggle (OPLA), the People's National Guard (EP), and the Guardforce. Of these the OPLA was the most ruthless; in December 1944, after the Germans withdrew, the OPLA killed over five thousand people in an at-

tempt to eliminate resistance to a Communist takeover of the country. Later, after this takeover failed, Communists created Aftoamyna (Self-Defense), a network of terrorist cells that worked against the government, kidnapping or assassinating public officials and destroying government and commercial buildings and equipment. Eventually, after a 1946 civil war between Communist forces and non-Communist forces that included the Greek army, Aftoamyna was effectively destroyed, and in 1948–49, military troops killed nine thousand terrorists in an attack on a Communist stronghold on Mount Grammos, an action that temporarily ended Communist terrorism in Greece.

Such terrorism resumed, however, during the 1970s and '80s because of a group called the Revolutionary People's Struggle (ELA). Formed in 1973 by people wanting to trigger a Communist revolution in the country, the ELA committed hundreds of bombings primarily against targets connected to capitalism and Western influences in Greece, including banks, major corporations, and U.S. military bases. The group's attacks apparently ended in the late 1990s, though experts disagree on whether it dissolved at that time or has simply become inactive, but another Greek terrorist group, the Revolutionary Nuclei, recently began engaging in similar activities, though on a much smaller scale.

Greece is also significant in terms of terrorism because of its capture of a key member of a Palestinian terrorist group called the 15 May Organization. In 1988 this member, Mohammad Rashid, was arrested by Greek authorities for trying to enter the country using a false passport. At the time, he was wanted by the U.S. government as a terrorist bomber, having attacked several airlines from various countries, but Greece refused to release him to U.S. authorities so he could stand trial in America. Instead the Greeks tried him themselves, and in 1992 they convicted him of being a bomber. Four years later, they chose to extradite Rashid to the United States, where he was then held responsible for his crimes against U.S. interests.

SEE ALSO: Greek Communist Party

Greek Communist Party (KKE)

In 1941, while the Germans were occupying Greece, the Greek Communist Party (KKE) created a guerrilla organization, the People's National Army of Liberation (ELAS), which it used to eliminate rival political parties and to terrorize citizens who did not support its actions. At the same time, KKE took care not to challenge the Germans, though in 1942–44 it tortured or executed Greeks in rural communities who had offered aid to German forces. Nonetheless, by 1944, ELAS terrorism in southern Greece had become so severe that many of the Greeks in this area openly joined with the Germans in fighting the KKE. That same year, the KKE began an aggressive campaign in Athens, intending to position itself so that once the Germans pulled out of the city—an action that seemed imminent—the Communists would be ready to seize power there. To this end, the KKE established three terrorist organizations in Athens: the Organization for the Protection of the People's Struggle (OPLA), the People's National Guard (EP), and the Guardforce. Of these the OPLA was the most ruthless; in December 1944, after the Germans withdrew, it killed over five thousand people in an attempt to eliminate resistance to communism. Despite this effort, the KKE was driven from Athens in January 1945, tak-

ing with it a few thousand kidnapped Athenians who were forced to march to central Greece; many died along the way, but the remainder were held hostage in exchange for a peace agreement that ensured the Greek government would not pursue the KKE or ELAS. Later that year, the KKE created Aftoamyna (Self-Defense), a network of terrorist cells that worked against the government, kidnapping or assassinating public officials and destroying government and commercial buildings and equipment. In rural areas, these officials might include teachers and community leaders. As a result of this terrorism, in March 1946 civil war broke out in Greece between Communist forces and non-Communist forces, the latter of which included the Greek army. The Communists had roughly twenty-five thousand fighters and at least fifty thousand supporters, as well as the backing of the Communist regimes in Albania, Yugoslavia, and Bulgaria. In 1947 the Greek army received U.S. backing, and the following year the Communists began losing their foreign support. By this time, the Athens police had eliminated most of the Aftoamyna from their city (the remainder were gone by 1953), and the following year the Aftoamyna was effectively destroyed elsewhere as well, after more than five thousand were arrested and eight thousand fled to Albania. In 1948–49, military troops killed nine thousand terrorists in an attack on a Communist stronghold on Mount Grammos, an action that marked the end of the KKE's terrorism in Greece.

SEE ALSO: Greece, terrorism in

Grenzschutzgruppe 9 (GSG-9)

The Grenzschutzgruppe 9, or GSG-9, is a paramilitary unit in Germany that performs domestic and international counterterrorist operations and hostage rescues. It was created after the 1972 Olympics Games in Munich, Germany, when the German government discovered that it was not equipped to deal with terrorist attacks and hostage crises. At the Olympics, Palestinian terrorists kidnapped nine Israeli athletes after shooting two others, and during an attempt to rescue the hostages, German forces accidentally killed all of the Israelis. The first major operation of GSG-9 was the successful rescue of hostages, again taken by Palestinian terrorists, in Mogadishu, Somalia, in October 1977. The hostages were aboard a Boeing 737 jet that had been hijacked while flying from Majorca, Spain, to Frankfurt, Germany; while the plane was over Germany, another plane filled with a GSG-9 counterterrorist team began following it. After both planes landed in Somalia, the GSG-9 team staged its rescue, killing three terrorists in the process.

See Also: Munich Olympics crisis

Griffin, Michael
(1962–)

In 1994 antiabortion activist Michael Griffin was sentenced to life in prison for killing an abortion provider in Pensacola, Florida, the year before. He was the first person to commit this type of terrorist act; others had protested in front of abortion clinics, but none had yet resorted to violence against the physicians. Griffin shot his victim, Dr. David Gunn, three times in the back as Gunn walked through a crowd of protestors in front of a clinic run by Pensacola Women's Medical Services, then surrendered himself to a police officer at the scene. Gunn had worked at clinics in Georgia and Alabama in addition to the one in Florida. Prior to his murder several antiabortionists had de-

clared that he deserved to be killed; Griffin learned of this a few days before the murder, while visiting the home of another antiabortionist, John Burt, who was the leader of the antiabortion groups Our Father's House and Rescue America. After the murder, other antiabortionists, led by Presbyterian minister Paul Hill (who later committed an antiabortion murder as well), released a signed statement to the press that declared Griffin was justified in committing the murder because it was in defense of innocent children. Nonetheless, in 1995 Griffin accused antiabortionist activists of framing him for the murder, in collusion with his lawyers and the police officers involved in his arrest.

See Also: antiabortion movement; Hill, Paul

Grivas, Georgios
(1898–1974)

In the 1950s Cypriot patriot Georgios Grivas led a right-wing resistance group (the Ethnikí Orgánosis Kipriakoú Agónos, or National Organization of Cypriot Fighters) in a guerrilla war against the British-controlled Cyprus at the time. After Cyprus achieved its independence from Great Britain in 1960, he led a terrorist campaign for a cause known as *eonosis* (union)—the merging of Cyprus with Greece. As part of *eonosis*, he fostered an underground movement against the leader of Cyprus, Makarios III, who had been his friend and ally during the war for Cyprus independence.

See Also: National Organization of Cypriot Fighters

Guatemala, terrorism in

Guatemala has not been notably plagued by terrorism in recent years, but during the late 1960s and early 1970s there were two terrorist acts there that gained world-wide attention. On August 28, 1968, gunmen killed the U.S. ambassador to Guatemala, John G. Mein, in Guatemala City, and on March 31, 1970, the West German ambassador to Guatemala, Count Karl von Spreti, was kidnapped from the same city and was found dead five days later. Guatemala is also known for engaging in state-sponsored terrorism in the 1966–67 military campaign known as el-Contra-Terror, in which the government squelched a guerrilla movement by sending its troops to kill over eight thousand people, most of them innocent civilians, in two provinces said to shelter guerrillas.

SEE ALSO: assassination, political; guerrilla warfare

guerrilla warfare

Guerrilla warfare is periodic warfare conducted by independent bands of civilian fighters against an organized army of the state. There are two types of guerrilla warfare, rural and urban. Rural guerrillas plan their operations from bases in remote geographical regions such as jungles or mountains, whereas urban guerrillas operate in cities, blending in with ordinary civilians.

The word *guerrilla*, meaning "little war" in Spanish, was first used in reference to a style of warfare employed by Spanish civilians resisting the French troops that occupied their lands during the Peninsular War of 1808–1814. During this war, the guerrillas received aid from the British government, which found it easier to arm the guerrillas than to fight the French themselves using British troops. Foreign support is common in guerrilla wars; for example, the United States provided aid to guerrillas opposed to the regimes of Fidel Castro in Cuba and the Sandinistas in Nicaragua. Also common is the support of civilians, but the food and supplies they might provide is not always given willingly. In many cases, guerrillas have threatened civilians who do not cooperate with them.

Guerrilla warfare has existed throughout history and throughout the world, to varying degrees of success. In the American colonies, for example, guerrillas participated in a revolution that resulted in the ousting of British forces and the establishment of the United States. The Cuban Revolution and the Chinese Civil War also involved guerrilla warfare that resulted in a regime change; other countries where guerrillas have been successful include Algeria, Afghanistan, Indonesia, Iraq, Mozambique, Lebanon, and Vietnam. In Malaya, Argentina, Bolivia, and the Philippines, however, guerrilla warfare has been largely unsuccessful. In South Africa during the Second Boer War (1899–1902), it appeared as though guerrilla warfare would be the undoing of the British forces occupying the region, but as the conflict wore on, the guerrillas ran out of food and ammunition and eventually were forced to surrender.

Guerrillas have operated during most major wars, including the Irish Confederate Wars, the American Civil War, World War I, and World War II. In fact, even in ancient Rome, guerrilla tactics were used during some battles. Certain parts of the world, though, have seen more guerrilla warfare than others. For example, during the 1960s, '70s, and '80s, Latin America experienced a great deal of guerrilla warfare, most of it urban. Much of this warfare was inspired by Brazilian revolutionary Carlos Marighella whose 1969 book *Minimanual of the Urban Guerrilla* provided a guide to guerrilla warfare in cities. Today the hot spots for urban guerrilla warfare are Iraq, where insurgents are fighting against occupying U.S. forces, and Chechnya, where Chechen separatists are seeking to drive out Russian forces. In recent years, U.S. forces have also fought against guerrillas in Kosovo (during the late 1990s) and Afghanistan (in the early 2000s).

SEE ALSO: Chechen separatists; Marighella, Carlos; Roman Empire

Guevara, Che (Ernesto Guevara de la Serna) (1928–1967)

Though born in Argentina, Che Guevara was heavily involved in the Cuban Revolution (1956–1959), and later he became a guerrilla leader in South America, hoping that a revolution there would create a climate of change that would encourage revolution in Latin America as well. This idea, known as *foquismo*, was one of several theories and tactics related to guerrilla warfare that Guevara developed during his lifetime. As a young man, while studying to be a doctor, he became convinced of the need for violent revolution after seeing a great deal of poverty, particularly during his vacations in Latin America. During a visit to Mexico in 1955 he met Cuban revolutionaries Fidel and Raúl Castro, and the following year he traveled with them to Cuba to participate in their attempt to overthrow the dictatorship of Fulgencio Batista. During this effort, Batista's army killed most of Castro's men, and Guevara was wounded; he and the other survivors retreated to the mountains, where they formed a guerrilla army that slowly grew in number and strength. In January 1959 Castro's forces finally took control of

Che Guevara was a devout revolutionist during the Cuban Revolution from 1956–1959, and later became a guerrilla leader in South America. AP IMAGES

Cuba's government, in which Guevara served in various capacities until 1965. During this period he also wrote about guerrilla warfare in such works as *La guerra de guerrillas* (*Guerilla Warfare*, 1961) and "El socialismo y el hombre en Cuba" ("Man and Socialism in Cuba," 1965). In 1966 he traveled to Bolivia to start a revolution there, creating a guerrilla group and leading it against forces of the Bolivian Army in the Santa Cruz area. During one of these skirmishes, Guevara was injured and captured, after which he was executed.

SEE ALSO: *foquismo*; guerrilla warfare

Habash, George
(1925–)

A Marxist politician and physician from Palestine, George Habash was one of the founders of the Arab nationalist movement, which supported the idea that the Arab nations should join together to work toward their common goals, particularly the destruction of Israel. After Israel defeated the Arab nations in the Six-Day War of 1967, Habash decided that Israel's destruction would only come about through terrorist attacks, and to this end he founded the Popular Front for the Liberation of Palestine (PFLP), whose members all supported a Marxist-Leninist ideology. This militant group became a faction of the Palestine Liberation Organization (PLO), and Habash became the lifelong rival of another faction's leader, Yasir Arafat, who later became head of the PLO. Wanting to distinguish the PFLP from other Palestinian groups, Habash staged a series of sensational airplane hijackings during the 1960s and '70s. Of these, the most extreme involved simultaneous attacks on one jet from each of four airlines from four countries (the United States, Great Britain, Israel, and Switzerland) in September 1970. Habash is also known for teaching terrorist tactics to one of the world's most famous terrorists, Carlos the Jackal, in 1970 at a PFLP training camp in Amman, Jordan. Also in 1970 Habash visited China, where he was dismayed to learn that other Marxists there disapproved of his terrorist activities. He had a similar experience in Russia two years later. In 1973 he became the spokesperson for four Palestinian groups, known collectively as the Rejection Front, that opposed any diplomatic settlement in Arab conflicts with Israel. Habash also spoke out against the PLO for its attempts to reconcile with King Hussein of Jordan, who had been engaging in a crackdown on terrorists operating in his country. In 1993 Habash led the PFLP in resigning from the PLO after Arafat signed a peace agreement between the PLO and Israel. By this time, Habash had organized terrorist cells in the Israeli-occupied West Bank and Gaza, and after he visited a French hospital for three days of medical treatment in 1992, several public officials there were chastised for allowing a terrorist into the country. Habash had many health problems and was the target of several assassination attempts, one of which caused injuries that ultimately led to his partial paralysis in 1980. Nonetheless, he is still alive.

SEE ALSO: Carlos the Jackal; Popular Front for the Liberation of Palestine

Haganah

Operating in Palestine from 1920 to 1948, Haganah ("Defense" in Hebrew) was a Zionist military organization that arose to protect Jewish settlers in Palestine from attacks by Palestinian Arabs. At first the group embraced the Jewish concept of *havlaga*, or "self-restraint," which meant that it did not engage in unnecessary violence, but after World War II it began bombing bridges, rail lines, and ships that the British, who then controlled the region, were using to transport some of the Jewish immigrants out of Palestine, and in 1947 Haganah engaged in armed conflicts with British and Palestinian Arab military forces in an attempt to defend the Jewish state in Palestine. Soon the Haganah controlled most of the lands that, in 1948, officially became the State of Israel, and when the government of Israel was established, the Haganah became its national army.

SEE ALSO: Zionism

Hamas

A militant Palestinian Islamic fundamentalist organization founded in 1987, Hamas (a name derived from Harakat al-Muqawama al-Islamia, or Islamic Resistance Movement) has committed numerous acts of violence—particularly suicide bombings—with the aim of eliminating Israel and establishing an independent Palestinian state run by Islamic fundamentalists. (This state would include what is now Israel, the West Bank, and the Gaza Strip.) In January 2006, however, after Israel relinquished control of the Gaza Strip to the Palestinians, Hamas gained control, via a democratic election, of the first Palestinian Parliament and therefore also of the newly created government, the Palestinian Authority; in the election Hamas received seventy-six seats in Parliament, whereas its rival, al Fatah, received forty-three. When this outcome was announced, al Fatah, whose leader Mahmoud Abbas had previously been elected president of the Palestinian Authority with the support of the Western world, threatened to end its participation in the coalition government rather than work with Hamas, even though Abbas agreed to remain president. Western nations were just as unhappy with the re-

sults, given Hamas's support of terrorism, and a few months later, Israel attacked Palestine, blaming Hamas for the capture of an Israeli soldier by Palestinian militants in June 2006. Immediate international outcry against Israel's attack resulted in a shaky peace between the Palestinian and Israeli governments, but afterward the tensions between the two countries continued.

This tension is understandable given the history of Hamas. The organization, which developed out of the Palestinian branch of a militant Islamic group called the Muslim Brotherhood, has engaged in countless attacks on Israeli targets, killing hundreds of people in various bombings and shootings. In 1996, for example, a Hamas bombing of Israeli buses resulted in over fifty deaths. Because of such acts, the Palestinian Authority and al Fatah publicly denounced Hamas during the 1990s. Now, however, they must work with Hamas in order to create an effective Palestinian government.

In fact, both Hamas and al Fatah announced a cease-fire in February 2007, but days later the fighting continued, with members of both factions battling with rocket-propelled grenade launchers, rockets, and assault rifles. Two universities were damaged by fire, a radio station was blown up, and dozens of people were killed or injured during the fighting in the Gaza Strip over control of the Palestinian provisional government.

SEE ALSO: al Fatah; Palestine

Hanafi Muslims

Followers of the Hanafi school, an institution created in eighth-century Baghdad to develop and interpret laws related to the Islamic religion in much of the Middle East, the Hanafi Muslims were connected to a hostage incident in the 1970s. One of these followers, a Black Muslim named Khalifa Hamaas Abdul Khaalis (born in the United States as Ernest McGee), had established his own branch of the Hanafi school in the 1950s, and in 1977 he led several members of his Hanafi Madh-Hab Center in taking 124 hostages in order to protest an upcoming motion picture, *Mohammed: Messenger of God*, about the prophet Mohammed. (The Hanafi school promoted the belief of most Muslims that it was blasphemy to depict Mohammed in movies or artwork.) These hostages were held at three locations in Washington, D.C.: the Islamic Center, the chamber of the City Council, and the center of a Jewish organization called the B'nai B'rith. Various people worked to negotiate their release, including diplomats from Iran, Pakistan, and Egypt, and after more than thirty hours and the murder of one of the hostages, Khaalis finally ended the standoff and turned himself in to police. Afterward he was sent to prison, where he remains, and the movie was shelved.

SEE ALSO: hostages

Harakat ul-Mujahideen (HUM)

Created in 1993 as Harakat ul-Ansar (Force of Helpers), the Harakat ul-Mujahideen ("Force of Holy Warriors," or HUM) is a militant group comprised of Muslims from the Sunni sect, primarily out of Pakistan, who have been involved in terrorist attacks in India and Kashmir. HUM targeted these locations because of a dispute between India and Pakistan over which of these two countries should govern Kashmir, and throughout the 1990s HUM received financial support, to varying degrees, from the Pakistani government. The group's members trained at guerrilla camps in Pakistan that had previ-

ously been used by Sunni Muslims (some of whom became the first members of HUM) attempting to oust Soviets from Afghanistan. In 1994 HUM launched its first major operation in Kashmir, kidnapping two British tourists there. Though the group soon released these hostages, within days it kidnapped four Western tourists in India; these hostages were rescued by police, who also arrested the kidnappers. HUM took six more Western tourists in Kashmir in July 1995. Shortly thereafter, the government of India received word that the hostages would be released only if several HUM members currently in jail were set free. (At the time, HUM denied being involved in the kidnappings.) The government refused to cooperate, and authorities subsequently discovered the headless body of one of the hostages. Another hostage managed to escape from his kidnappers, but the remaining victims were never seen again. Two years later the United States put HUM—then still called Harakat ul-Ansar—on its list of major terrorist organizations, and the group changed its name to avoid this recognition. In 1999 its leader, Pakistani terrorist Fazlur Rheman Khalil, declared war on the United States in response to the death of several HUM members in a U.S. cruise missile attack on terrorist training camps in Afghanistan the previous year. The United States subsequently froze the group's assets, and the Pakistani government ended its support for HUM. Pakistan also arrested many of the group's members, reducing HUM's numbers so severely that some experts on terrorism believe it no longer exists. Others, however, think that HUM has allied itself with the terrorist group al Qaeda or similar terrorist groups in the Middle East.

SEE ALSO: al Qaeda

Hawatmeh, Najib
(1937–)

Jordanian terrorist Najib Hawatmeh established the Democratic Front for the Liberation of Palestine (DFLP) in Damascus,
Syria, in 1970, after becoming disen-
chanted with a similar group, the Popular
Front for the Liberation of Palestine
(PFLP), the year before. Embracing Marxist and Leninist beliefs, Hawatmeh encouraged his followers, all militant revolutionaries, to use whatever means necessary to
oppose Israel and further the creation of a
Palestinian state. During the 1970s the
DFLP engaged in numerous terrorist activities, including hijackings and kidnappings, and in 1974 the group killed over
twenty Israeli schoolchildren after taking
over their school. By the 1990s, however,
Hawatmeh's position had apparently soft-
ened, which was evident at the 1999 funeral of King Hussein of Jordan when he
shook hands with Israeli president Ezer
Weizman. In recent years the DFLP has
apparently become inactive, though it is
still in existence, and Hawatmeh has not
been connected to any terrorist activities.

SEE ALSO: Palestine

Hearst, Patricia (Patty)
(1954–)

In 1974 Patty Hearst became famous for
her kidnapping by members of an American militant revolutionary group called
the Symbionese Liberation Army (SLA).
The stated goal of this group, which was
comprised of former prisoners and prison
activists, was to kill all fascist oppressors,
and to this end the SLA murdered a school
superintendent roughly three months prior
to abducting Hearst on February 4, 1974.
She was targeted because her family was
extremely wealthy (Patty's grandfather was

*Granddaughter of newspaper giant William
Randolph Hearst, Patricia Hearst was kidnapped by the Symbionese Liberation Army
(SLA) in 1974, and brainwashed into being
one of their revolutionaries.* AP IMAGES

newspaper giant William Randolph
Hearst). Three days after the SLA kidnapped her from her apartment near the
University of California in Berkeley, where
she was a sophomore, the SLA demanded,
via the media, that the Hearsts give food
to the poor if they wanted to see her again.
The Hearsts complied, but Patty was not
released. The SLA then distributed a photograph of her holding a weapon and said
that she had become one of their revolutionaries. Indeed, Hearst later said that she
had been converted to their cause through
brainwashing, a process during which she
was locked in a closet when not with her
captors. Under their influence, she took
the name of Tania, for the wife or girl-

friend (accounts vary as to whether they ever married) of Marxist revolutionary Che Guevara, and robbed the Hibernia Bank in San Francisco, California, on April 15, 1974. After bank cameras showed her participating in the robbery with apparent willingness rather than reluctance, the Federal Bureau of Investigation (FBI) put her on its Ten Most Wanted criminals list. By this time the SLA, which then had only eight members in addition to Hearst, had traveled to Southern California, where Hearst and two others attempted to rob a sporting-goods store. The next day police learned that the SLA had set up headquarters in a small house in Inglewood, California; they surrounded the place, a shootout ensued, the residence burst into flames, and in the end six SLA members were dead. Hearst and the remaining SLA members, plus one newcomer to the group (Kathleen Soliah, who joined the SLA after seeing the shoot-out on television), committed a few more robberies before Hearst was finally captured in September 1975. She was subsequently convicted of bank robbery, but in 1979 President Jimmy Carter commuted her sentence, and in 2001 President Bill Clinton granted her a full pardon; in the years after being released from prison, Hearst married and raised a family, worked as an actress, and wrote a book about her kidnapping, as well as a mystery novel.

SEE ALSO: Guevara, Che; hostages; Symbionese Liberation Army

Herzen, Alexander (1812–1870)

Russian socialist revolutionary Alexander Herzen wrote books and articles about revolutions and revolutionary movements, publishing radical journals such as *Kolokol* (*The Bell*) to express his views. His writings influenced the development of socialism and anarchism in the nineteenth century, though at times this influence was due more to discussions rather than adoptions of his ideas. Other revolutionaries often criticized Herzen for arguing that in terms of politics, change should be gradual but total rather than immediate and partial, because they wanted quick solutions to oppressive political situations. Herzen, however, was afraid that without using care in taking control of a government, revolutionaries would soon become as oppressive and corrupt as those they had removed from power. He also believed that perhaps the best hope for the future lay in peasant communes, from which would gradually develop ideal socialist societies. In addition to his writings for *Kolokol*, Herzen's other works include *From Another Shore* (1850), which provides his analysis of European revolutions, and *My Past and Thoughts* (1855), which focuses primarily on Russian revolutions and serfdoms.

SEE ALSO: Russian Civil War; Russian Revolution

Hezbollah (Hezbollah al-Hijaz; Hizb'allah)

The United States has declared that Hezbollah (Party of God) is a major terrorist organization, but public officials in Lebanon, where the group is based, have called it a national resistance movement. In either case, Hezbollah commits acts of violence against Israel, which it believes unjustly occupied Muslim lands and therefore has no right to exist. Hezbollah was formed in response to the 1982 Israeli invasion of Lebanon; its founders were radical Islamic clerics from Amal, a political party comprised of Shiite Muslims, whose aim was to forcibly drive Israeli forces from Lebanon. In support of this cause, that same year the Iranian government sent roughly two thousand soldiers from the Iranian Revolutionary Guard to Lebanon, and many of these men became the first members of Hezbollah.

Over the next two decades, while Israel continued to occupy parts of Lebanon, Hezbollah engaged in acts of terrorism that included suicide bombings and kidnappings. Initially, these attacks were against Israeli targets, but soon the group was choosing Western targets as well, largely because of Israel's ties to the United States. The group also kidnapped Westerners in order to exchange these people for Islamic militants held in Western prisons on various offenses. Their victims included an agent of the U.S. Central Intelligence Agency (CIA), William Buckley; a reporter for the Associated Press, Terry Anderson; an American university professor, Thomas Sutherland; an Irish national, Brian Keenan; and a British journalist, John McCarthy, who had been sent to Beirut, Lebanon, to cover the Keenan kidnapping. (Hezbollah has denied responsibility for these kidnappings, but terrorism experts remain convinced that the group was behind them.) In 1983 Hezbollah used suicide bombers to attack several targets in Beirut, most notably the U.S. embassy, where 63 people were killed, and U.S. and French military facilities, where over 350 were killed. Two years later terrorists connected to Hezbollah hijacked a TWA airplane en route to Rome, Italy, from Athens, Greece, and subsequently exchanged its passengers for the release of certain Muslims being held in Israeli prisons.

In the 1990s Hezbollah fired rockets over the Lebanese-Israeli border on several occasions, and Israel responded in kind, sending fighter planes to bomb suspected Hezbollah strongholds without concern for the lives of innocent civilians. This violence continued off and on into the early 2000s, even after Israel withdrew troops from south Lebanon, and in the summer of 2006 a brief war broke out between Hezbollah and Israel. This war was prompted by the July 2006 Hezbollah ambush of two Israeli army Humvees near the Israeli village of Shtula, near the border between Lebanon and Israel. In this attack, two Israeli solders were captured, three killed outright, and five more killed while attempting to pursue the attackers. Hezbollah had apparently intended to release the captured soldiers in exchange for the release of certain Muslims imprisoned in Israel, which is what happened after it kidnapped three Israeli soldiers in October 2000. But because eight Israeli soldiers were killed as a result of the 2006 kidnapping, Israel responded to this event by bombing a Hezbollah-controlled television station, as well as other targets in Lebanon that were either connected to the group or might benefit the group (such as an airport and seaports). Hezbollah countered by lobbing rocket bombs over the border at Israel until Israel called off its attacks.

Terrorism experts disagree on the current strength of Hezbollah; some say that the group has less than three thousand fighters, others that it has as many as ten thousand. There is ample evidence, however, that the group has received support from Syria and Iran, and that it has cells in many parts of Europe, Africa, South America, and the United States. In addition, the group has received financial assistance, in the amount of at least $50 million since 1995, from an Islamic charity organization called Bonyad-e Shahid (the Martyr's Charity), which was established to give money to the families of suicide bombers killed for Muslim causes.

An airplane hijacked by terrorists about to crash into the second tower of the World Trade Center on September 11, 2001. AP IMAGES

SEE ALSO: embassy bombings; bombers, suicide

hijackings, aircraft

Modern terrorists have often used aircraft hijackings—the forcible taking of airplanes—as a way to get governments to accede to their demands or pay them money in exchange for the release of the airplane passengers who have become their hostages. During the September 11, 2001, terrorist attacks on America, though, terrorists hijacked airplanes for a different reason: to use as weapons by flying them into buildings. This event triggered a strengthening of security measures already in place to prevent planes from getting hijacked; for example, in the aftermath of September 11, airlines ordered pilots to keep cockpit doors locked throughout the entire flight, no matter what was happening among the passengers, and these doors were replaced with new models that were impossible to break through.

The first airplane hijacker, in Peru in 1931, had no security measures to thwart, nor did the hijackers who seized planes in the oppressive countries of Eastern Europe during the 1950s in order to fly to free nations elsewhere. The same was true for hijackers who, during the 1960s, took planes to fly to Cuba, which by then had become a draw to those in the United States and Mexico who supported left-wing ideologies like socialism and communism. It was not until the late 1960s and 1970s when airlines began to take airplane security seriously, prompted by several hijackings by Islamic terrorists. The first of these hijackings took place in 1968, when members of the Popular Front for the Liberation of Palestine (PFLP) took control of an airplane owned by an Israeli company, El Al, after it left Rome, Italy, and forced its pilot to fly it to Algiers instead of Israel in order to call attention to their cause, which was the creation of a Palestinian state. The following year, members of the same group took control of TWA Flight 840 from Rome, Italy, rerouting it from Tel Aviv, Israel, to Damascus, Greece, for the same purpose. The year after that, on September 6, 1970, the PFLP coordinated four hijackings involving four different airlines (TWA, El Al, Pan Am, and Swiss Air) so that they all took place at the same time. All of these hijackings went as planned except for one; after the first PFLP hijacking, El Al had started putting armed guards on its planes, and one of these guards thwarted the new hijacking, killing a hijacker in the process. Meanwhile the other three planes were rerouted to Amman, Jordan, where the hostages were safely exchanged for some Palestinians imprisoned there. (In previous PFLP hijackings, the hostages were also released without incident.)

Afterward other airlines also started putting armed guards on their planes, though not on every flight, and making it difficult for would-be hijackers to smuggle weapons on board. Still the hijackings continued until September 2001, whereupon security measures became so extreme that no other hijackings of a major airline have taken place since then. Other notable airplane hijackings by terrorists include:

- the 1976 taking of an Air France Airbus by PFLP members shortly after takeoff from Athens, Greece, en route to Paris, France, after originating in Tel Aviv, Israel; after the plane landed in Entebbe, Uganda, Israeli military commandos raided the airport against the wishes of the Ugandan government, stormed the plane, and gunned down all of the terrorists.
- the 1976 taking of Japan Airlines Flight 472 while it was en route to Tokyo, Japan, from Mumbai, India; after takeoff, the plane was diverted to Dhaka, Bangladesh, by members of the terrorist group Japanese Red Army, who then exchanged its 156 passengers and crew after five days for ransom money and the release of several political prisoners.
- the 1977 taking of Lufthansa Flight 181 after it left Frankfurt, Germany, by four PFLP members who wanted the release of several members of the Red Army Faction (RAF) imprisoned in Germany; after being refused landing in several countries, the PFLP finally put the plane down in Mogadishu, Somalia, whereupon it was stormed, the hostages saved, and all

but one of the hijackers killed. (The RAF prisoners later committed suicide under questionable circumstances.)
- the 1985 taking of TWA Flight 847 while it was en route from Athens, Greece, to Rome, Italy, by two members of the Organization for the Oppressed of the Earth, which was subsequently linked to the Lebanese terrorist group Hezbollah; after landing in Beirut, Lebanon, to refuel, the terrorists flew the plane to Algiers, released some of their hostages, flew back to Beirut, picked up several more armed terrorists, and negotiated the release of the remaining hostages in exchange for several demands, including the release of some imprisoned Shiite Muslims.
- the 1991 taking of Singapore Airlines Flight 117 while en route from Kuala Lumpur, Pakistan, to Singapore by terrorists from the Pakistan People's Party who wanted some of their members released from prison; after the plane landed in Singapore for refueling (because the terrorists planned to fly it to Australia), military forces stormed the plane and killed the hijackers.
- the 1994 taking of Air France Flight 8969 while it was on the runway in Algiers by terrorists from the Armed Islamic Group, who killed three of the passengers after the plane was not allowed to take off; after a long, tense delay, they were finally permitted to fly to France, and when they landed in Marseilles to refuel (with authorities believing that they intended to fly the fully fueled plane into the Eiffel Tower) the plane was stormed and the hijackers killed.

- the 1999 taking of Indian Airlines Flight 814 while it was en route to Delhi, India, from Kathmandu, Nepal, by five Pakistani nationals who diverted the plane to Afghanistan and exchanged the hostages for three imprisoned associates, two Pakistani and one Indian.

Terrorists have also hijacked trains and ships, including the cruise ship *Achille Lauro*, and taken hostages at theaters, hospitals, and other buildings as well, in attempts to have their demands met. In addition, they have planted bombs on planes in acts of destruction intended to call attention to a particular cause or to create fear among travelers.

SEE ALSO: *Achille Lauro*, the; Entebbe raid; hostages

Hill, Joe
(1879–1915)

Born Joel Emmanuel Hägglund and also known as Joe Hillstrom, Joe Hill was a Swedish immigrant to America who became involved in the radical labor movement and engaged in terrorist acts on behalf of his labor union, the IWW (the Industrial Workers of the World, also known as the Wobblies). Hill joined the IWW in 1910, a few years after he tried to start his own labor union in Chicago. By this time he was a radical Marxist who wrote popular songs in support of labor unions and against capitalism. Immediately upon joining the IWW, however, he turned to violence, working with members of IWW and other unions to plant a bomb at the offices of the *Los Angeles Times* newspaper. (Two members of the Bridge and Structural Iron Workers Union, John J. and James McNamara, and two IWW anarchists, David Caplan and Matthew Schmidt, were later convicted of the crime,

which killed twenty newspaper workers; Hill's involvement was never proved.) In fact, there is evidence that he was hired by IWW leader Bill Hayward specifically to commit terrorist acts, including murder, against anyone who was antiunion. On January 10, 1914, Hill—accompanied by another IWW terrorist, Otto Applequist—gunned down one such person in Salt Lake City, Utah: grocery store owner John Morrison, who as a former police officer had arrested several IWW members for committing or plotting to commit violent acts. During this attack, which took place in Morrison's store, Morrison and his two sons (one of whom was also killed) tried to defend themselves with guns they kept for protection, and Hill was shot in the lung. His subsequent trip to a doctor resulted in his arrest, and he was eventually sentenced to death. The IWW used this sentence to its advantage, portraying Hill as a victim of capitalism and promoting the idea that unionization would prevent others from turning to such violence in the future. Largely because of this campaign, after Hill was executed by firing squad on November 19, 1915, he was viewed as both a martyr and hero among union activists and others who opposed capitalism.

SEE ALSO: anarchism; *Los Angeles Times* bombing

Hill, Paul
(1954–2003)

Anti-abortion activist Paul Hill shot and killed abortion provider Dr. John Britton and Britton's bodyguard, James Barrett, outside the Ladies Center abortion clinic in Pensacola, Florida, on July 29, 1994. In the aftermath, Hill became the first person to be tried under a new federal law addressing crimes committed outside such clinics, the Freedom of Access to Clinic Entrances law, and the first person executed in the United States for antiabortion violence. The Freedom of Access law was passed a year earlier in response to the shooting of abortion provider Dr. David Gunn by antiabortionist Michael Griffin outside the Pensacola Women's Medical Services clinic. After this killing, Hill made media appearances to defend Griffin's actions and formed an antiabortion group, Defensive Action, dedicated to committing similar murders. At the time, Hill was a Presbyterian minister, but his actions led to his expulsion from the church. Shortly thereafter, Hill killed Britton and Barrett and was immediately arrested for their murders. Hill was sentenced to both life in prison and death, and was executed by means of lethal injection on September 3, 2003.

SEE ALSO: antiabortion movement; Griffin, Michael

Hiroshima

The bombing of Hiroshima by the U.S. Army Air Forces on August 6, 1945, influenced American opinion in regard to nuclear weapons. Located on the Japanese island of Honshu, this city was the first in the world to be struck by an atomic bomb, and the result was devastating. Approximately seventy thousand to eighty thousand people were killed and many others were seriously injured; in subsequent years, some died of their injuries while many others died of radiation poisoning, despite the efforts of the Atomic Bomb Casualty Commission established in Hiroshima in 1947 to study and treat radiation victims. Consequently, although many people believe that the bombing was necessary in order to end World War II, many also believe that such an attack should never hap-

Adolf Hitler became known as a cruel Nazi dictator during the 1930s with his hatred toward the Jewish population, and launched a genocide against them, which became known as the Holocaust. THE LIBRARY OF CONGRESS

pen again. As a result, countries that have nuclear weapons have committed not to use them and to prevent terrorists from acquiring them.

SEE ALSO: bomb, atom; bombs, types of

Hitler, Adolf
(1889–1945)

After taking control of Germany in 1933, Adolf Hitler became a ruthless dictator whose regime supported terrorism against anyone he deemed "undesirable" to German society. As part of this state-sponsored terrorism, he launched a genocide campaign against Jews, known as the Holocaust, that killed millions. He was also ultimately responsible for the millions of deaths that occurred during the battles of World War II, because it was his aggressive military policies that triggered the start of the conflict. Before coming to power, Hitler served as a soldier in World War I; he was wounded on the battlefield in 1916 and gassed in 1918. After the war, in 1919, he joined the German Workers' Party, and the following year he became the head of its propaganda unit. In 1921 he became leader of the party, which had been renamed the National Socialists, or Nazi, Party, and he reorganized it into a paramilitary organization. In November 1923 Hitler attempted to use this force to overthrow the German government, but this effort failed and he was imprisoned for nine months. While in jail he wrote *Mein Kampf* (My Struggle), in which he expressed fascist and anti-Semitic views. His ideas brought him much political support, largely because the economy was in bad shape and some Germans were eager to blame the Jews and the current government system for their troubles, and in 1933 Hitler was appointed chancellor of Germany. By this time, the Nazi Party was the largest party in the country, and the following year, after the offices of chancellor and president were merged, he turned his position into a dictatorship. Hitler's regime, known as the Third Reich, began employing a special police force, the Gestapo, to kill or imprison his political enemies, including many socialists and Communists, as well as Jews, homosexuals, Gypsies, and others whom he considered to be undesirables. After Hitler invaded Poland in 1939, thereby starting World War II, he stepped up his campaign against the Jews, establishing death camps dedicated to exterminating as many as possible. Meanwhile, though, his military campaigns were not progressing, despite the

fact that Hitler had struck an alliance with Italian dictator Benito Mussolini. In 1945 it was clear he had lost the war, and as enemy forces were advancing on his location, he committed suicide.

SEE ALSO: Germany, terrorism in; Gestapo, the; Holocaust, the; Nazi terrorism

Ho Chi Minh (1890–1969)

The Communist leader of North Vietnam from 1945 to 1969 and its president from 1954 to 1969, Ho Chi Minh ("He Who Enlightens"; his birth name is believed to have been Nguyen That Thanh or Nguyen Sinh Cung) took control of Vietnam via a group called Vietminh (Viet-Nam Doc-Lap Dong-Minh or League for the Independence of Vietnam), which he founded in 1941. In fighting for a Vietnam that was independent from foreign colonial powers, his Vietminh routinely used suicide bombers to assassinate its enemies and engaged in other forms of terrorism as well. Aided by a peasant militia, the group attacked French colonial forces until 1953, when France decided to pull out of the region, and then launched a guerrilla war against South Vietnam. By this time, Ho Chi Minh had become an important symbol of the Communist struggle.

Ho Chi Minh first became involved in activism in Paris after World War I. Though he was born in a Vietnamese village, he traveled throughout Europe before the war and stayed in England during the war. In Paris he joined several socialist organizations, and in the 1920s he visited Russia to learn more about Communist revolution, then went to China to become involved in the Communist movement there. In 1930 he created the Indochinese Communist Party that would eventually evolve into the Vietminh.

SEE ALSO: communism; decolonization campaigns; Vietminh, the

Holocaust, the

In the fourteenth century, when it was first coined, the word "holocaust" meant a burnt offering, but by the seventeenth century it had come to refer to anything totally destroyed by fire, and by the late nineteenth century it was being used in reference to complete annihilation by any method. "The Holocaust," however, generally refers to a period in the twentieth century when the Nazi regime of Germany at first persecuted and then tried to exterminate all European Jews. This genocide, which took place under the regime of Adolf Hitler (1933–1945), was motivated largely by anti-Semitism, though greed also played a part in Nazi persecution of the Jews because the government seized the property of those they killed. The seizures were part of a process of persecution that began in 1933 with the firing of Jewish workers from government positions and the boycotting of Jewish-run businesses. Next came arson attacks on such businesses, as well as on Jewish places of worship, and individual attacks on Jews, often during anti-Semitic riots known as pogroms. By this point the seizure of Jewish property had begun, and Jews were sent to live in urban ghettos or in concentration camps, where they became slave laborers. Once World War II broke out, the Nazis established death camps whose sole purpose was to exterminate Jews by the thousands. At the same time, Jews in Russia, Poland, and the Balkans were murdered by death squads that accompanied German troops into these regions. By some estimates, over 6 million Jews were killed during the Holocaust, along with members of other groups the Nazis considered "undesirable" (such as Gypsies and homo-

sexuals). After the war, many of those who had persecuted the Jews stood trial for their crimes, and victims of the Holocaust were compensated financially for their suffering. In the late 1990s certain financial institutions that had benefited from the seizures of Jewish assets established a fund to compensate Holocaust survivors and their families, and in 2000 the German government and certain German businesses established a similar fund; together these funds amount to over $6 billion. However, this money cannot begin to repair the damage caused by the state-sponsored terrorism of the Holocaust.

SEE ALSO: anti-Semitism; Germany, terrorism in; Hitler, Adolf; Nazi terrorism

Homeland Security, U.S. Department of

Officially created in November 2002, the U.S. Department of Homeland Security (DHS) is a federal agency charged with keeping the United States secure from terrorist attacks and handling the aftermath of such attacks should they occur. The department is also responsible for dealing with natural disasters. DHS has several divisions, including the Border and Transportation Security division, which is primarily concerned with border security and immigration issues; the Emergency Preparedness and Response division, which oversees national-disaster readiness, emergency medical services, and weaponry stockpiles; the Information Analysis and Infrastructure Protection division, which is in charge of intelligence-gathering and protecting roads, bridges, and similar resources; and the Science and Technology division, whose main concerns are research and development projects related to science, engineering, and technology intended to predict and prevent disasters.

Within these divisions are other federal agencies whose duties are in some way related to terrorism or natural disasters. For example, within the Emergency Preparedness and Response Division is the Federal Emergency Management Agency (FEMA), which handles relief and rescue operations in the aftermath of such natural disasters as hurricanes and earthquakes. (FEMA is considered to have performed so poorly in the aftermath of Hurricane Katrina in 2005, however, that some government officials have suggested that this agency be eliminated so that the DHS is directly rather than indirectly responsible for such duties.) The DHS is also in control of certain security entities, such as the Secret Service, which guards the president of the United States, and the Coast Guard, which protects the nation's coastlines and waterways. Prior to its official creation, the DHS operated as the Office of Homeland Security, established almost immediately after the terrorist attacks of September 11, 2001. This office's major contribution was the Homeland Security Advisory System, which informed the public of the risk level (severe, high, elevated, guarded, or low) for terrorist attacks within the United States on any given day.

SEE ALSO: Federal Emergency Management Agency

hostages

Hostage taking has existed since ancient times, but in terms of modern terrorism, it was first employed in earnest during the 1960s with the rise of urban guerrilla warfare. Since then modern terrorists have hijacked airplanes, ships, trains, busses, and other vehicles and stormed buildings in order to take their passengers or occupants hostage. In many cases, these hostages are then exchanged for imprisoned terrorists or ransom money, though in a few cases the hostages are released or killed for no apparent reason. Hostages can come from all walks of life; however, certain types of people have been targeted more than others: public officials, diplomats, journalists, airline passengers, and Western tourists. In South America wealthy businessmen are the primary targets, because of the large ransoms they can bring; this was also the reason for the kidnapping of American heiress Patty Hearst by U.S. terrorists in 1974. In Russia people assembled in large groups, such as schoolchildren, theatergoers, and hospital patients, are commonly seized, whereas in Iraq, common targets are individual Western journalists, construction workers, or aid workers. Several of those kidnapped by terrorists in Iraq have been beheaded or otherwise executed while being videotaped, and tapes have then been released to the media, as have tapes showing hostages pleading for their lives and asking the United States or other nations to meet the terrorists' demands. Muslim fundamentalists have also kidnapped journalists, scientists, and industrial workers in various parts of the Middle East under the belief that these people are really spies. In Lebanon, for example, American reporter Terry Anderson was kidnapped in March 1985 and held for 2,454 days by Muslim fundamentalists associated with the group Hezbollah because these terrorists thought that he was not a journalist but an agent of the U.S. government.

Other notable hostage-taking incidents in recent years, excluding airline hijackings, are as follows:

- On October 13, 2005, an Islamic terrorist group called Yarmuk took more than one hundred hostages in Nalchik, Russia, as part of an attack on the town in protest of anti-Muslim sentiments in the region; the terrorists were killed in a shoot-out by hostage-rescue forces.

- On September 1, 2004, Chechen separatists (people from the Russian-controlled region of Chechnya who wanted Chechnyan independence) abducted over twelve hundred people, many of them children, at a school in Beslan, Russia, during a violent shoot-out that left many dead, then wired the school with explosives; after a three-day standoff during which the hostages had no food or water, Russian troops trying to collect the dead unintentionally triggered an explosion, followed by a shoot-out in which over three hundred people, including several of the terrorists, died and over seven hundred were wounded.

- On October 23, 2002, Chechen separatists took roughly 900 hostages at a theater in Moscow, Russia, and held them for two and a half days before Russian forces raided the theater and gassed its occupants; during this rescue operation, 129 hostages and forty-two terrorists were killed.

- On December 17, 1996, fourteen members of the Tupac Amaru Revolutionary Movement (MRTA) took hundreds of hostages at the Japanese embassy in Lima, Peru, and held them for 126 days before Peruvian forces raided the building and rescued the hostages.

- In June 1995, approximately fifty Chechen separatists took at least fifteen hundred people hostage in a hospital in Budyonnovsk, Russia, af-

ter killing several policemen and others in the town, and held them for fifteen days before Russian forces stormed the building; after more than one hundred hostages were killed and hundreds more wounded, a cease-fire was declared and the terrorists were allowed to leave, but they were later tracked down and either killed or arrested.

- On November 6, 1985, members of the Colombian guerrilla group M-19 stormed the Palace of Justice in the city of Bogotá and took everyone there hostage, declaring it would not release them until the country's president was put on trial; when Colombian forces attacked the building two days later, all of the guerrillas and eleven Supreme Court justices were killed.

- On October 7, 1985, four terrorists from the Palestine Liberation Front (PLF) took over the Italian cruise ship *Achille Lauro* while it was en route from Genoa, Italy, to Ashod, Israel, and held its 427 passengers, plus 80 crewmembers, for two days, killing 1 of the hostages before being allowed to leave the ship as a result of international negotiations. Other notable hostage crises include several embassy attacks in 1979–1980 (one of which, at the embassy in Tehran, Iran, resulted in a failed U.S. rescue attempt called Operation Eagle Claw), the seizure and fourteen-day holding of the Grand Mosque in Mecca, Saudi Arabia, in November 1979, the taking and twelve-day holding of a train in the Netherlands in December 1975, and an attack on Israeli Olympic athletes at the Munich, Germany, Olympics in 1972.

Saddam Hussein was the Iraqi ruler from 1979–2003, and was known for his terrorist attacks against the Kurds and Shiite Muslims. On December 30, 2006, Hussein was put to death by hanging. AP IMAGES

SEE ALSO: *Achille Lauro*, the; Chechen separatists; embassy bombings; Hearst, Patricia; hijackings, airline; Munich Olympics crisis; Operation Eagle Claw

Hussein, Saddam
(1937–2006)

As ruler of Iraq from 1979 to 2003, Saddam Hussein supported international terrorism and engaged in widespread terrorism in his own country, particularly against two groups of Iraqis, the Kurds and the Shiite Muslims, who did not support his regime. Hussein rose to power through his association with the Baath (Arab Socialist Resurrection) Party, which supported not only socialism but the establishment of a single, secular Arab state with no ties to Western nations—a position that put the party at odds with both

the secular rulers of Arab nations like Saudi Arabia and with the radical Islamic fundamentalists who wanted to establish an Islamic state in the Middle East. Hussein also had ties to the United States, which helped him achieve power so that Islamic clerics would not gain control of the region.

Hussein first joined the Baath Party in the 1950s, and in 1959 he participated in a Baath attempt to assassinate the leader of Iraq's military dictatorship, General Abdul Karim Kassam. When this failed, he and several other Baaths fled to Syria, after which he went to Cairo, Egypt, to study law. Throughout this period, he continued his association with the Baaths, holding several important positions in the party, so when one of the Baath leaders took control of the Iraqi government in 1968,

Hussein became the head of the country's security forces. Over the next several years, he gained power in the government, and by the late 1970s he was effectively ruling the country. He officially became president in 1979. By this time, he had already been involved in efforts to weaken the Kurds, a group of Muslims in northern Iraq who had long been demanding their independence from Iraq. To destroy their cultural identity, he forced many of them to relocate to southern Iraq during the 1970s, and in the late 1980s he bombed the villages of those who remained, using toxic gasses that have never completely been identified. He also established a blockade that prevented economic aid from getting into Kurdish regions. As a result, many Kurds left Iraq for Turkey or Iran.

From 1980 to 1988 Hussein fought a war against Iran, and in 1990 he took over Kuwait but retreated in 1991 after being attacked by U.S. forces there. (These forces had been sent to defend Kuwait at the request of the Saudi Arabian government, which did not want Hussein to control Kuwaiti oil fields.) This six-week war between Iraq and a coalition led by the United States is known as the Gulf War, or Operation Desert Storm. As part of the terms that ended this conflict, Hussein agreed to destroy all of Iraq's chemical, biological, and nuclear weapons and its long-range missiles, and to allow inspectors from the United Nations (UN) (specifically, from the UN Special Commission, or UNSCOM) and the International Atomic Energy Agency to physically verify that he had complied with this agreement. Until this verification could be made, international forces would maintain trade sanctions and an oil embargo against Iraq, making it impossible for Hussein to receive money acquired by means of terror-

ism—his own or others. (In the 1970s and '80s he supported the operations of several terrorist groups, including the Abu Nidal Organization and the Palestine Liberation Organization.)

Also in the 1990s Hussein began destroying the villages of Shiite Muslims, even going so far as to drain marshlands around their homes. Those Shiites who refused to leave their lands after this destruction were typically executed. By some estimates, 200,000 Shiites living in marshlands were forced from their villages, and 150,000 were killed. Hussein then turned his attention from marshland villages to the cities of Najaf and Karbala, which the Shiites considered holy. After attacking these cities with conventional weapons, he attacked them with chemical weapons dropped from helicopters, killing hundreds. In 1994 a committee of the U.S. Senate concerned over these attacks investigated whether U.S. soldiers might have been unknowingly harmed by chemical weapons during the Gulf War. As part of this investigation, the committee discovered that Iraq's chemical weapons had been purchased from U.S. firms in 1985–89, along with other toxic and biological research materials. It also determined that several high-level U.S. government officials had known about these shipments.

In 1995 UNSCOM inspectors received reliable information that Hussein was developing weapons of mass destruction, including biological weapons such as anthrax, and this information led them to several stockpiles of these weapons, which they then destroyed. Over the next few years, weapons inspections continued, as did Hussein's terrorism against Kurds, and thousands of chemical weapons were destroyed, as were missiles and any equipment and supplies that could be used to make biological or nuclear weapons. In 1998 the inspectors found evidence that Iraq was developing a weapon using nerve gas, and after this discovery Hussein refused to allow any more inspections. In response, U.S. and British forces bombed sites that they suspected were weapons manufacturing plants or weapons storehouses.

Meanwhile Hussein's people had descended into poverty, and in 1999 the international community partially lifted the oil embargo to allow him to trade oil for food and other supplies to aid Iraqi citizens. Consequently in 2000 Iraq began sending large amounts of oil to Syria, but soon the Western world began to suspect that Hussein was using this exchange to enrich himself rather than his people. By some estimates, the oil-for-food program earned him $2 billion, which he spent to decorate several palaces; in addition, Hussein donated over $800 million to Palestinian terrorists who were trying to destroy Israel. Also in 2000 human-rights advocates accused him of torturing or unjustly executing Iraqi prisoners at various facilities, including Abu Ghraib prison. In early 2001 they accused him of engaging in widespread torture against his political enemies.

Because of Hussein's actions, when U.S. president George W. Bush took office at the beginning of 2001, he told his secretary of defense, Donald Rumsfeld, and others that he wanted to find a way to remove Hussein from power. This opportunity occurred after the terrorist attacks on America on September 11, 2001. As part of his "War on Terror," Bush demanded that the international community force Hussein to allow weapons inspectors back

into his country to ensure that all Iraqi weapons of mass destruction had indeed been destroyed, as Hussein claimed. When Hussein agreed to allow limited inspections, Bush said that this was not good enough, and he called for Hussein to be removed from office and tried for war crimes. When this suggestion received no support in the international community, the United States drafted a UN resolution that would allow the UN to conduct unlimited weapons inspections and unsupervised interviews with Iraqi scientists. Hussein accepted this resolution and allowed the weapons inspections to begin. In 2003 the UN inspectors announced that Hussein had no weapons of mass destruction; the U.S. government rejected this position, saying that Hussein had tricked the inspectors and was therefore in violation of the UN resolution. Such a violation would give the United States the justification it needed to invade Iraq, and indeed on March 20, 2003, U.S. forces, with cooperation from other international forces, attacked Iraq with an aggressive military campaign dubbed Operation Iraqi Freedom; this campaign, which included aerial bombing and ground invasions from Kuwait, captured the city of Baghdad on April 9, and the rest of Iraq by April 14. Thousands of Iraqis were killed in the process, while Hussein went into hiding.

For several months, the United States received various tips regarding Hussein's whereabouts, but he was ultimately discovered in a "spider hole," a small, camouflaged, underground hideout, on a farm near the city of Tikrit. He was subsequently put on trial in Iraq for his attacks on Kurds and Shiites. The trial endured many delays due to assassinations and assassination attempts against various officials involved in the proceedings. In

November 2006, however, Hussein was sentenced to death, and on December 30, 2006, he was hanged for his crimes. Terrorist attacks are widespread in Iraq, despite years of Iraqi occupation by U.S. forces, but no weapons of mass destruction have been found there.

SEE ALSO: Abu Nidal Organization; Palestine Liberation Organization

Indonesian terrorism

Indonesian terrorism has primarily been state terrorism (i.e., terrorism perpetrated by the government) or communal terrorism (terrorism in which rival demographic groups attack one another). As an example of the latter, in 1965 after the Indonesian Communist Party (PKI) tried but failed to take over the country, anti-Communist Indonesians began attacking Communist Indonesians in the streets, killing over five hundred thousand. Another example of communal terrorism occurred in 1998, when anti-Chinese Indonesians looted Chinese neighborhoods in the city of Jakarta and raped innocent Chinese women in the streets. In 1999 and 2000 the two groups that fought were Christians and Muslims on Indonesia's Molucca Islands; this conflict, which was fueled by a militant Islamic group called Lashkar Jihad (Militia of the Holy War), resulted in thousands of deaths, and both sides engaged in numerous acts of violence.

Much of Indonesia's state terrorism was connected to the suppression of an independence movement on the island of Timor. Beginning in the fifteenth century, the eastern end of the island was a colony of Portugal, but in 1975 the Portuguese decided to grant it its independence. Before they could remove their troops, however, the Indonesian army invaded the region and made it a province of Indonesia, East Timor. For the next two decades, East Timor was plagued with violence, as army forces attacked anyone protesting the new

government. Hundreds of thousands were killed, including hundreds attending a pro-democracy demonstration in 1991. In addition, the government supported the actions of pro-government paramilitary groups that also killed people involved in the independence movement. Such attacks continued until 1999, when Indonesia responded to international condemnation of its actions by agreeing to let the United Nations take over East Timor in preparation for democratic elections there; these elections finally took place in 2002.

SEE ALSO: state terrorism

insurgencies

Insurgencies are organized acts of rebellion or revolt in which citizens rise up against a civil or political authority, typically under the belief that the authority is illegitimate. Insurgent terrorism is therefore typically intended to overthrow the government, but it differs from revolutionary terrorism in that revolutionary terrorism typically seeks radical, total, immediate, irreversible change not only in regard to the governing authority but in terms of all political and social institutions and policies within a society. (In contrast, sub-revolutionary terrorism is intended merely to change various elements within an existing political system, while still keeping that system.)

People engaged in insurgency, known as insurgents, use a variety of tactics to directly attack the governing authority, including shootings, bombings, kidnappings, and hijackings. Insurgent terrorism is therefore more confrontational than guerrilla warfare, which is typically a lengthy, low-intensity campaign intended to destabilize an authority in order to allow a rebellion to take place. However, insurgents can use guerrilla tactics as well, conducting raids and engaging in sabotage to weaken the governing authority. Also like guerrillas, insurgents might ally themselves with criminal elements, foreign governments, or international terrorist groups.

In fact, the similarities between guerrillas and insurgents are so strong that the Western media sometimes disagree on which conflicts are guerrilla wars and which are insurgencies. However, most have called the violence in Iraq against multinational occupying forces, beginning in 2003, the result of an insurgency. Another such conflict was the Taliban insurgency, which occurred in Afghanistan in 2001 after its leaders, Muslim fundamentalists known as the Taliban, fell from power, then began attacking NATO (North Atlantic Treaty Organization) forces controlling the country.

SEE ALSO: guerrilla warfare; Iraq; Taliban

Internal Macedonian Revolutionary Organization (IMRO)

Originating in 1893 among revolutionaries in Salonica (Thessaloniki), Macedonia (then a part of the Ottoman Turkish Empire), the Internal Macedonian Revolutionary Organization (IMRO; so named in 1906) was established in 1903 as a membership organization dedicated to driving the Turks out of Macedonia. Most IMRO members were professionals or academics who, though dues-paying members, did not participate in the group's many terrorist acts, which included attacks on and kidnappings of Turkish officials and Macedonians supporting their rule as well as the destruction of bridges and other structures. In committing such acts, the organization hoped to publicize Turkish oppression in Macedonia and to encourage others to join their fight against it; this oppression often took the form of random attacks on and rapes and murders of innocent civilians. Turkish officials, with a force of over three hundred thousand troops in the region, responded to these attacks, and those of other anti-Turk terrorist groups in Macedonia, with attacks on terrorist strongholds, but this only served to escalate the violence, and in August 1903 IMRO led a peasant rebellion in both Illinden and Preobrazhenski, Macedonia. When these failed to end or even soften Ottoman rule, the IMRO lost thousands of members and much of its influence in the region. (By some estimates the group numbered less than thirty-five thousand by late 1903.) Nonetheless, the IMRO continued to engage in terrorist acts in various parts of Macedonia until 1923, when the Bulgarian government (which by then controlled one part of Macedonia, with Serbia and Greece each controlling an additional part) responded to the IMRO's assassination of its prime minister by launching an aggressive campaign to destroy the group. This effort apparently succeeded in the early 1930s, though in the 1990s the IMRO resurfaced as a political party dedicated to supporting Macedonian nationalism.

SEE ALSO: Macedonia

international versus domestic terrorism

Terrorism experts generally define international terrorism as attacks on targets that have some international significance and that affect the global community. Such international terrorism, however, often grows out of domestic terrorism, which involves attacks on targets with domestic significance that only affect the people living in the region or country of the attacks. This outgrowth is often intended to call international attention to a domestic problem; it occurs, for example, when terrorists fighting for the independence of their country hijack an international airline flight or attack a foreign diplomat stationed within their country. International terrorism is also at play when one country offers aid or other support to terrorists from another country, even when those terrorists only engage in domestic terrorism. Terrorist attacks that occur in foreign countries are categorized as international terrorism as well, the most prominent example being the September 11, 2001, attacks on America by the al Qaeda terrorist group.

In contrast, the 1995 attack on the Alfred P. Murrah Federal Building in Oklahoma City, Oklahoma, by American terrorist Timothy McVeigh was an incidence of domestic terrorism. Other examples of domestic terrorism include American terrorists' bombings of U.S. abortion clinics and attacks on U.S. animal-testing facilities in order to protest abortion and animal cruelty, respectively. Most terrorism today, however, occurs on the world stage, because terrorists have decided that international pressure is among the best tools for creating political or social change.

SEE ALSO: al Qaeda; antiabortion movement; ecoterrorism; McVeigh, Timothy; Oklahoma City bombing; September 11 attacks on America

Interpol

The International Criminal Police Organization, more commonly known as Interpol, is an organization that coordinates criminal investigations concerning suspects whose actions involve multiple countries and therefore multiple law-enforcement agencies. Over 125 such agencies work with Interpol to apprehend international criminals, including terrorists, though before 1990, Interpol refused to work on investigations involving terrorists acts.

Intifada, the

The Intifada (in Arabic, the "shaking off") is the name commonly given to a time of civil unrest in Palestine that lasted from December 1987 through the early 1990s. It began with an uprising in the West Bank and Gaza Strip that was triggered by a traffic accident in which an Israeli driver killed several Palestinians. This incident ignited anti-Israeli sentiments in the region, and the resulting riots, demonstrations, and strikes quickly led to violent attacks against dozens of Israeli soldiers and settlers, though dozens of innocent Palestinian civilians were also injured or killed. There was no single organization behind the violence; most of the attacks, which included stabbings, stonings, shootings, minor bombings, and arson, were conducted by small groups of Palestinian youth dissatisfied with established Palestinian anti-Israeli organizations such as the PLO (Palestine Liberation Organization). While trying to quell the unrest, Israeli forces repressed the populace, routinely beat Palestinian youths, and killed hundreds of Palestinians. When these actions reduced support for the Israeli occupation of Palestine, both within Israel and in the international community, Israeli forces scaled back their attacks on Palestinians, and in response the civil unrest was gradually reduced.

SEE ALSO: Israel; Palestine; Palestine Liberation Organization

Iran

A country in which over 90 percent of the population is Shiite Muslim (an unusually high figure, given that only about 10 percent of all Muslims are Shiite), Iran is a leading sponsor of religious terrorism, promoting Islamic revolutionary movements in many countries and providing money, training, and other aid to international terrorists connected to radical Islamic fundamentalism. It disperses some of this money through a charity group called the Fund for the Martyrs, which was established to provide economic support to the families of suicide bombers. Iran supports Muslim terrorists throughout the world wishing to attack Jews, because it is opposed to the existence of Israel. To this end, the Iranian government has given substantial funds to organizations dedicated to destroying Israel, such as Hamas, Hezbollah, and the Palestinian Islamic Jihad. Iran has also supported terrorists who want to strike out at U.S. targets, having dubbed the United States a Satanic nation. One such group, the Mujahideen-e Khalq Organization (MEK), killed several members of the U.S. military during the 1970s, along with American scientists working on defense projects in Tehran, Iran. This group was formed in the 1960s to oppose American influences in Iran.

Prior to 1979 Iran was an ally of the United States under the Shah of Iran, Mohammad Reza Pahlavi, who ruled the country from 1953 to 1979. Pahlavi was a ruthless leader who used army, secret police, and other forces to quell public dissent. These forces routinely shot people

engaged in political protests and arrested and tortured people suspected of supporting or encouraging such protests. Thousands were killed at the hands of the shah's government, but even with this level of suppression, a religious leader, Ayatollah Ruhollah Khomeini, was still able to inspire Iranians to rise up against him, and in 1979 a revolution forced the shah out of the country. When he was allowed into the United States despite the atrocities he had committed, Iranian student protestors attacked the U.S. embassy in Iran and took several American diplomats hostage.

Iran then embarked on a war with Iraq (1980–1988). During this conflict, in 1986, the president of the United States, Ronald Reagan, secretly authorized the sale of arms to Iran in order to acquire money to support the Contras revolutionaries in Nicaragua. When information about the transaction was leaked to the press, the result was widespread condemnation of what became known as the Iran-Contra scandal.

SEE ALSO: Contras; Iraq; religious terrorism

Iraq

Most of Iraq's terrorism is associated with the rule of Saddam Hussein (1979–2003) and the subsequent invasion and occupation of the country by a U.S.-led coalition of forces. Hussein was a ruthless dictator who employed terrorism to keep Iraq's citizens in line and allowed torture in his prisons. He also used chemical weapons against the Kurds, a culturally distinct group within Iraq, who wanted their native lands to become independent from the rest of the country. At the same time, Hussein provided weapons and facilities to various terrorist groups, including several devoted to the Palestinian cause; he was opposed to the existence of Israel, though in the early years of his rule he had strong ties to the United States.

During the 1980s, however, the relationship between Hussein and America weakened, and U.S. forces subsequently fought two major wars against Iraq. The first, known as the Gulf War or Operation Desert Storm, occurred after Hussein invaded Kuwait in 1990. This invasion concerned the leaders of Saudi Arabia, who did not want Iraq to gain control of Kuwait's oil fields, so they asked U.S. president George H. W. Bush, with whom they had close ties, to send troops into the region to defend the oil fields. The result was a six-week war between Iraq and a coalition led by the United States that drove Hussein from Kuwait. At the end of this conflict, Hussein agreed to destroy all of Iraq's chemical, biological, and nuclear weapons and its long-range missiles, and to allow inspectors from the United Nations (UN) (specifically, from the UN Special Commission, or UNSCOM) and the International Atomic Energy Agency to physically verify that he had complied with this agreement.

In 1994 a committee of the U.S. Senate investigated whether U.S. soldiers might have been unknowingly harmed by chemical weapons during the Gulf War. As part of this investigation, it discovered that Iraq's chemical weapons had been purchased from U.S. firms in 1985–89, along with other toxic and biological research materials. It also determined that several high-level U.S. government officials had known about these shipments. In 1995 UNSCOM inspectors received reliable information that Hussein was developing weapons of mass destruction, including biological weapons such as anthrax, and this information led them to several stockpiles of these weapons, which they then destroyed. In 1998 the inspectors found evidence that Iraq was developing a weapon using nerve gas, and after this discovery Hussein refused to allow any more inspections. In response, U.S. and British forces bombed sites that they suspected were weapons manufacturing plants or weapons storehouses.

Consequently when U.S. president George W. Bush took office in January 2001, he told his secretary of defense, Donald Rumsfeld, and others that he wanted to find a way to remove Hussein from power. This opportunity occurred after the terrorist attacks on America on September 11, 2001. As part of his "War on Terror," Bush demanded that the international community force Hussein to allow weapons inspectors back into his country to ensure that all Iraqi weapons of mass destruction had indeed been destroyed, as Hussein claimed. After many negotiations, Hussein eventually agreed to allow the weapons inspectors to resume their activities in Iraq without restriction, and in 2003 the inspectors announced that Hussein had no weapons of mass destruction. The U.S. government immediately rejected this position, saying that Hussein had tricked the inspectors, and on March 20, 2003, U.S. forces, with cooperation from other international forces that Bush called a "coalition of the willing," attacked Iraq in an aggressive military campaign dubbed Operation Iraqi Freedom. This campaign, which included aerial bombings and ground invasions launched from Kuwait, captured the city of Baghdad on April 9, and the rest of Iraq by April 14. Thousands of Iraqis were killed in the process, while Hussein went into hiding; he was ultimately captured near the city of Tikrit and put on trial for various acts of terrorism committed during his rule.

Even after Hussein was removed from power and executed for crimes against humanity in 2006, however, the U.S.-Iraq conflict continued, not as a war but as a troubled occupation. The U.S.-led coalition forces struggled to restore order as terrorists continued to attack foreign troops, Iraqis who supported those troops, and innocent civilians. In regard to civilian attacks, much of the violence is sectarian, between the Sunni Muslims and the Shiite Muslims (who currently hold the majority in the post-Hussein Iraqi government, which was created, with U.S. help, through democratic elections) and against the Kurds. Experts disagree on how many Iraqi civilians died during the war and its aftermath; in 2005 the Bush administration claimed that approximately 30,000 had been killed since the war began, but in 2006 experts put the number at anywhere from 150,000 to 650,000. It is known, however, that over 3,100 U.S. soldiers had been killed in Iraq by mid-February 2007 (which is more than the number of people killed in the September 11, 2001, attacks on America that ultimately led to the war), and that 112 U.S. soldiers died in the month of December 2006 alone, the bloodiest month of that year.

SEE ALSO: Abu Nidal Organization; Hussein, Saddam; Palestine Liberation Organization

Irgun Zvai Leumi (IZL)

An extremist terrorist organization dedicated to Zionism (though its leaders continually insisted that it was a military group rather than a terrorist group), the Irgun Zvai Leumi (IZL) was established in the early 1930s to fight against British control of Palestine because at the time, British authorities refused to let Jews fleeing Nazi persecution in Europe immigrate to Palestine. Nonetheless during World War II, the IZL suspended its activities to allow the British to concentrate on fighting Nazi leader Adolf Hitler. (This suspension caused dissention in the organization that ultimately led one of its most prominent members, Abraham Stern, to create a more militant anti-British terrorist group, the Stern Gang, which was responsible for several murders.) Immediately after World War II, when the British refused to allow Holocaust survivors to immigrate to Palestine, the IZL resumed its activities, attacking a variety of British targets that included roads, railroad lines, airfields, and ships. (Other Zionist groups engaged in such attacks as well.) The IZL also engaged in murder, by some estimates killing over three hundred people by 1946. Then led by Menachem Begin (1913–1992), who later became the prime minister of Israel (1977–1983), the IZL murdered nine British military men in December 1945, and in July 1946 the group killed ninety-one people by bombing Jerusalem's King David Hotel, which then housed British troops and administration officials. In 1947, after the IZL murdered two British soldiers and hung their bodies from a tree, the British government offered to pay anyone who captured or killed Begin ten thousand pounds. That same year the IZL broke several of its members out of a British prison, and in 1947 the group killed over two hundred pro-British Palestinians in Palestine. In 1948, after Israel became a Jewish state, some members of the IZL—most notably Menachem Begin—refused to accept the new Israeli government, but when this government attacked an IZL ship, the *Altalena*, in June of that year, the IZL declared the government legitimate and became a political party, the Herut

(Freedom) Party. During the late 1970s this party, also known as Likud, gained great power in the Israeli government. By this time, however, the Israeli government had ordered that the military arm of the IZL be dissolved, and the group complied.

SEE ALSO: Begin, Menachem; King David Hotel bombing; Stern Gang, the

Irish National Liberation Army (INLA)

Formed in late 1974 by a faction of the Official Irish Republican Army, or Official IRA, which was itself a faction of the Irish Republican Army (IRA), the Irish National Liberation Army (INLA) is a socialist group dedicated to seeing Northern Ireland break away from the United Kingdom in order to join with the Republic of Ireland. To this end, during the 1970s and '80s the group engaged in terrorist attacks on British targets, most notably a March 1979 car bombing in the British House of Commons parking lot that killed a member of British Parliament (Airey Neave of the British Conservative Party, who was the spokesperson for Northern Ireland affairs). By some estimates, the group was either directly or indirectly responsible for as many as 150 deaths between 1974 and 1998, when it became inactive. In addition, several of its members were killed as a result of disputes between the INLA and other IRA factions. The INLA currently has less than fifty members, though it also has a political party, the Irish Republican Socialist Party.

SEE ALSO: Irish Republican Army

Irish Northern Aid (NORAID)

Irish Northern Aid, commonly known as NORAID, was established in New York in 1969 by Michael Flannery, a member of the Irish Republican Army (IRA) who wanted to funnel American money to the IRA in Ireland. NORAID was immediately successful in this regard, using fundraisers and other means to provide more than half of the IRA's operating budget during the 1970s. During the early 1980s, NORAID also sent weapons to the IRA, a practice that ultimately led to its downfall. In 1984 the British government, with help from the U.S. Central Intelligence Agency (CIA), discovered that a NORAID ship from Boston, Massachusetts, was rendezvousing at sea with an Irish trawler in order to transfer guns, rifles, grenades, and other weaponry to the IRA; after British authorities informed the Irish government of this plot, Irish authorities seized the trawler before any weapons could be off-loaded. This incident had a serious impact on NORAID's ability to provide other weapons to the IRA, not only because of increased law-enforcement scrutiny on its actions, but because once the public became aware of NORAID's involvement with the IRA, people who had been injured in IRA attacks began suing NORAID in U.S. courts for the group's procurement of IRA weapons. These lawsuits drained NORAID of cash and scared away many of its financial backers. Consequently by the 1990s, NORAID was providing the IRA with almost no weapons and very little money.

SEE ALSO: Irish Republican Army

Irish Republican Army (IRA)

The Irish Republican Army (IRA) is an Irish terrorist group whose goal is to force the United Kingdom to give up one of its provinces, Northern Ireland, so that this province can become a part of the Republic of Ireland. When the IRA was originally formed in 1919, however, the

A member of the Irish Republican Army (IRA), an Irish terrorist group who sought leadership over Northern Ireland, reads an Easter message from the IRA at a rally at Crossmaglen, Northern Ireland, on April 7, 1996. AP IMAGES

Republic of Ireland did not yet exist. At that time the IRA's goal was to break all of Ireland away from the United Kingdom of Great Britain and Ireland, which had been created in 1801. The British, who had controlled Ireland since King Henry II seized it in 1171, resisted this independence movement, so the IRA started a war, the Anglo-Irish War of 1919–1921, to gain freedom. In the subsequent peace settlement, England kept Northern Ireland.

Many of the people living in Northern Ireland were happy with this development, because at the time of the peace agreement, the province was primarily populated by Protestants whose ancestors had been British and Scottish settlers; in con-

trast, over 90 percent of Ireland is Roman Catholic, most of them natives of the region. The Roman Catholics in Northern Ireland, however, were miserable over the settlement, because as the minority they were discriminated against and had few rights, and as time went on they became more restive. Finally, by the mid-1960s, they started forming groups to fight for their rights, and as they increasingly engaged in public protests, the Protestants in Northern Ireland formed similar groups. In 1968–69, these Catholic and Protestant groups began to clash with one another, with the Catholics, being in the minority, taking the brunt of the violence. The IRA stepped in to protect the Catholics, but the attacks on them escalated. In an attempt to regain and keep control, the British increased their presence in the region, sending additional troops into Northern Ireland to quell the violence. At this point, a faction that called itself the Provisional IRA split off from the main group, which then began calling itself the Official IRA, though later it went back to using IRA again. The Provisional IRA was far more militant than the official IRA, engaging in extreme acts of violence, though it continued its association with the political arm of the IRA, Sinn Féin, which was also the largest Catholic political party in Northern Ireland.

During the 1970s the Provisional IRA became the dominant faction in Northern Ireland, where it attacked and sometimes killed any civilians who harmed Catholics, attacked British targets with car bombs and other types of explosives, and supported public protests and strikes. In 1974 it began bombing in Great Britain as well. After one such attack, in November 1974, when twenty-one people were killed in a Birmingham, England, pub, the British government enacted tougher laws to deal with terrorism and began to treat political protests as crimes. The Provisional IRA made some changes as well, restructuring itself into a collection of small, isolated, independent groups, or cells, so that if police caught some of its members it would not lead them to others. This restructuring was necessary because during the 1980s several arrested IRA members provided the police with information about IRA activities in an attempt to avoid long prison sentences. Nonetheless the Provisional IRA continued its operations, and in 1979 it assassinated a British lord. The group also planted a bomb at a meeting place in Brighton, England, in 1984, that came close to killing the entire British Cabinet, including the prime minister.

In the early 1990s, however, some members of the IRA realized that the violence was getting out of hand, and they asked Sinn Féin to negotiate a peace treaty with the British government. Other members, however, continued to engage in violence, bombing numerous sites in London. Therefore the British government was reluctant to enter into negotiations with the IRA, and even after they began, the process was rocky. Finally, though, the two sides came up with the Good Friday Accords of 1998, which gave Catholics equal say with Protestants in the government of Northern Ireland. This agreement and subsequent ones made other improvements in the situation as well, and in 2001 the IRA agreed to destroy its weapons. Though for a few years after this the Provisional IRA still attacked people in Northern Ireland who persecuted Catholics, the peace agreement held, and as of October 2006, according to a report issued by a nonpartisan group monitoring the situation (the Independent Monitoring Commission),

the IRA is no longer engaging in terrorism or supporting criminal activities connected to terrorism.

SEE ALSO: Sinn Féin

Islamic extremists

Islamic extremists are believers in the Islamic faith whose goal is to achieve a culture guided wholly by Sharia, or God's Law, in accordance with Islam. This spiritually pure culture would, by definition, exclude all nonbelievers, including Christians and Jews; consequently radical Muslims (adherents to the Islamic faith) seek to eliminate nonbelievers from any places where they want Sharia to hold sway. For example, radical Muslims in Lebanon have sought to drive Jews from their lands, committing murder if necessary, in order to create a pure Muslim state there. In regard to this and similar struggles in the Middle East, Islamic extremists have called for a *jihad* against Westerners. In the Quran (the holy book of Islam), the term *jihad* refers to two kinds of sacred struggle: one is within the self, as the individual tries to determine which actions would be in keeping with the will of God, and the other is with others, to defend the faith and the faithful from attack. Islamic extremists, however, have interpreted *jihad* as a holy war against nonbelievers, seeing *jihad* as a justification for violent attacks rather than as a defensive position.

SEE ALSO: *jihad*

Islamic Movement of Uzbekistan (IMU)

Established in 1999, the Islamic Movement of Uzbekistan (IMU) is actually a terrorist organization rather than a movement. Its members, fundamentalist Islamic militants primarily from central Asia, originally sought to turn the central Asian country of Uzbekistan into an Islamic state. Now, however, the group's goal is not only to overthrow the current Uzbekistan government but to establish an Islamic state in every other central Asian country as well. To reflect the fact that its activities are no longer confined to Uzbekistan, in 2001 the IMU changed its name to the Islamic Party of Turkestan, but its tactics have remained the same throughout its history. From its inception, the IMU has attacked villages, taken hostages, and planted car bombs in attempts to call attention to its cause. Though its operations were initially confined to Uzbekistan and along both sides of the border between Uzbekistan and Kyrgyzstan, today the group also operates within Kyrgyzstan and Tajikistan. Many terrorism experts believe that the IMU currently has training camps in Tajikistan and Afghanistan and might have ties to al Qaeda and the Taliban. Two of IMU's leaders, Tahir Yuldashev and Juma Namangani, fled to Afghanistan in 1999 after participating in five car bombings in Uzbekistan, where a court subsequently sentenced them to death in absentia. The two are possibly involved in drug trafficking in Afghanistan in order to finance IMU operations.

SEE ALSO: al Qaeda; Taliban

Israel

From the beginning of its creation in 1948, Israel has been the target of Arab terrorists who do not believe it has a right to exist. In fact, for more than a decade before this Jewish state was established, Palestinian Arabs had been attacking Jews in the region. But during the 1950s this violence grew more organized, as Palestinian terrorists based in Egypt and Jordan—who called themselves *fedayeen*, or fighters—began crossing into Israel to attack facilities necessary to keep the country running, such as electricity plants, irrigation systems, and transportation systems, as well as innocent civilians. Israel responded to these attacks immediately, in a variety of ways: It hid military and police forces along the border to ambush any terrorists venturing into the country; it strengthened its borders with additional troops, watchtowers, barbed wire, and similar features; and it sent its forces across the border to attack terrorist training camps and villages that sheltered terrorists. Nonetheless, one Palestinian group based in Jordan, al Fatah, continued its assaults on Israel into the 1960s, and in late 1966 Israel reacted by launching massive attacks on border villages. This soon led to the Six-Day War of 1967, during which Israel inflicted serious damage on the armies and air forces of Jordan, Syria, and Egypt and occupied the West Bank and the Gaza Strip. Israel then began military operations, both overt and covert, in these newly occupied areas to restrict the freedoms of Muslims there and stamp out Arab terrorists. Meanwhile, terrorists from the Palestine Liberation Organization (PLO), operating from bases in Jordan, continued to strike out at Israeli targets, and when the Jordanian government forced the PLO from its country, the PLO launched its anti-Israel attacks from Lebanon. Other Palestinian terrorist groups attacked Israelis as well, both inside and outside of Israeli; for example, in 1976 a terrorist group called the Popular Front for the Liberation of Palestine (PFLP) hijacked an Air France Airbus whose passengers included Israelis. After the terrorists landed the plane at the Entebbe Airport in Uganda and refused to let any Jewish passengers disembark, saying they wanted to exchange these prisoners for fifty-three terrorists held in Israeli prisons, Israeli forces raided the plane and rescued most of the hostages.

Faced with increasing terrorism from groups operating out of Lebanon, Israel began bombing that country, without regard for the many civilians its forces would kill in the process of trying to destroy terrorist bases. In March 1978 Israel went one step further, invading southern Lebanon and taking control of a small area there. This area was expanded via a more aggressive invasion in June 1982. Israel's military operation, called "Operation Peace for Galilee," drove the PLO from Lebanon and into Tunisia; however, the absence of the PLO soon allowed another terrorist group, Hezbollah, to grow powerful in the region, and when Israel decided to abandon most of Lebanon a few years later, this group began attacking Israel. Other groups continued to attack it as well. For example, in October 1985 four terrorists from the Palestine Liberation Front (PLF) took over the Italian cruise ship *Achille Lauro* while it was en route from Genoa, Italy, to Ashod, Israel, with the stated intent of holding any Israeli passengers hostage while demanding the release of fifty Palestinians imprisoned in Israel. However, terrorism experts believe that the hijacking of the *Achille Lauro* was actually in retaliation for an Israeli air attack on the PLO's headquarters in Tunis, Tunisia, earlier that month, which killed at least fifty PLO members.

Indeed, Israel's military actions have always tended to increase its problems with terrorism rather than end them. Its counterterrorism activities, however, have had better results. The Israeli Defense Force (IDF), which is the government's military arm, the Israeli National Police Force, the

Border Police, and two Israeli intelligence agencies, the General Security Services (also known as Shin Bet) and the Central Institute for Intelligence and Security (also known as Mossad), have all engaged in such activities. Mossad is particularly skilled at rescuing hostages and protecting foreign dignitaries and embassies, but it has also engaged in assassination as acts of retribution against terrorists or prevention against future terrorism. Covert operatives from this agency, for example, tracked down and killed the terrorists who attacked Israeli athletes at the Olympics Games in Munich, Germany, in 1972. Shin Bet is primarily known for its aggressive interrogation tactics; for example, after an uprising of Palestinian Arabs in the West Bank and the Gaza Strip in 1987—an incident known as the Intifada—Shin Bet rounded up anyone suspected of being involved in the uprising, including teenagers, and tortured them in order to find the rebellion's leaders, while Israeli security forces imposed curfews and more severe restrictions that limited the freedom of all Palestinians in the region. Israeli intelligence agents also pretended to be Arabs in order to gain information about possible terrorist activities. But despite such measures, terrorism continues to be a major problem for Israel, even though it pulled out of the West Bank and Gaza Strip in the 1990s and the Palestinians now have their own government in the region. Radical Muslims believe that Israel has no right to exist, and because of this belief they continue to try to destroy the Jewish state and establish a Muslim state in its place.

SEE ALSO: *Achille Lauro*, the; counterterrorism; Entebbe raid; Munich Olympics crisis; Palestine Liberation Organization; Popular Front for the Liberation of Palestine

Italy

Italy has experienced terrorism throughout its history, but two periods—the Roman Empire and World War II—and two groups—the Mafia and the Red Brigades—are especially associated with such violence.

The Roman Empire. In ancient times, political assassinations were especially common. In the sixth century B.C., the assassinations of Rome's last three kings, Tarquin I, Servius Tullius, and Tarquin II, established the Roman republic. In 82 B.C., a Roman general, Sulla, killed over two thousand of his political enemies, and in 44 B.C., Julius Caesar was assassinated after turning the republic into a dictatorship by becoming emperor. During the first century, various Roman emperors killed and were killed over struggles for political power within the Roman Empire, and as the Roman Empire expanded, its soldiers exported terror elsewhere, killing tribal leaders after conquering their lands. In fact, during some of these conquests, the Romans slaughtered entire tribes. They also killed anyone who rebelled against Roman rule, either in foreign lands or in Rome itself, as well as any of their own soldiers who displayed cowardice on the battlefield. In fact, terrorism was a common tool for military commanders wanting to keep troops in line. Soldiers were beaten and tortured if they disobeyed, and if an entire unit performed badly, then one-tenth of its men were killed, with the victims chosen at random. Similarly, if a Roman was killed by one of his slaves, then four hundred of his slaves were put to death. Christians were also murdered en masse, often in front of crowds who watched them die in horrible ways.

World War II. During World War II, it was not the Italians but the Germans who were responsible for most of the terrorism in Italy. The country had entered the war as a German ally in 1940 under Italian leader Benito Mussolini. After Mussolini was deposed in 1943, however, the new government officially sided with the Allies, and Germany immediately seized control of Italy, killing thousands of Italian officers who had ordered their men to resist German occupation. The Germans then established a new government, the Italian Social Republic, and put Mussolini at its head, with forces trained by the Nazis. These forces engaged in attacks on Jews, just as Nazi troops did in other German-occupied areas, but they also attacked the many Communist partisans who opposed the Nazis. These partisans planted bombs, ambushed troops, and assassinated political and military leaders, and when the Nazis were unable to stop them, they began murdering innocent people in retaliation for partisan attacks. For example, after a 1944 bombing that killed thirty-three German policemen, the Nazis killed several civilians, including women, children, and Italian priests. By the end of the year, Mussolini's fascist militia, the Blackshirts, had started destroying entire villages hoping to end partisan violence, sometimes conducting mass executions of all men at a particular site. Nonetheless, the partisans stepped up their attacks and launched a paramilitary campaign against the Nazis. As a result by April 1945 the partisans had taken control of several northern Italian towns and cities; shortly thereafter, Germany surrendered to Allied forces.

The Mafia. The Mafia is a crime organization that began in the Middle Ages in Sicily, where wealthy landowners established their own armies to protect their property. Some of the men in these armies soon became so powerful that they were able to terrorize the landowners, extorting money from them in exchange for their protection. The men then banded together to form a society, the Mafia, with a hierarchical structure and a rigid code of behavior. As part of this code, Mafia members and those they protected were forbidden from contacting law-enforcement authorities for any reason whatsoever. If a person wanted justice, they had to seek it from the Mafia, which would not hesitate to kill to avenge a death.

Gradually the Mafia spread from Sicily to Italy, where in the 1920s the government of Benito Mussolini tried to destroy the group by jailing thousands of its members, or mafiosi. At the end of World War II, however, these prisoners were released by U.S. officials, whereupon they were free to strengthen their crime organization—which by this time had also spread to the United States via Italian immigrants.

The Red Brigades. The Red Brigades (BR) was a left-wing secret organization that committed terrorist acts in Italy for more than three decades. Upon its founding in 1969, its main goals were to stage a violent revolution, forcing the creation of an Italian state that was based on Marxism and Leninism and to cut ties between Italy and the Western world. The group's first acts, in 1970, were firebombings of factories and other buildings in the city of Milan; the following year, the group turned to kidnapping businessmen and public officials, and then to assassinating such people. For example, the group assassinated the former prime minister of Italy, Aldo Moro, in 1978 and kidnapped a U.S. general, James Dozier, in 1981. By the late 1980s, however, the Italian police had managed to arrest many of the group's most prominent members, and as a result it stopped its attacks, though its few remaining members continue to support other terrorist groups.

SEE ALSO: Mafia, the; Mussolini, Benito; Nazi terrorism; Red Brigades

Jacobins

The Jacobins were members of a French political group, the Jacobin Club (formally known as the Society of the Friends of the Constitution from 1789 to 1792 and the Society of the Jacobins, Friends of Liberty and Equality from 1792 to 1794), that engaged in terrorism during a period of the French Revolution called the Reign of Terror. The group was formed prior to the revolution by radical politicians and other learned men opposed to the aristocracy. Though this group did not participate in the overthrow of King Louis XVI in August 1792, it did call for the king's execution and the removal of members of the Girondins (moderate republicans) from the Legislative Assembly of the new revolutionary government in early 1793, and by the middle of that year some of its members had become agents of the Reign of Terror, during which anyone who had once supported the monarchy or opposed the new government was executed. This was particularly true in Paris, where a Jacobin named Maximilien de Robespierre operated as a member of France's Committee of Public Safety to eliminate France's enemies. There were anywhere from five thousand to eight thousand individual groups, or clubs, of Jacobins in cities throughout France, with the Parisian club being the most powerful and the most involved in terrorism. Throughout France, however, Jacobins spied on people to determine whether or not they were loyal to France, raised money and supplies for the army, and helped keep order at the local level, where many of them ended up supplanting city leaders. When Robespierre fell from power in 1794, the Parisian club was closed; over the next few years, others were closed as well, and the government forbade them to reopen. Nonetheless a few clubs continued to operate at the local level.

SEE ALSO: Reign of Terror; Robespierre, Maximilien

Jaish-e Mohammed (JEM)

Established in the late 1990s by Islamic fundamentalist Maulana Masood Azhar, Jaish-e Mohammed (JEM), or "The Army of Muhammad," is a Pakistani Islamic group that commits terrorist acts in support of its goal to reunite Kashmir, now controlled by India, with Pakistan. To this end the group has attacked Indian Army forces and government officials in Kashmir as well as civilian targets in India. For example, in July 2000 JEM members fired a rocket grenade at the office of Kashmir's chief minister, and in December 2000 they threw grenades at a bus stop and a marketplace in India, killing over two dozen people. In October 2001 a JEM suicide bomber killed more than thirty people at a political gathering in Kashmir. In 2002 JEM began attacking Pakistani targets, believing that their government had become a puppet of the United States. Some terrorism experts suspect that the group has also been involved in violent attacks on Americans in Pakistan, including the kidnapping and murder of *Wall Street Journal* reporter Daniel Pearl, along with a similar group, Jamaat ul-Fuqra. Many of JEM's members previously belonged to another terrorist group founded by Azhar, Harakat ul-Mujahideen, which had the same goal of Kashmir-Pakistan reunification and, during the early 1990s kidnapped several Americans and Britons in India and Kashmir. After Azhar was arrested in 1994, Harakat ul-Mujahideen hijacked an Indian Airlines jet, landed in Afghanistan, and swapped its 155 passengers and crew for Azhar. He continues to head JEM today, although in October 2001 the group took a new name, Tehrik-al-Firquan, as part of a legal maneuver to keep its financial assets from being seized by the United States, Great Britain, and Pakistan.

SEE ALSO: Jamaat ul-Fuqra; Pearl, Daniel

Jamaat ul-Fuqra (Community of the Impoverished)

Established in the late 1970s in Pakistan by Sheik Mubarak Ali Gilani, Jamaat ul-Fuqra (Community of the Impoverished) is an Islamic group that commits terrorist acts, including murder and arson, in support of its goal to reunite Kashmir, now controlled by India, with Pakistan. In this way, it is similar to another group devoted to Kashmir-Pakistan reunification, Jaish-e Mohammed (JEM). However, whereas JEM primarily operates in India, Pakistan, and Kashmir, Jamaat ul-Fuqra primarily operates in the United States, most often targeting Hindus and Muslims whom they believe have not stayed true to their religion or their people. Terrorism experts suspect that Jamaat ul-Fuqra has killed at least thirteen men and firebombed several temples and other buildings for this reason. Because of its emphasis on U.S. missions, in the 1980s the group began establishing military compounds in remote areas of the country where members could train, make bombs, and stockpile weaponry. During this period, the group came to the attention of federal authorities, and in 1992 several members were indicted on various charges, including murder and arson. In 2001 more members were arrested for having illegal weapons and for engaging in workers' compensation fraud to finance their activities. Federal authorities now know that Jamaat ul-Fuqra has ties to a group called Muslims of the Americas, led by Sheik Mubarak Ali Gilani, who was suspected of being involved in the kidnapping and murder of *Wall Street Journal* reporter Daniel Pearl in Pakistan. (Gilani was arrested for the crime but later released for lack of evidence, and in 2002 another Islamic militant, Ahmed Omar Sheikh, was convicted of the murder.) At the time of his murder, Pearl was trying to find out whether Jamaat ul-Fuqra had any ties to Richard Reid, also known as "the Shoe Bomber," an al Qaeda member who tried to blow up an American Airlines plane in 2001.

SEE ALSO: Jaish-e Mohammed; Pearl, Daniel; Reid, Richard

Japan

The history of Japan is riddled with incidents of terrorism, much of it connected to gangs and crime organizations like the Yakuza (sometimes referred to as the Japanese Mafia). In terms of terrorism that is politically based, however, much of the terrorism associated with Japan has been related either to World War II or to two Japanese terrorist groups, the Japanese Red Army (JRA) and Aum Shinrikyō. In regard to the war, the Japanese engaged in bioterrorism when they attempted to decimate the Chinese by delivering plague-ridden fleas to Chinese towns via air drops of flea-ridden wheat, but they were also the victims of violence when the United States attacked them with atom bombs. As for the two terrorist groups, the Japanese anarchists of the JRA operated outside of Japan from the 1970s to the 1990s (it is now defunct) and is primarily known for engaging in airplane hijackings and embassy attacks, while Aum Shinrikyō operated inside the country and is best known for a 1995 sarin gas attack on the Japanese subway.

SEE ALSO: bomb, atom; Aum Shinrikyō; bioterrorism; Hiroshima; Japanese Red Army; Yakuza, the

Japanese Red Army (JRA)

The Japanese Red Army (JRA) emerged in Japan in the 1960s as one of many student groups protesting the Vietnam War and the Japanese government's relationship with the United States. By 1969 the group had turned from political protest to terrorism while embracing the Communist movement, and in March 1970 six of its members hijacked a Japan Airlines jet, surrendering its passengers and crew only after the plane landed in Communist North Korea. After this, a few other JRA members decided to leave Japan as well, and in 1971 they traveled to Lebanon to offer their support to the Popular Front for the Liberation of Palestine (PFLP). In the 1970s this branch of the JRA, which was led by a woman named Fusako Shigenobu, was involved in numerous terrorist actions in support of the Palestine cause, including airplane hijackings, an attack on a French embassy in the Netherlands, an attack on an American and a Swedish consulate in Malaysia, an attack on a Shell Oil facility in Singapore, and a massacre at the Tel Aviv, Israel, airport in which twenty-

three people waiting in a terminal were gunned down and seventy-six others were injured. All of the embassy attacks involved the taking of hostages who were later released in exchange for the release of various JRA members from prison. The JRA also received money in exchange for hostages, in both the Netherlands embassy attack and a 1977 hijacking of a Japanese Airlines jet after it left the Bombay, India, airport. Nonetheless, the JRA had difficulty sustaining itself financially, and the group lost members to internal disputes and to imprisonment. For example, in 1972 fourteen members were killed by more militant JRA members, and in 1973 one member was arrested (along with several PFLP members) after hijacking a Japanese airplane during its flight from Amsterdam to Tokyo, then landing it in Libya, blowing it up, and surrendering to Libyan authorities. During the 1980s and '90s, several of the group's key members were arrested for such crimes as smuggling and the possession of bomb-making components. By this time, the group had no more than forty active members, most operating out of a base in Lebanon, as well as about one hundred sympathizers in Japan. In 1997 Lebanon deported several JRA members to Japan, and in 2000 Shigenobu was arrested for terrorist activities after entering Japan using a false passport. The following year the JRA, which by then had less than a dozen members, officially dissolved.

SEE ALSO: Popular Front for the Liberation of Palestine

Jemaah Islamiyah

Jemaah Islamiyah (the Islamic Group) was the name taken by a cell of the al Qaeda terrorist group located in Singapore. Another cell, based in Malaysia, called itself

The Jewish Defense League (JDL), and their founder, Rabbi Meir Kahane, rally together at one of many protests. © BETTMANN/CORBIS

the Kumpulan Militan Malaysia. Members of both cells, and another cell in the Philippines, were arrested in Singapore in December 2001 and January 2002, right before launching attacks on various targets connected to the U.S. military and American, British, Australian, and Israeli corporations in Singapore; the cells were betrayed by an informant in Afghanistan, where its members attended al Qaeda terrorist-training camps.

SEE ALSO: al Qaeda

Jewish Defense League (JDL)

The Jewish Defense League (JDL) was founded in 1968 in Brooklyn, New York, to defend elderly Jews in the area from being attacked on the streets. Although its founder, Meir Kahane, was an orthodox rabbi, the group did not hesitate to use

violence to combat violence. Soon, however, it decided to expand its activities to include the cause of Russian Jews in the Soviet Union, where the government was not allowing Jews to immigrate to Israel. To call attention to this situation, in 1969 the JDL began planting bombs at places in the United States that were connected to the Soviet Union, such as a Russian mission and an office promoting trade with the Soviet Union. They also bombed offices and private residences of people with ties to the American Arab Anti-Discrimination Committee (ADC) and to men they suspected of having been Nazi war criminals. Some of these bombings caused serious injuries and deaths; for example, a letter bomb sent to an office in California in 1980 killed a secretary, and the bombing of an ADC office in Massachusetts in 1985 injured two policemen. As a result of such activities, in the 1980s the U.S. government dubbed the JDL one of the most active and violent terrorist groups in America. By this time, Meir Kahane had gone to Israel to establish his own political party, Kach, and two offshoots of the JDL soon formed there: Kach (Only Thus) and Kahane Chai (Kahane Lives). Both of these groups, whose aim is to eliminate all Arabs from Israel, remain active, and both have supporters in the United States and Europe.

The JDL remains active as well. In 2001, two members of the group were arrested before carrying out bombing attacks on Islamic centers in the United States, including the King Fahd Mosque in Culver City, California; they were also planning to bomb the office of a U.S. congressman of Arab descent, Darrell Issa. During the 1990s, however, the JDL was nearly inactive, possibly as a result of Kahane's being assassinated in 1990 by a Muslim, El Sayyid Nosair, who was angry over the JDL's anti-Arab activities.

SEE ALSO: Israel; Kach Movement, the

jihad

In the holy book of the Islamic faith, the Quran, the term *jihad* refers to two kinds of sacred struggle: one is within the self, as the individual tries to determine which actions would be in keeping with the will of God, and the other is with others, to defend the faith and the faithful from attack. Islamic extremists, however, have interpreted *jihad* as a holy war against nonbelievers, seeing *jihad* as a justification for committing unprovoked violence from an offensive rather than a defensive position. For example, some radical Muslims have declared a *jihad* against Westerners, whereby Islamic clerics have called upon the faithful to kill any Westerners they come across, even innocent civilians.

SEE ALSO: Islamic extremists

Justinian II
(ca. 669–711)

A Byzantine emperor who inherited the throne in September 685 when his father, Emperor Constantine IV, died, Justinian II used fear and violence to keep his subjects in line while forcing them to pay him exorbitant amounts of money. Consequently in 695 his people rebelled and removed him from the throne, whereupon he was banished to Cherson, on the Crimean Peninsula, after having his nose hacked off. Justinian subsequently escaped to the Khazars (a confederation of tribes in a region north of the Black Sea), where he married the sister of the khan, or ruler, there. However, when he learned that the khan was plotting to kill him, Justinian went to live with the khan of another kingdom, Bulgar, and with this ruler's help, in 705 he captured the city of Constantinople and again became an emperor. Once again, though, Justinian created a climate of fear, committing mass executions in order to enact revenge against those who had opposed him. As a result, in 711 his people again rebelled, and this time their new emperor, Bardanes (also known as Philippicus), made sure that Justinian would never rule again—by killing him and his family.

Kach Movement, the

Established by Rabbi Meir Kahane in the late 1980s, the Kach Movement—more commonly known simply as Kach—was an anti-Arab group dedicated to Zionism (the creation of a Jewish state in Palestine) and to the expulsion of all Arabs from lands that, according to the Old Testament of the Bible, had once belonged to the Jews: Israel, the West Bank, Gaza, and the Golan Heights. At first the group functioned as a political party, and Kahane earned a seat in Israel's Parliament. But after Kahane was murdered in New York in 1990 by a fundamentalist Muslim, Kach became a terrorist organization. At this point, its members began calling it Kahane Chai, or "Kahane Lives" in Hebrew, and Kahane's son, Binyamin, stepped forward to become its new leader. Among Kahane Chai's first acts was to threaten to kill several prominent Israelis and Palestinians who were promoting peace between Arabs and Jews. Its members also attacked Palestinians in the West Bank, killing four in 1993. A year earlier the group also attempted to kill a Palestinian leader, Faisal Husseini, in Jerusalem, and subsequently exploded a grenade in a marketplace there as well, in addition to detonating bombs near the French embassy in Tel Aviv, Israel. In 1994 a Kach member named Baruch Goldstein gunned down nearly thirty Palestinian worshippers and injured over two hundred more at the Ibrahimi Mosque in Hebron, a city on the West Bank occupied by Arabs; this mosque is located on a Jewish religious site known as the Tomb of the Patriarchs. Afterward Israel condemned the attack and arrested Kahane Chai leaders and former Kach members who, speaking in support of the massacre, called for further attacks on Palestinians. Nonetheless, Kahane Chai continued to operate throughout. the 1990s, even after being banned from Israel. The group still exists—in Hebron and perhaps elsewhere as well—though terrorism experts do not know how many members it currently has.

SEE ALSO: Israel; Zionism

Khmer Rouge (Party of Democratic Kampuchea)

A political party of radical Communists, the Khmer Rouge came to power in Cambodia in 1975, after which its leader, Pol Pot, engaged in terrorism as part of his plan to convert the country into an agricultural society. To this end, he sent thousands of city dwellers, including the old and the sick, into the countryside, where they were forced to labor in fields and as builders of agricultural villages. Thousands of these people died from overwork, malnutrition, starvation, dysentery, or disease, or they were executed for refusing to work. Also executed were people who opposed the new government, as well as academics, teachers, journalists, engineers, and other intellectuals and professionals—even physicians—because the Khmer Rouge felt that such people did not belong in an agricultural society. As a result of such poli-

A Khmer Rouge soldier demonstrates his dedication to the radical Communist political party in Phnom Penh, Cambodia, in 1975. CHRISTOPH FROEHDER. © AP IMAGES

cies, the Khmer Rouge was responsible for over 2 million deaths between 1975 and 1979, when Vietnam invaded Cambodia and drove the Khmer Rouge from power. The group continued to exist for another twenty years, however, though it split into two factions, one that remained loyal to Pol Pot (who was arrested when his government was overthrown) and the other that expressed anti–Pol Pot sentiments. Both of these factions tried to regain control of the country through guerrilla warfare against government troops in several provinces. The Khmer Rouge also attacked ethnic Vietnamese civilians, along with Western tourists and foreigners who worked for Cambodian businesses. For example, in July 1994 the Khmer Rouge kidnapped several train passengers who were from Western countries; in January 1995 the group attacked a sightseeing convoy,

killing an American tourist and wounding her husband; and in March 1996 Khmer Rouge guerrillas kidnapped twenty-six men who were disposing of mines near the Angkor War temple, along with their British boss. To counter this violence, the new Cambodian government offered amnesty to any Khmer Rouge fighter who turned in his weapons; during the 1990s many complied, and according to terrorism experts, by 1999 the group had dissolved. (In 1998 Pol Pot died of an illness suffered in prison.)

SEE ALSO: Cambodian killing fields

Khobar Towers attack

In June 1996 a group of Islamic terrorists used a truck bomb to attack the Khobar Towers in Dharan, Saudi Arabia, which were being used as a barracks for approxi-

The aftermath of the Islamic terrorist attacks on the Khobar Towers in Dharan, Saudi Arabia, in 1996, which killed 2,000 members of the U.S. Air Force. AP IMAGES

mately two thousand members of the U.S. Air Force. In executing the attack, the terrorists parked and then abandoned a tanker truck filled with a high-grade plastic explosive, C-4 (Composite-4), beside one of the high-rise towers. The resulting explosion killed nineteen people and injured over five hundred more. Because the military personnel housed at the towers had been flying patrols out of a nearby airbase to enforce a no-fly zone over Iraq (a consequence of the Persian Gulf War), the U.S. government at first assumed that Iraqis had committed the bombing. A subsequent investigation, however, determined that the terrorist group Hezbollah had instead been involved, and that the explosives had come from its headquarters in Beirut, Lebanon, though most of the bombers had been Saudis. These bombers were also Shiite Muslims, and because Iran

is a Shiite Muslim country that supports terrorism, some terrorism experts believe that the Iranian government was involved in the bombing as well, but this has never been proved. However, the Saudi government imprisoned eleven people for participating in the bombing. (Several other suspects remain at large.)

SEE ALSO: Hezbollah; Iran

Khomeini, Ayatollah Ruhollah (1902–1989)

As a high-ranking Shiite leader, or ayatollah, with both religious and administrative authority over the people of his Islamic sect, Ruhollah Khomeini took control of Iran after its shah was deposed in 1979, then proceeded to vilify Western secularism in general and the United States in particular. His regime, known as the Islamic Republic, supported terrorist acts against Western nations, such as the 1979 attack on the American embassy in Iran, and encouraged suicide bombing against Iraqis during the Iran-Iraq War of 1980–88. A religious zealot, Khomeini came to power after spending many years in exile (in Turkey from 1963 to 1964, in Iraq from 1964 to 1978, and in France from 1978 to 1979) because of its outspoken opposition to the shah, Reza Pahlavi, whom he believed had not been following the Islamic faith properly. Once he became ruler of Iran, the ayatollah used his interpretations of the Islamic holy book, the Quran, as a guide for all of the country's political and social policies.

SEE ALSO: embassy bombings; Iran; Iraq.

Kidnappings

Terrorists engage in kidnappings primarily to acquire money for their cause, to gain certain concessions related to their cause, or to attract media attention. This attention might be intended to publicize their grievances, or it might be used for propaganda purposes, in order to convince like-minded people to join their cause. It might also be used to instill fear in the international community or to affect the global economy. For example, kidnappings of Western tourists in certain parts of Africa have frightened away foreign visitors and have been detrimental to the tourism industry there. The concessions demanded in exchange for the release of hostages often include the release of the kidnappers' associates or other terrorists imprisoned in the countries of the hostages. In some cases, however, the hostage negotiations result in a nation providing weapons to people it would not normally arm. For example, in 1985 the U.S. government secretly sold weapons to Iran so that the Ira-

nian government would work to convince Shiite terrorists in Lebanon to release a group of American hostages they held there. (The United States subsequently sent the profits from this, sale, also secretly, to Contras guerrillas in Nicaragua.) After this crisis was over, though, the Shiite terrorists immediately kidnapped more Americans. This consequence is the justification that many nations give in refusing to negotiate with terrorists. It is also the reason that some nations, particularly Israel, deal quickly and harshly with hostage crises. For example, in 1976 it conducted a military operation, the Entebbe raid, to rescue hostages from terrorists at the Entebbe Airport in Uganda. The terrorists, most of whom were members of an organization called the Popular Front for the Liberation of Palestine (PFLP), said they would release their 106 Jewish hostages only if Israel released 53 men held as terrorists in Israeli prisons. Instead, Israeli military commandos attacked the airplane on which the hostages were being held and rescued all but three of them, gunning down all of the terrorists in the process. Similarly, in 1996, after the terrorist group Tupac Amaru Revolutionary Movement (MRTA) took over 600 people hostage at the Japanese embassy in Lima, Peru, the Peruvian military stormed the embassy, released the hostages, and killed all of the terrorists. In this case, however, the reaction was slow; the hostages were held for four months before their rescue. Far more often, hostages wait for a rescue that never comes. For example, American journalist Terry Anderson was held in Lebanon for 2,454 days (from March 16, 1985, to December 4, 1991) before his kidnappers, who were Muslims connected to the groups Hezbollah and Islamic Jihad, released him because some Muslims they had wanted freed from prison were indeed let go for unrelated reasons.

SEE ALSO: hijackings, aircraft; Contras; embassy bombings; Entebbe raid; hostages; Iran

Kim Jong II
(1942–)

As the leader of North Korea, Kim Jong II came into conflict with the international community in 2006 when he began test-firing missiles to assess their ability to carry nuclear weapons. At that time Kim insisted that he was close to having such weapons, and that they were needed to defend his country. The leaders of several other governments, however, expressed the fear that he would use them as offensive rather than defensive weapons, and they imposed economic and trade sanctions against North Korea in order to force Kim to give up his pursuit of nuclear missiles. However, the international community's past attempts to pressure Kim over his policies, such as human rights violations against his own people, have been unsuccessful. Lacking concern for the plight of ordinary citizens, he has engaged in policies that have thrown the majority of his populace into poverty and starvation. He has also sometimes attacked South Korea, with which he has been in conflict since 1950.

SEE ALSO: bombs, types of

King David Hotel bombing

On July 22, 1946, terrorists from the Jewish group Irgun Zvai Leumi, led by Menachem Begin (who later was prime minister of Israel from 1977 to 1983), bombed the King David Hotel in Jerusalem. To commit the attack, the terrorists disguised themselves dressed as waiters in order to bring seven milk churns filled with explosives into a hotel restaurant. In all, twenty-eight British, forty-one Arabs, and seventeen Jews died in the bombing, while 46 people were injured. At the time, the hotel was being used as the headquarters for British government and military personnel. The British had occupied Palestine since just after World War I, but during the 1930s the Arabs and Jews had been fighting with one another to such an extent that British forces were having trouble keeping the peace. Consequently in planning their attack, the terrorists hoped that it would drive the British out of Palestine, thereby giving the Jews an opportunity to seize control of the region. Instead, the British responded by limiting the freedom of the Jews, engaging in mass searches and arrests, instigating curfews, and establishing roadblocks, and it executed three members of the Irgun who had been involved in the incident. Then in July 1947 the Irgun hanged two British sergeants and sent photographs of the scene to the British media. This outraged the British public, and the following year, in May 1948, the British did indeed pull out of Palestine.

SEE ALSO: Begin, Menachem; Irgun Zvai Leumi

Kosovo

A province of Serbia and once a part of Yugoslavia, Kosovo has experienced violence between its ethnic Albanians and its Serbs for centuries. (Albania borders Kosovo on the west, Serbia on the north and east.) In medieval times, Kosovo was the center not only of the Serbian empire but of the Serbian culture. Then in 1389 the Ottoman Turks captured the region and crushed the empire, and Muslims from Albania began moving into Kosovo, forcing the Serbians, who were Orthodox Christian, from their native lands. By the early 1980s, nine-tenths of Kosovo's population was ethnic Albanian. Nonetheless, the Serbs believed that Kosovo was still rightfully theirs, and in the late 1980s Serbia, then a republic of Yugoslavia, took control of the government of the province. In response, in 1992 the Albanians voted to secede from both Serbia and Yugoslavia, but the Serb-dominated Yugoslavian government refused to allow this. Instead it strengthened its forces in the region. Shortly thereafter, however, another of Yugoslavia's provinces, Bosnia, declared its independence, whereupon Bosnia and Serbia went to war. In 1995 a peace accord settled this conflict, but it did not resolve the situation in Kosovo. Consequently the following year, some of the Albanian Muslims who had been involved in the Bosnian war formed a terrorist group, the Kosovo Liberation Army (KLA), dedicated to breaking Kosovo away from Serbia. (By this time, Yugoslavia's Communist government had collapsed.) In 1997 the KLA began attacking the Serbian police, who responded in kind, and soon many Serbian and Albanian civilians had joined the fight. In response, Serbian security forces began arresting and torturing Albanians, or in some cases killing them outright. Many of these victims were innocent of any wrongdoing, and their persecution increased support for Kosovo's independence. At the same time, approximately two hundred thousand Albanians fled Kosovo, putting a strain on the resources of surrounding countries. Consequently in early 1999, the member nations of NATO (North Atlantic Treaty Organization), including the United States and Russia, insisted that the Serbian security forces in Kosovo be replaced with an international peacekeeping force; when the Serbian forces refused to relinquish control, NATO launched a campaign of air strikes against them. During the bombings, thousands more Albanians left Kosovo, but they returned once NATO was victorious. With the conflict over and United Nations and Russian forces installed to keep the peace, Albanian nationalist political parties took control of the region, where Serbs now number less than 5 percent. However, Kosovo is still not independent.

SEE ALSO: Bosnian genocide; Kosovo Liberation Army

Kosovo Liberation Army (KLA)

Formed in 1996, the Kosovo Liberation Army (KLA) is an ethnic Albanian nationalist group that has used terrorism in a war for the independence of Kosovo, a province of Serbia (which was once a republic within the former Yugoslavia). Kosovo was a part of the Serbian empire in medieval times, but after the Turks captured the region in the fourteenth century, Albanian Muslims gradually supplanted the Serbian Christians living there. As a result, only about 10 percent of the people in Kosovo are Serbs; nonetheless it is controlled by Serbs. In 1989, after the newly elected president of Serbia, Slobodan Milosovic, decreed that all public officials in Kosovo should be Serbian, an Albanian nationalist movement began to develop, promoting the idea that all Serbs should be driven out of Kosovo. In 1997 this nationalism led to fighting between the KLA and Serbian police, and soon many Serbian and Albanian civilians had joined the fight. In response, Serbian security forces began arresting and torturing Albanians, or in some cases killing them outright. Many of these victims were innocent of any wrongdoing, and their persecution increased support for the KLA; in 1998 the group gained thousands of new members and thousands of dollars in funding as well. At the same time, approximately two hundred thousand Albanians fled Kosovo, putting a strain on the resources of surrounding countries. Consequently the international community stepped in to end the conflict. In early 1999 the member nations of NATO (North Atlantic Treaty Organization), including the United States and Russia, insisted that the Serbian security forces in Kosovo be replaced with an international peacekeeping force; when the Serbian forces refused to relinquish control, NATO launched a campaign of air strikes against them. During the bombings, thousands more Albanians left Kosovo, but they returned once NATO was victorious. With the conflict over and United Nations and Russian forces installed to keep the peace, some of the members of the KLA created Albanian nationalist political parties that now control the region, where Serbs currently number less than 5 percent. However, Kosovo is still not independent, and the KLA still exists.

SEE ALSO: Kosovo

Kropotkin, Pyot
(1842–1921)

During the late nineteenth and early twentieth centuries, Russian anarchist Pyot Kropotkin wrote extensively on the need to establish a Communist or socialist society in Russia, which was then a *monarchy*. To this end, he was an outspoken supporter of the ideas of Russian revolutionary Mikhail Bakunin, who is sometimes called the grandfather of terrorism because he advocated the use of extreme violence to effect social and political change. Kropot-

kin was a member of the nobility, but in 1867 he turned his back on his family and became a revolutionary. Shortly thereafter he joined the First International Working Men's Association, a group dedicated to inciting revolution among the working-class masses, and was arrested as an agitator. He soon escaped from prison and went to Switzerland, then to France, where he was arrested in 1883 for encouraging revolution in that country. In 1885, while imprisoned in France, he wrote *Paroles d'un revolte (Words of a Rebel)* to promote anarchism, and two years later, after serving his sentence and settling in England, he wrote *In Russian and French Prisons* to complain about his treatment in prison. His other works include *Conquest of Bread* (1892), *Fields, Factories, and Workshops* (1899), and *The Great French Revolution 1789–1793* (1909). In 1917, after the Russian revolution finally toppled the monarchy, Kropotkin went to Russia hoping to see the kind of society he had been advocating for years, but instead he discovered that those now in control of Russia, the Bolsheviks, were repressing the populace rather than treating all citizens fairly. He complained about this repressive regime, but nonetheless remained in Russia for the rest of his life.

SEE ALSO: anarchism; Bakunin, Mikhail

Ku Klux Klan

The Ku Klux Klan (KKK) is a violent right-wing, white-supremacist organization in the United States whose members have engaged in vigilantism, conducting beatings and lynchings of blacks and attacks on Jews, Catholics, and immigrants of all kinds. Founded in late 1865 or early 1866, the group was originally a fellowship of American Southerners who, in the post–Civil War era of Reconstruction, were

The Ku Klux Klan, a white-supremacist group known for their violent acts against racial and religious minorities, march in front of the Capitol building in Washington, D.C. THE LIBRARY OF CONGRESS

angry over the freeing of black slaves and attacked not only African Americans but anyone who helped them. Its first leader, or Imperial Wizard, was a former slave trader, Nathan Bedford, who also served as a general for Southern forces (the Confederacy). Under his guidance, the group soon grew to include roughly four hundred thousand members. Located in individual bands throughout the South, KKK members operated secretly at night and, while engaging in violence, hid their identity via white hoods and robes. To combat their violence, the U.S. government sent troops into areas where the KKK was active and passed a law, the Ku Klux Klan

Act (1871), establishing strict penalties for anyone supporting Klan terrorism. Shortly thereafter Bedford called for the group to disband, and it appeared to do so. However, after Reconstruction ended and Union troops were gone from the South, the Klan began operating again in secret, at the local level, targeting Jews, Roman Catholics, foreigners, and members of labor unions and left-wing groups as well as blacks, while manipulating the politics of the region to ensure that blacks were segregated from white Southern society. It was not until 1915, however, that the Klan once again became a national organization. At that time, several Klansmen met in Stone Mountain, Georgia, to create what they called the Invisible Empire, with a burning cross as its symbol. When this new incarnation of the Klan engaged in violence, its members often left a burning cross at the scene or burned the shape of a cross on lawns or buildings. In the 1920s the group had nearly 4 million members, but the economic crisis known as the Great Depression in the 1930s caused membership to drop dramatically, as did news of corruption within the organization. The group was invigorated, however, by a 1945 meeting, again in Stone Mountain, that did away with the Invisible Empire, so that the Klan no longer had a national body overseeing local activities. Instead the Klan was reorganized into a collection of regional units that acted on their own, while adhering to a single ideology. Some of these units were more violent than others, with those in Mississippi and Alabama engaging in more terrorism—in the form of beatings, bombings, shootings, and lynchings—than elsewhere, and this violence increased dramatically in response to the Civil Rights movement of the 1960s. In response, the federal government cracked down on Klan criminal activities, aggressively pursuing and prosecuting anyone associated with it, and the Klan again lost members. Still the violence continued; for example, in 1979, Klansmen killed anti-Klan demonstrators in Greensboro, North Carolina, and in 1981 the Klan was responsible for the lynching of a black teenager, Michael Donald, in Mobile, Alabama. In the 1990s the group was behind racially and ethnically motivated church burnings throughout the United States, and several Klansmen were arrested for various plots involving bombings, water poisoning, bank robberies, and assassination. Today there are over a hun-

dred Klan units still operating at the local or regional rather than the national level. Some of these groups are allied with the Christian Identity movement or with other white-supremacist groups, including neo-Nazi or neo-Confederate groups.

SEE ALSO: Christian Identity movement; neo-Nazis; racism

Kurdistan Workers Party (PKK)

The Kurdistan Workers Party (PKK) was established in 1978 by Turkish terrorist Abdullah Ocalan to fight for the creation of an independent Kurdish state in southeastern Turkey. Originally a nomadic people, the Kurds settled into a region now known as Kurdistan—which lies within the borders of Turkey, Armenia, Syria, Iran, and Iraq—after World War I. Since then, Turkey has repeatedly repressed any attempts by the Turkish Kurds to establish their independence, murdering hundreds of Kurds, many of them innocent villagers, in the process. Ocalan responded to this violence by becoming an outspoken advocate of using terrorism to force Turkey to establish a Kurdish state. To this end he called for violent revolution in his statement "The National Road to the Kurdish Revolution," and established the PKK. In 1980 he left Turkey to avoid imprisonment and, from Syria and elsewhere in the Middle East, began orchestrating PKK bombings of various Turkish targets, including government and police buildings, kidnappings of government officials, and attacks on any Kurds known to support government policies. The first PKK bombing was in 1984, after which Turkish authorities began killing Kurds believed to be involved with the PKK. The government also tracked down Ocalan; in 1999 they captured him in Africa, brought him back to Turkey, put him on trial and sen-

Two young female guerrillas of the Kurdistan Workers Party use terrorist methods to fight for an independent Kurdish state in southeastern Turkey. BURHAN OZBILISI. © AP IMAGES

tenced him to death. In 2000 the PKK, which continues to exist, ended its terrorist activities in the hopes of forestalling Ocalan's execution.

SEE ALSO: Kurds, the

Kurds, the

The Kurds are members of an ethnic group whose native lands are in a region of mountains and plateaus that lie within parts of Iran, Iraq, Syria, Turkey, and Armenia. Approximately 17 million people live in this region, which is known as Kurdistan ("Land of the Kurds"), with another roughly 12 million Kurds in Turkey. Kurds of varying numbers also live in Georgia (in central Asia), Lebanon, and parts of Iran and Syria that lie outside of Kurdistan. Prior to World War I, the Kurds had a nomadic way of life, moving through Turkey and Iran to graze their herds of goats and sheep as the seasons allowed. At the end of the war, however, boundaries were established between nations that made it impossible for the Kurds to travel freely from place to place. A 1920 postwar pact, the Treaty of Sèvres, between the Allied nations that won the war and the government of Turkey, then part of the Ottoman Empire, both abolished the empire and established Kurdistan as an autonomous state. However, when the Turkish government that agreed to the treaty was replaced with a Turkish nationalist regime, this new government refused to honor the pact, and a replacement treaty (the Treaty of Lausanne), struck in 1923, did not address the Kurdish situation. As a result, various Kurdish groups rose up to fight for independence, and from 1931 to 1932 and 1944 to 1945 they engaged in violent attacks in the Iraqi part of Kurdistan. Meanwhile the Kurds in Turkey were undergoing severe oppression at the hands of the government, which banned the Kurdish language, Kurdish clothing, and other elements of the Kurdish way of life in an attempt at cultural genocide. In Iran the government took a similar approach and persecuted Kurds for their religious beliefs. In 1970 the Iraqi government decided to grant the Kurds a limited autonomy within Iraqi lands, but the Kurds continued to demand their own independent state, preferably encompassing Kurdistan and southeastern Turkey. In the 1980s a Turkish Kurd terrorist group, the Kurdistan Workers Party (PKK), bombed various Turkish targets, including government and police buildings, kidnapped government officials, and attacked any Kurds known to support government policies. In response to these activities, Turkish authorities killed Kurds believed to be involved with the PKK. By this time, Iraq had also lost tolerance for the Kurds, who were engaged in an armed insurrection for independence. Consequently in 1987 Iraq's leader, Saddam Hussein, charged his cousin, Ali Hassan al-Majid, with stamping out the Kurdish threat in northern Iraq. Al-Majid responded with a campaign of genocide, during which he dropped chemical weapons on Kurdish villages, then killed any males who survived. He killed male Kurds elsewhere as well, and forced the women and children off their lands. As a result of this campaign, roughly 2.5 million Kurds were driven from Iraq, and fifty thousand to one hundred thousand Kurds died. The Kurds in Turkey, Syria, and Iran have also been subjected to forced migrations and massacres, though not on the scale of the violence in Iraq. Nonetheless they continue to call for their own independent state, and Kurdish rebels are particularly active in southeastern Turkey, even though the PKK is no longer engaging in terrorist attacks.

SEE ALSO: genocide; Hussein, Saddam; Kurdistan Workers Party

Lashkar-e-Taiba

Established in the early 1990s from within a Sunni religious group (the Markaz-ud-Dawa-wal-Irshad, or MDI) opposed to U.S. missionary activities in the Middle East, the terrorist group Lashkar-e-Taiba (Army of the Righteous) is comprised of militant Muslims who want Pakistan to control two states, Jammu and Kashmir, that lie along the borders of Pakistan and India (the former primarily Muslim, the latter Hindu and Sikh), both of which have laid claim to the states. To this end, Lashkar-e-Taiba has attempted to drive non-Muslims out of Jammu and Kashmir, terrorizing them and killing hundreds of innocent civilians, including children; it has also attacked Hindus in other parts of India. For example, in 1998 the group murdered twenty-five Hindus at a wedding in the Doda region, and in 2000 it killed over one hundred Hindus in various attacks and engaged in kidnappings as well. Lashkar-e-Taiba plans such operations from bases in Pakistan, Kashmir, and Afghanistan, where it has been connected to terrorist Osama bin Laden. However, since the beginning of 2002, the group has been officially banned from Pakistan, which was forced to take this action in response to pressure from the international community after a Lashkar-e-Taiba bombing at Parliament buildings in New Delhi, India.

SEE ALSO: Afghanistan, U.S. bombings in; bin laden, Osama; Pakistan

Latin America, terrorism in

From the 1950s to the 1980s, Latin America experienced Marxist revolutionary movements, most inspired by the Cuban Revolution or by Marxist revolutionary Che Guevara, that brought with them guerrilla warfare and terrorism in both rural and urban areas and included extreme anti-U.S. sentiments. In response to these movements and to other threats to Latin American governments, which were often backed by the United States, state authorities engaged in terrorism as well. In the early 1980s, for example, the government of Honduras suppressed any opposition to its policies, creating torture centers and death squads to deal with dissenters; hundreds of politicians, students, academics, and unionists were killed during this period. In the 1970s, under a military government, Argentina engaged in similar activities in response to terrorism instigated by a group called Montoneros, creating detention camps where tens of thousands were tortured and killed. Death squads terrorized civilians in El Salvador, Guatemala, and Chile as well. During the 1980s death squads in El Salvador were in response to a Marxist revolutionary movement that threatened to overthrow the government, which was backed by the United States, while the death squads in Guatemala were in response to a civil war and were part of a government campaign that involved not only mass executions but the razing of entire villages. In Chile a government death squad known as the Avengers of the

Martyrs killed over three thousand people. Today most of the terrorism in Latin America is in Colombia, where the government is under threat from leftist rebels, and to a lesser extent in Peru, where the remnants of two organizations, Shining Path and the Tupac Amaru Revolutionary Movement (MRTA), still operate on a small scale. Colombia also has a great deal of violence associated with the drug trade. In the 1980s two drug cartels (syndicates), Cali and Medellin, were the predominant cocaine dealers in the world, and they killed thousands of people—police, judges, soldiers, politicians, journalists, and others—in order to maintain their activities. These cartels now no longer exist, but the smaller criminal organizations that replaced them continue to engage in narcoterrorism, though to a much lesser extent and without calling attention to themselves.

SEE ALSO: Argentina, terrorism in; Chile, terrorism in; Colombia, terrorism in; Guatemala, terrorism in; Guevara, Che; Montoneros; Shining Path, the; Tupac Amaru Revolutionary Movement

Law of Hostages

Enacted by the Executive Directory of the French government in 1799, near the end of the French Revolution, the Law of Hostages allowed local authorities to identify "hostages" who would be held responsible for various crimes committed by others (usually relatives) in their community. Once identified, the hostages would be imprisoned and might be forced to pay fines, to give up their land, or to be expelled from the country; hostages who tried to escape might be executed. The Executive Directory hoped that this law would restore order in its provinces; however, local authorities were reluctant to enact such

serious punishments against their friends and neighbors, so the Law of Hostages was largely ineffective. Nonetheless the law was used again in 1871, by the socialist government that ruled Paris from March to May of that year. This government, known as the Paris Commune, massacred all of its hostages, including the archbishop of Paris, when the city was invaded by national forces.

SEE ALSO: hostages

Lawrence, T.E. (Lawrence of Arabia) (1888–1935)

Also known as Lawrence of Arabia, T(homas) E(dward) Lawrence was a British archaeological scholar and military strategist who, in 1916, became involved in an Arab uprising against the Turks and eventually stepped in to lead Arab guerrilla forces, in the hopes of helping them create an Arab nation. Lawrence's involvement began at the outset of World War I. By this time, he had visited the Middle East several times, spoke Arabic, and was an expert map-maker, so the Map Department of the War Office in London, England, hired him to go to Sinai and make a map that would help with British military attacks in the region. In 1914, after enlisting in the British army, Lawrence was sent to Cairo, Egypt, then a base for Great Britain's military operations in the Middle East, to work on other maps of the Middle East, to record militarily useful information provided by spies and prisoners of war, and to create a handbook on the Turkish army. In 1916 he accompanied a British diplomat, Sir Ronald Storrs, to Arabia, where they consulted with Arabs who had declared that they were in revolt against the Turks. When he returned to

Cairo, Lawrence convinced his superiors to provide these Arabs with military and financial aid in support of their cause, arguing that it would weaken Germany's influence in the Middle East. (Turkey was then a German ally.) He then went to help the Arab guerrillas personally, acting not only as their liaison with British headquarters in Cairo but also providing them with valuable information and advice related to military strategy. As a result, the Arab guerrillas were successful in taking the cities of Aqaba, Jordan, and Jerusalem, Israel, in 1917 and Damascus, Syria, in 1918. By this time, though, infighting among the Arabs had convinced Lawrence that they would never create a unified nation, and Great Britain and France would not allow this to happen in any case. Consequently Lawrence, who was already in poor health due to the hardships of his military campaigns, fell into despair and refused to accept the Distinguished Service Order and other honors that the British government tried to bestow on him after the war. In later years, he served as an adviser on Arab affairs, served in the Royal Air Force under an assumed name (John Hume Ross), served in the Royal Tank Corps under the name T.E. Shaw, and wrote several books, including *The Seven Pillars of Wisdom* (1926) about his experiences in the Middle East. (During World War I, war correspondent Lowell Thomas also publicized Lawrence's exploits in the Middle East.) Lawrence died in a motorcycle accident in 1935, at the age of 46.

SEE ALSO: guerrilla warfare

Lebanon

Lebanon is home to both Muslims and Christians of various sects and denominations, as well as hundreds of thousands of refugees from Palestine, and it is adjacent to both Israel and Syria, two countries whose people loath one another. Consequently Lebanon has long been a place of conflict, with Shiite and Sunni Muslims attacking one another, Muslims attacking Christians, and Palestinian terrorists using Lebanon as a base of operations from which to attack Israelis and others. In addition, Lebanon has strong ties to Syria, a longtime supporter of international terrorism, because in ancient times Lebanon's lands were a part of Syria; consequently Syria has permanently stationed thousands of its troops in Lebanon.

The southern part of Lebanon has long been controlled by a Lebanese Islamic militant group, Hezbollah. Ever since the early 1980s, this group has engaged in or been linked to numerous terrorist attacks, such as the 1985 hijacking of TWA Flight 847. (After landing in Beirut, Lebanon to refuel, the hijackers flew the plane to Algiers, released some of their hostages, flew back to Beirut, picked up several more armed terrorists, and negotiated the release of the remaining hostages in exchange for several demands, including the release of some imprisoned Shiite Muslims.) In the summer of 2006, Hezbollah waged a thirty-four-day war with Israel, and afterward, the United Nations established an embargo on Lebanon intended to keep Hezbollah from rearming. This conflict made it clear that the democratically elected government of Lebanon, which was backed by the United States, was weak in comparison to Hezbollah. In fact, in November 2006, the U.S. government accused Syria, Iran, and the terrorist group Hezbollah of trying to topple Palestine's government. U.S. officials also accused Syria and Iran of violating the embargo, and Syria of being involved in the assassination of Rafik Hariri, a Lebanese politician who was trying to lessen Syria's influence in Lebanon. In response, Hezbollah's leader, Sheik Hassan Nasrallah, demanded that Lebanon's prime minister, Fuad Saniora, establish a cabinet that included Islamic militants and their allies in large enough numbers to give them veto power. Meanwhile Syria and Iran denied the U.S. government's accusations.

SEE ALSO: Hezbollah; hijackings, aircraft; Iran; Syria

left-wing terrorism, U.S.

In the United States, left-wing terrorism most commonly relates to animal rights, environmentalism, labor activism, antiwar activism, and antigovernment movements that arise from left-wing ideology. In addition, although the civil rights movement was largely nonviolent, a few groups—most notably the Black Panthers and other entities within the Black Power and Black Liberation movements—did assault police and other government authorities, and many civil rights protests turned into riots. The same was the case for antiwar activism during the Vietnam War. For example, in 1968 members of the Students for a Democratic Society (SDS) antiwar group seized several buildings at Columbia University in New York and then rioted when, five days later, police tried to break up the demonstration; by the time order was restored, roughly 150 people had been hurt and over 700 people were arrested. An offshoot of the SDS, the Weatherman group, also engaged in violent confrontations, as well as acts of vandalism, street fights, and bombings that targeted symbols of government and corporate au-

thority, such as National Guard facilities and the headquarters of the Gulf Oil corporation in Pittsburgh, Pennsylvania. Another left-wing terrorist group, the Symbionese Liberation Army, targeted the Hearst Corporation in 1974 by kidnapping a member of the Hearst family, Patty Hearst, and demanding that the corporation distribute food to the poor in exchange for her release. (After the food was distributed, however, they failed to release her.) Beginning in the 1970s, terrorist groups involved in the animal-rights movement, such as the Animal Liberation Front (ALF), have bombed facilities that use animals to test medicines and cosmetics and attacked researchers involved in such work, while terrorist groups connected to the environmental movement, such as the Earth Liberation Front (ELF), have sabotaged construction and logging equipment, set fire to development projects, and engaged in other types of ecoterrorism involving attacks on businesses and institutions that environmentalists believe are harmful to the environment. Violence associated with labor activism occurred during the late nineteenth and early twentieth centuries, as unions, labor activists, and workers attacked businesses and government authorities who did not support their views. For example, in October 1910 union members bombed the offices of the antiunion *Los Angeles Times* newspaper in Los Angeles, California, killing twenty people.

SEE ALSO: Animal Liberation Front; animal-rights movement; Black Power movement; Earth Liberation Front; ecoterrorism; extremism, right-wing versus left-wing; Hearst, Patricia; *Los Angeles Times* bombing; Students for a Democratic Society; Symbionese Liberation Army; Weatherman

Lenin, Vladimir (1870–1924)

Born Vladimir Ilyich Ulyanov, Russian revolutionary Vladimir Lenin was the founder of the Russian Communist Party and led the Bolshevik Revolution in 1917. Afterward he became the first head of state of the Soviet Union, a position he held until his death in 1924. Lenin first became a revolutionary in the late 1880s, when he studied Marxism. In 1895 the Russian government arrested him for being a subversive and sentenced him to a term of exile in Siberia; five years later he went to western Europe and became the leader of the Bolsheviks, then a faction of the Russian Social Democrats. After the czar was overthrown in Russia in 1917, Lenin went to Russia and took charge of the Bolsheviks, who soon became the dominant political group in the country.

As a Marxist, Lenin had long been committed to replacing capitalism with socialism. But whereas Marxists believed that the working classes would, of their own accord, eventually rise up to eliminate capitalism, Lenin felt that the Communist elite—intellectuals, rather than workers—had to act as a catalyst to bring about revolution, using violence as necessary. He also believed that the Communist elite and not the workers should be in control of the government, and so his Bolsheviks established a dictatorship as soon as they came to power. Under Lenin's leadership, the new government abolished a market economy, though in 1921 this economy was restored (later it would once again be eliminated), and he added other elements of socialism to the government as well; the principles and beliefs that guided him later became known as Leninism.

SEE ALSO: Marx, Karl

Libya

Beginning in the 1970s under the rule of General Mu'ammar Qaddafi, Libya has been a major supporter of terrorism, providing funds to such groups as the Popular Front for the Liberation of Palestine (PFLP), the Abu Nidal Organization (ANO), the Irish Republican Army (IRA), the Basque Homeland and Liberty (ETA), the Japanese Red Army (JRA), and the Tupac Amaru Revolutionary Movement (MRTA). Qaddafi has also been accused of paying bonuses to the families of suicide bombers and to individual terrorists who have accomplished things that he considers worthy of reward, including the murder of American hostages.

During the 1980s, Libya established ties with various Communist and other anti-U.S. governments around the world, while declaring that it was opposed to Israel and the West, and began creating terrorist-training camps, while buying and stockpiling weapons, particularly plastic explosives, intended for the hands of terrorists. In fact, during this period many of the revolutionary groups in Central and South America received weapons from Libya, as did the Sandinista government of Nicaragua. Also in the 1980s Libyans were associated with several major terrorist attacks, including ones at the Rome, Italy, and Vienna, Austria, airports in 1985.

In response to such activities, in 1986 the United States stationed military ships off the Libyan coast, and shortly thereafter Libyan terrorists bombed a TWA airplane in Greece and a discotheque in West Berlin, Germany; both bombings killed Americans (four on the plane, one at the discotheque). The United States then attacked the cities of Benghazi and Tripoli, Libya, killing over one hundred civilians in air strikes, an action that many Europeans protested. In 1991 the United States uncovered evidence that two Libyan nationals had been behind the 1988 bombing of Pan Am Flight 103 as it flew over Lockerbie, Scotland. Two hundred and seventy people were killed in this attack, including everyone on the plane and eleven people on the ground. The American government accused these two nationals, Abdel Basset al-Megrahi and Al-Amin Khalifa, of acting on behalf of the Libyan state security agency, Jamahiriya Security Organization (JSO). Indeed the two men were agents of the JSO, which was subsequently connected to other terrorist acts as well (especially assassinations and bombings), but Qaddafi denied that his government had anything to do with these acts. Nonetheless the United States and Great Britain imposed economic sanctions on Libya because of its sponsorship of international terrorism (the United Nations Security Council [UNSC] approved and enhanced these sanctions in 1993), and in May 2002 Libya agreed to pay the victims of the Lockerbie bombing $10 million in exchange for the lifting of the sanctions. Moreover after the September 11, 2001, terrorist attacks on American soil, Libya denounced terrorism, and Libyan officials now say that their country no longer sponsors terrorism.

SEE ALSO: Abu Nidal Organization; Basque Homeland and Liberty; funding terrorism; Irish Republican Army; Japanese Red Army; Popular Front for the Liberation of Palestine; Qaddafi, Mu'ammar; Tupac Amaru Revolutionary Movement

Lidice, Czechoslovakia

The village of Lidice, Czechoslovakia, was "liquidated" by the Germans on June 10, 1942, six days after the deputy leader of

the German SS (Schutzstaffel), Reinhard Heydrich, died from injuries he received during a bombing by Czech underground forces intending to assassinate him. To the Germans, "liquidation" meant total destruction of the town and all of its people, and to this end, on June 9 they rounded up everyone in Lidice. The next day they shot all 172 of the men and 7 women who had either tried to escape or were hysterical. They then sent the remaining 52 women to a concentration camp in Ravensbrück, Germany, where according to German records, all but 3 died or were executed. (The 3 "survivors" were never seen again.) Later the Germans discovered that they had neglected to round up 19 men from the village who were working in a nearby mine, but they eventually executed them as well. Meanwhile, 89 of the village's 90 children were carefully examined to determine whether they were "racially pure," and when it was decided that they were as white as the Germans, they were given German "parents" and new names; the remaining child was shot while trying to run away. After this process was complete, the Germans set fire to Lidice, and when certain structures failed to burn down, they dynamited them, then leveled the ground to make it look as though no village had ever existed there.

SEE ALSO: Nazi terrorism; Schutzstaffel (SS), the

Los Angeles Times bombing (1910)

On October 1, 1910, twenty workers at the *Los Angeles Times* newspaper offices in California, were killed and dozens more injured when a bomb planted in the *Los Angeles Times* building exploded. The owner of the newspaper, Harrison Gray Otis, immediately suspected that the bombers were members of a labor union, because Otis had published several anti-union editorials. Otis told the police that he had been receiving bomb threats from labor leaders, whom he called anarchists, and he insisted that the mayor do whatever it took to track down the bombers. In response, the mayor hired William J. Burns, then a famous detective, and shortly thereafter he uncovered evidence that the *Times* bombing had many elements in common with several other bombings that had already been linked to the Bridge and Structural Workers Union. This led him to suspect that two members of the union, brothers John and James McNamara, were behind the *Times* bombing. Through careful detective work, Burns determined that they had used a third party, Ortie Mc-Manigal, to hire anarchist bomb experts, David Caplan and Matthew Schmidt, to do the job. Burns convinced McManigal that the McNamaras were going to put all the blame for the crime on him, so Mc-Manigal confessed and agreed to testify against them. Burns arrested the brothers in Indianapolis, Indiana, with the help of state police there, then forced them to travel to Los Angeles, an illegal extradition that their union cohorts later protested. The union hired noted attorney Clarence Darrow to defend the McNamaras, and he accepted under the belief that they were innocent. During the course of preparing for trial, however, Darrow realized that the men were guilty. Consequently Darrow went to Otis and made a plea bargain: his clients would plead guilty if Otis would agree not to request the death penalty. Otis accepted the deal, and James McNamara was sentenced to life in prison, as were Caplan and Schmidt, while his brother John received a fifteen-year sentence.

Luddites

In modern times, Luddites are people who shun technology, generally out of the belief that it is harmful to the environment and the human spirit; however, the original Luddites were nineteenth-century English craftsmen who banded together to destroy textile machinery and weaving looms at wool and cotton mills because this equipment was making it harder for them to find work. They began their actions around Nottingham, England, in 1811, but soon the violence spread to other cities as well. During their attacks, which took place in the middle of the night, the Luddites were careful not to harm any people, only machines. (In this way, they were similar to modern-day environmental activists, or ecoterrorists, who sabotage construction equipment in wilderness areas under cover of darkness.) The Luddites also concealed their identities by wearing masks and claimed that their leader was King Ludd or Ned Ludd. (Historians disagree on whether Ludd was a real person.) To combat Luddite attacks, the British government decreed that "machine breaking" was a crime punishable by death, and mill owners began hiring people to protect their machinery. In 1812 several Luddites were killed by mill guards during an attack, and in 1813 seventeen were arrested, put on trial, and subsequently hanged. Because of these events and other instances of strict policing by government officials, the Luddite attacks soon ended, although there was a brief flare-up of activity in 1816 during a period of economic depression.

SEE ALSO: ecoterrorism

lynching

Lynching occurs when a violent mob executes someone without first determining, through due process of law, whether that person is guilty of a crime. The word "lynch" comes from the name Charles Lynch, a Virginia patriot who, during the American Revolution, created his own court to punish those loyal to the crown of England. His victims, then, were killed for their political beliefs, while others have been lynched because the mob believes they have committed a crime. More commonly, however, lynching victims have been targeted because of their race or religion. For example, from the late nineteenth century to the advent of World War II, anti-Semitic groups in many parts of eastern and western Europe routinely attacked Jews, and some of these attacks resulted in lynchings, particularly in Russia and Poland. In the United States the victims of lynching have most commonly been African American; in fact, of the more than forty-five hundred people who were lynched in America between 1882 and 1951, approximately thirty-five hundred were black, with hanging being the most common method. In the United States and elsewhere, lynch mobs typically torture the victim before killing him, perhaps by dragging him behind a moving car or horse, and afterward the mob might mutilate his body or set fire to it.

SEE ALSO: anti-Semitism; racism; revolutionary terrorism

Macedonia

A country in the southern Balkans, Macedonia has been home to Christian terrorists as well as Muslim ones. The country is primarily occupied by Christian Slavonic peoples, though Muslim Slavs, Muslim Albanians, and Christian Serbs, Greeks, and Turks also reside there. In the late nineteenth century, when the land was ruled by Turkey, a group of Christian Slavs formed the Internal Macedonian Revolutionary Organization (IMRO) in order to force Turkey into granting Macedonia its independence; the group's slogan was "freedom or death." Like modern terrorist groups, the IMRO structured itself into a network of relatively autonomous cells and committed terrorist acts including violent attacks, kidnappings, and assassinations. Also in the late nineteenth century, Serbian and Greek guerrilla units formed for the same purpose; these groups fought with the IMRO even as they encouraged widespread revolution against the Turkish government; however, the peasantry did not support these revolutionary activities.

In 1919 Macedonia became a part of Yugoslavia, but this did not end IMRO's drive for independence or its terrorism. The group's violent attacks continued until 1990, when it reformed itself into a national political party. By this time, a new group had appeared to fight for nationalism: the National Liberation Army (NLA), a rebel force of Muslim Albanians. After Macedonia finally declared its independence from Yugoslavia in 1991, the NLA became associated with international Islamic terrorism, largely because of Iran. In the late 1990s the Iranian government decided to try to turn Macedonia, Kosovo, and Albania into an Islamic stronghold because of these countries' proximity to Europe. To this end, radical Muslim began flooding into the region, recruiting Albanian Muslims into such Islamic militant groups as al Qaeda and establishing multinational terrorist cells in the country. As these cells began operating, Macedonian authorities struggled to destroy them. For example, in February 2002 police arrested four terrorists, who had originally come from Jordan and Bosnia, for plotting to bomb American, British, and German embassies in Macedonia, and the following month security officers killed seven members of the same terrorist cell who were also involved in the embassy-bombing plot.

In conducting such operations, terrorists in Macedonia receive funding via the "Balkan Route," whereby several tons of heroin are shipped from Turkey via the Balkans to Western Europe. Organized crime groups in the region, known as the Albanian Mafia, have not only gained control of drug transit along the Balkan Route, but have also smuggled arms into Macedonia from Serbia, Albania, Bulgaria, and Western Europe. In 1993 and 1994 Greece tried to prevent such activities by placing an embargo on Macedonia, but

A sign protesting the violence and criminal acts of the Italian Mafia in Sicily. © MARTINEZ PAZ RICARDO/CORBIS

narcotics and weapons still managed to pass through the country.

SEE ALSO: al Qaeda; funding terrorism; Internal Macedonian Revolutionary Organization; Iran

Macheteros

Created in the late 1970s by a faction of the Puerto Rican nationalist group known as FALN (Fuerzas Armadas de Liberación Nacional), the Macheteros engaged in bombing attacks on military and government targets in Puerto Rico during the 1980s. The group also killed a Puerto Rican police officer in 1978 and two U.S. Navy sailors in 1979. In September 1983 it stole $7 million from a Wells Fargo bank in West Hartford, Connecticut, to fund its activities. The Macheteros—which means "machete wielders" in Spanish—took

credit for the attack in a letter to a local newspaper. At other times, the group left a machete near the site of an attack to claim responsibility for the action. In 1985 most of the men who had taken part in the bank robbery, including one who had worked there as a guard, were captured and sentenced to prison; most were released in 1999 as part of a U.S. push to pardon Puerto Rican nationalists.

SEE ALSO: Fuerzas Armadas de Liberación Nacional

Mafia, the

A crime organization whose members are primarily of Italian or Sicilian ancestry, the Mafia has terrorized and murdered people in order to further its criminal acts. The group began in the Middle Ages in Sicily, where wealthy landowners established their own armies to protect their property. Some of the men in these armies soon became so powerful that they were able to terrorize the landowners, extorting money from them in exchange for their protection. (This type of extortion continues in the Mafia today.) The men then banded together to form what became the Mafia, a society with a hierarchical structure and a rigid code of behavior. As part of this code, people in the Mafia—and those they protected—were forbidden from contacting law-enforcement authorities for any reason whatsoever. If a person wanted justice, they had to seek it from the Mafia, which would not hesitate to kill to avenge a death.

Gradually the Mafia spread from Sicily to Italy, where in the 1920s the government of Benito Mussolini tried to destroy the group by jailing thousands of its members, or mafiosi. At the end of World War II, however, these prisoners were released by U.S. officials. By this time, the Mafia also existed in the United States, having been brought there in the nineteenth century by Italian and Sicilian immigrants who settled in such cities as New York, Boston, Philadelphia, Detroit, Chicago, New Orleans, St. Louis, Kansas City, and San Francisco. At first the Mafia had to compete with Irish and Jewish gangs who were also engaging in illegal activities, but by the 1930s the Mafia had become the most powerful crime organization in America, and by the 1950s, most major cities had a Mafia "family." In fact, New York City had five families: Gambino, Genovese, Lucchese, Colombo, and Bonanno. There were approximately twenty-four Mafia families in all, each one headed by a man known as the don who had a hierarchy of underlings to do his bidding. Along

with its illegal operations, each family also had one or more legal businesses under its control, in order to hide assets gained from the criminal activity. For example, a family might run a legal vending-machine business in addition to engaging in gambling and prostitution. This system still exists today, though most crime experts believe that the Mafia is far less powerful now than it was in the twentieth century. However, the word "mafia" is often used to refer to crime syndicates elsewhere that have similar characteristics as the original Mafia. For example, the Yakuza crime organization of Japan is often called "the Japanese Mafia."

SEE ALSO: criminal terrorism; Yakuza, the

Malayan Races Liberation Army (MRLA)

The Malayan Races Liberation Army (MRLA) arose out of the Malayan Communist Party (MCP) in Malaya during the 1940s. The British government had donated with arms and advisers to the MCP during World War II to defend the island against the invading Japanese. After the war, however, the MCP turned against the British colonial government, developing a military wing known as the Malayan People's Anti-British Army. This was renamed the Malayan Races Liberation Army in 1949, a year after the British colonial government had declared a state of emergency in order to counter a wave of guerrilla terrorism. The state of emergency, which lasted until 1960, allowed the government to arrest, deport, or even execute anyone who was involved in guerrilla warfare, but it didn't deter the MRLA. Operating from bases in the jungle, the group engaged in numerous attacks not only on government officials and supporters but on businessmen and other innocent civilians; approximately eleven thousand died as a result of these attacks. The MRLA also raided or machine-gunned villages, burned down factories, damaged machinery, bombed or fired upon police stations and military buses, and derailed military trains. By the middle of 1951, such attacks were occurring at the rate of approximately four hundred a month.

To counter this activity, the British built new villages far from the old ones for the Chinese Malayans who had been providing food to the MRLA (sometimes against their will) and controlled how much rice was sent to each village. But although this made it more difficult for the MRLA to operate, it did not end the terrorism. In late 1951 the group assassinated British high commissioner Sir Henry Gurney by machine-gunning his motorcade, blew up a mail train, and killed several people in roadside attacks; their youngest victim was a two-year-old girl shot in the head while riding in a car. Consequently the British colonial government stepped up its efforts to capture the guerrillas, launching a propaganda campaign to convince Malayans that it was unwise to support terrorists and offering rewards to anyone who turned them in. This, along with problems acquiring food, reduced the strength of MRLA to only a few hundred, whereas in 1948, at its peak, the group had contained roughly three thousand active members and seven thousand part-time supporters. In 1957 the group's numbers dwindled still further after Malaya became independent from Great Britain, and three years later the new government lifted the state of emergency.

SEE ALSO: Asia, terrorism in; guerrilla warfare

Mao Tse-tung
(1893–1976)

Mao Tse-tung was a Chinese Marxist who led his people in a Communist revolution that resulted in the establishment of the People's Republic of China, which he led from 1949 to 1959. He also helped found the Chinese Communist Party in 1921 and led this group from 1931 until his death in 1976. In bringing about the Communist revolution, from 1927 to 1934 he organized peasants into Communist guerrilla groups that attacked the forces of General Chiang Kai-shek, then leader of the Chinese government and its Nationalist Party. When the general's armies began assaulting Mao's main base, he took his guerrillas on a considerable journey, later dubbed the Long March (1934–1935), from southeastern to northwestern China. In April 1949, however, he overcame the general's forces in the city of Nanking, and shortly thereafter his People's Republic was established.

SEE ALSO: communism; guerrilla warfare

Marighella, Carlos
(1911–1969)

Brazilian revolutionary Carlos Marighella was the head of the Brazilian terrorist group Acao Libertadora Nacional (Action for National Liberation, or ALN) and authored the *Minimanual of the Urban Guerrilla* (1969), a guide to guerrilla warfare in cities. Translated into many languages, this book has been used by terrorists in many parts of the world, and in Brazil it was read aloud on public radio. Marighella's revolutionary activities began after he joined the Brazilian Communist Party (PCB) in 1930; he became a member of the Central Committee of the Communist Party in 1952. However, he was expelled from the party in 1960 after criticizing it for failing to strike out at the military dictatorship then in place in Brazil. The following year, Marighella formed the ALN and began leading the group in attacks on urban targets connected to the government. These attacks, which included bombings, kidnappings, and assassinations of ambassadors and other officials, prompted Brazil to create the Department of Social and Political Order, charged with arresting urban terrorists in citywide sweeps. Marighella was killed by the police in November 1967, and his group soon dissolved.

SEE ALSO: Brazil, terrorism in

martyrs

A martyr is someone who dies for his beliefs (often religious) and afterward is revered by people who share those beliefs. For example, some terrorists consider suicide bombers to be martyrs to their cause. In most major faiths, martyrs are believed to receive special honors in the afterlife. For example, Muslims believe that martyrs stand nearest the throne of God in heaven. In the Islamic faith, there are two basic types of martyrs among the faithful: those who have been killed unjustly, and those who have been killed during a holy war, or *jihad*. Among Jews, martyrs are typically people who have died for holding true to their religion when others want them to go against their beliefs; for example, in ancient times, Jews were martyred for refusing to work on the Sabbath. However, in modern Jewish literature, the word "martyr" has also been used to refer to Jews who died simply for being Jews, such as those killed during the Holocaust. In most cases, though, martyrs are given the opportunity to abandon their faith to escape death. Such was the case, for ex-

Karl Marx's socialist ideas, which were expressed in his 1848 The Communist Manifesto, *served as the springboard for communism and revolutionary terrorists.* THE LIBRARY OF CONGRESS

ample, in ancient Rome, when Christians arrested for their beliefs could avoid martyrdom by publicly worshipping Roman gods.

SEE ALSO: bombers, suicide; Holocaust, the

Marx, Karl
(1818–1883)

The writings of sociologist, economist, and political theorist Karl Marx inspired many revolutionaries seeking to establish socialism throughout Europe during the nineteenth century. Born in Prussia, Marx studied history and philosophy at German universities and in 1842 became an editor of the newspaper *Rheinische Zeitung* in Cologne, Germany. The following year, the government silenced his newspaper, and shortly thereafter he moved to Paris, France, where he became an associate of

French socialist writers, including Friederich Engels. In 1848, after relocating to Brussels, Belgium, Marx and Engels created *Manifest der Kommunistischen Partei*, commonly known as *The Communist Manifesto*, which expressed Marx's socialist views; this work served as the platform for the Communist League. By this time, the political climate in Germany had changed, so Marx returned to work on his newspaper, but shortly thereafter the government expelled him for expressing his views. He then went to London, England, where in 1867 he wrote his major work, *Das Kapital*, concerning economics and capitalism. (Marx also discussed economics in an earlier work, *La misère de la philosophie*—or *The Poverty of Philosophy*,—which was published in French in 1847 and in English in 1900.)

SEE ALSO: communism; Engels, Friederich

Matuschka, Sylvestre (dates unknown)

During the early 1930s, Hungarian World War I veteran Sylvestre Matuschka bombed trains in Austria and Hungary, frightening the public and therefore earning himself the label of terrorist. However, his motives were not political but financial. Having failed at several business ventures, Matuschka planned to defraud insurance companies by pretending to be an injured passenger on the trains that he bombed. The first bomb struck the Vienna-Passau Express on January 1, 1931, but did minimal damage, and when Matuschka went to join the passengers he discovered that they were all soldiers in uniform. He then struck a train near Juelerboy, Hungary, on August 8, 1931, but this time he was unable to pass as one of the twenty-five injured train passengers because they were at the bottom of a steep cliff. After both this incident and the previous one, authorities recognized that the bombing was intentional and sought to prevent future attacks and catch the person responsible. To this end, they placed guards on trains, inspected tracks, added lights to the front of trains that would travel at night, registered all train passengers so they would know who was on board, and searched train passengers and their luggage as well as suspicious people at train stations. Because of these measures, Matuschka waited until September 12, 1932, to try his scheme again. This time he bombed a Hungarian Railways train, killing twenty-two people and injuring dozens more. Afterward he successfully joined the injured and smeared blood on himself to make it look as though he were wounded. Later when he put in a claim against the railroad for his injuries, authorities discovered that he had not been on board. They then went to arrest him at his home, where they discovered explosives, as well as detailed plans to blow up trains in other countries. At his trial for the three train bombings, Matuschka blamed a mental illness for his actions, but he was found guilty and sentenced to death. Later, however, his sentence was commuted to life in prison, and in 1944 he was released from prison by the Russians who took over Hungary that year.

SEE ALSO: bombs, types of

Mau Mau

A militant African national movement, Mau Mau developed among the Kikuyu people of Kenya in the early 1950s in opposition to the British who controlled the country; throughout the 1950s, Mau Mau terrorists engaged in various acts of sabotage and assassinated government officials. In 1952 the government declared a state of emergency and ordered its military to track down these terrorists. British Kenyan forces then rounded up over twenty thousand Kikuyu and confined them in detention camps. Another eleven thousand or more were killed as terrorists, along with over two thousand people who had aided the terrorists. The government also used propaganda to try to end the Mau Mau movement, but it refused to die. Instead it spawned a move for Kenyan independence from Great Britain, and when this independence came to pass in the 1960s, a former Mau Mau leader, Jomo Kenyatta, became Kenya's prime minister.

McKinley, William (1843–1901)

The twenty-fifth president of the United States, William McKinley was shot and killed on September 6, 1901, by anarchist Leon Czolgosz at the Pan-American Exposition in Buffalo, New York. This assassination was one of several committed during the late nineteenth and early twentieth centuries; anarchists also killed France's president Said Carnot in 1894, Austria's empress Elizabeth in 1898, Italy's king Umberto in 1900, and Spain's prime minister Canalejas y Mendez in 1912. Among these world leaders, McKinley was perhaps the most popular with his people. At the time of his death, the United States was enjoying great prosperity, and McKinley had recently been reelected to a second term by a landslide. However, he was also accused of being an imperialist for his decision to take control of Puerto Rico, the Philippines, and certain other islands in the aftermath of a U.S. victory in a war with Spain in 1898. After McKinley's death, his vice president, Theodore Roosevelt, became president.

The twenty-fifth president of the United States, William McKinley was assassinated by anarchist Leon Czolgosz on September 6, 1901. THE LIBRARY OF CONGRESS

SEE ALSO: anarchism; assassinations, political

McVeigh, Timothy (1968–2001)

In June 2001 Timothy McVeigh was executed for a major act of domestic terrorism in the United States: the bombing of the Alfred P. Murrah Federal Building in Oklahoma City, Oklahoma, on April 19, 1995. One hundred sixty-eight people, including nineteen children, were killed in the blast that destroyed a day-care center on the ground floor; over five hundred people were injured. McVeigh planned the bombing for April 19 because on that exact day two years earlier, agents from the U.S. Bureau of Alcohol, Tobacco, and Firearms (ATF) had tried to force their way into the Waco, Texas, compound of a religious group, the Branch Davidians, which had stockpiled illegal weapons, and in the resulting violence several people were killed. McVeigh believed that these people had done nothing wrong, and that the government had infringed upon their right to bear arms. He chose to retaliate by bombing the Murrah Federal Building because he mistakenly believed that it housed the offices of the ATF. His inspiration was one of his favorite novels, *The Turner Diaries* (1978), in which a character bombs the headquarters of the Federal Bureau of Investigation (FBI) in order to protest gun-control laws.

In planning the bombing, McVeigh enlisted the help of two friends, Terry Lynn Nichols and Michael Fortier, who had served with him in the U.S. Army in the late 1980s. (McVeigh had spent forty-three months in military service and served in the Gulf War before resigning from the army.) McVeigh and Nichols committed robberies in order to acquire enough money to build a truck bomb, and together they purchased the thousands of pounds of explosives it required. At Fortier's home in Kingman, Arizona, they discussed how McVeigh would drive the truck, filled with over four thousand pounds of explosives, to the building, where he would park it for maximum destruction, and how he would escape undetected in another vehicle before the bomb detonated. The men rented lockers in which to store the materials for the bomb, including ammonium nitrate fertilizer and race car fuel. They also created a fake driver's license for McVeigh so that he could use an alias when renting the truck. Despite these precautions, McVeigh made a serious error after leaving the bomb site. Just eighty minutes after the bomb ex-

ploded, McVeigh was pulled over by an Oklahoma state trooper for having no license plates on the getaway vehicle. The trooper noticed a gun in McVeigh's pocket and arrested him for illegally carrying a firearm. But before bail could be arranged for his release, he was linked to the bombing by federal authorities who had begun investigating the rental truck that carried the explosives as well as the storage lockers that housed them. Soon Nichols and Fortier were implicated and Fortier agreed to testify against his coconspirators in exchange for leniency. During McVeigh's trial (Nichols was tried separately), witnesses placed him at the rental offices and other locations connected to the crime, but not at the site of the bombing itself. Moreover federal investigators were unable to prove that explosives had ever been in the storage lockers, though they could prove that McVeigh's clothes had once come in contact with explosives. Nonetheless in June 1997, after only four days of deliberations, the jury convicted McVeigh on eight counts of first-degree murder, conspiracy to use a weapon of mass destruction, and the detonation of an explosive. (Nichols was found guilty on one count of conspiracy and eight counts of manslaughter and was sentenced to life in prison.) McVeigh was subsequently sentenced to die by lethal injection, and after his appeal of this sentence failed, he was executed on June 11, 2001.

SEE ALSO: Alcohol, Tobacco, and Firearms, U.S. Bureau of; *Turner Diaries, The*

media-oriented terrorism

Media-oriented terrorism is violence perpetrated specifically to attract the attention of the media, in order to deliver the terrorists' message to the largest possible audience. This message might be the terrorists' attempt to gain sympathy for their cause, to instill fear in the general population, to demoralize their enemies, or to influence government policies. Or the message might be intended as a show of strength or a way to encourage other terrorists to take the same actions. In many cases, media-oriented terrorism involves symbolic targets; for example, terrorists attacked the World Trade Center in New York on September 11, 2001, because, as the home to many financial institutions, this site symbolized American capitalism. Similarly airplane hijackings and embassy bombings are terrorists' attempts to strike out at the countries associated with these planes and embassies, as was the 1972 attack at the Olympic Games in Munich, Germany, during which Israeli athletes were targeted. One of the most successful terrorist groups to use the media for its cause is Hezbollah. When this Lebanese group attacks an Israeli target, its supporters often give interviews or distribute press releases to the media that present the attack as justified, the Israelis as villains, or the Hezbollah members as freedom fighters and patriots. Another group that routinely issued press releases after a terrorist attack was the Red Brigades in Italy in the 1970s. They timed these releases to arrive at newspaper offices just before it was time to print the edition, so that reporters could not verify the facts provided by the Red Brigades or interview anyone opposed to its version of what occurred.

SEE ALSO: embassy bombings; Hezbollah; hijackings, aircraft; Munich Olympics crisis; Olympics Games as terrorist targets; Red Brigades; September 11 attacks on America

medieval terrorism

In the Middle Ages, most terrorism was conducted by one party on an enemy's castles, fortresses, fortified towns. (Most medieval towns were encircled by walls with gates that were locked against intruders.) In many cases, attackers would lay siege to such places while trying to frighten inhabitants into opening their locked gates. For example, in many cases besiegers beheaded people they caught outside of fortified towns and placed their heads in plain view of the towns' walls. Attackers might also employ crude forms of bioterrorism, using catapults to fling diseased human corpses over the walls of a castle, fortress, or town or intentionally contaminating their food and water sources with rotting carcasses. If these tactics worked and the castle, fortress, or town surrendered, the terrorism often continued; surrendering citizens might be slaughtered, their possessions taken, and their homes burned to the ground. Often such actions served as a warning to others who might force a siege. For example, in 1105, after King Henry I of England attacked and burned down the town of Bayeux, France, several nearby towns surrendered to him immediately. In other cases, however, the conquerors did not care about the message sent by their actions, only about how much loot they could pillage. Alternatively they might be motivated by religious concerns. For example, in 1099, during the Crusades, Christian soldiers laid siege to the city of Jerusalem in order to claim it for Christianity, and when they captured it five weeks later, they slaughtered all of its inhabitants for being non-Christian.

SEE ALSO: bioterrorism

Metesky, George Peter (The Mad Bomber)
(1903–1994)

Dubbed "The Mad Bomber" by New York newspapers, George Peter Metesky terrorized the people of New York City by planting thirty-seven bombs at various places in the Manhattan area from 1940 to 1956. His first attack occurred on November 16, 1940, when he put a pipe bomb in a tool box and left it at the Edison Building on West Sixty-Fourth Street in Manhattan. Alongside the bomb, which was found and defused before it went off, was a note reading, "Con Edison crooks, this is for you," alluding to the reason Metesky planted the bombs. Several years earlier, in September 1931, he had been exposed to harmful gasses while working at a power plant owned by Consolidated Edison, but doctors could find nothing wrong with him; nonetheless Metesky demanded that the company put him on disability leave, and when they refused, he tried to persuade the city to force Edison to consider him disabled. When this failed, his anger against the company and the city led him to violence.

In December 1941, however, Metesky sent an anonymous note to New York police saying that he would not be planting any bombs until World War II was over. He was true to his word, but he still continued sending letters to newspapers, theaters, and restaurants, stating that New York City would eventually be terrorized again. In March 1950 he did indeed start planting bombs again, first at Grand Central Station, then in a phone booth near the New York Public Library, then at the Grand Hotel. All of these were defused or detonated by police before they could harm anyone, and the next several bombs that Metesky planted were duds. A bomb left at the Radio City Music Hall in 1954, however, did go off, damaging the building and injuring two people. Another, left at Grand Central Station in 1955, exploded and injured one person. Other targets included Macy's department store, the RCA (Radio Corporation of America) building, the Paramount Theater, and the Staten Island Ferry.

With each bombing, police noted that the bomber was improving on his devices and doing more damage, and they were desperate to stop him. Consequently they devoted a large amount of resources to the case and interviewed dozens of witnesses and suspects. In the end, though, it was Consolidated Edison that identified the bomber. Based on the note left with the first bomb, the company examined its records for complaints by people angry with its business practices. This search led them to Metesky, and police were soon able to prove that he was the Mad Bomber. In 1957 a judge ordered him to be sent to a mental institution, where he remained until December 1973.

SEE ALSO: bombs, types of

Mexico

In 1994 Mexico experienced a rebellion in which leftist rebels from a group called the Zapatista National Liberation Front attacked army troops and police in protest of the country's poor treatment of Indian peasants. At first its attacks were direct armed conflicts, resulting in the deaths of 145 people, but the group then turned to guerrilla warfare; today, however, it no longer engages in such violence, having become a political movement emphasizing civil rights. Consequently Mexico is now connected to terrorism primarily through the drug trade. Its major drug-smuggling cartel, the Arellano-Felix cartel based in the city of Tijuana, has engaged in terrorist violence against government authorities seeking to end the group's illegal activities. In addition, there is evidence that the Arellano-Felix cartel has ties to the Marxist Forces of National Liberation (FARC), a revolutionary group in Colombia that supports its own terrorist activities through the drug trade.

See Also: Colombia, terrorism in; guerrilla warfare

Middle East, terrorism in the

Traditionally, the Middle East has been defined as the countries of southwestern Asia and northeastern Africa; terrorism experts, however, generally consider some parts of central Asia—Afghanistan, Pakistan, and the former Islamic republics of the Soviet Union (Uzbekistan, Turkmenistan, Tajikistan, Kyrgystan, and Kazakhstan)—to belong to the Middle East as well. The entire region both supports and suffers from terrorism, but Israel, Lebanon, Iraq, Iran, and Syria have been especially associated with terrorist activities in recent years. Other countries, most notably Libya and Jordan, once sponsored terrorist groups but lately have insisted that they want to stamp out international terrorism.

Much of the violence in the Middle East has its origins in the aftermath of World War I, when the British and French divided up the region. At the time, Arabs and Jews both insisted that they had the right to live in Palestine; most of the people then living in Palestine were Arab, but the Jews still considered it to be their ancestral homeland. (The ancient Romans had destroyed the Jewish kingdoms in Palestine and forced the Jews out of these lands during the first and second centuries A.D.) In 1917 Great Britain, which took control of Palestine, Jordan, and Mesopotamia (while France took Syria and Lebanon), promised the Jews that they could establish a Jewish state in Palestine. However, British diplomats also promised Arabs control over their territories. Consequently when Jews began to move from elsewhere in Europe into Palestine in significant numbers in the 1920s, Arabs began to attack Jews and Jewish settlements, and the Jews responded in kind.

This violence escalated just before and during World War II, when Jews escaping Nazi persecution streamed into Palestine. In 1947 the United Nations (UN) decided that the only way to end the violence in Palestine was to partition the country into Arab lands and Jewish lands by creating the independent state of Israel. The following year, Israel was officially founded, and immediately thereafter it was at war with neighboring Arab states. Though the Arab-Israeli War only lasted until early 1949, it set the stage for all future terrorism in the region, because the victorious Israelis mercilessly drove thousands of Arabs from Palestine, taking their homes, businesses, possessions, and historical treasures, and the Arabs responded by randomly attacking Jewish civilians. In addition, Arabs outside of Palestine decided to band together against the Israelis, and an Arab nationalist movement began in the Middle East. This movement led to the creation of many Arab terrorist groups, including al Fatah and the Palestine Liberation Organization (PLO), and to another brief Arab-Israeli war, which resulted in another Arab defeat in 1967 and more Arab anger over the existence of Israel.

This anger, however, soon grew to encompass hatred for all countries that supported Israel. Consequently between 1970 and the late 1980s, Arab terrorists not only continued to attack Israeli targets and individual Jews but also struck out at the

United States and other western nations that recognized Israel's right to exist. Increasingly these terrorists engaged in large-scale operations, such as airline hijackings, that brought media attention to their cause. However, such operations also brought Israeli reprisals and aggressive attacks from law-enforcement and military personnel in various countries seeking to end Arab terrorism. As a result, some terrorists began rejecting violence, arguing that a better way to force change was through politics, while others became even more militant, particularly after Israel invaded Lebanon in 1982. Moreover these militants increasingly viewed their struggle in religious terms as the involvement of predominantly Christian nations, particularly the United States, grew in the region. Religious terrorism grew as secular Arab governments, such as Iraq under the regime of Saddam Hussein, became more oppressive and, in some cases, engaged in state-sponsored terrorism to keep citizens under control or to mete out punishments to those who opposed the state. (For example, during the 1990s Hussein used chemical weapons to kill Iraqis who were not of his religious sect or did not support the ruling Ba'-ath Party.)

Also fueling religious terrorism was the Islamic fundamentalist government of Iran, which sponsored terrorist attacks against Arab Gulf states, including Saudi Arabia and Kuwait, by Muslims of the Shiite sect, and promoted the idea that terrorist attacks on U.S. targets were justified because America was a satanic nation. During the late 1980s Iran funded such Shiite terrorist groups as the Supreme Council for the Islamic Revolution in Iraq, the Organization of the Islamic Revolution in the Arabian Peninsula, the Islamic Call Party, and the Islamic Front for the Liberation of Bahrain. Iran also helped terrorists establish training camps in the country, as did Sudan. These and other countries controlled by Islamic fundamentalists sponsored the activities of such terrorist groups as Hezbollah and the Abu Nidal Organization. For example, Afghanistan was a safe haven for many terrorists, including members of the al Qaeda terrorist network; this changed, however, after the September 11, 2001, terrorist attacks on the United States, after which American troops attacked Afghanistan and destroyed its Islamic government. Fearing the same fate, many countries that had previously supported terrorism now rejected it. But with the 2003 attack on Iraq by American- and British-led forces came a resurgence of Arab support for terrorism, because many Muslim extremists viewed this attack as part of a war not on terrorism but on Muslims by Western Christians intent on destroying the Islamic faith. This view was strengthened by the refusal of the United States to condemn Israel for attacking Arabs in Lebanon in 2006. Today anti-U.S. sentiment is at an all-time high in the Middle East, and dozens of terrorist attacks occur in the region each day.

SEE ALSO: Abu Nidal Organization; Hezbollah; Hussein, Saddam; Iran; Iraq; Lebanon; Pakistan; Syria

militias

Militias are armies of citizens rather than soldiers. These armed groups might be state-sponsored, in response to a terrorist or guerrilla threat, or they might be formed independently of a government by people unhappy with the way the government is handling a particular threat or under the belief that citizens need to defend themselves against a corrupt government.

For example, in the United States during the 1990s, some right-wing Christians and white supremacists formed militias because they believed that the American government was planning to infringe upon their constitutional rights, particularly their right to bear arms. Some of these militias also bombed abortion clinics, gay bars, and government offices by way of protesting activities at such places. In fact, after the federal government tried to seize weapons from a religious group, the Branch Davidians, in Waco, Texas, in 1993—a conflict that resulted in many deaths—anti-U.S. sentiments among right-wing extremists created a militia movement that spread to at least twenty-five states. Some of the members of this movement believe that the U.S. government is planning not only to take away various rights and freedoms but wants to end democracy altogether, so that America would be controlled by a military government with ties to one or more foreign countries.

SEE ALSO: Branch Davidians; right-wing terrorists, U.S.

millennium beliefs

A millennium is a period of a thousand years; therefore the end of the year 2000 was the end of the millennium. As this moment approached, some people feared that between the last second of 2000 and the first second of 2001 the world would end. Others thought that this transition would launch a battle between good and evil known as Armageddon, which itself would lead to the end of the world as we know it and the return of Jesus Christ. In fact, the word "millennium" can also refer to a thousand-year period during which, according to the New Testament of the Bible, Jesus Christ will rule on earth. Because of millennium beliefs, some right-

wing domestic terrorists in the United States (particularly white supremacists) commit acts of violence intending to trigger the war between good and evil. Consequently as 2001 approached, government authorities stepped up their surveillance of such terrorists in order to prevent millennium-based attacks, and they managed to thwart several such plots.

SEE ALSO: apocalypticism

missiles, rockets, and mortars

Terrorists use a variety of weapons, including missiles and other rocket-propelled devices. Among these weapons, one of the most common is the RPG-7 rocket-propelled grenade launcher, which is used to attack armored vehicles, bunkers, and buildings. When the Soviet Union existed, it manufactured thousands of RPG-7 grenade launchers, so these weapons have been fairly easy for terrorist organizations to obtain. Less prevalent but also used by terrorists are light-weight guided anti-tank missiles like the American M72.750 LAW, or Light Anti-tank Weapon, which can fire projectiles through armor that is nearly two inches thick but weighs only seven pounds, and Russian multibarreled rocket launchers known as Katyushas, which must be mounted on a vehicle. Many terrorists have also used handheld, guided surface-to-air missiles, or SAMs. For example, in Afghanistan during the 1980s, the mujahideen employed the Stinger surface-to-air missile, manufactured in the United States, which is fired after being positioned on a person's shoulder and can bring down a low-flying plane. A similar missile is the SA-7, manufactured by the Soviet Union. Mortars, which have front-loading muzzles that fire shells, are also popular weapons. For example, Islamic fundamentalists in the terrorist group

Hezbollah have often used conventionally manufactured mortars to attack Israeli villages from just over the border in Lebanon, while the Irish Republican Army (IRA) has used homemade mortars to strike police stations and other government and military facilities in Northern Ireland.

SEE ALSO: weapons, types of terrorist

Molly Maguires, the

A secret organization that operated in eastern Pennsylvania in the 1860s and '70s, the Molly Maguires murdered at least sixteen people and engaged in numerous terrorist attacks related to the coal-mining industry and to antiwar sentiments related to the Civil War. Their violence began with a July 4, 1862, protest against the draft in Carbon County, Pennsylvania, during which someone believed to be a member of the Molly Maguires killed the foreman of a coal mine who was not only pro-draft but had been treating his workers badly. Over the next few years, several more abusive, pro-draft foremen were murdered, as well as some mine owners. In most cases, the workers being abused were Irish Catholic, which was no coincidence; the Molly Maguires originated in Ireland, where it fought ill treatment by English Protestant landowners, and was brought to the United States by Irish immigrants. In 1874–1875, after coal-mining workers went on strike in Pennsylvania, the Molly Maguires apparently began sabotaging mining equipment and facilities and detonating bombs along rail lines, roads, and bridges so that mine owners could not bring in replacement workers. By this time, a leader in the coal industry, Franklin B. Gowen, had hired an agent for a private detective agency, Pinkerton, to infiltrate the group, and in 1876, this agent, James McParlan

(under the alias James McKenna), provided enough evidence to bring several members of the Molly Maguires to justice for their crimes; ten of them were executed in 1877, and another in 1879. Several years later, however, additional evidence surfaced that suggested Gowen was behind the acts of sabotage, explosions, and perhaps even some of the murders attributed to the Molly Maguires, apparently to make it easier for him to destroy the group.

Mongols, the

In the thirteenth century, the leader of Mongolia, Gengis Khan, terrorized thousands of people in the lands he conquered in China, central Asia, and the Middle East. When he and his soldiers captured a city after a long battle or siege, they would often execute everyone living there, except perhaps for craftsmen with skills valuable to the Mongol armies. (If the townspeople surrendered quickly, they might be spared.) In China, however, they forced civilians to march with Mongolian soldiers as shields against Chinese armies. Khan also burned crops in order to starve his enemies. Eventually he became so well known for his ruthlessness that when people in a particular area heard that he was on his way to conquer them, they were already prepared to surrender.

Montagnards, the

The Montagnards controlled the French government at the peak of the French Revolution, from 1793 to 1794; on September 5, 1793, they declared that terror would be "the order of the day," thereby launching what became known as the Reign of Terror. At the outset of this period, the Montagnards cracked down on rebellion via harsh laws and policies, imprisoned their political enemies, and confiscated the lands and money of any nobles and clergymen who fled the country. In June and July of 1794 they executed over fifteen hundred people; in most cases the method of death was the guillotine, but in one city, Lyon, so many people were sentenced to death (over seven hundred) that the guillotine could not kill them fast enough, and mass executions by cannon fire were employed instead. Many of the victims were Girondins, the main political opponents of the Montagnards. Before the Reign of Terror, in the fall of 1792, both the Montagnards, who were radicals, and the Girondins, who were moderates, had been members (deputies) of the National Convention. (The Montagnards sat on the highest benches at the gathering, which is how they received their name; "Montagnards" means "mountain men"—i.e., men who are atop a peak.) Shortly thereafter, however, a popular uprising drove the Girondins from the National Convention, and the Montagnards took control of this assembly and of the Committee of Public Safety as well, which was established in April 1793. Comprised of twelve members of the Convention, this body essentially governed France. But soon the public grew tired of its executions, and at the Convention on July 27, 1794, the Montagnards fell from power, after some of the deputies rose up against the committee's most influential member, Maximilien Robespierre. In the aftermath, many of the Montagnards were sent to the guillotine.

SEE ALSO: Reign of Terror

Montana Freemen

A right-wing extremist group in eastern Montana, the Montana Freemen were involved in a confrontation with the Federal Bureau of Investigation (FBI) in March 1996. At that time, the FBI sent agents to the group's headquarters at a ranch near the town of Jordan, because the government had warrants for the arrest of some of its members. The group had been forging money orders and committing other financial crimes out of its belief that it was exempt from various U.S. laws, including those related to taxation; this belief arose from its interpretation of the U.S. Constitution, the Bible, and other writings, which led the Freemen to consider its lands to be sovereign territory. Consequently when federal agents went to the Freemen's ranch (called Justus Township by the Freemen and Clark Ranch by others), the Freemen refused to allow the FBI on their property. In response, the FBI decided not to force their way inside, because during two previous, similar incidents (one in Waco, Texas, and the other in Ruby Ridge, Idaho), people were killed or injured when this occurred. So instead, the agents simply cut off all electricity, water, and phone service to the ranch, then waited for the Freemen to give up. This occurred on June 13, 1996, when the wanted members of the group were then arrested.

SEE ALSO: Ruby Ridge; Waco incident

Mooney, Thomas Jeremiah (1882–1939?)

In the early 1900s, American labor leader and socialist Thomas Jeremiah Mooney was falsely accused and convicted of being a terrorist bomber. A member of the IWW (Industrial Workers of the World) as of 1910, Mooney was one of the founders of a militant publication, *Revolt: The Voice of the Militant Worker*, and a vocal supporter of the labor movement in San Francisco, California. In 1913 he became involved in a labor dispute between the Electrical Workers' Union and the Pacific Gas and

Electric Company of California (PG&E). After some of the striking workers bombed property owned by PG&E, Mooney spoke in their favor, and shortly thereafter he was accused of being a bomber himself. He was arrested for planning to bomb two of the electric company's towers but was soon released because there was no evidence that he had ever possessed or used any dynamite.

Nonetheless three years later the government again went after Mooney. At that time, a bomb exploded during a parade supporting U.S. allies fighting in what would become World War I (which the United States had not yet entered). The explosion, near the intersection of Market Street and Steuart Street, killed ten people and injured at least fifty more. Several people were suspected of planting the bomb, including German agents, but a detective for United Railroads convinced the police that Mooney was the person responsible; United Railroads wanted Mooney out of the way, because he had been trying to convince its workers to unionize. As a motive, the company suggested that Mooney was not really targeting the parade, but instead wanted to blow up the offices of United Railroads, which was only a short distance from the point of explosion. The police therefore arrested Mooney, and witnesses soon came forward to say that they had seen him near the site of the bombing; some even said that Mooney was carrying a suitcase that must have contained the bomb.

During the trial, however, Mooney's attorneys presented photographic evidence that he was not on the street, but on a rooftop watching the parade. Jurors ignored the photographs of Mooney on the roof, accepting the prosecution's position that the photos had been doctored, and

found him guilty. He was sentenced to death by hanging, but the governor of California changed the sentence to life in prison at the request of President Woodrow Wilson. Then, one by one, those who had testified as witnesses against Mooney began to admit that they had lied during their testimony after being threatened by the police. Despite these confessions, the governor refused to set Mooney free, but after he was voted out of office his successor immediately gave Mooney a full pardon, and in January 1939, Mooney was released from prison.

SEE ALSO: bombs, types of

Moro Islamic Liberation Front (MILF)

The Muslim terrorist group known as the Moro Islamic Liberation Front (MILF) was created in 1978 by members of the Moro National Liberation Front (MNLF) who disagreed with a truce agreement reached between the MNLF and the Philippine government. Established in the late 1960s, the MNLF had been waging a guerrilla war against the government because of a long-standing conflict between Muslims and Christians in the Philippines. This conflict began in the sixteenth century, when the Spanish converted many of the islands' inhabitants to Christianity; Muslims who refused to convert were treated badly and therefore generally kept to themselves. However, in the late 1950s the government began encouraging Christians, by then the majority, to move into Muslim-dominated lands, particularly on the island of Mindanao, and dismissed any Muslim complaints about these incursions. Consequently the MNLF was formed with the intent of forcing the creation of an independent Muslim state within the Philippines. The group's truce agreement with the government seemed to support this goal, because it included the provision that certain lands would be declared exclusively Muslim and, within limits, be given over to Muslim control. The government, however, did not honor this part of the agreement, and it was this failure that led to the disagreement which created the MILF. Roughly fourteen thousand-strong, the MILF launched a series of attacks against government forces, and it continued these attacks even after the government negotiated a new peace agreement with the MNLF in 1996. This agreement gave the leader of the MNLF, Nur Misuari, only limited control of four Muslim regions on Mindanao, and afterward the government reneged on promises to improve living conditions in these regions. As a result, the MILF gained support in these and other Muslim areas throughout the Philippines, and the group's attacks increased in number and severity. In the late 1990s the Philippine Army began an aggressive military campaign against the MILF guerrillas, and in July 2000 its troops captured the group's main base. Nonetheless the MILF continued its attacks until the following year, when Philippine vice president Gloria Arroyo seized control of the government. Arroyo convinced MILF leaders to come to the negotiating table, and in June 2001 the MILF signed a peace agreement. However, the government still did not allow the creation of an independent Muslim state, and tensions soon began building again in the region. In 2002 the Philippine government, with U.S. funding and expertise, established a military unit dedicated to combating terrorism on the islands; the MILF has strongly objected to the existence of this unit, though it has not launched attacks against it. In 2003 the leader and founder of the MILF, Salamat Hashim,

died, and the group's leadership was taken over by Al Haj Murad Ebrahim. Little else is known, however, about the current operations of MILF. In 1998 the group claimed to have 90,000 fully armed members, but today terrorism experts believe the number is far less. It does appear, though, that MILF's military wing, the Bangsamoro Islamic Armed Forces, has about 12,500 members.

SEE ALSO: Philippines, the

Mossad

Also known as the Central Institute for Intelligence and Security, Mossad is an Israeli intelligence agency dedicated to fighting terrorism. Its agents protect Israeli embassies and diplomats, rescue hostages, and engage in espionage, and on occasion they have been known to assassinate terrorists. The agency also consults with other counterterrorism agencies and security forces throughout the world.

SEE ALSO: Israel

Moussaoui, Zacarias (1968–)

Born in France but of Moroccan descent, Zacarias Moussaoui was the sole person, as of December 2006, to be convicted for involvement in the September 11, 2001, terrorist attacks on America, during which terrorists flew airplanes into the buildings of New York's World Trade Center and the U.S. Pentagon in Washington, D.C. Moussaoui apparently was supposed to pilot one of these planes, but he was arrested in August 2001 for being in the United States illegally; his arrest was prompted by a Minnesota flight instructor who found Moussaoui's determination to learn to fly a 747 passenger jet suspicious. After the September 11 attacks involving nineteen hijackers, Moussaoui was deemed "the twentieth hijacker," and in April 2005 he pleaded guilty to conspiring with the other men. In May 2006 he was sentenced to life in prison, despite the fact that the leader of the al Qaeda terrorist group responsible for the attack, Osama bin Laden, had issued a statement that Moussaoui was not involved in the September 11 attacks. However, there is ample evidence that Moussaoui was involved with radical Islamists while studying for a graduate degree in business in England in the 1990s.

SEE ALSO: al Qaeda; bin laden, Osama; September 11 attacks on America

Mozambique Liberation Front (FRELIMO)

The Mozambique Liberation Front (FRELIMO) engaged in terrorism during the 1960s and '70s as part of a struggle for independence in Mozambique against the Portuguese forces then controlling the country. At the beginning of this struggle, in 1964, the group attacked militarily strategic targets, such as dams and roads. By 1973, however, it had begun attacking villages and civilians. That year, the group was responsible for the death of over three hundred civilians, the injury of at least that many more, and the kidnapping of over seventeen hundred. In response to these attacks, the Portuguese government sent additional troops into Mozambique and became extremely aggressive in tracking down FRELIMO members. Nonetheless in 1975 Portugal decided to grant Mozambique its independence.

SEE ALSO: decolonization campaigns

Mughniyah, Imad Fayez (1962–)

Lebanese terrorist Imad Fayez Mughniyah is wanted by the United States for partici-

pating in the hijacking of TWA Flight 847 in 1985, during which one person was killed. He is also wanted in Argentina for the bombing of the Israeli embassy in Buenos Aires in 1992 that killed twenty-nine people, and the bombing of a community center in the same city in 1994 that killed eighty-five people. He has been connected to several kidnappings and bombings in Lebanon in the late 1980s and early 1990s as well, including the 1983 suicide bombing of the U.S. embassy in Beirut. Mughniyah has belonged to several terrorist groups, including the Palestine Liberation Organization (PLO) and Hezbollah. In 1985, after the TWA hijacking, U.S. authorities were thwarted twice in their attempts to capture Mughniyah, both times when foreign governments—first France and then Saudi Arabia—refused to help them arrest the terrorist. In France's case, the French government released Mughniyah in exchange for the release of a French hostage being held by Mughniyah's associates.

SEE ALSO: embassy bombings; hijackings, aircraft

mujahideen

From the late 1970s to the early 1990s, an Afghan Islamic rebel group known as the mujahideen (holy warriors) attacked the forces of the Afghanistan government, which had strong ties to the Soviet Union, out of a desire to defend Islam against Marxism and communism. In 1979 the Soviet Union sent troops into Afghanistan in order to defend its interests there, and in response several governments opposed to the Soviet Union began supporting the activities of the mujahideen. For example, the United States sent more than $2 billion in weapons and supplies to the mujahideen, including Stinger surface-to-air missiles that could take down airplanes. In addition, other Islamic militants went to Afghanistan to join the mujahideens' fight, including Saudi terrorist Osama bin Laden; he also started an organization dedicated to recruiting fighters for the conflict, and this organization later became al Qaeda. As a result of this activity, in 1989 the Soviet Union pulled out of Afghanistan, but the Soviet-allied Afghan government, which was controlled by the Marxist People's Democratic Party of Afghanistan (PDPA), remained in place. Consequently the mujahideen kept up its attacks until it overthrew this government in 1992. After this, however, the group splintered into several factions that began fighting with one another. This allowed a different Islamic group, the Taliban, to take control of the country in 1996.

SEE ALSO: al Qaeda; bin laden, Osama; funding terrorism; Taliban

Munich Olympics crisis

The Munich Olympics crisis occurred at the 1972 Olympic Games in Munich, Germany, when eight Palestinian members of the Black September terrorist group attacked Israeli athletes in their quarters at the Olympic Village. When the terrorists stormed the Israelis' apartment at approximately 5 AM on September 5, 1972, they shot the Israeli wrestling coach and a weightlifter outright, wounding the former and killing the latter. Amidst the gunfire, several other athletes escaped through windows, but nine were taken hostage. Meanwhile German police surrounded the building. In the subsequent negotiations between the terrorists and the police, the terrorists demanded that two hundred Arabs being held in Israeli prisons be released or the athletes would be shot one after another. After the Israeli government refused

to comply, the German government managed to convince the terrorists to release the hostages in exchange for safe passage to Tunisia. They emerged from the building at around 10 PM and got into waiting helicopters with their hostages; they then flew to a German military base, where the terrorists tried to board an airplane but were fired upon by a German counterterrorist force. The terrorists fought back with gunfire and grenades, and in the end all of the hostages and all but three of the terrorists were dead. These three terrorists were subsequently released by the German government, but then tracked down and assassinated by agents of the Israeli government. Israeli agents assassinated at least five other terrorists associated with the Munich crisis as well.

SEE ALSO: Black September; Olympic Games as terrorist targets

Mussolini, Benito
(1883–1945)

As the leader of Italy from 1922 to 1943, first as its prime minister and then as its dictator (though at the time, Italy also had a king), Benito Mussolini created the first fascist state, a development that inspired Adolf Hitler to establish a similar fascist regime in Germany in 1933. But whereas Hitler's fascism was based strongly on racism, Mussolini's fascism arose from a desire to return Italy to the glory days of the Roman Empire, when the state inspired powerful nationalist sentiments in its citizens and increased its territories through expansionist policies and a strong military. The Italian people largely welcomed Mussolini's dictatorship, because at the time that he took control of the country, Italy was plagued by strikes and riots. As he restored order and embarked on a series of domestic projects to improve work-

Benito Mussolini created the first fascist state during his dictatorship of Italy in the 1920s, which became the basis of Adolf Hitler's fascist regime in Germany in 1933. THE LIBRARY OF CONGRESS

ing conditions and other aspects of daily life, Mussolini's citizens hailed him as a hero. But when he began invading other countries (beginning with Abyssinia in the mid-1930s), he angered many in the international community and his people began to question his leadership. Their doubts deepened after he joined the German war effort in 1940. As soon as Italy entered World War II, it became clear that Hitler was not interested in Mussolini's opinions about how the war should progress; Hitler ignored Mussolini's requests that Italy be apprised of Germany's attacks prior to their execution. By 1943 most Italian politicians, as well as Italy's monarch, had decided that Mussolini no longer deserved to rule the country, and in July of that year the king sent royal troops to arrest Mussolini. He was imprisoned on a series of islands and then at a retreat in the Abruzzi Mountains, where a German commando force freed him in September 1943 and flew him to Munich, Germany. There Mussolini agreed with Hitler's request that he establish a new fascist Italian government in northern Italy, which was at the time under the control of Germany. Mussolini had hoped that his government would be independent of Germany's, but he soon realized that he was no more than a figurehead. He also realized that allied forces would soon have control of all of Italy, and as these forces encroached on his territory in the north, he decided to relocate to a mountainous area where it would be more difficult for his enemies to reach him. En route to this retreat, he was assassinated by Italian Communists.

SEE ALSO: Hitler, Adolf

Narodnaya Volya (The People's Will)

Between 1878 and 1881, the Russian militant group Narodnaya Volya (The People's Will) engaged in terrorism, particularly assassinations, in an attempt to get rid of the czar. Its members argued that such violence was a necessary component of revolution, serving as a rallying cry for the cause, and that it ultimately saved more lives than rebellion because it targeted specific people. This thinking soon spread to other revolutionaries elsewhere, inspiring a rash of political assassinations in the late nineteenth and early twentieth centuries; at least ten world leaders were assassinated during this period.

SEE ALSO: assassination, political

National Liberation Army (Ejército de Liberación Nacional, or ELN)

There have been two terrorist groups in South America with the name National Liberation Army (Ejército de Liberación Nacional, or ELN), one in Bolivia and the other in Colombia. The Bolivian group, which was founded in March 1966 by Cuban revolutionary Che Guevara, was destroyed in 1967 when the Bolivian government arrested and executed Guevara and most of his followers; consequently it never realized its goal of bringing about a Communist revolution in Bolivia that would spread to other parts of the world. The Colombian group, however, still exists and continues to engage in guerrilla attacks against the Colombian government. Embracing Marxist ideology, this ELN was founded by student activists in the early 1960s; its first guerrilla attacks were in 1965, when membership numbered in the hundreds. The Colombian army responded to this threat in the 1970s by tracking down and arresting or killing most of these members, but the group soon rebounded, and in 1983 it again began staging guerrilla attacks. This time the government responded by entering into peace negotiations with the group in 1984, but after two years no agreement had been reached and the violence began again. Now the ELN targeted the oil industry, destroying equipment and pipelines, kidnapping executives, and profiting from ransom money and protection money paid by companies wanting to end the attacks. In 1998 the government again tried to end the violence through a peace negotiation, but this time the authorities spoke not with the ELN but with another, larger Colombian guerrilla group, the Revolutionary Armed Forces of Colombia (FARC), under the assumption that if the FARC declared peace then the ELN would too. When this approach failed to bring any sort of peace to the country, Colombian officials decided to use military force against both the FARC and the ELN. To date, however, the government has still not eliminated either group, and the ELN numbers at least five thousand.

SEE ALSO: Colombia, terrorism in; Revolutionary Armed Forces of Colombia

National Liberation Front of Corsica (FLNC)

Established in 1976, the National Liberation Front of Corsica (FLNC) has committed numerous acts of violence in hopes of forcing France to grant Corsica its complete independence. (The island, which has been under French rule since 1769, has only limited autonomy, and its official language is French rather than Corsican.) Most of FLNC's attacks have been bombings, with their customary targets being government offices, police stations, and buildings owned by the French who have settled on Corsica. In the 1990s, however, the group increasingly targeted individual public officials and employees, though it also committed an average of five hundred bombings a year. Still, few people have died as a result of the FLNC's actions; the most notable death was that of Prefect Claude Erignac, the highest-ranking French public official at the time of his 1998 assassination. Terrorism experts estimate that the FLNC currently has five hundred members operating in several independent cells.

National Organization of Cypriot Fighters (EOKA)

From April 1955 through 1958, the National Organization of Cypriot Fighters (EOKA) engaged in a terrorist campaign against military forces on the island of Cyprus, which was then under British rule; the group's attacks involved over fifteen hundred bombings, resulted in several million dollars in damages, and killed 238 civilians, 104 soldiers, 50 police, and at least 90 EOKA members. The group was founded in 1955 by a former colonel in the Greek army, Georgios Grivas, who as a Greek Cypriot nationalist believed the island of Cyprus should become a part of Greece. To this end, when public demonstrations in Cyprus's capital city, Nicosia, failed to convince the British to leave Cyprus, and the United Nations (UN) refused to intervene in the situation despite Greece's requests to do so, the EOKA started bombing British offices and other places where British soldiers and public officials were likely to be. For example, in May 1955 the group planted explosives in a theater where the governor of Cyprus, Sir Robert Armitage, had been watching a movie, but he left before the bomb exploded. In November 1955, the British government declared a state of emergency on the island and established curfews and other restrictions to prevent more bombings. Nonetheless, the violence continued, especially in Nicosia. For example, a hotel there was bombed, wounding several British who were partying in its ballroom, and an airplane was destroyed, though the passengers had not yet boarded when the explosion occurred. In March 1956 the EOKA planted a bomb in the home of Armitage's successor, Sir John Harding, but it failed to explode. Meanwhile bands of EOKA guerrillas attacked British military members and policemen, not only in urban areas but in rural areas and mountain regions as well. In November 1956 alone—a month still referred to as "Black November" in Cyprus—there were over 416 terrorist attacks resulting in over 35 deaths. In April 1957 the EOKA was responsible for at least 50 bombings; later that same year, the group killed 2 British soldiers, bombed another plane, and tried to assassinate a military commander. The following year it killed a soldier's wife, an attack that incited British soldiers to brutalize Greek Cypriots, whether or not they were known members of EOKA. By this time, the island was on the brink of civil war, because its Turks, who were in the minority compared to its Greeks, did not want Cyprus to become part of Greece. Consequently Britain decided to abandon its claims on the island and allow Cyprus to become an independent republic. At the end of 1958, after this decision was made, the EOKA disbanded.

SEE ALSO: Black November; Grivas, Georgios

National Security Council (NSC)

The National Security Council (NSC) is a U.S. government agency charged with advising the president of the United States on matters related to national security. To this end, it oversees all government policies on national security issues. Members of the NSC include the vice president, secretary of state, and secretary of defense, along with dozens of experts in domestic, international, and military affairs. The NSC also includes several subcommittees devoted to various issues and programs related to national security, antiterrorism, and counterterrorism.

SEE ALSO: counterterrorism

nationalism

Nationalism is the belief that one's country or nation is more important than any individual within that nation; nationalists are intensely loyal to their country, though not necessarily to its leaders, and their nationalist movements are typically dedicated to promoting a national identity while ousting outsiders. Such movements might also promote certain cultural, ethnic, or religious identities seen as tied to the national identity. In fact, nationalist dissident terrorism is typically defined as violence committed by members of ethno-national groups seeking political autonomy. For example, in the late 1960s and early 1970s the Ibo tribe of Nigeria attacked members

of other tribes in an attempt to establish an independent Ibo nation, Biafra, in southern Nigeria, while Palestinian nationalists began attacking Israelis and others in an attempt to establish an independent Palestinian state. Throughout the twentieth century, nationalist movements arose in various places, particularly in Asia and Africa, where people sought to drive out a colonial power. For example, ever since the 1960s, Corsican nationalists have attacked French settlers in Corsica in an attempt to make that island independent from France. Other nationalists have committed terrorist attacks while seeking to "cleanse" their lands of a particular ethnic or religious group. For example, in Bosnia during the 1990s Serbian nationalists, who were of the Orthodox Christian faith, massacred, raped, and tortured thousands of Bosnian Muslims in a campaign of genocide (which they dubbed "ethnic cleansing") intended to drive all but Serbs from the country. Nationalism generally did not exist until the eighteenth century, because prior to this time, people showed loyalty to a town, a church, or some other small local entity—or perhaps several such entities—but not to a nation. However, the late eighteenth and early nineteenth centuries brought the first nationalist movements in Europe and Russia. The revolutionaries who participated in these movements confined their activities to their own nations; however, in recent years nationalist movements have often taken place on the international stage. For example, Palestinian nationalist revolutionaries have conducted airplane hijackings and other large-scale operations designed to attract global media attention in order to further their cause, thereby promoting international terrorism.

SEE ALSO: Bosnian genocide; decolonialization campaigns; ethnic cleansing; Palestine

Nazi terrorism

Under the leadership of German dictator Adolf Hitler from 1933 to 1945, the Nazi Party, which was the only political party in Germany during that period, engaged in and supported terrorism that was largely based on racism and scapegoating, the latter of which—common among right-wing extremists—occurs when one group of people is blamed for all the troubles suffered by others in a community. The Nazi Party engaged in violent attacks on not only Jews and other racial minorities but also foreigners, homosexuals, and leftists. In 1940–1941, these attacks became part of a master plan whereby the Germans intended to rid their society of anyone who was not of the white or Aryan race; to this end, they established death camps where they sent thousands of Jews to die. This approach was based primarily on nationalism and race rather than on religion. (In fact, at the time, many Nazis were rejecting Christianity in favor of occultism, mysticism, paganism, and other unconventional beliefs and practices, though outwardly the state continued to support the Christian religion for the order and traditions it represented.) Nonetheless, far-right extremists who have embraced the Nazi ideology in recent years do engage in anti-Semitic violence based on religious beliefs; these people, known as neo-Nazis, are generally Christian white supremacists with little or no nationalist sentiments.

SEE ALSO: Hitler, Adolf; neo-Nazis; Schutzstaffel (SS), the; Waffen, SS, the

Nechayev, Sergey (1847–1882)

Russian revolutionary Sergey Nechayev was a close associate of Mikhail Bakunin, who is sometimes called the grandfather of terrorism, and perhaps with Bakunin's help wrote "Catechism of a Revolutionary," a statement of his anarchist ideology that essentially states that the ends justify the means in regard to terrorist acts. This document subsequently inspired other terrorists, and in the late 1960s a translated version of the work was popular among American dissidents, including some in the Black Power movement. Nechayev created his "Catechism" in 1869, while participating in a student revolutionary movement in Saint Petersburg, Russia. That same year, he founded a secret revolutionary group, the People's Will (Narodnaya Rasprava), based on the principles of revolution that he had espoused in "Catechism." When one of the group's members, a student named I.I. Ivanov, disagreed with Nechayev on key points of his ideology, Nechayev murdered him at a group meeting. Shortly thereafter, Nechayev fled to Switzerland to escape arrest by Russian authorities, but sixty-seven members of his group were arrested for doing nothing to stop the crime. In 1872 Swiss police arrested Nechayev as well, then sent him back to Russia to stand trial. He was sentenced to twenty years in prison but died halfway through his term of imprisonment.

SEE ALSO: anarchism; Bakunin, Mikhail; Black Power movement

neocolonialism

The word "neocolonialism" has been used by terrorism experts to refer to instances where major international or multinational corporations function in a country much the way colonial powers once did, thereby triggering terrorism intended to drive out such foreign forces. Terrorists acting out

Members of the Aryan National Alliance, a white-supremacist neo-Nazi group, protest with Nazi flags. Tom Davenport. © AP Images

of neocolonialist sentiments typically attack targets either directly or symbolically connected to the offending corporations not only in their own country but elsewhere in the world as well, attempting to destroy the economic well-being of the corporations.

See Also: decolonization campaigns

neo-Nazis

Neo-Nazis are anti-Semitic, racist people living today who ascribe to the white-supremacist ideology of the Nazi regime that controlled Germany during World War II. They primarily exist in Europe and North America but are particularly active in the United States, where they are allied with other right-wing, white-supremacist extremists like those in the Christian Identity movement. American neo-Nazis typically insist that there is a Jewish conspiracy to take over the U.S. government, and some also believe that the country will one day experience a racial holy war, which they call Rahowa. To this end, they stockpile weapons and engage in terrorist acts against Jews and African Americans. They might also participate in racist gatherings such as those of the Ku Klux Klan. Many collect Nazi memorabilia, uniforms, helmets and other items associated with the Nazis and their leader, Adolf Hitler, whom they revere.

See Also: Christian Identity movement; Ku Klux Klan; Nazi terrorism; white supremacists

The Greenhaven Encyclopedia of Terrorism

Ferdinand Marcos was the tenth president of the Philippines from 1965–1986, and halted the New People's Army attempts to take over the Philippines in the early 1980s.
THE LIBRARY OF CONGRESS

New People's Army (NPA)

The militant arm of the Communist Party in the Philippines, the New People's Army (NPA) seeks to overthrow the Philippine government. Beginning with its formation in 1968, the group has engaged in guerrilla warfare against government forces, operating out of rural areas and relying on peasants for support. In fact, many members of the NPA came to the group after belonging to village militias that attacked the government on their own. The NPA hoped to use this support to drive the Philippine military completely out of certain areas, but despite hundreds of terror-

ist attacks during the early 1980s, when the group numbered over twenty-five thousand, it was unable to prevail against the government, then controlled by Ferdinand Marcos. When Marcos was ousted in a 1986 revolution that established a less-oppressive government, NPA membership fell to approximately five thousand, and declined still further through several successive governments. Nonetheless the group still exists today, though its attacks are few.

SEE ALSO: Philippines, the

Nicaragua

During the 1980s the Sandinista government of Nicaragua was linked to Middle Eastern terrorist networks and activities. Specifically the Libyan government, which then supported international terrorism in several countries, sent Nicaragua military supplies and equipment, including missiles, bombs, and fighter planes, and at least $100 million in aid. Libya also used Nicaragua as a conduit to supply international terrorists, particularly those based in Central and South America, with money and weapons. There is also evidence that in 1987, the government of Iran offered to give Nicaragua an additional $50 million a year in aid on top of its existing $100 million a year, if the Nicaraguan government would help encourage Latin Americans living in the United States to join terrorist cells dedicated to attacking U.S. targets if America attacked Iraq. Meanwhile the United States was secretly funding a Nicaraguan guerrilla group, the Contras, dedicated to overthrowing the Sandinista government; by doing so, U.S. president Ronald Reagan hoped to destabilize the country, but when his actions became known, Americans were outraged and his administration suffered from the Iran-

Contras scandal, which involved investigations into his illegal diversion of monies into the support of terrorism. The Contras also made news in May 1996, when several former Contras guerrillas kidnapped an American aid worker in Nicaragua who was helping with preparations for an upcoming election (she was released the following day). In November 2006 the Sandinistas again took control of Nicaragua, after Sandinista commander and Marxist revolutionary Daniel Ortega won the country's presidency in a democratic election. Before the election, U.S. officials expressed opposition to Ortega, who as an ally of both Cuba's dictator Fidel Castro and Venezuela's left-wing president Hugo Chavez harbors anti-U.S. sentiments.

SEE ALSO: Contras; Libya

Nichols, Terry Lynn (1955–)

Three years after the 1995 bombing of the Alfred P. Murrah Federal Building in Oklahoma City, Oklahoma, Terry Lynn Nichols was convicted of manslaughter and conspiracy involving the use of explosive materials for helping the man who bombed the building, Timothy McVeigh, obtain sticks of dynamite, detonating cord, and hundreds of pounds of ammonium nitrate fertilizer, which can be highly explosive. According to the federal officials who prosecuted the case, Nichols also encouraged McVeigh to commit the crime, which injured over 500 people and killed 168 people, including nineteen children who had been attending a day-care center on the first floor of the building.

SEE ALSO: McVeigh, Timothy

Northern Ireland

In Northern Ireland, members of nationalist groups have employed terrorism in attempts to force the British government to remove its troops from the country. The British first occupied Ireland in the twelfth century, but it was not until the sixteenth and seventeenth centuries that large numbers of English immigrants moved into the region. This angered the Irish, who already resented British rule, because England is a Protestant country and Ireland a Catholic one. In the 1640s anti-Protestant sentiment among the Irish led to a Catholic revolt in Ireland. This revolt was soon put down by British troops, but Irish Catholics continued to seethe over being forced to share their lands with Protestants. In the mid- to late nineteenth century, an Irish revolutionary group, the Fenians, engaged in bombing attacks on British targets not only in Ireland but in England and Canada, which was then a British colony. In the early twentieth century, violent rebellions in Ireland, as well as guerrilla attacks led by a group called the Irish Republican Army (IRA), led the British Parliament to agree to the creation of an independent Irish state, Ireland, which was predominantly Catholic; however, the same agreement also created Northern Ireland, which was predominantly Protestant and would remain under British rule as part of the United Kingdom. The IRA opposed this decision and it continued to attack British targets in hopes of forcing the United Kingdom to relinquish Northern Ireland, even though the many Protestants living in the region did not want this to occur. At the same time, Protestants in Northern Ireland known as Loyalists (because they remained loyal to the United Kingdom) formed paramilitary groups that engaged in anti-Catholic violence. For several decades, the nationalists fought with the Loyalists over the issue of whether Northern Ireland would reunite with Ireland, with both groups engaging in violence against innocent civilians. In addition, during the 1970s and 1980s Loyalists assassinated prominent nationalists and vice versa.

By this time, the IRA had splintered into two groups, the original IRA and the Provisional IRA. The former group largely abandoned violence in favor of political activism that included a Catholic civil rights movement aimed at weakening Protestant political power in Northern Ireland, whereas the latter group continued the militant activism established by the IRA. The Provisional IRA not only firebombed and car bombed British targets in Northern Ireland but also fired upon Protestants there, with the aim of threatening both security and commerce, and the British responded by sending additional military forces into Northern Ireland, even though this inflamed Catholic citizens who then rioted. One such riot in January 1972 became known as Bloody Sunday because the military quelled the violence by firing into the crowds, killing at least thirteen. That year, nearly five hundred people were killed in Northern Ireland, roughly half by the Provisional IRA (which, on one day alone, exploded twenty-two bombs in the Northern Ireland city of Belfast) and the remainder by either British forces or Loyalist paramilitary groups. The Provisional IRA also killed Protestant peasants in rural areas of Northern Ireland where British troops were scarce, policed fellow Catholics in urban areas of Northern Ireland by engaging in violent attacks known as kneecappings, which punished Catholics by shooting or striking them in the knees, and bombed tourist sites, hotels, pubs, and restaurants in England, especially in the city of London, as well as military and police facilities.

From the mid-1980s to the early 1990s, the British government made some inroads into lessening the violence in Northern Ireland by arresting or killing several terrorists, while civilians rioted in protest of the Provisional IRA bomb attacks. Nonetheless the bombings and assassinations continued until 1993, when several innocent people, including two children, were killed. In December of that year, the governments of England and Ireland began negotiating with the Provisional IRA, and eight months later the group agreed to end its violent activities. Two years later, however, the bombings began again. Then in 1998, the United Kingdom agreed to give Catholics equal say with Protestants in the government of Northern Ireland. This agreement and subsequent ones made other improvements in the situation as well, and in 2001 the IRA agreed to destroy its weapons. Though for a few years after this the Provisional IRA still attacked people in Northern Ireland who persecuted Catholics, the peace agreement held, and as of October 2006, according to a report issued by an independent group monitoring the situation (the Independent Monitoring Commission), the IRA is no longer engaging in terrorism or supporting criminal activities connected to terrorism. Other nationalist groups in the region, as well as Loyalist paramilitary groups, have also ceased their violent activities.

SEE ALSO: Irish Republican Army

nuclear weapons

Nuclear weapons are bombs or missile warheads that derive their force from the energy released during an atomic reaction—either the fission or fusion of the nuclei, or cores, within atoms. In fission, the nuclei are split into fragments, whereas in fusion, the nuclei are pressed so that they fuse together. Fission bombs are called atom or atomic bombs; fusion bombs are called hydrogen or thermonuclear bombs. Fusion bombs use hydrogen in their reaction, whereas atom bombs use either uranium or plutonium; together these two types of bombs are called nuclear weapons.

All nuclear weapons produce massive damage, but not always of the same kind. Small fusion bombs called neutron bombs produce only a small amount of blast and heat, which means that they leave most buildings in the "blast zone" standing, but they release massive amounts of lethal radiation, which means that they kill all living things within the zone (either immediately or later as the radiation poisoning takes effect). In contrast, atom bombs cause massive devastation to both people and buildings. Larger fusion bombs are far more destructive than atom bombs, but they are also more difficult to work with. Highly advanced calculations are necessary in order to make the fusion process occur, and because the fusion process only occurs at extremely high temperatures, fusion bombs must use fission bombs as detonators. Consequently most nations wanting nuclear weapons have concentrated their efforts on developing atom bombs.

See Also: bombs, atom

Nuremberg (also Nürnberg) trials

In 1945–46, a series of trials were conducted in the town of Nuremberg (or Nürnberg), Germany, in order to bring Nazi war criminals to justice. Handled by the International Military Tribunal, which was given its power by the agreement of twenty-three nations and was comprised of one representative (and an alternate) each from the United States, Great Britain, Russia, and France, these trials involved twenty-four individuals and several groups deemed by the tribunal to be criminal in nature, including the Gestapo, a Nazi police force. There were 216 court sessions in all, and in the end, nineteen of the defendants were found guilty; three were found innocent, one killed himself in prison before his verdict was reached, and one was deemed mentally incompetent to stand trial. Of those found guilty, twelve were sentenced to hang, three to serve life in prison, and the remainder to serve various sentences ranging from ten to twenty years.

See Also: Nazi terrorism

Oklahoma City bombing

The bombing of the Alfred P. Murrah Federal Building in Oklahoma City, Oklahoma, on April 19, 1995, was a major act of domestic terrorism that killed 168 people, including women and children in a day-care center on the first floor, and injured over 500 more. The explosion was caused by a four-thousand-pound fertilizer bomb in a rental truck that had been detonated next to the federal building af-

ter the driver, 26-year-old Timothy James McVeigh, had walked away from it. A former soldier who had served in the U.S. Army during the Gulf War, McVeigh had scheduled his attack to take place two years, to the day, after an attack by agents of the U.S. Bureau of Alcohol, Tobacco, and Firearms (ATF) on the Waco, Texas, compound of a religious group called the Branch Davidians. McVeigh felt that this incident, which had been prompted by the

Destruction wrought by the bombing of the Alfred P. Murrah Federal Building in Oklahoma City, Oklahoma, on April 19, 1995. Eric Draper. © AP Images

Branch Davidians' possession of illegal firearms, was an infringement on Americans' right to bear arms, and he wanted to punish the ATF for its actions. (He incorrectly believed that the agency had offices in the Alfred P. Murrah Federal Building.) McVeigh was arrested eighty minutes after the explosion by an Oklahoma state trooper who spotted him driving a car with no license plates. He was soon connected to the bombing. McVeigh was put on trial on April 24, 1997, in Denver, Colorado, where his defense attorneys suggested that others might have been involved in the crime, including Islamic militants, neo-Nazis, and members of the Christian Identity movement, and that the U.S. government had advance knowledge of McVeigh's plans but failed to stop him from carrying them out. The defense claimed that federal authorities were suppressing evidence of a broader conspiracy in which McVeigh was only a minor player, and indeed there is evidence that an associate of McVeigh, Terry Nichols, who helped him make the bomb, also met with Islamic terrorists, some of them linked to the al Qaeda network of terrorist Osama bin Laden, to discuss the manufacture of explosive devices. The defense also showed that McVeigh had been in contact with neo-Nazis who might have received funds from the Iraqi government and that several Christian Identity terrorists had been planning to blow up the Murrah Federal Building for several years. Nonetheless the judge refused to allow most aspects of the conspiracy defense to be introduced into the trial, and in 1997 McVeigh was convicted and sentenced to die by lethal injection. He was executed in 2001. McVeigh's associate, Terry Lynn Nichols, was also put on trial for his involvement in the manufacture of the bomb; found guilty on one count of conspiracy and eight counts of manslaughter, he was sentenced to life in prison.

SEE ALSO: Alcohol, Tobacco; and Firearms, U.S. Bureau of; al Qaeda; Christian Identity movement; McVeigh, Timothy; neo-Nazis; Nichols, Terry Lynn; Waco incident

Olympic Games as terrorist targets

Because the eyes of the world are on the Olympic Games, terrorists know that an attack on any aspect of an Olympic event or on its athletes will bring attention to their cause. Moreover the athletes are viewed as symbols of their countries, which makes them symbolic targets for terrorists wanting to strike out at certain nations. This was the case, for example, with the 1972 Summer Olympics in Munich, Germany, where Palestinian terrorists killed several Israeli athletes.

An attack on the Olympics might also result from the terrorist's feelings about the host country. For example, when anti-abortion activist Eric Rudolph was arrested for planting bombs at a site connected to the 1996 Olympics Games in Atlanta, Georgia, he said that he had wanted to stop the Olympics in order to embarrass the United States, as Rudolph believed the country deserved given its stance on abortion. But although terrorists are motivated to target the Olympics, the Munich and Atlanta incidents are the only such attacks to take place so far because the games have extremely tight security measures.

SEE ALSO: Atlanta's Centennial Park bombing; Munich Olympics crisis

Omega 7

Established in 1974 in the United States among Cuban exiles there, the terrorist group Omega 7 engaged in bombing attacks during the 1970s and 1980s against anyone who supported the Communist dictatorship of Fidel Castro in Cuba. Its name comes from the fact that it began with just seven members, all of whom had fought in the Bay of Pigs invasion of Cuba in 1961. (This failed U.S.-backed invasion sent a guerrilla force of Cuban exiles from the United States to Cuba in an attempt to overthrow Castro.) The group's first attack was against the Venezuelan consulate in New York City in 1975; there were thirty attacks in all in several U.S. states, and in 1980 the group bombed the Cuban consulate in Montreal, Canada. That same year, Omega 7 assassinated a Cuban diplomat, and nearly assassinated the Cuban ambassador to the United Nations (UN), Dr. Raul Roa Kouri. The following year, however, the group's members began fighting among themselves, and its leader, Eduardo Arocena, spoke to the Federal Bureau of Investigation (FBI) in an attempt to convince the U.S. government to arrest Omega 7 members who disagreed with him. Shortly thereafter, Arocena realized that the government was planning to arrest not only the other Omega 7 members but him as well. He went underground, but in 1983 the FBI tracked him down and arrested him. Arocena is now serving life in prison, and the Omega 7 has disbanded.

Operation Backfire

Operation Backfire was a U.S. investigation into more than twenty cases of ecoterrorism in Oregon, Washington, California, Wyoming, and Colorado, where firebombs damaged or destroyed lumber mills, research facilities involved in the genetic engineering of plants, an electrical tower, a ski resort encroaching on the habitat of endangered lynx, a horse slaughterhouse, wild-horse roundup facilities, and sport utility vehicles (SUVs) known for getting poor gas mileage and causing pollution. Two radical environmental groups, the Earth Liberation Front (ELF) and the Animal Liberation Front (ALF), took credit for these attacks, which took place during a five-year period ending in September 2001 and caused over $30 million in damages. However, the agents of the Federal Bureau of Investigation (FBI) who investigated the violence attributed most of the firebombings to an ecoterrorist cell only loosely associated with both environmental groups. Known as The Family and based in Eugene, Oregon, this cell was led by a bookstore owner from Prescott, Arizona, named William C. Rodgers, who committed suicide in jail after being arrested by the FBI for the crimes. As of November 2006, twelve other people had been arrested for the attacks and received varying sentences; they pleaded guilty to arson and conspiracy in order to avoid trials that might have resulted in life sentences. The FBI would probably not have connected any of these people to the firebombings had it not been for the girlfriend of one of the bombers, who was uncomfortable keeping the bombers' activities a secret because her father was a state fire marshal. Before the informant came forward the FBI had found no clues regarding the bombers' identities because the ecoterrorists had been careful not to leave fingerprints, DNA, or other evidence on their firebombs, which were typically made using five-gallon (19L) buckets of diesel fuel. Another informant—a former member of The Family who had been involved in the bombing—agreed to help the FBI gather additional information about the group by wearing a hidden recording device while talking to various ecoterrorists. As a result of this aspect of the investigation, Operation Backfire led to the breakup of several other ALF and ELF-associated cells in the Pacific Northwest.

See Also: Animal Liberation Front; Earth Liberation Front; ecoterrorism

Operation Eagle Claw

Operation Eagle Claw was a failed 1980 U.S. military mission to rescue sixty-six hostages from militant students in Tehran, Iran. The hostage crisis began on November 4, 1979, when approximately five hundred students surrounded the city's U.S. embassy to protest American meddling in Iranian politics. (The trigger for this protest was the fact that the United States had helped the former ruler of Iran, deposed in a revolution the year before, leave Iran and come to the United States for medical treatment, after which the new leader of Iran, Ayatollah Ruhollah Khomeini, demanded his return.) Suddenly the crowd surged into the building and took it over. A few days later, the students released thirteen of the hostages, keeping only white males, whom they held for almost six months while the United States tried to negotiate their release. Eventually the U.S. president, Jimmy Carter, decided that the only way to resolve the situation was by force. He authorized a secret rescue mission that would employ personnel from the army, air force, and marines; navy helicopters and air force planes would take troops to a staging area in a desert near Tehran, and from there the assault on the embassy would begin. Instead, though, a dust storm made it impossible for all of the helicopters to reach the site, and one of them slammed into one of the airplanes, killing five air force men and three

marines. Knowing that the disaster would attract the attention of the Iranian government, which would never have given permission for U.S. forces to enter its borders, the U.S. military immediately evacuated everyone at the staging area, but they had to leave their equipment and the bodies of those killed in the crash behind. Afterward President Carter was severely criticized for authorizing such a mission, and an evaluation of its failures showed that it was necessary for the U.S. government to do more to coordinate the operations of all branches of the military and to train all members of all armed forces in the same way. Operation Eagle Claw also led the United States to devote more resources to developing military units dedicated to counterterrorist activities.

Operation Enduring Freedom

"Operation Enduring Freedom" is the name that the U.S. government, under the administration of George W. Bush, gave to the military campaign against the Taliban in Afghanistan in 2001–2002. Primarily a U.S. action but with the cooperation of a coalition of forces from other countries, this campaign was originally named Operation Infinite Justice, but this wording was changed because to Muslims, only God can deliver "infinite justice." The intent of the operation was to destroy the Afghani bases of the terrorist group al Qaeda in response to this group's September 11, 2001, attack on the World Trade Center in New York and the Pentagon in Washington, D.C. But while the assault on Afghanistan did destroy some al Qaeda strongholds, others remain, and the group's leader, Osama bin Laden, is believed to still be in the country.

See Also: Afghanistan; bin laden, Osama; September 11 attacks on America; Taliban

General Tommy Ray Franks speaks at the one-year anniversary of Operation Enduring Freedom at MacDill Air Force Base in Florida. SCOTT MARTIN. © AP IMAGES

Order, the

An American white-supremacist terrorist group comprised of neo-Nazis and members of the Christian Identity movement, the Order was established in 1983 by Robert Mathews, an anti-Semite who had spent time in jail for tax evasion. Mathews believed that taxation was not only illegal but that it had been created by Jews who wanted to steal the money of Christians. He formed the Order, whose name he took from a terrorist group in a novel called *The Turner Diaries* by William Pierce, with the intent of using it to spark a revolution that would overthrow the U.S. government. However, from the beginning the

Order was primarily focused on committing for-profit crimes, supposedly to finance its revolution. They started out by robbing individuals that they had deemed immoral, such as drug dealers and prostitutes. They next turned to bank robbery, armored-car robbery, and counterfeiting. Then in the spring of 1984 the group turned to violence. In April two of its members, without authorization from the Order as a whole, planted a bomb at a synagogue, and the following month the group killed a member of another white-supremacist group, the Aryan Nations, who was divulging the Order's activities. The following month, the Order assassinated Alan Berg, a Jewish radio host who had often spoken out against white-supremacist groups. This was to be the first in a series of assassinations of prominent Jews, but shortly thereafter the Federal Bureau of Investigation (FBI) arrested a member of the Order for counterfeiting and he put the FBI on the trail of the rest. By the late 1980s most members were in custody; Mathews, however, resisted arrest and was killed in a standoff with police.

SEE ALSO: anti-Semitism; Aryan Nations; Christian Identity movement; neo-Nazis

Organization for the Oppressed Earth

The Organization for the Oppressed Earth took credit for the 1985 hijacking of TWA Flight 847 while it was en route from Athens, Greece, to Rome, Italy. After landing in Beirut, Lebanon, to refuel, the two hijackers flew this plane to Algiers, Algeria, released some of their hostages, flew back to Beirut, picked up several more armed terrorists, and negotiated the release of the remaining hostages in exchange for several demands, including the release of some imprisoned Shiite Muslims. Later, however, the Organization for the Oppressed Earth was linked to the Lebanese terrorist group Hezbollah, and some terrorism experts believe that the hijackers were really Hezbollah members operating under an assumed group name.

SEE ALSO: Hezbollah; hijackings, aircraft

Pakistan

Pakistan has long been in conflict with neighboring India, largely because the former is primarily Muslim and the latter primarily Hindu; the two groups began attacking one another after British colonial forces withdrew from the region in 1947, and today the animosity between Pakistanis and Indians is so strong that terrorism experts have compared it to that between Arabs and Israelis. Because of such feelings, Pakistan has supported numerous anti-Indian terrorist groups (just as India has supported numerous anti-Pakistani terrorist groups). One of the most active is the radical Islamic group Jaish-e-Mohammed (JEM), or the "Army of Muhammad." In the late 1990s this group began attacking targets connected to India with the goal of forcing India to allow the region of Kashmir, now controlled by India, to join with Pakistan, but in 2002 JEM began attacking Pakistani targets as well, believing that the Pakistani government had become a puppet of the United States. A similar group is the Harakat ul-Mujahideen ("Force of Holy Warriors," or HUM), whose terrorist attacks in India and Kashmir have been supported by the Pakistani government. During the 1990s the group's members trained at guerrilla camps in Pakistan, but in 1999 the Pakistani government ended its support for HUM and arrested so many of the group's members that some experts on terrorism believe it no longer exists. The government took these actions under pressure from the United States, which has severely criticized Pakistan for its support of terrorists, many of whom the Pakistani government calls "freedom fighters" instead. The United States has also criticized Pakistan for maintaining a connection with the radical Muslims of the Taliban who were once in control of Afghanistan.

SEE ALSO: Harakat ul-Mujahideen; Jaish-e-Mohammed; Taliban

Palestine

A region of southwest Asia along the eastern shore of the Mediterranean Sea, Palestine has long been a source of conflict. Historians disagree on where its boundaries were in ancient times, when it was a province of the Roman Empire, and on whether it might have previously been an ancient land known as Philistinia, whose people were enemies of the Israelites. In any case, by the end of the nineteenth century, Palestine consisted of what are now Jordan and Israel as well as the West Bank and the Gaza Strip, and Arabs generally believed that only Muslims had the right to live there. Consequently after the independent Jewish state of Israel was established in 1948 (the Muslim country of Jordan received its independence in 1922), Palestinian Arabs began attacking Jews in the region. During the 1950s, this violence grew more organized, as Palestinian *fedayeen*, or fighters, based in Egypt and Jordan began crossing into Israel to attack facilities necessary to keep the country running, such as electric plants, irrigation systems, and transportation systems, as well as innocent civilians. As these assaults continued into the 1960s, Israel reacted by triggering the Six-Day War of 1967, during which it inflicted serious damage on the armies and air forces of Jordan, Syria, and Egypt. Israeli forces also occupied the West Bank and the Gaza Strip, where they restricted the freedoms of Muslims there in an attempt to stamp out Arab terrorism.

Meanwhile terrorists associated with the Palestine Liberation Organization (PLO) kept striking out at Israeli targets, first from Jordan and then from Lebanon. The PLO was established in 1964 as a central organization for militant Arab groups whose shared goal was the creation of an independent Palestinian state, either by the destruction of Israel or, after 1967, by the retaking of the Israeli-controlled West Bank and Gaza Strip; among the groups within the PLO were al Fatah, the Abu Nidal Organization (ANO), and the Popular Front for the Liberation of Palestine. Al Fatah was the dominant member of the PLO, and al Fatah's leader, Yasir Arafat, was its head. Under his leadership, which lasted until his death in 2004, the PLO was transformed into a political organization, and in the early 1990s it officially renounced terrorism, as did al Fatah. Arafat then began participating in negotiations that eventually convinced Israel to withdraw from the lands it took in 1967 (the West Bank and the Gaza Strip), where Israeli authority would be replaced by a governing body known as the Palestinian Authority. In other words, a Palestinian state would finally exist; nonetheless the radical Islamic groups within the PLO, including Hamas, continued to engage in violent attacks against Israel, and Israel responded in kind, although there were brief periods of uneasy peace. Then, in January 2006, Hamas became the majority party in the Palestinian Authority, and tensions between Palestine and Israel quickly escalated. Israel and the West urged Hamas to officially renounce terrorism and recognize Israel's right to exist; when Hamas refused, the international community placed economic sanctions on Palestine.

On June 25, 2006, Palestinian militants linked to Hamas captured a soldier during a raid along the Israeli border, and a few days later—only a year after Israel had withdrawn its troops from the Gaza Strip—Israel began a military offensive in Gaza to force the terrorists to release the captive soldier; in response Palestinian militants fired rockets into Israel. Over three hundred Palestinians were killed during this five-month offensive, along with three Israeli soldiers and two Israeli civilians. But although Israel had the upper hand, it declared a cease-fire in November 2006 in response to international outrage over its killing of a family of nineteen civilians during one of its attacks. The president of the Palestinian Authority, Mahmoud Abbas, convinced the radical Palestinian groups to honor this cease-fire. However, the sanctions remained in place, despite Abbas's pleas that they be lifted. A member of al Fatah, Abbas then began working to replace the Hamas-led Palestinian government with one that was more moderate, hoping that this would someday change the West's position on Palestine.

A cease-fire was agreed upon by both al Fatah and Hamas in February 2007, but just days later a battle broke out in the Gaza Strip between members of the two groups. Using assault rifles and launching rocket-propelled missiles, militants damaged two universities, blew up a radio station, and destroyed other buildings. Dozens of people were killed in the melee over control of the new Palestinian provisional government.

SEE ALSO: Abu Nidal Organization; al Fatah; Arafat, Yasir; Hamas; Israel; Palestine Liberation Organization; Popular Front for the Liberation of Palestine

Palestine Liberation Front (PLF)

Founded in the mid-1970s, the Palestine Liberation Front (PLF) is best known for its involvement in the 1985 hijacking of the Italian cruise ship *Achille Lauro* and the murder of one of the ship's passengers, a wheelchair-bound, elderly New Yorker named Leon Klinghoffer who was targeted for being both American and Jewish. After this incident, some of the hijackers were captured, while others escaped from Italy into Yugoslavia; these escapees included the group's leader, Muhammad (also known as Abu) Abbas. Abbas created the PLF from dissatisfied members of the Popular Front for the Liberation of Palestine-General Command, which sought to drive Israelis from Palestinian lands. The PLF was originally based in Tunisia, but relocated to Iraq after the hijacking. By this time, Italy had sentenced Abbas in absentia to life in prison for Klinghoffer's murder, and dozens of PLF members had been arrested for engaging in various terrorist attacks in Israel. Nonetheless in the mid-1990s Israel allowed Abbas to participate in Palestinian-Israeli peace negotiations in the Gaza Strip after he openly supported the peace process. According to Abbas at the time, the PLF had abandoned terrorism, and the group still denies that it engages in terrorism. However, the U.S. government has never accepted this claim, and Israel continues to arrest individual PLF members suspected of plotting terrorist attacks.

SEE ALSO: Palestine

Palestine Liberation Organization (PLO)

The Palestine Liberation Organization (PLO) was established in 1964 as a central organization for all Palestinian movements. In other words, the organization was formed by militant Arab groups whose shared goal was the creation of an independent Palestinian state, by the destruction of Israel or by the retaking of the Israeli-controlled West Bank and Gaza Strip. Among the groups within the PLO were al Fatah, the Abu Nidal Organization (ANO), and the Popular Front for the Liberation of Palestine (PFLP). Al Fatah quickly became the dominant member of the PLO, and al Fatah's leader, Yasir Arafat, was named head of the PLO's forces; in 1973 he became head of the political branch of the PLO as well. Under his leadership, which lasted until his death in 2004, the PLO was transformed from a loose association of militant groups into a tightly structured, well-managed, and well-funded organization. In 1988, for example, the group had a budget of $674 million, and its investments alone were bringing in an income of $300 million; in 1990, according to estimates by the U.S. government, the PLO's total wealth was at least $8 billion and possibly as much as $14 billion.

As the PLO made the transition to a powerful, wealthy organization, it also changed its approach toward violence. In its early years, operating first from Jordan and then from Lebanon, the organization launched several attacks on Israel, and in September 1972 one of the PLO groups, Black September, killed eleven Israeli athletes at the Olympic Games in Munich, Germany. Worldwide public outrage over this incident led Arafat to decree that in the future the PLO would only commit acts of violence in lands held by Israelis. When Israel invaded Lebanon in 1982, after many Palestinian refugees had settled there, the organization concentrated much of its efforts in that country, using physical violence to protect the Palestinian refugees and to drive others out of areas where the Palestinians wanted to settle. PLO attacks here and elsewhere in the region continued until the early 1990s, when Arafat officially denounced terrorism and began concentrating the PLO's efforts in the political arena. At this time, he participated in negotiations that convinced Israel to withdraw from parts of the West Bank, where its authority would be replaced by the Palestinian Authority, a political body that was soon dominated by the PLO. Today the PLO remains a political rather than a terrorist organization; however, in 2000 some of its member groups again began engaging in violent attacks as part of a 2000–2001 Palestinian uprising, or intifada, in protest of Israeli occupation. (This event is known as the second intifada, because a similar uprising occurred in 1987.)

SEE ALSO: Abu Nidal Organization; al Fatah; Arafat, Yasir; Black September; Munich Olympics crisis; Popular Front for the Liberation of Palestine

Palestinian Islamic Jihad (PIJ)

Also called the Palestine Islamic Jihad, the Palestinian Islamic Jihad (PIJ) is a radical Islamic terrorist group that has launched numerous attacks against Israeli targets, possibly with funding from Iran, in opposition to Israel's occupation of the Gaza Strip and the West Bank. It has bombed military and government targets, including a crowded military bus in 1995, and assas-

sinated military and government personnel. It has also attacked civilians in Israel, particularly via suicide bombs. The group was created in the late 1970s in Egypt by three Palestinian college students who, because of their religious rather than political beliefs, felt that Israel had no right to exist. In the early 1980s the PIJ began operating out of Palestine and Israeli-occupied territories, but by the late 1980s it had moved its base to Syria, where it remains today. The group has threatened to attack targets associated with the United States because of its support of Israel, but terrorism experts disagree on whether it has actually been responsible for any such attacks.

SEE ALSO: Palestine

Pan Am Flight 103 bombing (Lockerbie bombing)

Pan Am Flight 103, a Boeing 747 en route from London, England, to New York, crashed in Lockerbie, Scotland, on December 21, 1988, after a bomb in the plane's cargo hold went off at around 7 PM. At the time of the explosion, the plane was flying at approximately thirty-one thousand feet; when it hit the ground, it destroyed twenty-one homes, scattered wreckage over 845 miles (1360 km), and killed 11 residents of Lockerbie and all 259 passengers on board. The bomb had apparently been hidden inside a cassette recorder, which in turn had been placed inside a suitcase; remnants of this suitcase, along with scraps of the clothing it contained, ultimately led investigators to two Libyan nationalists, Abdel Baset Ali Mohamed al-Megrahi and Al-Amin Khalifa Fhimah, who worked for an airline owned by Libya and had apparently used their access to baggage-loading areas to get the bomb onto the plane. By the time these men were connected to the Lockerbie bombing, they were also suspected of killing 171 people in the bombing of a French airplane over Niger in 1989. In 1991 the United States, Scotland, and France all demanded that the Libyan government produce al-Megrahi and Fhimah so they could stand trial. Libya's leader, Mu'ammar Qaddafi, refused. Over the next three years, the United Nations put various sanctions in place to force Libya to comply, but it was not until 1999 that the government finally turned the terrorists over to the United Nations, which then lifted the sanctions. Their trial was held in the Netherlands, where al-Megrahi was sentenced to life in prison and Fhimah was acquitted for lack of evidence against him. Since then, al-Megrahi has insisted that he is innocent as well. But regardless of who carried out the attack, some people believe that Iran was ultimately responsible for it, funding the bombing as revenge for the deaths of 290 people on an Iranian Airbus destroyed by a U.S. military ship in 1988, four months before the Lockerbie bombing.

SEE ALSO: Qaddafi, Mu'ammar

Paraguay, Ciudad del Este

The port city of Ciudad del Este, Paraguay, is home to several terrorist cells connected to radical Islamic organizations like Hezbollah and Hamas. These groups were attracted to the region not only because it has a growing Muslim community (currently a little more than 3 percent of the population) but also, more importantly, because it is the center of a $12-billion-a-year smuggling business. This business provides terrorists with weapons, forged or stolen passports and other illegal documents, and cash. For example, between 1998 and 2005, supporters of the

terrorist group Hezbollah who were living in Ciudad del Este sent the group over $50 million generated by the smuggling of pirated software and CDs. Ciudad del Este also supports terrorism via a banking system that allows foreigners to launder their money, or hide the source and destination of their funds. This money-laundering business brings a variety of terrorists (including not just radical Muslims but other types as well) to the town, as well as drug dealers and other criminals.

SEE ALSO: funding terrorism; Hamas; Hezbollah; narco-terrorism

Patriot Act, the U.S.

Enacted by the U.S. Congress in 2001, the Patriot Act was proposed by the administration of President George W. Bush as a way to combat terrorism in the aftermath of the September 11, 2001, terrorist attacks on the United States. The act is complex, but among its features are the establishment of new laws and policies that make it easier for federal authorities to prevent terrorism and to track down, arrest, and prosecute terrorists. For example, the act permits the federal government to freeze the bank accounts and other assets of people suspected of being terrorists so that they cannot fund their activities, and it makes it a crime for anyone to knowingly shelter a terrorist. Some of the act's laws and policies, however, are controversial because they infringe upon long-held individual rights, such as the right to privacy. For example, the Patriot Act allows federal authorities to listen in on people's phone conversations and voice mail messages without first obtaining a warrant. Opponents of such provisions hoped that Congress would not vote to renew them when the opportunity arose in early 2006,

After Wall Street Journal *reporter Daniel Pearl was kidnapped, in Karachi, Pakistan, photographed in captivity, and beheaded, a group called the National Movement for the Restoration of Pakistani Sovereignty claimed sole responsibility for his death, but terrorism experts disagree on whether this was the case.* CNN/GETTY IMAGES

but Congress ultimately decided to keep all aspects of the Patriot Act in place.

SEE ALSO: funding terrorism; September 11 attacks on America

Pearl, Daniel
(1963–2002)

On January 23, 2002, American journalist Daniel Pearl was kidnapped by radical Islamic terrorists while he was in Pakistan working on an article for the *Wall Street Journal*. At the time he was taken, Pearl was en route to a meeting with Sheik Mubarak, Ali Gilani, an Islamic extremist whom Pearl believed had information that would connect terrorist Richard Reid (also known as the Shoe Bomber because he tried to smuggle explosives on an airplane

by hiding them in his basketball shoes) with the al Qaeda terrorist group. Pearl had written other articles about al Qaeda—particularly in regard to how it funded terrorist activities—and after he was kidnapped this group was suspected of being responsible for his disappearance. However, the National Movement for the Restoration of Pakistani Sovereignty soon took credit for the kidnapping and released photographs of Pearl, taken in captivity, to prove their claim. Insisting that Pearl was a spy working for both Americans and Israelis, the Pakistani terrorists said that they would execute him unless Pakistani terrorists held at the U.S. military prison at Guantánamo Bay, Cuba, were released. When these prisoners were not released, the terrorist group sent the media a video of Pearl being decapitated. Even before this tape surfaced, Pakistani police had arrested Islamic radical Ahmed Omar Sheikh for the kidnapping, based on reliable witnesses who said that he had been seen with Pearl prior to his disappearance; three other men were subsequently arrested as well. They were eventually sentenced to life in prison, while Sheikh was sentenced to death. Terrorism experts disagree, however, on which terrorist group or groups were behind these men's actions. Some think that in addition to or instead of the National Movement for the Restoration of Pakistani Sovereignty, they were working for Jaish-e-Mohammed (JEM), or the "Army of Mohammad." (When formed in the late 1990s, this radical Islamic group only attacked targets connected with India, but in 2002 it began attacking targets connected with Pakistan and the United States as well.) Others continue to believe that al Qaeda was responsible, and indeed at least one al Qaeda member has insisted that his group was involved in Pearl's death.

SEE ALSO: al Qaeda; Jaish-e-Mohammed; Pakistan; Reid, Richard

People for the Ethical Treatment of Animals (PETA)

Some people have accused the animal-rights group People for the Ethical Treatment of Animals (PETA) of being a terrorist organization because its members have, on occasion, thrown paint and other substances on people wearing fur; forced disturbing photographs of animals at medical-research facilities, slaughterhouses, and fur factories upon unwilling passersby; and engaged in passionate demonstrations and protests intended to interfere with businesses that exploit animals. However, PETA's acts are generally nonviolent, in accordance with the group's stated philosophy of pacifism. Its members primarily engage in political activism and public-information campaigns in order to protect the well-being of animals, particularly those animals used by the fur industry, the entertainment industry, medical researchers, and slaughterhouses. Therefore most terrorism experts do not classify PETA as a terrorist organization, and some believe that much of the violence attributed to the group has actually been caused by another, more radical animal-rights group, the Animal Liberation Front (ALF).

SEE ALSO: Animal Liberation Front

Persian Gulf War

A 1991 conflict between Iraq and the United States—the latter of which had support from an international coalition of forces—the Persian Gulf War (also known more simply as the Gulf War) was triggered when Iraq invaded one of its neighbors, Kuwait. Iraq and Kuwait had previously fought against each other in the Iran-Iraq War of 1980–1988, triggered in large part by Iraq's belief that Kuwait was stealing its oil along the Iraq-Kuwait border. Just prior to the Persian Gulf War, Iraq accused Kuwait of manipulating oil prices so that Iraq would profit less on the international market. In August 1990 Iraq invaded Kuwait in an attempt to control Kuwaiti oil fields. The United Nations (UN) officially condemned this action, calling for Iraq to withdraw its troops from Kuwait immediately, and established an economic embargo on Iraq.

Meanwhile, the United States sent troops to protect Saudi Arabia, which feared that Iraq might invade its country to seize oil fields as well. There the U.S. troops joined with troops from other nations to launch Operation Desert Shield, which became Operation Desert Storm on January 16, 1991, when it attacked Iraq. This attack—which began only after the UN issued an ultimatum giving Iraq until January 15 to withdraw from Kuwait—was initially an air assault, but in late February it became a ground campaign; most of the troops were American, though several other nations contributed both men and money to the effort. Four days after this ground assault began, the U.S.-led coalition forces had driven the Iraqi forces from Kuwait. However, this victory, as well as the buildup leading to the Persian Gulf War, ultimately caused the United States many problems, because it increased Iraqi support for international terrorist groups and angered Muslims who felt that the United States had no business becoming involved in Arab disputes. Before, during, and after the war, terrorism against targets associated with the United States became much more frequent, and anti-U.S. sentiment in the Middle East rose. In fact, the continuing presence of U.S. troops in

Saudi Arabia after the Gulf War was one of the factors responsible for the development and growth of al Qaeda, the radical Islamic terrorist group responsible for the attacks on the World Trade Center in New York and the Pentagon in Washington, D.C., on September 11, 2001.

Some people also believe that the Persian Gulf War was the reason that U.S. president George W. Bush attacked Iraq after the September 11, 2001, terrorist attacks, even though Iraq was not responsible for the events of September 11. Bush's father, George H.W. Bush, was president during the Gulf War, and at that time he was criticized for not going on to capture the Iraqi capital of Baghdad after taking Kuwait, thereby leaving a brutal dictator, Saddam Hussein, in control of Iraq. As part of the surrender agreement that ended the Gulf War, Hussein promised to allow international inspectors into his country to ensure that he was not developing weapons of mass destruction, but on many occasions he made it difficult or even impossible for the inspectors to do their work. In addition, there is some evidence that Hussein tried to have the senior Bush assassinated. Consequently even before the September 11 attacks, according to some of the younger Bush's confidants, President George W. Bush expressed a desire to finish his father's work by ridding Iraq of Hussein—a desire that was fulfilled via the 2003 U.S. attack on and occupation of Iraq and the subsequent trial, conviction, and execution of Hussein by the Iraqi Special Tribunal in 2006.

SEE ALSO: Hussein, Saddam; Iraq

Peru

Peru experienced a great deal of terrorism from the 1960s through the 1990s, thanks in large part to two militant Marxist groups. The first was Sendero Luminoso (Shining Path), whose goal was to destroy all existing political, economic, and social institutions in the country so that they could be replaced by an agricultural society similar to one that existed there under the Inca Empire prior to the sixteenth century; the second was the Tupac Amaru Revolutionary Movement (MRTA), which bombed urban targets in hopes of triggering a revolution that would ultimately create a society similar to Cuba's under Communist leader Fidel Castro. In 1997 the latter attacked the Japanese ambassador's residence and took seventy-two people hostage. After a standoff of over four months, the Peruvian military stormed the embassy and killed most of the group's leaders before rescuing the hostages. This act was the beginning of a more aggressive approach to terrorism in Peru, and by 2000 the government had managed to arrest many of the members of Sendero Luminoso and the MRTA and to break up many other terrorist groups as well. Consequently although there are still terrorists operating in Peru, they are much less active than they were prior to 2000.

SEE ALSO: embassy bombings; Tupac Amaru Revolutionary Movement (MRTA)

Philippines, the

Several terrorist groups currently operate on the islands of the Philippines, though some have signed peace agreements with the government. The Moro National Liberation Front (MNLF), for example, signed such an agreement first in 1978 and again in 1996. Another group, the Moro Islamic Liberation Front (MILF), signed a peace agreement in 2001, after an aggressive military campaign against its guerrillas nearly destroyed the group. One of the most notorious terrorist groups in the region, however, has refused to negotiate with the government: Abu Sayyaf (Bearer of the Sword), which is connected to the Islamic terrorist network al Qaeda. Like most other terrorist groups in the Philippines, including MNLF and MILF, Abu Sayyaf's existence arose out of a desire to create an independent Muslim state within the Philippines, where approximately 5 percent of the population is Muslim. To this end, in March 2000 Abu Sayyaf took twenty-seven schoolchildren and their teachers hostage until an Army attack forced the terrorists to flee, and in April 2000 the group kidnapped twenty-three people, including foreign tourists and journalists, from a Malaysian resort and released them in exchange for $25 million in ransom money. In May 2001 they kidnapped another twenty people and again held them for ransom; the following month they beheaded one of these hostages after failing to receive their demands. As a result of this act and Abu Sayyaf's known connection with al Qaeda, in 2001 the U.S. government provided the Philippine government with $100 million and military training to further their efforts to eliminate Abu Sayyaf. By 2002 so many of the group's members had been killed or driven from the country that terrorism experts disagree on whether it remains a viable organization today. Two other groups that have engaged in terrorism in the Philippines, the New People's Army (NPA) and the Alex Boncayao Brigade, were primarily active in the mid-1980s and throughout the 1990s, when they sought to eliminate the U.S. presence in the region; these groups were Communist rather than Muslim.

SEE ALSO: Abu Sayyaf; Moro Islamic Liberation Front

pirates

Beginning in the sixteenth century, pirates sometimes used terrorism to instill fear in the seafaring population and enhance their own reputations for fierceness. Their aim in doing so was primarily to reduce the amount of effort and weaponry it would take to seize a particular ship, because they made it known that they would refrain from their acts of barbarism, which included various forms of torture as well as murder, if their victims surrendered without a fight. In this way they were similar to medieval warriors who laid siege to castles, fortresses, and fortified towns.

SEE ALSO: medieval terrorism

Popular Front for the Liberation of Palestine (PFLP)

A group within the Palestine Liberation Organization (PLO), the Popular Front for the Liberation of Palestine (PFLP) was established in 1967 by George Habash, a supporter of Marxist-Leninist ideology who wanted to see Arabs from many nations participate in a revolution that would establish a single Arab state encompassing all of the Middle East. Under Habash's leadership, during the 1960s and '70s the PFLP staged several airplane hijackings while operating from Jordan, and in September 1970 the group coordinated the hijackings of one jet from each of four airlines based in four countries: the United States, Great Britain, Israel, and Switzerland. The U.S. jet was blown up during this attack, after the planes landed in Amman, Jordan; afterward the head of Jordan, King Hussein, launched a crackdown on Palestinian guerrillas in his country. The group then declared it would no longer engage in hijackings, and for a time it disappeared, though some of its members took part in projects designed to benefit Palestinians, such as the establishment of health clinics. Meanwhile Habash established a new headquarters in Damascus, Syria, and bases in both Syria and the West Bank. In the early 1990s the PFLP again became active, resurfacing to reject a PLO peace agreement with Israel. Over the next few years, the PFLP spoke out against any such attempts at peace, and in 2000, after Habash retired from leading the group and was replaced by the more militant Mustafa Zibri, also known as Abu Ali Mustafa, it began engaging in roadside bombings and other attacks on Israelis. In 2001 Israeli agents assassinated Mustafa, and in response the PFLP assassinated an Israeli cabinet minister. Israel then pressed the Palestinian Authority to arrest the new head of the PFLP, Ahmed Saadat; afterward some PFLP members threatened to assassinate Palestinian Authority members if Saadat was not released. Not only were they unsuccessful in achieving this, but their threat against fellow Palestinians led other members of the PFLP to denounce violence and distance themselves from the group. Still, militants within the group continue to engage in violence. It is unclear how many people currently belong to the PFLP, though in the 1990s it had roughly eight hundred members.

SEE ALSO: Habash, George

Posse Comitatus (Power of the Country)

Created in 1969, the Posse Comitatus, or Power of the Country, is an Oregon group of right-wing Christian extremists who do not recognize the powers of the federal government, particularly in regard to tax collection. Instead the group only recognizes the power of the county, saying that local governments alone have legitimate authority over citizens. The posse also op-

poses desegregation and believes that Jews and Communists are plotting to seize control of America through its financial institutions. Posse members therefore stockpile weapons and engage in military training in preparation for a war against a future Jewish government. During the 1980s some members plotted attacks on federal judges, while another, Gordon Kahl, shot two federal officials who were trying to arrest him in 1985 for tax evasion after having already served time for the same offense. Kahl was subsequently shot while continuing to resist arrest; his death inspired many other right-wing extremists to join the Posse Comitatus, and the group subsequently established dozens of chapters throughout the American West and Midwest. This was its most active period, but the Posse Comitatus still exists today and is an ally of several neo-Nazi and other white-supremacist and anti-Semitic groups.

SEE ALSO: anti-Semitism; neo-Nazis; white supremacists

propaganda

Propaganda is a systematic, deliberate attempt to convince people to adopt a particular cause, set of beliefs, or course of action. Often based on a political agenda, this type of indoctrination is used by governments or organizations that might distort the truth in order to manipulate public sentiments. Propaganda is typically spread via the media (radio, newspapers, and television), reaching a domestic or international audience. In many cases the propagandist message is disseminated through persuasive writing, but most terrorists prefer armed propaganda, which is propaganda that sends a message through symbolic violence. Examples of armed propaganda include hostage beheadings, embassy bombings, airplane hijackings, assaults on occupying troops, and other attacks intended to attract more supporters to the perpetrators' cause. Armed propaganda falls into the category of what terrorism experts call "propaganda by deed," or propaganda that uses actions to demonstrate the strength of the perpetrators and the weakness of the opposition. The intent of propaganda by deed is often to attract others to the cause. For example, many radical Islamic terrorists attack Western targets in an attempt to convince Muslims that God favors them in a battle against Christian forces and will reward those who join the fight. Propaganda by deed is also employed in order to sow discontent in a society against its government. In other words, by disrupting daily life in a particular country, terrorists hope that its citizens will demand that their government accommodate the terrorists' wishes. This was the case, for example, when Puerto Rican nationalists bombed various sites in the United States during the 1980s in an unsuccessful attempt to convince the American public to demand that Puerto Rico, a U.S. commonwealth, be granted its independence. Propaganda by deed might be the only way that terrorists can influence the population in totalitarian regimes and other places where media reports are suppressed. Indeed, many such places have government-controlled propaganda machines that prevent any antigovernment messages from getting through to the public.

SEE ALSO: Islamic extremists; Puerto Rico, anti-U.S. sentiments in

Proudhon, Pierre-Joseph (1809–1865)

The writings of nineteenth-century French socialist Pierre-Joseph Proudhon influ-

Nineteenth-century French socialist Pierre-Joseph Proudhon influenced many radicals through his writings, which inspired the development of anarchist theory. THE LIBRARY OF CONGRESS

enced many radicals, including Mikhail Bakunin, and inspired the development of anarchist theory. The son of a cooper, Proudhon was raised among rural peasants who convinced him that it was better to be poor than rich; nonetheless he accepted a college scholarship that took him to the city of Besançon, France. While a student there, he apprenticed himself to a printer to help support his family, and in the print shop he befriended several socialists. In 1838 he received another scholarship to study in Paris, where in 1840 he wrote *Qu'est-ce que la propriété?* (published in English as *What Is Property?* in 1876); this book, in which Proudhon declared himself to be an anarchist, expressed his view that it was theft to exploit the labor of others and also theft to own property unless the owner actually farmed the land himself. This latter point—that property could be privately owned by farmers—ran counter to the position of many Communists and Marxists, who felt that everything should be communally owned. Similarly Proudhon argued that craftsmen and laborers should retain private ownership of their tools because they had the right to control their own ability to work, whereas many Communists and Marxists felt that tools should also be communally owned. Still, Communists and Marxists embraced the slogan of "*Qu'est-ce que la propriété?,*" or "Property is theft."

In 1843 Proudhon took a job as a clerk in the city of Lyon, where he became involved with a group of weavers who had formed a secret society promoting the idea that workers should control their own factories. He also encountered Karl Marx, Mikhail Bakunin, and other socialists and revolutionaries, with whom he argued over his ideas. In 1846 he published *Système des contradictions économiques, ou Philosophie de la misère (System of Economic Contradictions, or the Philosophy of Poverty*, translated into English in 1888), in which he argued against many of Marx's beliefs; Marx responded with *La misère de la philosophie* (1847), or *The Poverty of Philosophy* (translated into English in 1910), in which he attacked Proudhon on a more personal level. This exchange caused arguments among socialists about the best way to achieve an ideal society, and it divided anarchists from Marxists.

In 1848–1849, Proudhon published his own anarchist periodicals in Paris, where he also participated in revolutionary activities and criticized Napoleon III shortly before Napoleon became the emperor of France. These criticisms led to Proudhon's imprisonment from 1849 to 1852, but while in jail he was able to marry, father a child, and continue his writings, which now focused on issues related to revolu-tion. After leaving prison he had trouble getting these works published, and when some of them did go to print, he was again threatened with arrest and fled to Belgium. He returned to Paris in 1862, even though he had been sentenced to prison during his absence, but managed to evade arrest for the next three years, when he died from an illness.

SEE ALSO: anarchism; Bakunin, Mikhail; Marx, Karl

Puerto Rico, anti-U.S. sentiments in

Anti-U.S. sentiments in Puerto Rico have caused several nationalist movements there, and in some cases these have triggered violence both in Puerto Rico and in the United States. The first violent nationalism occurred in Puerto Rico in the 1930s, when the island was owned by the United States. At that time, some of the politicians in Puerto Rico began arguing that it should become a U.S. state, while others insisted that it should receive its independence from the United States. Amid these debates, a group of nationalists (or *independencistas*, as they are called in Puerto Rico) formed the Puerto Rican Nationalist Party (NPPR) to encourage radical activism that would force the United States to allow Puerto Rico to become independent. This political group supported student protest, and after police killed some of the protestors, NPPR assassinated the police commander. When the leader of the NPPR, Pedro Albizu Campos, was arrested shortly after this 1936 assassination, his supporters staged massive protests and demonstrations, and the police responded by attacking those who participated, killing 30 and injuring over 150. During the 1940s, the violence abated a bit as politicians worked on an agreement with the

United States that would make Puerto Rico a commonwealth tied to the United States in such a way that its residents would be U.S. citizens. However, in 1950—two years before this commonwealth was finally created—over two thousand nationalists on the island participated in a violent protest against any political maneuverings that would not result in Puerto Rican independence. Two days after U.S. troops quelled this violence, one group of nationalists tried unsuccessfully to assassinate U.S. president Harry Truman in Washington, D.C., killing a Secret Service agent (one of the terrorists was killed as well), and four years later, another group attacked a session of the U.S. House of Representatives, firing upon its members and injuring five. (All four of the attackers were subsequently arrested.) In the 1960s and '70s, a Puerto Rican nationalist group called Omega 7 continued to engage in violent attacks in the United States, including attempted assassinations and the bombing of a crowded New York airport, hoping to frighten American citizens into demanding that their government grant Puerto Rico its independence. In the mid-1970s, two similar groups began engaging in such violence as well, Fuerzas Armadas de Liberación Nacional (FALN) and Macheteros;

the former primarily attacked on U.S. soil, the latter in Puerto Rico. In addition, FALN typically bombed buildings housing government agencies and public services, whereas Macheteros concentrated on targets affiliated with the U.S. military. During the 1980s, while these groups continued to operate, other Puerto Rican nationalist groups began engaging in terrorist activities as well, though to a much lesser extent; these include the Committee of Revolutionary Workers (COR), the Armed Forces of the Popular Resistance (FARP), the Movement for the National Liberation (MLN), and the Organization of Volunteers for the Puerto Rican Revolution. By the end of the decade, however, federal investigators had managed to arrest many of the leaders of these groups, while others abandoned their terrorist activities and went into hiding. Today most Puerto Rican nationals shun violence, preferring instead to promote their cause of independence through nonviolent means. This is also the goal of the Puerto Rican Independence Party, a leftist political movement comprised primarily of nonviolent nationals.

SEE ALSO: Fuerzas Armadas de Liberación Nacional; Macheteros; Omega 7

Qaddafi, Mu'ammar
(1942–)

The dictator of Libya since seizing power from its king in September 1969, army colonel Mu'ammar Qaddafi has provided financial aid to many terrorist groups, including the Irish Republican Army (IRA) and the Palestine Liberation Organization (PLO). He has also established terrorist-training camps in his country and made it a safe haven for terrorists escaping arrest by other governments. Because some of the terrorists linked to Qaddafi have targeted America, the United States briefly attacked Libya in 1986; nonetheless Libya continued to support terrorism, and in 1991 Qaddafi refused to turn two Libyan terrorists believed responsible for the 1988 explosion of Pan Am Flight 103 over to the United Nations (UN) for trial. Qaddafi was also connected to an unsuccessful assassination attempt on the leader of Egypt, Anwar Sadat (who was later assassinated by others). In 1976–1980 he published a two-volume work entitled *Green Book*, which expressed his views on Islamic socialism and interpretations of Islamic teachings.

SEE ALSO: Irish Republican Army; Libya; Palestine Liberation Organization; Pan Am Flight 103 bombing; Sadat, Anwar

Quisling, Vidkun
(1887–1945)

During World War II, Norwegian army officer Vidkun Quisling was a notorious trai-

tor who enabled German terrorism in Norway. In December 1939, as the head of the fascist Nasjonal Samling (National Union) Party, he met with German dictator Adolf Hitler and urged him to invade Norway. After this occurred in early 1940, Quisling declared himself the leader of Norway, but Hitler quickly replaced Quisling's government with an occupying German one. Nonetheless, Quisling still had a role in

Norwegian army officer Vidkun Quisling was a notorious traitor who persuaded Adolf Hitler to invade Norway with German terrorist attack methods. ARCHIVE PHOTOS/GETTY IMAGES

Norwegian affairs. He decided that his Nasjonal Samling Party should engage in a show of force that would keep Norwegians from rejecting German occupation, and, to this end, his followers launched a campaign of violence against teachers, intellectuals, and others who spoke out against the situation. Nonetheless, in December 1940 in the city of Oslo, there were mass protests against German collaboration, and in September 1941 most of the workers in Oslo went on strike. The Germans responded by ordering its secret police, the Gestapo, and its Nazi Party paramilitary force, the Schutzstaffel (SS), to arrest and torture strikers. Shortly thereafter, the Germans sent five hundred male teachers to forced-labor camps in the Arctic and thirteen hundred uncooperative Norwegian police officers to a concentration camp in Poland. Both of these actions had been encouraged by Quisling, and in February 1942 the Germans allowed him to become Norway's president, though the government remained under the control of German commissioner Josef Terboven. Quisling then collaborated with the Nazis in sending approximately one thousand Norwegian Jews to concentration camps to die. (Of these, the majority went to the Auschwitz death camp.) Quisling was executed after the war by an international court that found him guilty of treason and other war crimes.

SEE ALSO: Nazi terrorism

Qutb, Sayyid
(1906–1966)

The written works of Egyptian radical Islamic intellectual Sayyid Qutb inspired an anti-Western, anti-secular school of thought, Qutbism, which includes the notions that any government not guided by a strict interpretation of the Quran is ille-

gitimate and that any non-Islamic government is evil. Qutb's most influential works are *Fi zilal al-Qur'an* (*In the Shade of the Quran*), a thirty-volume commentary on various aspects of Muslim society and politics, including the Quran and westernization, and *Ma'alim fi-l-Tariq* (*Milestones*), a manifesto calling for political activism in support of his views on Islam. Specifically, Qutb believed that truly faithful Muslims should fight a holy war, or *jihad*, against secular Muslim regimes like that of Egypt's in order to replace them with religious Islamic states, ruled by the Sharia laws and principles of Islam, that would unite and spread throughout the world. Qutb developed a hatred for all things Western while studying for two years (1948–1950) in the United States, where he received a master's degree in education from the Colorado State College of Education (now the University of Northern Colorado) in 1950. Prior to studying abroad, he worked for Egypt's Ministry of Education, but afterward he rejected his country's embrace of westernization, quit his job, and joined a radical Islamic group, the Egyptian Muslim Brotherhood. In 1952, when Egypt's government was overthrown by Gamal Abdel Nasser, Qutb hoped that a religious government would take its place. However, Nasser proved himself a secularist, and after someone attempted to assassinate him in 1954, his forces arrested many members of the Muslim Brotherhood for speaking out against his failure to adopt Sharia law. Qutb was one of those arrested, and while in prison he wrote both *Fi zilal al-Qur'an* and *Ma'alim fi-l-Tariq*. These works led to his trial in 1965 for plotting to overthrow the government, and in August 1966 he was hanged for this crime. After his death, his brother, Muhammad Qutb, who had also spent some time in prison, moved to Saudi Arabia, became a professor of Islamic studies there, and published and disseminated Sayyid Qutb's writings, which eventually made their way to Islamic terrorist Osama bin Laden. Consequently Sayyid Qutb is considered one of the most important influences on the course of modern Islamic terrorism.

SEE ALSO: bin laden, Osama; Islamic extremists; religious terrorism

Rabin, Yitzhak
(1923–1995)

Prime minister of Israel from 1974 to 1977 and again from 1993 to 1995, as well as defense minister in between these periods, Yitzhak Rabin participated in peace negotiations with the Palestine Liberation Organization (PLO) in 1993 and agreed to pull Israeli forces out of the West Bank and Gaza Strip. As a former military officer, he commanded great respect from Israeli troops; this, combined with his popularity among the general public, made a permanent peace between Palestine and Israel seem attainable. However, in November 1995, Yigal Amir, a Jewish zealot angered by the pullout agreement, assassinated Rabin, thereby dealing a serious blow to Israel-Palestine relations. Amir be-

Yitzhak Rabin, prime minister of Israel from 1974–1977 and 1993–1995, tried to maintain peace between Palestine and Israel, but was assassinated in November 1995. JACQUELINE ARZT. © AP IMAGES

longed to a radical Orthodox Jewish group called Eyal, whose members believed that Jews had to occupy the West Bank and Gaza Strip in order for the Messiah (the king of the Jews, sent by God) to appear on earth. This view was shared by many right-wing Israelis, who were not saddened by Rabin's death, though the majority of Israelis mourned his passage.

SEE ALSO: Israel; Palestine; Palestine Liberation Organization

racism

Many right-wing extremists promote racism, the belief that one race is superior to others; white supremacy is currently the most prevalent form of racism, and the most common victims of white-supremacist violence in Europe and the United States are Jews and African Americans, respectively. During World War II, millions of Jews in Europe were killed by Nazis who considered them naturally inferior to the white, Aryan race. Also, during the years following the American Civil War, racists in Southern states lynched or otherwise attacked hundreds of African Americans, with many more being assaulted there during the civil rights movement of the 1960s. In both of these periods, many racists belonged to a white-supremacist group called the Ku Klux Klan; other such groups in the United States include Aryan Nations, formed in Idaho in the mid-1970s; White Aryan Resistance, formed in California in the early 1980s; and various groups associated with the Christian Identity movement, which is affiliated with neo-Nazi terrorism.

SEE ALSO: anti-Semitism; Christian Identity movement; Ku Klux Klan; neo-Nazis

Rahman, Omar Abdel (1939–)

As one of the most prominent members of the Egyptian terrorist organization Gama'a al-Islamiyya, Sheik Omar Abdel Rahman supported the overthrow of the Egyptian government because of its secular nature, but after being forced from his native country in 1990 he began speaking out against American authorities as well. In the early 1990s, while the religious leader was at a mosque in New Jersey, he was put on trial for encouraging others to destroy the United States government, prosecuted under a rarely used sedition law created during the Civil War. He was arrested for the crime after investigators discovered that three of the men involved in the 1993 bombing of the World Trade Center in New York City worshipped at Rahman's mosque and that, at these worship services, Rahman had been calling on faithful Muslims to attack the United States. Federal authorities later learned that Rahman had also suggested targets to people that he apparently knew to be terrorists. Rahman was eventually connected to plots to bomb a variety of sites, including the United Nations building in New York, as well as to at least one attempted assassination and the assassination of Jewish radical Rabbi Meir Kahane, who was the leader of an anti-Arab group called the Kach Movement. (When he was arrested, Kahane's assassin, Egyptian radical El Sayyid Nosair, was found in possession of pro-terrorism literature from Rahman.) Convicted and sentenced to life in prison, Rahman continued to encourage terrorism, sending messages to Gama'a al-Islamiyya members who then engaged in various attacks. In one such attack, on tourists in Luxor, Egypt, the terrorists killed several people while apparently trying to take hostages whom the group planned to exchange for Rahman's release from prison.

SEE ALSO: Kach Movement, the; World Trade Center bombings

Rape of Nanking

From December 1937 to February 1938, the Japanese killed over two hundred thousand people in China during what became known as the Rape of Nanking. The murders took place in the city of Nanking after it was captured by Japanese forces at war with China. These forces went on a rampage, raping thousands of women in the streets, killing innocent civilians of both genders, looting shops, and destroying buildings. After World War II, in the late 1940s, a war crimes trial found Japanese general Iswane Matsui responsible for the Rape of Nanking and sentenced him to death.

SEE ALSO: Japan

reactionaries versus radicals

Terrorism experts typically call right-wing extremists reactionaries and left-wing extremists radicals. These names come from the way that each form of extremism arises. Members of the right wing generally react to perceived threats to the status quo, whereas members of the left wing seek radical changes.

SEE ALSO: extremism, right-wing versus left-wing

Real Irish Republican Army (Real IRA, or RIRA)

Established in 1998 out of a political group called the 32-County Sovereignty Movement, the Real Irish Republican Army

(Real IRA, or RIRA) is a militant group led by a former member of the Irish Republican Army (IRA). Both the IRA and the Real IRA share the same goal: making Northern Ireland once again part of the Republic of Ireland, rather than part of the United Kingdom. To this end, both have engaged in bombings, assassinations, and other acts of terrorism, but when in 1997 the IRA decided to abandon violence, some of its members abandoned the IRA to join the Real IRA. In 1997 and 1998, the Real IRA engaged in a series of bombings in Northern Ireland, but its intent was to destroy property rather than people. Consequently the group issued a public apology after one of its car bombings, in August 1998, killed twenty-nine people despite the group's having issued a prior warning to police. The following month, the Real IRA declared that it was no longer going to engage in violence, but in 2002 its members were once again involved in bombing and assassination attempts. Today the group has approximately forty members.

SEE ALSO: Irish Republican Army

Red Army Faction (RAF, or Baader-Meinhof Gang)

Also called the Baader-Meinhof Gang in recognition of its creators, Andreas Baader and Ulrike Meinhof, the Red Army Faction (RAF) was formed in 1968 by left-wing extremists initially dedicated to attacking the facilities and representatives of West German and American corporations and military forces in West Germany. After bombing and setting fire to various facilities and assassinating several businessmen and politicians, however, the group turned its attention to international affairs, sometimes allying itself with Palestinian groups in order to commit acts of terrorism outside of Germany. Its most notable terrorist act during this period was a 1976 incident that became known as the Entebbe raid, in which two RAF members helped a terrorist organization called the Popular Front for the Liberation of Palestine (PFLP) to hijack an Air France Airbus and land it at the Entebbe Airport in Uganda, where Israeli military commandos then rescued most of the hostages and gunned down all of the terrorists. The same year, Ulrike Meinhof committed suicide in her jail cell, having been arrested—along with many other members of the RAF—during a crack-down on terrorists by West German authorities in 1972. In October 1977 Andreas Baader and two other members of the RAF were also found dead in their jail cells, though it is unclear whether they had shot themselves or been killed. Once its leaders were dead, the group began working even more extensively with other left-wing terrorist groups, including the Red Brigades, and participated in several bombings and assassinations. During this period, many RAF members operated out of East Germany, but when the Communist regime there fell in 1989–1990, they fled to various other countries. Today their whereabouts and activities are unknown, but some terrorism experts believe that the RAF still exists, its purpose solely to offer support to other groups engaged in international terrorism.

SEE ALSO: Entebbe raid; Popular Front for the Liberation of Palestine; Red Brigades

Red Brigades (BR)

Created in 1969 or 1970 in Italy, possibly by Marxist-Leninist Renato Curcio (1945–), the Red Brigades (BR) was a left-wing group that committed firebombings, assassinations, kidnappings, and other ter-

Andreas Baader was a member of the Red Brigades (BR), a left-wing group that committed terrorist acts in many Italian cities in order to overthrow the Italian government. AP IMAGES

rorist acts in various Italian cities out of a desire to isolate Italy from its allies, destroy the Italian government, and establish a revolutionary government in its place. Among its murder victims were one of the heads of an antiterrorist agency in the city of Turin in 1974, a former prime minister in 1978, and a U.S. diplomat in 1984. The group also kidnapped a U.S. Army brigadier general, James Dozier, in 1981, holding him for ransom until he was rescued by Italian police in the city of Padua. In the late 1970s, Italian authorities estimated that members of the Red Brigades were responsible for thousands of terrorist attacks, with nearly three thousand in 1978 alone, but some terrorism experts question this assessment. However, a crackdown by Italian law enforcement resulted in many suspected BR members being arrested, and by the end of the 1980s the group was largely inactive, though it apparently still has a few dozen members.

SEE ALSO: Italy

Reid, Richard (the Shoe Bomber) (1973–)

British terrorist Richard Reid, who has also gone by the names Abdel Rahim and Abu Ibrahim, is best known as "the Shoe Bomber" because in December 2001 he sneaked explosives onto an airplane by hiding them in his basketball shoes. His plan was to ignite the explosives by touching a lit match to his shoes, but when he struck the match a stewardess intervened, telling him that matches are not allowed on airplanes. Reid and the stewardess then got into a struggle, first verbal and then physical, whereupon another stewardess and some of the plane's passengers jumped in to subdue Reid. Eventually they tied him up and one of the passengers, a doctor, injected him with a drug to keep him calm until the plane—American Airlines Flight 63 from Paris, France, to Miami, Florida—could land at the Boston, Massachusetts, airport. Later, U.S. authorities determined that Reid was a member of al Qaeda and had worked for the terrorist organization as a scout for potential attack targets, traveling extensively in Europe and the Middle East while based in London during the late 1990s. In the late 1980s and '90s he spent several years in jail for various crimes, and it was during this period that he became a Muslim; he joined al Qaeda in late 1997, and the following year he went to Pakistan and Afghanistan to train at terrorist camps. Investigators found that Reid had

been receiving e-mails from someone in Pakistan prior to his bombing attempt, telling him what to do. This person was never captured, but in January 2003, Reid was sentenced to life in prison, after pleading guilty to the attempted use of a weapon of mass destruction, attempted homicide, and carrying explosives onto a plane. At the time of his plea agreement, Reid denied that al Qaeda was involved in the shoe-bombing incident.

SEE ALSO: al Qaeda

Reign of Terror

The Reign of Terror was a period of the French Revolution when the Revolutionary government, largely at the urging of politician Maximilien Robespierre, systematically arrested and executed those who opposed its existence and policies. During this period, which lasted from September 5, 1793, to July 27, 1794, government officials terrorized local authorities and rounded up nobles, priests, and others in both the right wing and the left. At least three hundred thousand people were executed, and hundreds more died in prison. In the summer of 1794, a time known as the Great Terror, the Revolutionary government suspended the people's right to stand trial and executed fourteen hundred people. Shortly thereafter, Robespierre's opponents seized control of the government and, in July 1794, executed him, thus ending the Reign of Terror.

SEE ALSO: France, terrorism in; Robespierre, Maximilien

religious terrorism

Religious terrorism is terrorism committed under the belief that God or another deity supports violence that serves a particular faith-driven agenda. In other words, religious terrorists think that they have an otherworldly mandate to commit their terrorist acts; many also think that they will be richly rewarded in the afterlife for their deeds. Terrorists of the Christian faith might further believe that their violence will hasten Armageddon and the apocalypse, a battle between good and evil that will ultimately bring about a new and better world. In fact, the goal of all religious terrorists is a new society, which they believe, by virtue of their faith, will be vastly improved. They are also generally more indiscriminate and unrestrained in their violence than are secular terrorists, killing innocent people without qualms because it is for a higher purpose. Examples of religious terrorists include Islamic extremists in the Middle East, like those who belong to the al Qaeda terrorist network, members of the Christian Identity movement in the United States, Aum Shinrikyō cultists in Japan, and in thirteenth- through nineteenth-century India, members of the Hindu murder cults, the latter of whom killed approximately twenty thousand people a year in the name of the Hindu goddess Kali.

SEE ALSO: al Qaeda, Aum Shinrikyō, Christian Identity movement; Islamic extremists

responses to terrorism

In response to terrorism, governments have engaged in counterterrorism, which involves trying to eliminate terrorists and terrorist groups, and antiterrorism, which involves improving security systems in an attempt to prevent terrorist attacks. Counterterrorism can employ diplomacy, legal systems, financial systems, espionage, and various types of violence, including assassination, military attacks, and sabotage.

Diplomatic approaches might involve making concessions to terrorists, perhaps by changing political or social systems in order to appease them. Legal responses often involve strengthening laws against various types and aspects of terrorism, increasing sentences for such crimes, and, on an international level, making it difficult for countries to harbor terrorists. Financial responses include economic sanctions against countries that support terrorism and the freezing of bank accounts connected to individuals or organizations that fund terrorism. Espionage and other intelligence operations are employed to gather information about terrorists and their groups, and perhaps to infiltrate such groups in order to destroy them from within. Military or paramilitary force might be used to destroy terrorists or to punish them for particular acts of violence. Actions known as repressive responses, which include nonviolent covert operations and disinformation campaigns, are used to make it more difficult for terrorists to plan and find support for their attacks. Antiterrorist measures primarily involve increasing security at places where terrorists are likely to attack, through the use of such devices as X-ray machines, video cameras, and blockades to impede easy access to vulnerable areas.

SEE ALSO: antiterrorism; counterterrorism; funding terrorism

Ressam, Ahmed
(1967–)

Algerian terrorist Ahmed Ressam was arrested at the U.S.-Canadian border while en route to Los Angeles International Airport, which he planned to bomb during the last seconds of 1999 as part of a millennium attack on the United States. From

1994 to 1998, Ressam lived in Montreal, Canada, with members of an Algerian terrorist group, the Armed Islamic Group (GIA). In 1998 he traveled to the Middle East—first to Pakistan and then to Afghanistan—and attended terrorist-training camps run by al Qaeda. In early 1999 he returned to Canada, this time to the city of Vancouver, to prepare for his attack on the United States. On December 14, 1999, border guards caught him trying to drive into the United States with bomb-making materials in his car trunk. He was subsequently convicted of various crimes related to this act, including attempting to commit terrorism (a charge that made him the first person to be prosecuted under the then new crime of Terrorism Transcending National Boundaries) and illegally transporting explosives. Ressam subsequently provided information about other terrorists involved in his bombing plot and about the inner workings of al Qaeda.

SEE ALSO: al Qaeda; Armed Islamic Group

revolts

A revolt is an uprising or rebellion, typically against a state authority and often as part of an attempt to overthrow that authority. In many cases, revolts arise spontaneously after a long period of oppression, during which the victims' anger at their oppressors builds. For example, the Warsaw Ghetto Uprising sprang into existence in early 1943 among Jews in the city of Warsaw, Poland, who had been mistreated by German Nazis for months. The Germans had forced these Jews to live in ghettos that were walled off from the rest of the city; conditions in the ghettos were deplorable. Approximately five hundred thousand people, many of them without shelter, lived in an area of only 840 acres,

and thousands died of disease and starvation. After isolating the Jews, the Germans then began transporting them to death camps, while misleading their captives into believing that they were actually going to labor camps. When an underground information network provided the Jews with the truth, the next attempt to transport them, on January 18, 1943, triggered armed resistance, led by an underground group called the Jewish Combat Organization. Over the next four days, over fifty Germans and at least as many Jews were killed, and the Germans withdrew from the city only to return on April 19 with two thousand soldiers dedicated to killing the resisters. Instead, they were attacked by fifteen hundred armed Jews who held the Germans at bay for nearly a month until their ammunition was exhausted, whereupon the remaining fifty-six thousand Jews in the ghetto were either killed outright or sent to death camps.

A similar revolt occurred in Warsaw in 1944 as part of a Soviet plot to help Russian soldiers wrest control of the city from the Germans. This revolt, known as the Warsaw Uprising, began in August 1944 after Soviet authorities informed the Polish underground that if it staged an uprising against the Germans it would be given various types of aid. This revolt, involving over fifty thousand Polish troops, at first succeeded, but before the Soviets could move to a position that would allow them to take control of the city, the Germans sent more soldiers into Warsaw and quelled the rebellion, then deported everyone living there and destroyed the city. Two similarly unsuccessful Jewish revolts were the First and Second Jewish Revolts (A.D. 66–70 and A.D. 132–135, respectively), wherein Jews rebelled against forces of the Roman

Empire in an attempt to end Roman rule in Judea.

SEE ALSO: Nazi terrorism; Roman Empire

Revolutionary Armed Forces of Colombia (FARC)

Since the 1960s, the Revolutionary Armed Forces of Colombia, or Fuerzas Armadas Revolucionadas de Colombia (FARC), has engaged in guerrilla attacks against the government of Colombia. FARC is also heavily engaged in the drug trade, financing its operations primarily through cocaine sales. The group arose during a civil war in the 1950s, when peasants created armed militias to protect themselves. After the war was over, the militias became guerrilla groups that challenged the new government, and in 1964 several members of the Central Committee of the Communist Party of Colombia, including Marxist radical Manuel Marulanda Velez, established the FARC as a way to unite these groups. Their shared goal was the overthrow of the existing government and the defense of the poor; over time, the FARC also became dedicated to ending American influence in the country and driving out multinational corporations. In late 1985, the FARC tried to form a political party, but the Colombian army, angered by recent attacks from another guerrilla group, the M-19, launched an assault on all guerrillas that drove the leaders of the FARC into hiding. Nonetheless the group remained strong, largely because of its drug profits and the money it made from kidnapping and ransoming wealthy businessmen and government officials. Because of these and other illegal activities, including smuggling and money laundering, the FARC has an income of between $200 and $400 million a year and has been able to acquire more-

advanced weaponry and equipment than most other guerrilla groups. In addition, FARC forces, whose members (wearing uniforms and functioning much like an army) number approximately seven thousand, have wrested control of nearly half of Colombia from the army, though they primarily operate out of jungle bases. In 2001, Colombia asked the United States to help its military end terrorism and drug trafficking in the country, and the United States responded with a $1.3-billion aid package. In early 2002, the Colombian army began attacking FARC strongholds in earnest; the FARC fought back by bombing government facilities, killing dozens of civilians in the process.

SEE ALSO: Colombia, terrorism in; funding terrorism

revolutionary terrorism

Revolutionary terrorism is terrorism committed or threatened for the purpose of destroying a particular political system, but this purpose typically arises from a noble goal. Revolutionaries view the targeted system as evil and seek to replace it with something that, in their minds, will be for the good of the people. Many revolutionaries are Communists or socialists who oppose regimes run by the wealthy at the expense of the poor.

SEE ALSO: communism

right-wing terrorists, U.S.

In the United States, right-wing terrorists are typically white supremacists with anti-government sentiments and strong religious beliefs. They often live in rural areas or small towns and operate in small groups or alone, usually striking symbolic targets or taking individual human lives based on their religious or white-supremacist beliefs. For example, right-wing antiabortionists have killed abortion providers, while members of racist groups like the Ku Klux Klan have lynched African Americans. Since the 1990s, most members of the Christian right have been Protestant fundamentalists who connect their religious beliefs to a political agenda such as the right-to-life movement. The majority of these people are nonviolent, though they might engage in confrontational protests and demonstrations; some, however, have participated in bombings, assassinations, and similar acts. Particularly violent are some of the antigovernment groups, many of which arose as part of the Patriot movement of the 1990s. Members of this movement, known as Patriots, have argued that the U.S. government has strayed from the values embodied in the U.S. Constitution and therefore no longer represents the people; instead it is oppressive, infringing on individual freedoms and rights. Many Patriots support various conspiracy theories involving government plots to turn the American democratic system into a repressive regime, perhaps controlled by foreigners. Such beliefs have led Patriots to arm themselves and train in survivalist techniques so that they can defend themselves from government assaults. This was the case, for example, with members of the Branch Davidians, a religious cult in Waco, Texas, that in April 1993 engaged in a standoff with federal authorities trying to seize their illegal weapons. After this standoff turned into an assault on their compound, eighty Branch Davidians died—an event that provided proof of government oppression to other adherents of the Patriot movement.

SEE ALSO: antiabortion movement; Branch Davidians; Ku Klux Klan; racism; religious terrorism

Robespierre, Maximilien-François-Marie-Isidore de (1758–1794)

French radical Maximilien Robespierre was a driving force of the French Revolution and, as the leader of the Committee of Public Safety in 1793, was largely responsible for the Reign of Terror. A distinguished lawyer and philosopher, he served as an attorney, a judge, and a university president before becoming active in politics. He was elected a representative of the city of Arras in 1789 after writing a well-received political essay, and from this point he was increasingly involved in French government. As a member of the National Assembly from 1789 to 1791, he delivered over five hundred political speeches, and he was one of the leaders of the Jacobins, a political club encouraging revolution. He was an outspoken advocate of the rights of French society's most downtrodden, opposed discrimination, argued in favor of universal suffrage, and spoke out against the monarch's veto ability. In 1791, when many French citizens were calling for the king to abdicate his throne, someone tried to assassinate Robespierre for his antimonarchist views. By this time the National Assembly had dissolved, and Robespierre had become the public prosecutor of Paris. He remained active in politics, though, by speaking before the Jacobin Club over a hundred times between July 1791 and August 1792. He also established a political newspaper, *Le Défenseur de la Constitution* (The Defense of the Constitution). Among his writings were predictions that the French army was ill equipped for a proposed war against Austria and Prussia, and when Robespierre's predictions regarding how badly this war would go came true, he became the people's hero. Consequently, in August

1792, Paris elected Robespierre as the head of its delegation to the National Convention, and when this body put the king on trial four months later, Robespierre was a leading advocate of the king's execution. After the execution, Robespierre's political party, the Montagnards, gained control of the assembly, making him one of the most powerful figures in the revolutionary government. He also encouraged an escalation of the Reign of Terror, though he opposed random violence, calling for more attacks on the government's enemies. Still very popular with the public, Robespierre was elected president of the National Convention in May 1794. However, within this body, opposition to Robespierre grew, with some of his opponents labeling him too moderate and others saying he wanted a dictatorship. At the same time, he developed health problems that forced him to cut back on his activities right before the start of the most brutal period of the Reign of Terror, the summer of 1794 Great Terror. Shortly thereafter, his opponents had him and many of his supporters imprisoned as enemies of the state, and he and 108 of his followers were quickly executed.

SEE ALSO: Montagnards; Reign of Terror

Roman Empire

Established in 27 B.C. in Rome, Italy, the Roman Empire was created after the Roman Republic, itself created in 509 B.C., expanded its influence outside of Italy through a series of wars that earned Roman soldiers a reputation for brutality. In addition, the Roman Age embodied many examples of state-sponsored terrorism. Among these were the government's persecution of Christians, most of whom were tortured and executed via crucifixion, being fed to lions, or by other cruel means,

and the brutal treatment of followers of Spartacus in a slave rebellion known as the Servile War of 73–71 B.C. Political assassination was also common in the Roman Empire; murdered emperors include Julius Caesar (44 B.C.), Caligula (A.D. 41), Galba (A.D. 68), Domitian (A.D. 96), and Commodus (A.D. 193).

SEE ALSO: assassination, political; Spartacus

Romanian terrorism in World War II

During World War II, under the leadership of Ion Antonescu, the Romanian government engaged in terrorism against Jews and political opponents. During the 1930s, Antonescu, then a military general, joined with a fascist, anti-Semitic terrorist group called the Iron Guard to seize control of the government. With support from Germany's Nazi regime, the new government murdered hundreds in a subsequent Iron Guard reign of terror against former government members and Jews. In January 1941, the Iron Guard tried to take sole control of the government by ousting Antonescu, but he prevailed and eliminated the Iron Guard. With the advent of the war came a strengthening of Antonescu's alliance with Germany and an increase in state-sponsored persecution against Jews. In June 1941, Antonescu ordered thousands of Jews to relocate from their village homes to concentration camps and urban ghettos, brutally killing those who resisted (and some who did not). Meanwhile Russia's Red Army managed to plant activists in Odessa, a Ukrainian city taken over by Romanian soldiers, to act as partisans in attacking the Romanian military from within. In October 1941, these partisans, or perhaps other Russian agents, bombed an Odessa military headquarters; in retaliation, Antonescu burned the city, killing 25,000 Jews in the process. He also went after partisans elsewhere, attempting to kill as many as possible. Antonescu's brutal grip on his territories continued until August 1944, when Russian forces invaded them and returned control of the country to its former ruler, King Michael. Romania subsequently allied itself with Russia and declared war on Germany, and in 1946 Antonescu was executed as a war criminal. Historians estimate that he was responsible for the death of 110,000 to 220,000 Jews, as well as an unknown number of Romanian political opponents.

SEE ALSO: anti-Semitism; Antonescue, Ion; Reign of Terror; wartime terrorism

Ruby Ridge

Located in northern Idaho, Ruby Ridge was the site of a 1992 incident that fueled several subsequent acts of antigovernment terrorism in the United States. On August 21 and 22, 1992, federal authorities engaged in a shoot-out with members of a Christian fundamentalist family whose head, Randy Weaver, had moved his wife and children to a remote wilderness area of Idaho to avoid government interference. The groundwork for the shoot-out was laid when, in 1989, Randy Weaver sold illegal firearms unknowingly to undercover agents of the U.S. Bureau of Alcohol, Tobacco, and Firearms (ATF). Weaver had originally met these men at a meeting of a group called Aryan Nations, and after his arrest for illegal weapons sales the ATF asked him to work undercover as an informant on the activities of this group and other militants. Weaver not only refused but, while out on bail, failed to show up for his first court date. Federal agents consequently began a surveillance of his compound at Ruby Ridge, hoping to capture

him outside its perimeter. Instead, Weaver's son Sam spotted three of the agents while patrolling the grounds with his dog and another man, Kevin Harris. A shoot-out ensued, and Sam and the dog were killed, along with a U.S. marshal, William Degan. The federal government then sent additional forces into the area, some of whom were part of the U.S. Hostage Rescue Team (HRT). Shortly thereafter, an HRT sniper fired into the house, killing Randy's wife Vicki and wounding Harris, and one week later, those still alive in the house surrendered to authorities. Randy was tried and found innocent of all charges related to illegal weaponry, though he was found guilty of failing to appear for his original court date. Meanwhile the U.S. Congress launched an investigation into the actions of federal agents at Ruby Ridge, and in the end they condemned those agents for the way they had handled the situation, though they also found Randy Weaver partially responsible because he had created the circumstances of the shoot-out by avoiding his court date. In response to this condemnation, various federal agencies changed their policies regarding deadly force, but many right-wing extremists, particularly members of the antigovernment Patriot and Christian Identity movements, considered the Ruby Ridge incident as proof that the U.S. government was planning to end democracy and eliminate personal freedoms. As a result, some of these extremists cited Ruby Ridge as their reason for committing terrorist acts; such was the case, for example, with Timothy McVeigh, who bombed the Alfred P. Murrah Federal Building in Oklahoma City, Oklahoma in 1995.

SEE ALSO: Alcohol, Tobacco, and Firearms, U.S. Bureau of; Christian Patriots; Christian Identity movement; McVeigh, Timothy; Oklahoma City bombing

In 2005, antiabortion activist Eric Rudolph was convicted for various bombings from 1996–1998. AP IMAGES

Rudolph, Eric
(1966–)

In 2005, antiabortion activist Eric Rudolph was convicted of bombing one of the sites of the 1996 Olympic Games—Centennial Park in Atlanta, Georgia—as well as an abortion clinic and a nightclub for gays and lesbians in Atlanta in 1997, and an abortion clinic in Birmingham, Alabama, in 1998. One person was killed in the Birmingham bombing, while two died and more than a hundred were injured as a result of the Olympics bombing; Rudolph pleaded guilty to these crimes in exchange for a sentence of five consecutive life terms rather than the death penalty. He subsequently revealed that his motive for bombing the Olympic Games was connected to

his antiabortion views, because he hoped the attack would shame the United States in the eyes of the world for its legalization of abortion.

Despite his right-to-life stance, Rudolph created his bombs in an attempt to maximize harm to human life. In the Olympics bombing, he added screws and nails to the gunpowder in three pipe bombs hidden in a backpack, so that people would be struck by flying debris. As well, in the Atlanta abortion-clinic bombing, he planted two bombs so that the second would go off after rescue workers had arrived to help those people injured in the first explosion. After his 1997 attacks he sent a letter to various media representatives taking credit for the bombings, but signing it "the Army of God" in order to assign blame to a radical anti-abortion group. By this time, federal authorities had a suspect in the Olympics bombing case: Richard Jewell, a security guard who had spotted the backpack and alerted police to its whereabouts. The Birmingham bombing, however, led them to Rudolph, and during their investigation of that attack they concluded that the same person had committed the Olympics attack. In February 1998 they charged Rudolph with the Birmingham bombing and in October 1998 with the Centennial Park bombing, though he was then at large. Because he had survivalist skills, he was able to hide out in wilderness areas in North Carolina, thereby avoiding capture until 2005.

SEE ALSO: antiabortion movement; Atlanta's Centennial Park bombing

Rushdie, Salman
(1947–)

The publication of British Muslim novelist Salman Rushdie's book *The Satanic Verses* in late 1988 triggered worldwide Islamic violence in early 1989 after the leader of Iran, the Ayatollah Ruhollah Khomeini, called on all faithful Muslims to try to kill the author and anyone involved in the book's publication or distribution. As a result of this religious decree, or *fatwa*, booksellers, agents, and others in the publishing industry were attacked; for example, two translators of the book—one Japanese and one Italian—were stabbed, one of them to death. In addition, members of various Muslim groups, including the Popular Front for the Liberation of Palestine (PFLP), stated that they were planning to murder Rushdie, who subsequently went into hiding under the protection of the British government, and an Iranian charity group, 15 Khordad, offered a $2.5 million reward to anyone who carried out the *fatwa* against him. The reason for the Ayatollah's outrage was that Rushdie's novel made fun of the Islamic prophet Muhammad. The *fatwa* remains in effect today, even though the Ayatollah is no longer alive. However, in 1998 the Iranian government said that it has no intention of encouraging Rushdie's murder.

SEE ALSO: *fatwa*; Iran

Russian Civil War (1918–1920)

The Russian Civil War of 1918–1920 involved many acts of terrorism; among the most notable was the Red Terror, a period during which the government took hostages only to shoot them and executed prisoners without trial. At the beginning of the war, Russia's former ruler, the czar Nicholas II, and his wife and children were imprisoned, then shot en masse in the cellar of the home where they were being held. The war arose out of an attempt to keep the new Communist Bolshevik government in power—a government that had come into power during the Russian Revolution of 1917. During the Red Terror the Bolsheviks attempted to exterminate all Cossacks in southeast Russia, along with others who threatened or disagreed with their government, and maintained order by terrorizing the populace. Approximately fifty thousand to two hundred thousand people were killed during the Red Terror, but by the end of the civil war Russia was firmly in the hands of Communists who eventually became more oppressive than the monarchy they replaced.

SEE ALSO: Bolsheviks, the; Russian Revolution

Russian Revolution, 1905 and 1917

The Russian Revolution of 1905 led the country's ruler at the time, Nicholas II, to try to establish a constitutional monarchy, while the Russian Revolution of 1917, which was actually two revolutions, overthrew this government and put revolutionaries known as Bolsheviks in control of Russia. Both the 1905 and the 1917 revolutions involved a great deal of violence. The 1905 revolution was triggered by the government's slaughter of peaceful demonstrators in the city of Saint Petersburg, after which workers in several cities went on strike and peasants throughout the Russian Empire revolted. To quell this rebellion, Nicholas made several changes in his government, including the creation of a constitution and elections for legislative representatives, and gradually order was restored. In 1917, new riots broke out as a reaction to food shortages in the aftermath of several Russian defeats in World War I. Nicholas then lost control of his armies and was forced to leave the throne, whereupon a provisional government took over. This government was soon threatened by a group known as the Soviets, or Petrograd Soviets of Workers' and Soldiers' Deputies, which was controlled by radical socialists. One of these groups of socialists was the Bolsheviks, who eventually seized the government and, as the country was plunged into civil war, assassinated Nicholas and his family on the night of July 16–17, 1918.

SEE ALSO: Bolsheviks, the; Russian Civil War

Rwandan genocide

The Rwandan genocide was a case of state terrorism during the 1990s whereby the Rwandan army and Hutu militants murdered approximately five hundred thousand Tutsis in Rwanda in an attempt to exterminate that tribe. Members of the Hutu and Tutsi tribes had been fighting with each other for centuries, but in the early 1990s the Tutsis started attacking the Hutus, then in control of Rwanda, from bases across the border in Uganda, and the Hutus responded with genocide. Nonetheless within months the Tutsis had vanquished the Rwandan government and driven thousands of Hutus from the country, with most of them heading to the Congo. An international tribunal, the International Criminal Court for Rwanda, subsequently indicted several people for their role in the genocide and brought many details about the atrocities to light.

SEE ALSO: Africa, terrorism in postcolonial

Sadat, Anwar
(1918–1981)

Assassinated by Islamic extremists in 1981, Anwar Sadat incurred the wrath of fellow Muslims by working toward peace with Israel in the late 1970s. However, before meeting with Israel's prime minister, Menachim Begin, in 1977, Sadat had supported the long-standing Arab-Israeli conflict. He was an intense Arab nationalist when he came to power in 1970, having actively supported the Germans during World War II out of a desire to drive Great Britain from the Middle East. In 1973 he ordered Egypt's forces to attack Israel in the Sinai Peninsula, and shortly thereafter Israel invaded Egypt and took the Sinai Desert. During the peace negotiations, Sadat convinced Israel to give this land back to Egypt, in exchange for Egypt's officially recognizing Israel's right to exist, establishing limited trade relations between the two countries, and demilitarizing the Sinai. The peace process continued after Sadat's death.

SEE ALSO: assassination, political; Begin, Menachim; Israel

sarin gas

The Aum Shinrikyō religious cult used sarin, a powerful nerve gas, in a terrorist attack on the Tokyo, Japan, subway system in March 1995. A small amount of any nerve gas, possibly as little as a drop, can severely damage the body's nervous system if it is inhaled or absorbed through skin pores; in the case of the Aum Shinrikyō

attack, twelve people died and as many as six thousand were injured. To disperse the gas, on March 20, 1995, members of Aum Shinrikyō put sarin-filled packages on five subway trains, all en route through the Kasumigaseki train station in Tokyo, then poked holes in the packages before jumping off the trains at various stations along the route. The attacks were timed so that they all occurred simultaneously, making it more difficult for rescuers to respond to the crisis. Terrorism experts warn that sarin gas might be used again in similar attacks, because it is relatively easy to obtain and use as a weapon.

SEE ALSO: Aum Shinrikyō; bioterrorism

Saudi Arabia

Saudi Arabians have been both the victims of terrorism and sponsors of terrorism. In December 2006, U.S. officials uncovered evidence that various Saudi groups have been funding Sunni terrorists in Iraq, and one of the most prominent terrorists in the world is a Saudi, Osama bin Laden, who as the leader of the terrorist network al Qaeda planned the September 11, 2001, attacks on America. But although bin laden is a Saudi, he has opposed the Saudi government ever since 1991, when Saudi king Fahd allowed the United States to fight the Persian Gulf War from bases within Saudi Arabia. bin laden felt that Americans were not worthy to set foot on holy Islamic lands, and he and other radical Islamics grew angry at the Saudi royals for their close association with the United States. In 1996, some of these anti-Saudi Islamic revolutionaries bombed the Khobar Towers in Dharan, Saudi Arabia, because they were being used as barracks for U.S. military personnel. The previous year, Islamic militants car bombed a Saudi National Guard facility. The first large-scale terrorist attack of this nature occurred in November 1979, when three hundred Islamic radicals took over the Grand Mosque in the holy city of Mecca, where all able-bodied Muslims are expected to make a pilgrimage during their lifetimes. These radicals hoped that their seizure of the mosque would trigger an uprising against the Saudi monarchy. However, the Saudi government responded by bringing in a French counterterrorist squad, which eventually killed over one hundred of the terrorists. The remaining terrorists were executed after the mosque was retaken, two weeks after the attack.

SEE ALSO: bin laden, Osama; Khobar Towers attack

Sayaret Mat'kal

Part of the Israel Defense Forces (IDF), Sayaret are small, secretive reconnaissance units, the most notable of which is the Sayaret Mat'kal. This unit has engaged in numerous counterterrorist activities, including several 1973 assassinations of people involved in the attack on Israeli athletes at the Munich, Germany, Olympic Games in 1972 as well as the rescue of hostages from terrorists at the Entebbe Airport in Uganda. Another Sayaret unit, the Parachute Sayaret, was also involved in the Entebbe incident, and also fought against Hezbollah terrorists in Lebanon.

SEE ALSO: Entebbe raid; Munich Olympics crisis

Schutzstaffel (SS), the

An elite branch of the Nazi Party, the Schutzstaffel (SS, or Protective Echelon) was responsible for numerous acts of terrorism from the time Adolf Hitler gained control of Germany in 1933 until the end of World War II in 1945. SS members were chosen for their ruthlessness and trained to attack Jews and others that the Nazis deemed inferior. During the war, the SS slaughtered thousands of Jews, Gypsies, Poles, Communists, and Russian prisoners of war. The group began in 1925 as Hitler's bodyguards, but by 1939 this 300-man unit had grown to a 250,000-member organization with police and military powers. In 1946 a war crimes tribunal in Nuremberg, Germany, declared the SS to be a criminal organization.

SEE ALSO: Nazi terrorism

sectarian violence

Sectarian violence is violence that occurs between religious groups, sometimes of the same ethnic group and other times of different ethic groups. As an example of the former, members of two different Islamic sects, the Shiites (also known as the Shias) and the Sunnis, have committed acts of sectarian violence against one another ever since the founder of Islam, Muhammad, died in 632. (Prior to his death, there had been only one Islamic faith, but afterward, its members began fighting over who should succeed Muhammad as leader of the faith; the Sunnis felt that the successor should be chosen by election based on community agreement, whereas the Shiites felt that Muhammad would have wanted a favorite relative, Ali, to become his successor.) As an example of the latter, in Sri Lanka, members of two different ethnic groups, the Tamils and the Sinhalese, have been engaged in civil war for

The burning and exploding World Trade Towers in New York after terrorists hijacked American airplanes and crashed them into the towers on September 11, 2001. Todd Hollis. © AP Images

weapons. Nineteen Islamic extremists, fifteen of them from bin laden's native country of Saudi Arabia, were involved in the attack, which had been planned for years and killed over three thousand people. The terrorists prepared for September 11 by acquiring travel visas to the United States in 2000 and meeting there to set up the attack. Some of the terrorists traveled in and out of the country during this period, even though they were on a list of suspected al Qaeda members. Most established themselves in apartments in various U.S. states, and some attended flight school to learn how to pilot American passenger jets, particularly Boeing 747s, 757s, and 767s, while others bought knives and prepared to smuggle them onto planes. The terrorists made practice runs, seeing whether they could get onto certain flights without difficulty. One of the terrorists, Zacharias Moussaoui, was arrested on August 17, 2001, after his flight instructors became suspicious of his motives for wanting to learn to fly, but the Federal Bureau of Investigation (FBI) did not find any evidence that he was plotting a terrorist act, though they did jail him for overstaying his U.S. visa.

Shortly thereafter, the other terrorists carried out their plan. They bought first-class tickets—which gave them seats closest to each plane's cockpit—on four September 11, 2001, flights: American Airlines Flight 11, leaving from Logan Airport in Boston, Massachusetts, at 8 AM; American Airlines Flight 175, also leaving from Logan Airport but at 8:15 AM; United Airlines Flight 77, leaving from Dulles International Airport in Virginia at 8:20 AM; and United Airlines Flight 93, leaving Newark International Airport in New Jersey at 8:45 AM. All of these nonstop flights were scheduled to land in California, which required

years, largely because the Tamils are Hindu and the Sinhalese are Buddhist. Similarly, in Israel and Palestine, Jews and Muslims have always attacked one another, and in Bosnia in 1992–1995, three groups, the Orthodox Christian Serbs, the Muslim Bosnians, and the Roman Catholic Croats, slaughtered one another in large numbers.

See Also: Bosnian genocide; Iraq; Palestine; Sri Lanka; Tamil Tigers

September 11 attacks on America

On September 11, 2001, terrorists belonging to the al Qaeda terrorist network led by Osama bin Laden attacked the United States, using four hijacked airplanes as

a large amount of fuel on board that would maximize each plane's explosive damage.

The terrorists struck when each plane was airborne. Five terrorists on Flight 11—Mohamed Atta, Satam al-Suqami, Abdul Alomari, Waleed al-Shehri, and Wail al-Shehri—and five on Flight 175—Moahld al-Shehri, Ahmed al-Ghamdi, Hamza al-Ghamdi, Ahmed al-Haznaw, and Marwan al-Shehhi—used knives and box cutters to attack passengers and flight attendants, forced their way into the cockpit, killed or severely wounded the flight crew, took control of the plane, and then piloted it into the towers of the World Trade Center in New York City. Flight 11 hit the north Trade Center tower at 8:48 AM; Flight 175 hit the south tower at 9:06 AM. The impact ignited the jet fuel, and the 110-story buildings caught fire. People tried to escape, some by jumping to their death, others by struggling down smoke-filled stairwells. Shortly before 10 AM, however, the south tower collapsed, killing nearly everyone inside, including rescue personnel. Shortly before 10:30, the north tower collapsed as well. Several nearby buildings and streets were also seriously damaged, and only about a third of the bodies of those killed—approximately 3,000 in the Trade Center, 147 on the planes, and several hundred rescue workers—were recovered from the scene.

As this disaster was taking place, terrorists on board the other two planes were launching their attacks, attempting to coordinate their actions so that all of the airplanes hit their targets at once. On Flight 77, five terrorists—Salem al-Hazmi, Nawaf al-Hamzi, Majed Moqed, Hani Hanjour, and Khalid al-Midhar—took control of the plane in much the same way as the terrorists on Flights 11 and 175 and flew it into

the Pentagon in Arlington, Virginia, killing all 59 people on the plane and 184 in the building. The intended death toll was much larger; the terrorists had not realized that much of the section of the Pentagon struck by the plane had been closed for renovations at the time. Flight 93 was also unsuccessful in achieving the terrorists' aims. The terrorists on that flight—Ahmed al-Haznaw, Saaed al-Ghamdi, Ahmed al-Nami, and Zia al-Jarrah—who numbered four instead of five because Moussaoui had been jailed, took control of the plane as it flew over Ohio and forced it to turn back toward Washington, D.C., probably so it could strike the White House. Before it could reach its target, though, some of the passengers on board the plane had learned about the attacks on the World Trade Center through cell phone conversations with loved ones at home. Realizing that they were going to die in a similar attack, they decided to try to wrest control of the plane from the terrorists. During the ensuing battle, Flight 93 crashed into the ground, at approximately 10 AM in a western Pennsylvania field. All 40 people on the plane were killed, but no one on the ground was hurt.

As these attacks were taking place, U.S. officials grounded all other flights over the country so that no additional planes could take off (though there is evidence that the government allowed at least one private jet to violate this order: a plane carrying members of Saudi Arabia's royal family out of the country). Soon they also launched an investigation into what had happened, hoping to prevent further attacks. They quickly connected the terrorists to al Qaeda and demanded that the leaders of Afghanistan, the Taliban, who were sheltering, al Qaeda's leader, Osama bin Laden, turn him over to the U.S. government. When the Taliban refused, the United States attacked Afghanistan, and the Taliban was defeated. Nonetheless, the U.S. was unable to find bin laden, who continues to remain at large. Some critics of United States policy have blamed the failure to find bin laden on President George W. Bush, because he pulled troops out of Afghanistan in order to attack the leader of Iraq, Saddam Hussein, with whom he had long been at odds. At the time of this attack, in March 2003, Bush insisted that Hussein had also been involved in the September 11 attacks, though there was and continues to be no evidence of this, and bin laden has taken credit for the attacks.

SEE ALSO: al Qaeda; bin laden, Osama; Bush, U.S. president George W.; Hussein, Saddam; Taliban

Sharon, Ariel
(1928–)

As prime minister of Israel from March 2001 to April 2006, Ariel Sharon was accused by Palestinians of refusing to negotiate for peace between Arabs and Israelis, and in fact, some of his actions—most notably his insistence that a site holy to both Muslims and Jews (the al-Aqsa Mosque to Muslims, the Dome of the Rock to Jews) remain under Israeli control—were damaging to the peace process. However, he also ordered a withdrawal of Israelis from the Gaza Strip, a territory claimed by the Palestinians, an action that many scholars considered necessary to the furtherance of peace (though Israel retained control of the strip's airspace and coast). As a young man, Sharon was a member of a paramilitary organization, the Haganah, that was a forerunner to the Israel Defense Forces. During the 1950s, '60s, and '70s, he participated in numerous military raids and

battles against Arabs as an Israeli military officer; in 1983, while defense minister of Israel, he was held personally responsible for the massacre of innocent Palestinians during the 1982 Lebanon War, and lost his position in the government, but he soon rose to power again. His political influence came to an end, though, in 2006 when he had a stroke and fell into a coma.

SEE ALSO: Israel; Palestine

Shining Path, the

A Peruvian guerrilla group formed in the 1960s by philosophy professor Abimael Guzmán Reynoso, the Shining Path (Sendero Luminoso) has engaged in bombings, assassinations, arson, and other acts of violence, primarily in the 1980s, in an attempt to destroy the government of Peru and replace it with a Communist society modeled after the ideology of Mao Tse-tung, whom Reynoso revered. The group's first members were students who had attended Reynoso's discussion groups at San Cristobal de Huamanga University in Ayachucho, Peru, and initially it was nothing more than a political group, the Communist Party of Peru. By the 1970s, though, Reynoso had decided that violence was the only way to create meaningful change, and the Shining Path began arming and training itself for guerrilla warfare. Its first attacks occurred in 1980 in Ayachucho, where the group killed several landowners, interfered with local elections, and convinced many peasants that their cause was worth supporting. The Peruvian government responded by sending forces into Ayachucho to keep the peace and arresting thousands of Shining Path supporters; many of these people—some of whom had no connection whatsoever to the group—were never seen again. But despite—or perhaps because of—this threat, the group grew rapidly, and by the late 1980s it had over ten thousand active members, in addition to thousands of supporters among the peasantry. This allowed the Shining Path to expand its activities in the early 1990s into the capital city of Lima, where deplorable living conditions among the poor made people in the slums eager for revolution. In Lima, the group bombed dozens of targets, at the rate of at least one a day, and the government reacted by enacting various measures to make it easier for the military to imprison people. It also launched an attack on a Shining Path base that resulted in the arrest of fifteen key members of the group, including Reynoso. This nearly destroyed the group, but in the early 2000s it rebounded somewhat, attacking military and police facilities and, some terrorism experts believe, plotting to attack the American embassy and American tourists in Peru. The Shining Path funds itself primarily through the drug trade, giving it ample resources to rearm itself and add members in the future.

SEE ALSO: South America, terrorism in

Sicarii, the

The Sicarii were Jewish rebels who, during a Jewish rebellion against Roman occupiers in Palestine in 66–73 A.D., attacked representatives of authority, whether Roman or Jewish. The rebels' name came from their use of the sica, a type of dagger, to assassinate their enemies. The Sicarii were a faction of a larger group, the Zealots; both the Sicarii and the Zealots engaged in guerrilla warfare against the Romans, largely without success, for many years.

SEE ALSO: Palestine; Roman Empire

Sikh extremists

Sikh extremists are members of the Sikh religion, most of whom live in India, who want an independent Sikh state. Their faith arose in the 1500s in northern India, where a Sikh kingdom developed but was destroyed by the British in 1849. As part of the decolonization that occurred in the 1940s when the British finally gave India its independence, the Sikhs demanded that their Sikh autonomy be restored. India would not permit this, but it did create a state, Punjab, in an area dominated by Sikhs. Several Sikh militant groups then developed, sometimes fighting among themselves over who would control the battle for independence. When one of the most prominent Sikh radicals, Jarnail Singh Bhindranwale, was arrested for murdering a journalist who had criticized him, his followers demanded his release, and when the government did not comply, they began randomly attacking people of another Indian religion, Hinduism, as well as trains, planes, and other targets associated with the Indian government. Even after Bhindranwale was released for lack of evidence, however, the violence continued, with Sikhs not only attacking individual Hindus but now groups of them, primarily in the city of Punjab. For example, in October 1983, Sikh extremists murdered six Hindu passengers on a bus there. Indian authorities responded by attacking, and often killing, Sikhs throughout the city, but because many of the people they murdered were innocent of any wrongdoing, the citizens of Punjab increasingly supported the militants instead of the authorities, particularly after the military staged one of its largest assaults on the grounds of a sacred Sikh temple in 1984. Shortly thereafter, with the Sikh-against-Hindu violence escalating, Sikh extremists assassinated the prime minister of India, Indira Gandhi, in the capital city of New Delhi, because she had authorized the attack on the temple (Punjab's Golden Temple); her murderers were her bodyguards, both Sikhs. Gandhi's murder turned the international community against the Sikhs, many of whom were attacked in the streets throughout India by non-Sikhs. Nonetheless, Sikh extremists continued their attacks, the most notable of which were the bombing of Air India Flight 182 in June 1985 and several marketplace bombings in 1988. These attacks led India to undertake a massive crackdown on Sikh extremists, and by the end of the 1990s most had gone underground or lessened their activities.

SEE ALSO: decolonization campaigns

single-issue terrorist groups

Single-issue terrorist groups are those whose activities are all related to a single cause, such as antiabortionism, environmentalism, and animal rights. Many such groups arise out of the frustrations of members of conventional activist groups who feel that their legal, nonviolent methods of activism are not working, or at least not working fast enough. Single-issue terrorist groups might be allied with broader movements involving other causes; for example, in the United States many antiabortion groups are connected to Christian Identity and other religious movements. However, each single-issue group remains devoted to its one cause.

SEE ALSO: antiabortion movement; Christian Identity movement

Sinn Féin

An Irish Catholic political party, Sinn Féin (We Alone) has been linked to the Irish Republican Army (IRA) and other groups that have used violence to promote the reunification of Northern Ireland with the

Republic of Ireland. In fact, Sinn Féin has been called the political wing of the IRA, many of whose members also belong to Sinn Féin. In recent years, however, Sinn Féin has been involved in peace negotiations between the British, who control Northern Ireland, and various terrorists in the country. As well, in January 2007 Sinn Féin voted to support the police force in Northern Ireland, in an attempt to open the way toward a shared rule by Protestants and Catholics. (The organization has a history of distrust toward the British-run law-enforcement agencies, the courts, and the prison system.)

SEE ALSO: Irish Republican Army

skinheads

Named for their shaved heads, skinheads are white supremacists, and typically neo-Nazis as well, some of whom engage in racist attacks against nonwhites. Skinheads first appeared in Great Britain in the 1960s, where they shared certain tastes in music and clothing, but over time they became more diverse. Some formed skinhead gangs, others participated in white-supremacist or neo-Nazi groups, while still others preferred to engage in solitary acts of violence as "lone wolves." By the 1980s, skinheads had become established in North America. Most allied with violent U.S. neo-Nazi and white-supremacist groups like the Ku Klux Klan, but a few advocated nonviolence, forming the Skinheads Against Racial Prejudice (SHARP) in the 1990s. Today there are both violent and nonviolent skinheads throughout America, and it is difficult from appearances alone to tell one from the other. However, certain groups of skinheads, such as the Aryan Brotherhood, have been linked to hundreds of murders of various

Skinheads, a nickname inspired by their shaved heads, are usually white supremacists who participate in racist attacks against non-whites. CORBIS

minority groups, particularly blacks, Jews, and gays; some of these groups believe that their actions will trigger a racial holy war that eventually will leave whites in control of the world.

SEE ALSO: Aryan Nations; white supremacists

Snell, Richard
(1931–1995)

The execution of white-supremacist Richard Snell on April 19, 1995, has become an important symbol to other right-wing extremists in the United States who have conducted acts of terrorism on April 19 to honor his death. For example, Timothy McVeigh timed his bombing of the Alfred P. Murrah Federal Building in Oklahoma City, Oklahoma, to coincide with Snell's execution. Snell was a member of the Christian Identity movement and a right-wing terrorist group called the Covenant, the Sword, and the Arm of the Lord (CSA) when, in 1983, he killed the owner of a pawnshop, William Stumpp, in Arkansas. The following year, he shot and killed an Arkansas state trooper who was writing him a ticket for a traffic violation. When Snell was subsequently arrested, he had a variety of weapons and explosives in his possession. Terrorism experts believe that at the time of his arrest, Snell was plotting to blow up the Alfred P. Murrah Federal Building, but there is no evidence that he ever communicated with McVeigh.

SEE ALSO: McVeigh, Timothy

socialists

Socialists have been responsible for numerous violent revolutions throughout history, but some types of socialists lean more toward revolutionary activism than others. Specifically, Marxists and other radical socialists, as well as Communists, often emphasize revolution over reform, arguing that it is necessary to do away with existing governments in order to create meaningful, long-lasting change. In contrast, democratic socialists emphasize reform over revolution, believing that demonstrations, labor strikes, and other nonviolent forms of activism can create meaningful, long-lasting change. Many European democracies include democratic socialists, but in the United States most socialists are revolutionaries, often violent ones.

SEE ALSO: Marx, Karl

Somalian terrorism and the Mogadishu incident

Colonized by Great Britain, France, and Italy in the nineteenth century, Somalia became independent in 1960, after which it became the site of brutal violence and guerrilla warfare as various clans struggled for control of the country. In addition, a nomadic tribe of Somalians living in northeastern Ethiopia demanded that their land, the Ogaden, be included in the new Somali Republic, and when the Ethiopians refused to allow this, the Somali Republic funded a guerrilla force, the Western Somalia Liberation Front (WSLF), that engaged in terrorist attacks against Ethiopians in the Ogaden. By May 1977, a full-scale war had developed between the Ethiopian Army and the WSLF, the latter of which was soon joined by Somali Army forces. Before the year's end, the Ogaden was under the control of Somalia. However, the Soviets, who had been supporting Somalia in this conflict, suddenly decided to support Ethiopia instead, after Ethiopians ousted their pro-U.S. government in favor of an anti-U.S. one. As a result, the Soviets stopped supplying Somalia with military aid, and the Ethiopians, with help from Soviet and Cuban forces, were able to regain control of the Ogaden in March 1978. In 1982, Ethiopian guerrillas began engaging in terrorist attacks against the Somali government, and in 1988 they invaded northern Somalia. The resulting yearlong civil war killed over ten thousand people, and even after the Somali government drove the Ethiopians from the country, violence continued to plague the region. At the same time, Somalia suffered a severe drought, and the resulting famine only made conditions in the country worse. In the early 1990s, when the United Nations sent aid workers, food, and sup-

plies guarded by United Nations (UN) and U.S. troops into Somalia, rival clans immediately began fighting over control of these resources, and the situation deteriorated into guerrilla warfare. In 1993, guerrillas killed twenty-four UN soldiers and, in a separate incident, fifteen U.S. Rangers in the city of Mogadishu.

The Mogadishu incident. The incident in Mogadishu is often cited as an example of the media's ability to influence U.S. policy in regard to terrorism. The incident took place on October 3, 1993, during a U.S. military operation to arrest a Somali warlord, General Mohammed Farah Aideed, and his lieutenants. In addition to the fifteen U.S. Rangers being killed, seventy-seven other soldiers were wounded, including a U.S. Army helicopter pilot who was dragged through the streets by a mob of Somali militiamen. The U.S. president at the time, Bill Clinton, immediately sent reinforcements to the area, but after the news media showed the footage of the dragged pilot on U.S. television, the American public began calling for U.S. troops to withdraw from Somalia. According to a *USA Today*/CNN/Gallup poll taken at the time, 57 percent of the American public disagreed with Clinton's decision to send reinforcements, 50 percent wanted all U.S. troops withdrawn from Somalia immediately, and 52 percent believed that the previous administration, that of President George H.W. Bush, should never have sent troops to Somalia in the first place. Faced with such poll numbers, President Clinton decided to pull U.S. forces out of Somalia by March 1994, regardless of whether the UN had completed its humanitarian effort there. This effort was indeed not completed by that time, and in 1999, several UN and European aid workers were kidnapped from the village of

Elayo, though their guerrilla captors eventually released them unharmed. Today rival clans continue to fight over control of resources in Somalia, which is now called the Republic of Somaliland.

SEE ALSO: Africa, terrorism in post-colonial

South-West Africa People's Organization (SWAPO)

Founded in 1960, the South-West Africa People's Organization (SWAPO) was dedicated to forcing the South African government to allow Namibia to become an independent state; this did indeed occur in the late 1980s, and in 1990, after Namibia's first election, SWAPO formed the country's first government. Prior to this, however, the group committed many violent acts, training insurgents to fight against South African security forces. In 1966, when SWAPO had approximately one thousand members, the group attacked dozens of white civilians in Namibia. In the early 1970s, it received training and weapons from Communist guerrillas from the Soviet Union and Cuba. By 1978, the group had over ten thousand members, but it was nearly wiped out by South African counterterrorism forces. Nonetheless SWAPO was able to conduct bombings and other attacks that killed dozens of civilians, and eventually the South African government decided to abandon Namibia. Working with U.S. and Soviet diplomats, South Africa allowed Namibia its independence in exchange for the withdrawal of Communist forces from neighboring Angola.

SEE ALSO: Africa, terrorism in postcolonial; South Africa

South Africa

In South Africa a system of racial segregation known as apartheid was responsible for a huge amount of violence. This system was established by the country's all-white government, which was comprised primarily of Afrikaners (the descendants of the Dutch who colonized the country in the seventeenth century, though the ancestors of British colonists ruled as well). From 1948 until the early 1990s, this government ruled the country, even though most of the population was black or of mixed race, and enforced the laws and policies of apartheid. One of these laws was that every black person was required to carry an identification card that the police could demand to see at any time and for any reason; objectors to apartheid decided to target this law in a March 1960 demonstration. At that time, a crowd led by members of two groups dedicated to fighting for racial equality in South Africa, the nonviolent African National Congress (ANC) and the violent Pan-African Congress, publicly protested the ID card, whereupon the police fired at them, killing sixty-seven blacks and injuring over two hundred. Angered at this brutality, thousands of black South Africans rioted and marched in the streets, and the government responded by arresting as many ANC and Pan-African Congress members as it could find, including ANC leader Nelson Mandela. The Pan-African Congress did not recover from this assault, while the ANC created a military branch, known as the Umkhonto we Sizwe (Spear of the Nation), whose purpose was to strike back at the government through terrorism directed primarily at property; this group was largely ineffective.

During the early 1970s another force, the Black Consciousness movement, attempted to influence South African politics through nonviolent political demonstrations. This effort was also ineffective, because it only resulted in more police brutality. In June 1976 a Black Consciousness–led protest—this time against the government's decision to force black schoolchildren to learn Afrikaans, the language of the Dutch white minority— sparked rioting throughout South Africa, and hundreds of blacks were killed. Afterward the ANC and the Umkhonto we Sizwe gained many new members and established bases outside of South Africa, where it trained guerrillas and planned terrorist attacks, but these forces still were no match for the South African police. In most cases, terrorist attacks ended with the terrorists either arrested or dead.

Nonetheless in 1984 the ANC led several protests against the government, and in October 1984 their efforts sparked riots in the Vaal Triangle, a region encompassing the cities of Johannesburg and Pretoria, and over forty thousand mine workers there went on strike. When police tried to force them back to work, violence broke out, and the South African government sent the military into the region. Thousands of troops were deployed, but the violence quickly spread to other areas. In 1985 it reached the Cape Province, where police misinterpreted a funeral procession as a protest and shot at its participants, killing twenty innocent blacks. The military subsequently fired on other gatherings of blacks in the Cape, killing more than a thousand within the next three months. The ANC retaliated with terrorist bombings, often leaving bombs in trash cans around tourist areas. Meanwhile black workers continued to protest and to go on strike, and police brutality escalated. Arrests also increased; during 1986, over thirty thousand blacks, including children, had been jailed. The country would have continued on this course had it not been

for political leader F.W. de Klerk, who took over the government of South Africa in 1989. He ended apartheid and partnered with Nelson Mandela, after releasing him from prison, to establish a political system shared by blacks and whites. In 1994 blacks were finally allowed to vote, and Mandela and de Klerk were elected president and vice president, respectively.

SEE ALSO: Africa, terrorism in postcolonial

South America, terrorism in

As with the rest of Latin America, from the 1950s to the 1980s the countries of South America experienced Communist revolutionary movements. Most of these were inspired by the Cuban Revolution or Marxist revolutionary Che Guevara, and were represented by guerrilla warfare and terrorism in both rural and urban areas as well as extreme anti-U.S. sentiments. In response to these movements and to other threats, state authorities engaged in terrorism as well. In the 1970s, for example, Argentina, then under a military government, responded to terrorism instigated by a group called Montoneros by creating detention camps where tens of thousands were tortured and killed. Death squads terrorized civilians elsewhere in South America as well, particularly in Chile, where a government death squad known as the Avengers of the Martyrs killed over three thousand people. Today most of the terrorism in South America is in Colombia, where the government is under threat from leftist rebels, and to a lesser extent in Peru, where the remnants of two organizations, Shining Path and the Tupac Amaru Revolutionary Movement (MRTA), still operate on a small scale. Colombia also has a great deal of violence associated with the drug trade. In the 1980s, two drug cartels (syndicates), Cali and Medellin, were the predominant cocaine dealers in the world, and they killed thousands of people—police officers, judges, soldiers, politicians, journalists, and others—in order to maintain their activities. These cartels no longer exist, but the smaller criminal organizations that replaced them continue to engage in narco-terrorism, though to a much lesser extent and without calling attention to themselves.

SEE ALSO: Latin America, terrorism in

Spain

Most of Spain's experiences with domestic terrorism have arisen from its conflicts with the militant group Basque Homeland and Liberty ("Euskadi ta Askatasuna" in the Basque language of Euskara, or ETA). Formed in 1959, this group has used bombings, assassinations, kidnappings, and other attacks intended to force Spain to relinquish its hold on the Spanish Basque region. The Basque region is in the Pyrenees Mountains between Spain and France, as is the French Basque region; both regions were an independent land until approximately 1800, when Spain and France each took control of half of this land, but even then the Basques continued to have a unique culture and language and were allowed to manage their own affairs. Under Spain's dictator Francisco Franco, however, in the 1930s the Basques were denied their traditional autonomy and ordered to speak Spanish instead of their own language. As a result, a Basque separatist movement developed in Spain during the 1940s–1960s, and by the 1970s, the idea of Basque nationalism had many supporters, not only in Spain but in France, where the ETA established bases from which it could plan attacks on Spanish targets. The group killed several officials in the Spanish government, including the

prime minister in 1973. In 1975, after Franco died, the ETA increased its activities, hoping that the change in Spain's government would lead to the Basque separatism it sought, and indeed, the new government did return some of the autonomy to the Basques. Still, some ETA members continued to fight for full separatism, despite government efforts in the 1980s and '90s to convince members that their terrorist activities were no longer necessary given increased autonomy among the Basques. One of the ETA's most notable attacks occurred in 1987, when the group killed twenty-one people during a supermarket bombing in Barcelona, Spain, and in 2001, eight ETA members were arrested while planning a car bombing that was intended to target tourists and therefore disrupt Spain's tourism industry.

SEE ALSO: Basque Homeland and Liberty

Spartacus

In 73 B.C., Spartacus led a slave rebellion in which over 120,000 slaves in Italy rose up against their Roman masters. This rebellion lasted for two years, during which some of the slaves roamed the countryside attacking Roman citizens at random, while others reserved their brutality for those Romans who had oppressed them. In 71 B.C., the rebellion was finally extinguished by a Roman general named Crassus, who crucified over 6,000 of the slaves he captured. According to ancient Roman writings, the crosses of these crucified slaves dotted the road from the city of Capua to Rome, a distance of 100 miles (161 km).

SEE ALSO: Roman Empire

Special Operations units, U.S.

The United States has several Special Operations units, many of which can be called upon to deal with terrorist threats. The U.S. Army has three such units, the Special Forces, the Rangers, and Delta Force; the air force has one unit, the Air Force Special Operations Command (SOCOM); and the navy has one unit, the Sea Air Land (SEAL) Team. The Army's Special Forces has three teams, the A-team, the B-team, and the C-team, all working out of Fort Bragg, North Carolina. Of these, only the A-team goes on missions; the other two teams offer support for the A-team. Members of the A-team are therefore combat-trained soldiers, all male and all with the rank of sergeant or higher. They are experts in one of five specialties: weapons and tactics, demolitions and explosives, communications, medicine, or operational planning (team leaders). Together their main purpose is to work with and train members of foreign military groups to fight against terrorists and revolutionaries. The Army's Rangers are also well trained, though their training concentrates on teaching them how to patrol various harsh environments—such as deserts, jungles, swamps, forests, mountainous terrain, and deep valleys—so that they can lend support to military operations anywhere in the world. Delta Force is trained in more advanced skills, such as parachuting, rappelling down the sides of office buildings, and operating all sorts of vehicles, and it has been used to rescue hostages. SOCOM's duties are to evaluate an enemy's air power and to provide air support to other special operations units via the use of its sophisticated aircraft and well-trained pilots. The SEAL team conducts its operations under water, using advanced underwater breathing gear and other equipment suitable for use not only in oceans and seas of various temperatures but in swamps and other bodies of water. SEALs also are trained to work in various

land environments, and all know how to handle explosives and other weapons as well as a variety of military equipment, including parachutes.

SEE ALSO: Delta Force

Sri Lanka

Most of the terrorism in Sri Lanka has been committed by Tamils, an ethnic group whose people primarily practice the Hindu religion. They have their own language, Tamil, and comprise only 15 percent of the country's population; there are Tamils in India as well, predominantly in the southeastern Indian state of Tamil Nadu. Sri Lankan Tamils want their own state too, and in an attempt to force the government to create one, Tamil separatists have attacked numerous military, government, and civilian targets via bombings and assassinations. The largest and most powerful of these groups in Sri Lanka is the Liberation Tigers of Tamil Eelam (LTTE), more commonly known as the Tamil Tigers, which controls large sections of the northern and eastern countryside. Members of this and other Tamil groups have long engaged in a civil war against members of a different Sri Lankan ethno-religious group, the Buddhist Sinhalese, committing sectarian violence as part of their drive for Tamil separatism.

SEE ALSO: sectarian violence; Tamil Tigers

Stalin, Joseph
(1879–1953)

As the leader of the Soviet Union, Joseph Stalin was responsible for millions of people, many of whom died during one of Stalin's "purges" of anyone disloyal to the state. Stalin encouraged his citizens to inform on one another, whereupon those deemed suspect would be tortured, then either executed or sent to prisons in the

Joseph Stalin was the leader of the Soviet Union beginning in the mid-1920s, and was known for his ruthless acts of torture and execution against anyone not loyal to the Soviet Union. AP IMAGES

brutal climate of Siberia, an arctic region of Russia, where many died of hunger or disease. Stalin was also behind the assassination of his rival for control of the Soviet Union, Leon Trotsky, in 1940, even though Stalin had wrestled control of the government from Trotsky in the early 1920s and sent him into exile in 1929. The struggle for power between Trotsky and Stalin had arisen after the death of Vladimir Lenin, who led the Bolshevik revolution that destroyed the Russian monarchy in 1917. Some Russians revere Stalin for his role in this revolution and for his leadership during World War II in the fight against a Nazi invasion. Others, however, condemn him for his purges, particularly because the victims of these murders were often innocent of any wrongdoing.

SEE ALSO: Bolsheviks, the

state terrorism

State terrorism is terrorism conducted by a government. In many cases where nations have committed such violence, terrorism experts have disagreed on whether these acts did indeed constitute terrorism or instead were acts of war. However, experts generally agree that when state-sponsored violence is conducted secretly, unpredictably, and to a degree that is so severe it offends most human beings' sensibilities, then it is usually terrorism, even when carried out by known government agencies. For example, when a country's military or police forces randomly arrest and torture civilians whose only crime appears to be an outspokenness against government policies—as occurred in many Latin American countries in the 1970s and '80s—this constitutes state terrorism, particularly when the victims are given no legal rights and are never seen alive again. State terrorism also occurs when a government targets a particular group for persecution, such as the Nazi government did when it attacked Jews in the 1930s and '40s.

SEE ALSO: Latin America, terrorism in; Nazi terrorism

Stern Gang, the

Also known as the Fighters for the Freedom of Israel, the Stern Gang was a Jewish terrorist group dedicated to ousting the British from Palestine. Its founder, Avraham Stern, created the group in 1940 from dissatisfied members of another Jewish nationalist group, Irgun Zvai Leumi, that wanted to stop fighting the British in order to join their fight against the Nazis. Instead Stern felt that the Nazis could be persuaded to allow the Jews to settle in Palestine. Throughout the 1940s, the Stern

Gang committed assassinations, bombings, and other acts of terrorism against British targets, even after British forces killed Stern in 1942. One of the group's victims was Count Folke Bernadotte, a Swedish diplomat at the forefront of negotiating the dispute between Israel and Arab nations during the Israeli War of Independence; the Stern Gang gunned him down in 1948. After this, Israel banned the group, making it a crime for anyone to belong to or aid the Stern Gang, and its members drifted away.

SEE ALSO: Irgun Zvai Leumi

Stockholm syndrome

Stockholm syndrome is a condition that occurs in certain hostage situations, whereby a captive bonds with his or her captor(s) and becomes sympathetic to the cause behind the kidnapping. Experts in the psychology of hostage situations believe that it takes at least three days for the syndrome to develop, but they disagree on how easily or strongly it occurs. For example, after kidnap victim Patty Hearst bonded with her captors, who were members of a group called the Symbionese Liberation Army (SLA), experts argued over whether her case of Stockholm syndrome was powerful enough to cause her to rob banks for the group while armed and unsupervised, as she did after enduring more than fifty days of physical and psychological tortures.

The syndrome is named after a hostage situation that occurred in Stockholm, Sweden, in August 1973, when four bank employees were held in a bank vault by two men for six days. One of the employees not only bonded with her captors but became the lover of one of them and continued to consider herself his girlfriend even after he was sent to prison. (Hearst

had a similar relationship with one of her kidnappers.) Since this time, there have been several documented cases of terrorists' hostages coming to sympathize with their captors, and some psychologists have noted that the same type of syndrome occurs among victims whose lives are threatened in similar closed environments, such as prison camps, cult compounds, and homes with battering spouses. Psychologists have theorized that fear of imminent death is an important component of the Stockholm syndrome, perhaps because victims find themselves grateful to their captors for deciding not to kill them after all.

SEE ALSO: Hearst, Patricia; Symbionese Liberation Army

Students for a Democratic Society (SDS)

Established in 1962 by a group of middle-class students, most from the University of Michigan, the Students for a Democratic Society (SDS) was a left-wing activist organization dedicated to challenging the values of traditional American society. Originally the group advocated nonviolent demonstrations as a way to present its views, but by 1968 many of its members had turned to violence, and riots often broke out during SDS demonstrations on university campuses. That same year, the organization splintered into several factions that spawned groups with varying levels of tolerance for violence; among the most violent was the Weatherman group and the United Freedom Front (UFF), the latter of which committed at least twenty-five bombings and robberies in the northeastern United States. Most of the SDS-inspired groups were only active during the 1960s and early 1970s, but the UFF remained active until the mid-1980s.

SEE ALSO: left-wing terrorism, U.S.; Weatherman

Symbionese Liberation Army (SLA)

Established in California in the 1970s and led by Donald DeFreeze, an escaped convict who renamed himself General Field Marshal Cinque, the Symbionese Liberation Army (SLA) is best known for its kidnapping of Patty Hearst, the granddaughter of a millionaire newspaper magnate, as part of a campaign of violence against targets it connected to fascism. In November 1973, the SLA assassinated the superintendent of schools in Oakland, California, because he insisted that students carry identification cards (an insistence that the SLA considered fascist), and in 1974 it kidnapped Hearst, demanding that her wealthy family establish a feed-the-poor program in exchange for her release. After the Hearst family donated over $2 million worth of food, however, Hearst refused to leave her captors, probably as the result of a psychological condition known as the Stockholm syndrome, and began participating in the group's activities, including a bank robbery on April 15, 1974, during which she was videotaped brandishing a gun. The group then established a hideout in Los Angeles, California. While Hearst and two other SLA members, Bill and Emily Harris, were absent, the police attacked the home on May 16. During the shoot-out and subsequent fire that destroyed the house, six SLA members, including DeFreeze, were killed. Roughly five months later, police captured five more SLA members, including Hearst and the Harrises, all of whom were sent to prison. Later the Harrises and two other SLA members were charged with a death that occurred during an SLA bank robbery in Carmichael, California, on April 21, 1975, and another was charged with planting a bomb under police cars in August 1975. Hearst, however, has been released from prison and now leads a normal life.

SEE ALSO: Hearst, Patricia; Stockholm syndrome

Syria

In the 1960s, the secret service of Syria, along with that of Egypt, created the Palestinian militant group al Fatah, providing it with arms and training, and from 1971 to 2000, under the rule of Hafez el-Assad, the country continued to support Palestinians' efforts to create a Palestinian state. Syria has also offered aid to the Lebanese militant group Hezbollah, and it has apparently helped recruit terrorists for various Islamic extremist groups. Syria has also harbored and funded terrorist organizations, but terrorism experts have been unable to connect it to any specific acts of terrorism, nor can they find proof that Syria is directing the activities of an anti-Israeli militant group called the Popular Front for the Liberation of Palestine (PFLP). After the September 11, 2001, terrorist attacks on America, Syria spoke out against terrorism and vowed to help the United States capture those responsible for the attacks, but it continued to support Palestinian terrorists.

SEE ALSO: al Fatah; Palestine; Popular Front for the Liberation of Palestine

Taliban

From the mid-1990s to 2001, a religious group known as the Taliban controlled Afghanistan. It first developed as a religious movement in 1994 in the southern part of the country, where various warlords had been fighting for supremacy since defeating Soviet-backed forces there in 1992. One of the mujahideen, or Muslim fighters, who had been involved in this war, Mohammed Omar, eventually stepped forward to change this situation. A religious student, Omar was a member of the Sunni sect of Islam, as well as a member of the Pashtun ethnic group whose people lived in both Afghanistan and Pakistan; consequently he gained many supporters in these two countries when he spoke against the chaos in the region, and his group, the Taliban (meaning "religious students"), grew from thirty armed warriors to three thousand in only one month near the end of 1994. This force seized control of one place after another, eventually taking a ma-

A Taliban fighter sits near a Russian-built rocket launcher in Kabul, Afghanistan, in 1998.
AP Images

jor city, Kandahar, which gave them access to a large number of military weapons. Over the next two years the group gained thousands of members, and in early 1996 it took control of the capital city of Kabul. By this time, its enemies were concentrated in the northern part of the country, but although the Taliban often attacked this region, it was never able to seize control of it. Nonetheless it became the official government of Afghanistan.

Once in power, the Taliban adopted policies in accordance with the strictest interpretations of the Islamic faith from the Sunni perspective, and it persecuted Shiites. It also repressed women, restricting their movements and activities and forcing them to wear clothing that hid their faces and bodies from view. The Taliban also banned television, movies, and music from Afghan society. More importantly, the Taliban supported radical Islamic groups, including the al Qaeda terrorist network of Osama bin Laden, by providing such groups with funds, weapons, and training centers. The United States bombed one of these training camps in August 1998, after U.S. authorities determined that al Qaeda was responsible for the bombing of two American embassies—one in Kenya and the other in Tanzania—and offered support to the Taliban's enemies, a group called the Northern Alliance. The U.S. government also demanded that the Taliban end its support of al Qaeda, but the Taliban ignored this demand. In fact, some terrorism experts believe that this warning only strengthened the Taliban's resolve to support terrorism against Western targets. When the September 11, 2001, terrorist attacks on America that were masterminded by bin laden occurred, the United States demanded that the Taliban turn this terrorist over to American authorities. The Taliban repeatedly refused, so the United

States and some of its allies, including Great Britain, attacked Afghanistan—first with a wave of air bombings and then with ground forces—and in less than two months they had destroyed the Taliban and taken control of the country, establishing a new, U.S.-backed government in late December 2001. Today, however, the Taliban is once again gaining prominence in the country, and some terrorism experts believe that it will one day control the Afghanistan government again.

SEE ALSO: Afghanistan; al Qaeda; bin laden, Osama

Tamil Tigers (Liberation Tigers of Tamil Eelam), the

Established in 1976, the Liberation Tigers of Tamil Eelam, more commonly known as the LTTE or the Tamil Tigers, is dedicated to forcing the government of Sri Lanka to create an independent state for the Tamils, a Hindu people who have long been at odds with the Buddhist Sinhalese in the country. There are several such Tamil separatist groups in Sri Lanka, but the Tigers are the largest and most powerful, with perhaps as many as ten thousand men engaging regularly in guerrilla warfare and insurgent attacks on government targets. Some have assassinated important political and military figures, while others have bombed political and military facilities. The group currently controls the majority of the northern and eastern coastlines of Sri Lanka, as well as other areas within the country, and it funds its activities primarily through the drug trade. The Tigers also receive support from Tamil separatists living in other countries, many of whom have formed their own groups, such as the World Tamil Association (WTA) to further their cause.

SEE ALSO: Sri Lanka

tax protestors, U.S.

In the United States, some of the people protesting the mandatory payment of taxes have expressed their antigovernment sentiments through violence. For example, in the 1990s several tax protestors bombed, fired upon, set fire to, or gassed offices of the Internal Revenue Service (IRS), the U.S. agency in charge of collecting taxes. In the late 1990s, one of these terrorists, Charles Polk, was convicted of planning to blow up an Austin, Texas, IRS office. Many other tax protestors have been convicted of tax fraud; this was the case, for example, with the leader of an antitax group called the Your Heritage Protection Association (YHPA), Armen Condo. Members of the tax-protest movement, which is considered an element of right-wing activism, are often members of other right-wing groups as well, particularly those associated with the Patriot movement.

SEE ALSO: Christian Patriots; right-wing terrorists, U.S.

terror anniversaries

Some terrorists plan their attacks to coincide with the anniversary of previous attacks or with dates that are significant to their cause or otherwise have meaning to them. For example, Islamic terrorists chose to launch synchronized attacks on American embassies in Nairobi, Kenya, and Dar es Salaam, Tanzania, on August 7, 1998, because that date was the eighth anniversary of U.S. president George H.W. Bush's decision to establish an American military presence in Saudi Arabia. (Though the Saudi government welcomed this presence as a response to the threat of invasion by Iraq, which had just sent troops into Kuwait, the terrorists were offended by the idea of non-Muslims walking on holy Muslim ground.) An important date to right-wing extremists in the United States is April 19: The first battle of the American Revolution, at Lexington, took place on April 19, 1775; a standoff between federal officials and the American right-wing group the Covenant, the Sword, and the Arm of the Lord (CSA) transpired on April 19, 1985; a shoot-out between federal officials and white separatist Randy Weaver and his family occurred at Ruby Ridge, Idaho, on April 19, 1992; and a 1993 attack by federal officials on the Branch Davidian compound in Waco, Texas, also culminated on April 19. To many right-wing extremists, all of these events were battles between true patriots and an oppressive, unjust government that no longer represented the values of the U.S. Constitution. One such extremist, Timothy McVeigh, therefore planned his own attack on a symbol of the U.S. government—the Alfred P. Murrah Federal Building in Oklahoma City, Oklahoma—to coincide with this anniversary, in 1995. (McVeigh was aware that this was also the day of the execution of white separatist and right-wing extremist Richard Wayne Snell, a member of the CSA who had killed a pawnbroker in 1983.) Because of these events, federal authorities heighten their security measures every April 19, concerned that another terrorist attack might take place on the anniversary of the Oklahoma City bombing.

SEE ALSO: Branch Davidians; Covenant, the Sword, and the Arm of the Lord, the; embassy bombings; McVeigh, Timothy; Ruby Ridge

Terror, The

The name "The Terror" is sometimes used interchangeably with "The Reign of Terror," a period of the French Revolution when the Revolutionary government, largely at the urging of politician Maximilien Robespierre, systematically arrested and executed those who opposed its existence or policies. More commonly, however, "The Terror" refers to the most violent time of the Reign of Terror, June–July 1794, when the Revolutionary government suspended the people's right to stand trial and executed fourteen hundred people. (This time has also been called the Great Terror.) The name "The Terror" has also been used to refer to the full span of revolutionary violence—from the overthrow of King Louis XVI in 1792 to the creation of a new regime, the Directory, in 1795–99—but most historians refer to the violence of 1795–99 as the White Terror. In any case, an estimated two hundred thousand people died as a result of state terror during the 1790s.

SEE ALSO: Robespierre, Maximilien; Reign of Terror

terrorism, categories of

In an attempt to come up with a universal definition of terrorism (which does not yet exist), scholars and politicians have created categories of terrorism. Some have based these categories on the geographical region of either the terrorists' country of origin or their region of operation (Iraqi terrorism, for example, or Middle Eastern terrorism). Others have based their categories on the terrorists' ideology, goals, or targets. For example, the first scholar to categorize terrorism, Thomas P. Thornton, in 1964, broke it into two types, enforcement terror (designed to influence specific behaviors) and agitational terror (designed to create chaos), while in the 1970s it was popular to categorize terrorism according to whether it was selective (striking specifically chosen targets) or indiscriminate (striking random targets). Today it is more common to categorize terrorism as religious versus secular, right-wing or left-wing, or state-sponsored versus non-state-sponsored (revolutionary or insurgency). However, experts now recognize that terrorism is too complex an issue to discuss in terms of neat categories, and that the same act of terrorism can be categorized in several different ways.

SEE ALSO: terrorism, definitions of

terrorism, current geographical hot spots for

Terrorism occurs all over the world, but certain locations currently have more terrorist activity than others. Most of these hot spots are in the Middle East, where the U.S. invasion of Iraq and removal of its dictator, Saddam Hussein, destabilized the region. When this occurred, terrorists from other countries entered Iraq from Syria and Iran and began attacking American forces there on a daily basis, causing thousands of deaths. A large number of attacks have also occurred against Israel, perpetrated by terrorists in Palestine and Lebanon who oppose the idea of Jews occupying what they believe are Arab lands. In 2006, the terrorist group Hezbollah engaged in mortar and missile attacks against Israel, which in turn lobbed missiles at suspected Hezbollah strongholds in Lebanon. The African continent has also seen a great deal of terrorism, not just in recent years but throughout history, with much of it involving ethnic warfare and genocide. India is another hot spot for terrorism, largely because of ethnic and religious differences in the Kashmir region (a conflict that neighboring Pakistan, which wants control of the region, has encouraged), and similar ethnic violence has occurred in Indonesia. In Latin America, however, terrorism is on the decline, with the exception of violence related to criminal terrorism (especially the drug trade). This could change, however, at any time, as is the case for the status of other hot or cool spots as well, and experts often have trouble predicting whether a particular conflict will escalate or decline. For example, in Spain a terrorist group known as Basque Homeland and Liberty (ETA, or "Euskadi ta Askatasuna" in the Basque language of Euskara) had declared a cease-fire against the government despite its desire to liberate the Spanish Basque region from Spain, and terrorism experts believed that this cease-fire would hold. But in January 2007, police found a cache of explosives in the Basque region and connected these explosives both to a car bombing that killed two people at the Madrid International Airport and to the ETA, indicating that ETA intended to resume its violence. Terrorism in Somalia is also escalating, despite attempts by a transitional government to drive out radical Islamic militias there; in January 2007, unknown assailants launched grenades at Ethiopian troops, part of an international peacekeeping force helping to support the new government, and Muslim chieftains have protested the presence of these troops because they are Christian and because Ethiopia has fought two wars with Somalia.

SEE ALSO: Africa, terrorism in postcolonial; Basque Homeland and Liberty; criminal terrorism; genocide; Hezbollah; Hussein, Saddam; Indonesian terrorism; Iran; Iraq; Israel; Latin America, terrorism in; Pakistan; Palestine; Somalian terrorism and the Mogadishu incident; Syria

terrorism, definitions of

Among members of the general public, terrorism is typically defined as the unlaw-ful, deliberate use of violence against people or property in an attempt to instill fear in others and perhaps also influence individual behavior or government policy. However, scholars, historians, politicians, government agencies, and other experts in terrorism consider this definition too simplistic. At the same time, they cannot agree on an alternative definition; indeed, there are several dozen definitions of terrorism among such experts, based on their opinions of what constitutes a terrorist act. For example, while many experts say that guerrilla warfare is not a type of terrorism but instead a type of warfare, others insist that guerrilla warfare must be considered terrorism because it both instills fear in the populace and is tied to a political agenda. The notion that terrorism is motivated by a political agenda is an element of many terrorism definitions; however, some experts argue that motivation is a poor way to define terrorism, because terrorists can commit violence because of religious, ethnic, or cultural beliefs instead. Moreover defining terrorism in terms of goals can lead to problems related to the old adage: "One man's terrorist is another man's freedom fighter." For example, both the American Revolutionaries who fought for the creation of the United States and the Palestinians who fought for the creation of a Palestinian state could be said to have used violence in order to liberate their people from oppression, but the former have been called patriots and the latter terrorists. Therefore some experts have sought to define terrorism based not on the motivations of those who commit violence but on whether or not such people are operating within mainstream society. In other words, if those who perpetrate violence are extremists operating on the fringes of their society, with little support from their peers, then, some experts say, they are terrorists. But again, there are others who disagree with this approach to defining terrorism, this time under the argument that terrorism cannot be determined by a popularity contest.

Such struggles aside, though, scholars have managed to come to some agreement over the terms used to define various types of terrorism. In the broadest sense, these types are:

State terrorism: terrorism committed by a government, whether against its own citizens or against perceived enemies elsewhere.

Non-state or dissident terrorism: terrorism committed by groups or individuals not associated with the government, against other groups, individuals, or the government.

Religious terrorism: terrorism committed out of beliefs related to the terrorists' religious faith, usually as part of an attempt to glorify, protect, or promote the faith.

Criminal terrorism: terrorism committed to further illegal acts, usually connected to acquiring wealth either for its own sake or in order to fund other types of terrorism; most criminal terrorism is associated with the drug trade.

Some experts consider hate crimes to be terrorism as well, along with race-based violence, while others reject this view because such violence is often unconnected to any political, religious, or other sort of agenda. Similarly, a few scholars have called serial killers terrorists because their actions terrorize the population, but because such murderers have no agenda in committing their violence, most scholars would disagree with this notion.

In addition, experts typically classify terrorism in accordance with whether it is associated with left-wing or right-wing ideologies. They also note that certain ideologies—specifically anarchism, fascism, and Marxism—have been more strongly associated with terrorism throughout history than others. Historians further note that the connotation of the word "terrorism" has changed over the years. When the word was first used by participants in the French Revolution, it had a positive connotation; the public viewed terrorists as people dedicated to creating a democracy. From this point until the 1930s, terrorism was strongly associated with revolution, but during the 1930s and '40s it was increasingly associated with the actions of the state rather than of revolutionaries. At that time, governments that repressed the freedoms of citizens were increasingly called terrorist, and the word came to have a negative connotation. Then, after World War II, it was again viewed positively, as natives being repressed by colonial powers committed terrorist acts in order to drive out occupying governments. Terrorism inspired by nationalism in the 1960s and '70s was also viewed positively, but in the 1980s the word "terrorist" once again became pejorative, as the rise of religious terrorism led to many attacks on the West. This is still the situation today, when calling someone a terrorist is considered an attack on his or her character.

SEE ALSO: terrorism, motivations for

terrorism, motivations for

There are obviously as many motivations for terrorism as there are terrorists; however, certain generalizations can be made regarding why certain individuals or groups are likely to commit terrorist acts. First and foremost, terrorism begins with the belief that violence is necessary to create some kind of change, usually political, in a particular society. Often this belief comes after nonviolent political activism has failed to create the desired change; for example, in the United States, some right-wing extremists began committing terrorist acts against abortion providers after being frustrated in their attempts to have abortion declared illegal. Terrorism might also be a defensive response triggered by an attack or other violent event; for example, civil wars, foreign invasion, and periods of extreme government repression have all inspired terrorism at various times and places. But regardless of the trigger, most terrorists share a firm conviction that their cause is just and that their enemies are evil, or at least morally inferior. Many view the world in a simplistic way in regard to good and evil—that is, they see people as either being absolutely right or absolutely wrong, with no middle ground or subtle nuances. Moreover terrorists typically believe that the good of the many outweighs the good of the few, which means that it is acceptable to kill dozens or even hundreds of innocent people in order to end the oppression of the masses. And because terrorists consider themselves morally superior, they typically believe that they know what is best for the masses, and their violence is intended to encourage or frighten the public into supporting their views.

Often these views include the notion that a utopian society is possible, and that by joining the terrorist in violent revolution, the masses can create a perfect world. For religious terrorists, this world is typically one in which all of God's wishes, as expressed through the terrorists' faith, are strictly followed; for secular terrorists (anarchists and the like), the utopian society typically comes with the adoption of an egalitarian political system. Moreover, terrorists might seek to prove themselves worthy of utopia by following a rigid code of behavior; such self-sacrifice is particularly true of members of religious terrorist groups, but even secular groups like neo-Nazi organizations might also encourage their members to adopt a certain set of behaviors, because such codes serve to unite the group's members by providing them with a shared discipline to match their shared cause.

Most terrorists also share certain character traits: a single-minded dedication to their cause, a lack of concern for their physical well-being, a lack of remorse after committing murder or lesser crimes that benefit their cause, and a lack of sympathy or empathy for the victims of their violence. Many are also highly intelligent and well educated, particularly those who become leaders of terrorist groups. Historically, a large number of terrorists, especially anarchists and revolutionaries, have been students or intellectuals. In recent years, however, terrorists have increasingly been uneducated or barely educated young people who are not only willing but eager to die for their cause.

SEE ALSO: terrorism, definitions of

terrorist-threat warnings

After the September 11, 2001, terrorist attack on America, U.S. president George W. Bush created the Homeland Security Advisory System by presidential directive; this color-coded system provides terrorist-threat warnings to the general public and public officials. On a daily basis, the system indicates which of five levels of risk currently exist, with the following levels: Severe, indicated by the color red, means

The first U.S. Secretary of Homeland Security, Tom Ridge, unveils the five-level, color-coded warning system for terrorist threats and attacks. JOE MARQUETTE. © AP IMAGES

there is a severe risk of terrorist attack; High, indicated by the color orange, means there is a high risk of terrorist attack; Elevated, indicated by the color yellow, means there is a significant risk of terrorist attack; Guarded, indicated by the color blue, means there is a general risk of terrorist attack; and Low, indicated by the color green, means there is a low risk of terrorist attacks. In creating this daily assessment, federal experts in terrorism consider a variety of factors, such as whether intelligence agents have heard "chatter" over phone lines or other means of communication that suggest an attack is being planned or whether a particular date is the anniversary of something significant to terrorists. (For example, there is a greater than usual terrorist threat on April 19 be-

cause this day has meaning to right-wing extremists, one of whom bombed the Alfred P. Murrah Federal Building in Oklahoma City, Oklahoma, on April 19, 1995.) Prior to the establishment of this system, however, a terrorist-threat warning already existed; called FPCON (Force Protection Condition), it was used by the U.S. Department of Defense to inform federal agencies and the military of the degree of readiness necessary to defend the country from attack. Like the Homeland Security Advisory System, FPCON has five levels:

- Delta—Country at full readiness; military fully armed and guarding possible terrorist targets; important roads and buildings closed to civilians.

- Charlie—Country at heightened readiness; military armed and waiting to deploy, with all terrorism experts on duty, and military bases and other important facilities closed to unauthorized personnel.
- Bravo—Military on alert, conducting random searches and inspections of people and vehicles seeking to enter a military base or other important facility; no cars allowed near important buildings; all terrorism experts ready to respond but not necessarily on duty.
- Alpha—High level of alertness and suspicion, but no extra security measures taken.
- Normal—Business as usual.

SEE ALSO: Oklahoma City bombing; terrorism anniversaries

terrorist activities

Terrorists engage in many activities related to their goals, but the most common terrorist acts are bombings; assassinations; kidnappings and hijackings; rocket, missile, and mortar attacks; and chemical attacks. They also engage in criminal activities to fund their terrorism, and sometimes various terrorist groups work together to conduct large terrorist operations.

Bombings. By far, bombing is the most common terrorist activity, because bombs are relatively simple to make and use yet cause a great deal of death and destruction while enabling the bomber to avoid capture. A bomb is comprised of some sort of explosive material, a detonator, and a fuse. Gasoline and fertilizer are both popular explosives because they are easy to obtain, as are plastic explosives because they are small, malleable, and easy to transport. Terrorists can also obtain sophisticated

military materiel, either from governments or the black market, but these are more expensive and usually require an equally sophisticated detonator with a timing device that will ensure the bomb does not detonate prematurely. Simple detonators and timing devices can be homemade and might run on batteries alone. As for the method of delivery, the most common are letter and packable bombs and car and truck bombs. The car or truck bomb is most often exploded via a timing device after the driver has parked and left the vehicle, but in some cases (particularly in Iraq in recent years) a suicide bomber detonates the bomb while driving toward or into the intended target. Suicide bombers also strap bombs to their bodies and walk into crowded markets or other places intended to cause maximum casualties before detonating. Bombs might instead be planted in trash cans, suitcases, or other suitable objects. In most cases, the violence caused by the bomb is intended to be indiscriminate, but sometimes bombs are used to attack specific targets, as with assassinations carried out via a car bomb.

Assassinations. While assassinations have often been conducted by individuals with a personal grievance toward the victim, such murders sometimes occur as part of a terrorist campaign as a way to eliminate an obstacle to that campaign or to bring media attention to a related cause. The tactic is most common in countries in which the government is weak, because strong governments typically have powerful security forces that protect their public officials. However, even well-protected state officials, judges, police officers, and other symbols of authority have been the victims of assassins. Some of these victims were shot, stabbed, or poisoned, while others have been killed by bombs planted in their cars, homes, or places of business. In most cases, the death has little or no impact on the particular situation it was intended to influence.

Kidnappings and hijackings. Although kidnappings and hijackings have been used as political tools since ancient times, they became particularly popular among terrorists in the 1960s, when terrorists realized that hostages could be used as bargaining tools to gain certain concessions from governments. Sometimes the hostages have been exchanged for money, but more often they have been used to secure the release of imprisoned terrorists. Kidnappings and hijackings have also been used to attract media attention to a cause, particularly in cases where terrorists take control of airplanes or embassies. Between 1971 and 1980, there were more than fifty embassies seized by terrorists (twenty-six in 1979 alone), because of the media sensation caused by such operations. However, since many embassy seizures ended in the death of all terrorists involved, after the host government's military personnel stormed the building, most terrorists abandoned embassy seizures in favor of embassy bombings. After the September 11, 2001, terrorist attacks on America, however, increased security measures made it much more difficult for terrorists to get bombs near embassies. The same was true for airplanes; planting bombs on planes or hijacking them became extremely difficult in the weeks after September 11.

Other forms of attack. Terrorists who employ rockets, mortars, missiles, and chemical and biological weapons have the advantage of being able to strike from a distance, usually in anonymity, while causing a great deal of damage. However, long-range rockets, missiles, and mortars often lack accuracy, and chemical and biological weapons can be dangerous to handle as well as difficult to acquire and transport. The same is true for nuclear weapons, which many terrorists have tried unsuccessfully to obtain. So far, no terrorist has used a nuclear weapon for mass destruction, but terrorism experts fear that this will one day happen.

Fundraising activities. Modern terrorist organizations can require large amounts of cash to sustain themselves and carry out operations. Consequently such organizations often solicit donations from people sympathetic to their cause. In addition, terrorists might engage in criminal activities such as drug trafficking and kidnapping for ransom in an attempt to raise money. They also invest money in order to grow their funds.

Collaborative efforts. In the 1970s, terrorists with common enemies increasingly realized that they might accomplish more by pooling their resources for large operations, and an era of collaborative efforts between terrorist groups began. Most of the first such joint operations were conducted against Israelis. For example, in 1972 the Popular Front for the Liberation of Palestine (PFLP) joined with the Japanese Red Army to attack an Israeli airport, and in 1976 with the German Red Army Faction in hijacking an Israeli passenger jet. In recent years there have been several cooperative attacks against U.S. targets in the Middle East, by Islamic terrorists who have joined together to oppose the American presence in Iraq.

SEE ALSO: bombs, types of; criminal terrorism; embassy bombings; funding terrorism; hijackings, aircraft; Popular Front for the Liberation of Palestine

terrorist groups, internal organization of

While every terrorist group is unique, most share a typical structure, with rural groups usually taking a different approach to terrorist activities than urban ones. The primary focus of rural groups is guerrilla warfare, and to this end most adopt a military structure. Therefore rural groups are commonly comprised of small paramilitary units that band together for large operations, much the way an army would function. All members of the group usually know all commanding officers, and most have a general sense of what their upcoming operations and goals will be. In contrast, urban terrorist groups typically reject a conventional military structure in favor of a network of cells, which are units of usually three to five people who operate without much or any knowledge of the group as a whole. In fact, in most cases only one member of each cell has contact with superiors in the organization, who might be grouped in similar units and have limited knowledge of their superiors' activities and identities as well. This ensures that if one member of the organization is captured, that person will not be able to provide the enemy with any significant information about the group, its leaders, its plans, or the location of the group's bases. In some groups, even those with several layers of superiors, cells are encouraged to act independently and on their own initiative, while in others the leadership directs some, most, or all of the group's operations. But again, the key aspect of each urban terrorist group is compartmentalization, in order to minimize the risk of being destroyed by an informant. Because this approach has been highly successful, rural terrorist groups have begun adopting the same organizational structure, particularly in the Middle East.

SEE ALSO: cells, terrorist; guerrilla warfare

terrorist literature

Throughout history, terrorists have written about their beliefs and tactics, often in an attempt to justify their actions and to educate their followers. Among the most common such writings are manifestos and manuals. One of the foremost examples is *Minimanual of the Urban Guerrilla* by Brazilian revolutionary Carlos Marighella, the leader of the Brazilian terrorist group Acao Libertadora Nacional (Action for National Liberation, or ALN). Published in 1969, this guide to guerrilla warfare in cities has been translated into many languages and used by terrorists in many parts of the world. Another prominent example of a terrorist manual is "Military Studies in Jihad Against the Tyrants," which was discovered by British authorities in May 2000. This nearly two-hundred-page document, written in Arabic, is a terrorist manual for al Qaeda operations in foreign countries. It encourages kidnapping, assassination, and bombings of various types of sites, advises terrorists to have more than one form of fake identification, touts the use of cells (units within the structure of terrorist organizations) to ensure that one member cannot act as an informant against others, and cautions married terrorists not to talk to their spouses about their activities. A typical example of a manifesto is "The Philosophy of the Bomb," written by Indian revolutionary Bhagwat Charan and distributed illegally in India in 1930. This document is a call for revolution—nonviolent if possible but violent if necessary—in order to force the British colonial government in India to give the country its independence. This and other terrorist writings have been reprinted in one of the best, recent works on terrorism, *Voices of Terror: Manifestos, Writings and Manuals of al Qaeda, Hamas, and Other Terrorists from Around the World and Throughout the Ages*, edited by Walter Laqueur (Reed Press, New York: 2004).

SEE ALSO: al Qaeda; India; Marighella, Carlos

3-X Killer, the

Some terrorism experts have called the 3-X Killer a terrorist, though others have said he was nothing more than a common murderer; the difference between these two positions depends upon whether or not the expert thinks that the killer was motivated by a political agenda. The 3-X Killer first gained recognition because of a murder in New York City on June 11, 1930, when a grocery-store clerk named Joseph Moyzynsky was shot while sitting in his car with his girlfriend. This woman, Catherine May, later identified the shooter as well-known New York gangster Albert Lombardo, but he had an alibi, provided by many reliable witnesses, for the time of the murder. Six days later, a nearly identical murder took place when mechanic Noel Sowley was shot in his car while his girlfriend, Elizabeth Ring, looked on. This time, the killer—using the name 3-X—left a note at the crime scene, stating that he had committed this and the previous murder in an attempt to retrieve stolen documents. He also said that he was working for a secret international organization, and that the murders would continue until he found the documents. When this news reached the public, New Yorkers panicked, and the police launched a massive manhunt based on Ring's description of the shooter. Meanwhile the 3-X Killer continued to send notes to newspapers and to

people he believed might have the documents or might be preventing him from getting them. For example, he wrote to Moyzynsky's brother John, demanding that he produce the documents, and he wrote to the secretary of a local politician, demanding that the police manhunt be called off. Eventually the notes stopped appearing, and no other murders took place; the identity of the 3-X Killer was never determined.

SEE ALSO: terrorism, definitions of

Tōjō, Hideki
(1884–1948)

Prime minister of Japan and in control of the ministry of war during much of World War II (1941–1944), Tōjō Hideki was held responsible for many of the wartime cruelties of Japanese soldiers and for the treatment of Japan's prisoners of war. In April 1946 he was tried as a war criminal at the International Military Tribunal for the Far East. He was subsequently found guilty and hanged.

SEE ALSO: war-crimes trials

Ton Ton Macoutes, the

The Ton Ton Macoutes was a ten-thousand member special police force established by the brutal dictator of Haiti, Fransçois "Papa Doc" Duvalier, in the late 1950s or early 1960s. For over thirty years, the force used terrorism to keep the Haitian people in line and Duvalier in power. Carrying guns, machetes, and bolos, they accosted foreigners, robbed and raped innocent civilians, and murdered anyone who displeased them or threatened their regime. They also engaged in voodoo rituals, and the Haitian people consequently believed that anyone who crossed a member of the Ton Ton Macoutes risked becoming a zombie or suffering some other voodoo curse.

Duvalier supported the notion that his men could perform voodoo magic; for example, he ordered that all dogs in Haiti be executed after a Ton Ton Macoutes supposedly turned himself into a dog in order to escape punishment for disloyalty to the group. The Ton Ton Macoutes remained a fearsome force in Haiti until the end of Duvalier's reign.

Triads, the

A criminal terrorist group, the Triad Society, more commonly known as the Triads, originated in China in the late seventeenth century, when several Chinese bands joined together to rebel against corrupt rulers. In 1911, a Triad leader, Sun Yat-sen, came to power in China, and afterward the society's influence spread through Southeast Asia. In Malaya, Singapore, and Hong Kong the Triads established itself in the drug trade (especially dealing in opium) and made money on prostitution and gambling as well. Over time, the society became wealthy and gained powerful friends. Consequently when British authorities in Hong Kong tried to stamp out the Triads there in the 1950s, they were unable to gain convictions against the few Triads they were able to arrest. In the 1980s, the Triads' influence spread to Hawaii, then California, where the group trafficked in stolen cars, and then up the West Coast of the United States and into Canada. Today the Triad Society is among the largest criminal terrorist groups in the United States.

SEE ALSO: criminal terrorism; funding terrorism

Trotsky, Leon (Lev Davidovich Bronstein) (1879–1940)

One of the most significant Communist revolutionaries of the early twentieth century, Leon Trotsky was a leader of the October Revolution in Russia in 1917 and subsequently became commissar of foreign affairs and commissar of war in the Soviet Union (1917–24). However, he was sent into exile in 1929 after losing a political power struggle to Joseph Stalin in the aftermath of the death of Soviet leader Vladimir Lenin. While in asylum in Mexico, Trotsky was assassinated by a Spanish Communist, Ramón Mercader, believed to be working for Stalin. Trotsky left behind several writings on terrorism, including articles published in *Przeglad Socyal—demokratyczny* (The Collapse of Terrorism, I) in May 1909 and *Der Kampf* (The Collapse of Terrorism, II) in November 1911.

SEE ALSO: Lenin, Vladimir; Russian Revolution

Tupac Amaru Revolutionary Movement (MRTA)

Formed in Peru in 1983, the Tupac Amaru Revolutionary Movement (Movimiento Revolucionario Tupac Amaru, or MRTA) is a Marxist organization whose goal has been to overthrow the Peruvian government in order to establish a Marxist regime. In addition, the MRTA is dedicated to driving foreigners and their businesses from Peru. (The name "Tupac Amaru" is a reference to an Incan revolutionary who led a Peruvian uprising in the late eighteenth century.) Though the MRTA has few followers (perhaps less than a thousand), the group has been very active since its first attack, which occurred in 1984 when some MRTA members shot at the U.S. embassy in Lima, Peru. In cities the group bombed banks, government buildings, and other facilities associated with the government or foreign institutions, and in rural areas it engaged in guer-

Members of the Tupac Amaru Revolutionary Movement (MRTA), an organization formed in 1983 in Peru whose goal has been to overthrow the Peruvian government and establish a Marxist regime. AP IMAGES

rilla attacks against the Peruvian military. In 1990 the MRTA broke into a prison to free dozens of its members, and in 1996 fourteen MRTA members seized the Japanese embassy during a party, taking over six hundred people, including thirty ambassadors, hostage. After a four-month standoff with the Peruvian military, during which the MRTA released all but seventy-two of the hostages, all of the terrorists were killed, among them one of MRTA's leaders, Nestor Cerpa. Afterward the group became inactive.

SEE ALSO: embassy bombings

Turkey

Turkey is currently experiencing unrest among members of its Kurd population, a minority group that wants its own independent state. Terrorism experts are concerned that if the Kurds who live in Iraq

suddenly break away to create an independent Kurdistan, the Kurds in Turkey might do the same, taking ownership of an important Turkish oil center, Kirkuk. Turkey has long suffered from clashes between various ethnic groups in the country, including not only the Kurds but the Serbs, Armenians, and several others, and it has endured through Islamic terrorism as well. The members of such groups as the Kurdistan Workers Party (PKK) have engaged in bombings, assassinations, and other attacks on government targets, and there have also been bombing attempts against U.S., Russian, and NATO (North Atlantic Treaty Organization) facilities. In the early twentieth century, Turkey aggressively suppressed nationalist struggles by Armenians, and this resulted in an unusually large number of terrorist attacks by both groups and individuals. This was also the case in the late nineteenth and early twentieth centuries, when the Ottoman Turks occupying Macedonia experienced attacks by a revolutionary group called the Internal Macedonian Revolutionary Organization (IMRO). A crackdown against this violence by Turkish authorities resulted in the deaths of thousands of Turkish soldiers and Macedonian villagers.

SEE ALSO: Internal Macedonian Revolutionary Organization; Kurds, the

Turner Diaries, The

A 1978 novel entitled *The Turner Diaries* has had a significant impact on right-wing extremism in the United States. In fact, many terrorism experts believe that it has encouraged a great deal of white-supremacist violence in America, including the bombing of the Alfred P. Murrah Federal Building in Oklahoma City, Oklahoma, in 1995. Written by neo-Nazi William L. Pierce, a former physics professor at Oregon State University who died in July 2002, under the pseudonym Andrew Macdonald, the book is the fictional diary of a character named Earl Turner, describing a future time (beginning in 1991) after American society had been taken over by nonwhites, particularly Jews and blacks, because the government had previously confiscated all citizens' weapons. Turner joins a group called the Organization and becomes a member of its most elite faction, the Order, to fight a revolution by whites to regain control of the country by using terrorism. As part of this revolution, Turner explains, it was necessary for innocent civilians to die for the greater good, and much of the violence in the novel is indiscriminate. For example, when a federal building is bombed, many innocent people die. The novel also portrays blacks as violent cannibals, lauds the Organiza-

tion for hanging blacks, Jews, other minorities and those whites who support those minorities, and expresses great vitriol for whites who have married outside their race. At the end of the novel, Turner is a suicide bomber who destroys the Pentagon with a nuclear weapon.

In the decades since its publication, many white supremacists have cited *The Turner Diaries* as a cautionary tale of why the government should never be allowed to take guns of any kind away from ordinary citizens. Indeed, Timothy McVeigh, who blew up the Alfred P. Murrah Federal Building, said that the novel encouraged his antigun-control activism; a copy of *The Turner Diaries* was found with him when he was arrested, and the bomb he used to destroy the federal building was similar to one described in the novel. In addition, several individuals who have committed violent acts, including murder, against minorities later referred to the book or are believed to have been influenced by it, both in the United States and in other countries, One right-wing U.S. group, the Order, formed by fans of the book even attempted to duplicate some of its crimes during the 1980s. However, no acts of violence have been directly connected to the group that Pierce founded, the National Alliance, which is headquartered in West Virginia and continues to promote neo-Nazi, racist views. In addition, *The Turner Diaries* was reprinted in 1996, and has sold over 360,000.

SEE ALSO: McVeigh, Timothy; neo-Nazism; Oklahoma City bombing; Order, the

TWA Flight 840

Of the many airline hijackings conducted by Palestinian terrorists, the taking of Trans World Airlines (TWA) Flight 840 is particularly notable because it involved a

On August 29, 1969, Laila Khaled became the first female terrorist when she took part in the hijacking of TWA Flight 840. © BETTMANN/CORBIS

female terrorist, Leila Ali Khaled, who subsequently became famous for her participation in the hijacking, her first. The event took place on August 29, 1969, when Khaled and another Palestinian terrorist, Salim Issawi, both members of the Popular Front for the Liberation of Palestine (PFLP), brandished grenades and forced their way into the cockpit. At the time, the flight was en route from Rome, Italy, to Tel Aviv, Israel; the terrorists ordered its pilot to fly instead to Damascus, Syria, where the plane landed and its passengers and crew were forced off the plane. Then the terrorists blew up the cockpit, and Khaled and Issawi allowed themselves to be arrested, most likely knowing that Syria would not keep them in custody for very long. Indeed they were released five weeks later, whereupon Khaled—whose photograph had been in many newspapers im-

mediately after her arrest—began undergoing a series of surgeries to alter her appearance. The following year, she hijacked another plane, an El Al flight, using the same method; she and a partner, Patrick Arguello, used grenades to storm the cockpit. This time, however, there were armed guards on board; they killed Arguello and captured Khaled. Still, she was only jailed for twenty-eight days, in London, England, before members of the PFLP negotiated her release in exchange for the release of some hostages they had recently taken. After this, Khaled was not involved in any high-profile actions, but in 1973 she published a book, *My People Shall Live: The Autobiography of a Revolutionary* (edited by George Hajjar), about her exploits.

SEE ALSO: hijackings, aircraft; Popular Front for the Liberation of Palestine

tyrannicide

Tyrannicide is the murder of a tyrant, a cruel and oppressive ruler. Many of these who have committed this type of assassination have done so under the stated intent of freeing the masses from oppression. However, this was often just an excuse to seize power and usually resulted in a new ruler as oppressive as the former. The issue of whether tyrannicide is ever justified was discussed in many works of ancient and medieval literature. For example, in *Poycraticus*, John of Salisbury (ca. 1120–1180) argues that it is commendable for someone to slay a tyrant providing the killer commits the deed honorably, particularly when the tyrant has offended God. This thinking is often used by modern-day religious terrorists.

SEE ALSO: religious terrorism; terrorist literature

Ulster Defense Association (UDA)

Founded in 1971 in Northern Ireland, the Ulster Defense Association (UDA) is a paramilitary organization of Protestants dedicated to fighting for the independence of Ulster, a historical region of Northern Ireland now under the control of Great Britain and sought by the Republic of Ireland. Much of the group's violence, particularly during the 1970s and '80s, has been directed at Catholics, and in the 1990s it started targeting members of the Irish Republican Army (IRA) and the Provisional IRA as well. By the late 1980s, UDA death squads had killed approximately 450 people, but today the group is largely inactive.

SEE ALSO: Irish Republican Army

Unabomber, the (1942)

"The Unabomber" is the nickname of Theodore "Ted" Kaczynski, a former mathematics professors who killed several people from 1978 to 1995 via letter bombs and other explosives. Experts in terrorism disagree over whether he can be called a terrorist; many insist that he is nothing more than a common murderer, while others say that because he had a political agenda he should indeed be classified as a

Ted Kaczynski, known as the Unabomber, committed several murders from 1978–1995 using letter bombs and other explosives. JOHN YOUNGBEAR. © AP IMAGES

terrorist. The Unabomber's aim, as he later stated, was to use violence to trigger an antitechnology movement in the United States. To this end, he wrote a more than thirty-five-thousand-word political manifesto, "Industrial Society and Its Future," railing against modern technology, and in June 1995 sent it anonymously to the *Washington Post*, the *New York Times*, and *Penthouse* magazine, taking credit for the bombings and demanding that his words be published. The *Washington Post* complied with this demand on September 19, 1995 (splitting the cost of publication with the *Times*), and *Penthouse* in its October 1995 issue. When Ted's brother David read the manifesto, he realized who had written it and contacted federal authorities through a friend who worked as a detective. Ted was then arrested at his home in thick Montana woods, a ten-by-twelve foot (3m-by-3.6m), one-room plywood shack with no plumbing or electricity that was in keeping with his antitechnology beliefs. While Kaczynski was awaiting trial, the government determined that he had killed or injured at least fifteen people, most upon opening letter bombs. Among those killed were the owner of a computer rental store and the head of a forestry association; among those injured were an airline president, a computer scientist, and a geneticist. In 1996, Kaczynski pleaded guilty to the Unabomber attacks and received four life sentences with no parole. He tried unsuccessfully to kill himself two years later.

SEE ALSO: bombs, types of; terrorism, definitions of; terrorist literature

United Nations (UN)

An international organization established in New York City in 1945, the United Nations (UN) is charged with attempting to maintain peace between member nations and encouraging cooperative solutions between disputing countries. To this end, the UN regularly assembles its members to vote on how to handle various issues and crises; member nations can send up to five representatives to the General Assembly, though each nation is allowed only one vote. Decisions are made by either a simple majority vote or a two-thirds majority vote. Matters coming before the General Assembly are usually first discussed in various committees, which include the Security Council and the Economic and Social Council. The UN also has an International Court of Justice, and it assembles international peacekeeping forces to maintain order in areas plagued by violence.

Terrorist violence first became an issue at the UN in 1972, when the General Assembly discussed a recent Palestinian terrorist attack on Israeli athletes at the Olympic Games in Munich, Germany. At that time, the assembly felt a universal definition of terrorism was needed, and to this end they tried to develop one that all nations could agree upon. However, after ten years they were unable to come up with a definition that satisfied all members, because nations disagreed on how to determine whether a particular act of violence was a terrorist act or a legitimate act intended to fight oppression or injustice. Still, the UN has since condemned certain specific acts of violence as being terroristic in nature, thereby taking a case-by-case approach to recognizing terrorism. Moreover, in 1994 the General Assembly officially acknowledged that terrorist acts could threaten international peace and security and called upon all countries to fight terrorism, both alone and in cooperation with international counterterrorism efforts. Also in the 1990s the UN Security Council advised member nations to end the practice of harboring terrorists. In recent years the UN has spoken against funding terrorism and in favor of various nations' efforts to combat terrorism.

SEE ALSO: terrorism, definitions of

United Self-Defense Forces of Colombia (Autodefensas Unidas de Colombia, or AUC)

Established in 1997, the United Self-Defense Forces of Colombia (Autodefensas Unidas de Colombia, or AUC) is an umbrella organization comprised of several right-wing paramilitary groups dedicated to combating guerrilla militias in Colombia. Its members' training has been backed by businessmen and ranchers tired of being the victims of guerrilla attacks. However, the AUC also engages in drug trafficking and other forms of criminal terrorism, as well as attacks on rivals and innocent civilians. By some estimates, AUC members were behind over thirteen hundred deaths in the year 2000 alone, in addition to more than two hundred kidnappings for ransom. In 2001, the AUC killed over one thousand innocent civilians, sometimes after torturing them, as part of its efforts to destroy support for guerrillas. As a result, in 2001 the U.S. government declared the AUC to be a terrorist organization and urged the Colombian government to eradicate it. Nonetheless, today the AUC remains extremely powerful and well funded.

SEE ALSO: Colombia, terrorism in

United States, terrorism in the

Terrorist attacks on U.S. targets abroad are typically committed by religious terrorists and nationalists angered over the Ameri-

can presence in their lands. This was also the motivation for the terrorist attacks of September 11, 2001, when Islamic extremists flew airplanes into the World Trade Center in New York City and the Pentagon in Washington, D.C. These terrorists were members of al Qaeda, whose leader, Osama bin Laden, was violently opposed to the establishment of U.S. military bases in Saudi Arabia because he considered these bases to be on holy Muslim lands. A previous attack on the World Trade Center in 1993 was also committed by Middle Eastern terrorists opposed to U.S. actions abroad.

Most terrorist attacks in the United States, however, are committed not by foreigners but by American right-wing extremists, usually with racist or antigovernment beliefs. These include members of the Christian Identity movement and neo-Nazi and white-supremacist groups like the Ku Klux Klan and Aryan Nations. Homegrown terrorists were responsible for such attacks as the bombing of the Alfred P. Murrah Federal Building in Oklahoma City, Oklahoma, in 1995, a bombing at the 1996 Olympic Games in Atlanta, Georgia, and various bombings and killings at abortion clinics throughout the United States, some of which have been encouraged by such antiabortion extremist groups as the Army of God. Nonetheless in recent years most of the American public's attention has been on the threat of another attack by Islamic extremists, and the federal government has devoted many resources to addressing this issue, enacting new laws and security measures designed to protect airports, ports, and borders from foreigners seeking to enter the country to commit violent acts. It was with such terrorists in mind that the U.S. government created the Patriot Act,

The Pentagon, before Islamic terrorists flew an airplane into the building as part of the September 11, 2001, terrorist attacks. © UPI/CORBIS-Bettmann

which makes it easier to spy on and arrest suspected foreign as well as homegrown terrorists.

See Also: antiabortion terrorism; Army of God; Aryan Nations; Christian Identity movement; Ku Klux Klan; Oklahoma City bombing; Olympic Games as terrorist targets; Patriot Act, the U.S.

urban terrorism

Urban terrorism is terrorism that takes place in cities as opposed to the countryside. Because cities are more densely populated than rural villages, it is extremely difficult to destroy urban terrorists without harming noncombatants—a fact that gives terrorists an advantage against forces that do not want to hurt innocent people, whether because of morals or because of negative public opinion. Urban terrorists, however, typically do not care whether innocent people are hurt; indeed, in the early stages of an urban terrorism campaign, terrorists themselves often attack civilians in order to intimidate them into supporting the campaign or making them afraid to betray the plans or location of terrorists. Civilians are also killed in indiscriminate bombings intended to create chaos and destroy urban infrastructures so that the government cannot function.

See Also: insurgencies

victims of terrorism, types of

The aims of most terrorist campaigns are to disrupt society, instill fear in the public, and make it difficult or impossible for businesses and government agencies to function. Consequently many terrorist attacks are against public and corporate buildings, marketplaces, rail lines, and the like, but in strikes against such places, innocent people often get hurt. In these attacks, victims are said to have been felled by random violence, which is the most common type of terrorist violence. They also kill by selective violence, however, targeting specific businessmen, government or military officials, and others for assassination, kidnapping, or other types of assault. Both kinds of attacks—random and selective—might be intentionally performed in ways to attract maximum media attention, with victims chosen for their value to the press. This is the case, for example, with the murder of embassy ambassadors or famous public figures. Some victims are chosen for the message they send to the terrorists' enemies. For example, when terrorists assassinate a well-guarded person, they are sending the message that no one is safe from attack. Other times, victims are chosen for their financial or political value in regard to hostage negotiations. For example, many airline hijackings have been orchestrated with the intent of trading the hostages for terrorists imprisoned in the country associated with the airline, and during the 1970s and '80s many businessmen in Latin America were kidnapped and held for ransom in order to fund terrorist operations. (In one such kidnapping in Argentina, committed by a group called the Montoneros, two businessmen were ransomed for more than $50 million.) Another type of victim is the rival terrorist, particularly where criminal terrorism is involved. One drug lord might kill another, for example, to protect his illegal operation. Similarly, terrorists might choose victims because they are from an enemy country or tribe. For example, Palestinian terrorists at the 1972 Olympic Games in Munich, Germany, attacked a group of athletes because they were from Israel, and in the African country of Rwanda, members of the Hutu and the Tutsi tribes have been committing terrorist attacks against one another for more than a decade in an attempt to exterminate each other. Similar attacks have been committed out of anti-Semitism and other forms of racism, as with terrorism committed by the Nazis during World War II and by the Ku Klux Klan in mid-twentieth-century America, or out of religious prejudice, as with the ongoing violence between Arabs and Jews in the Middle East.

SEE ALSO: Africa, terrorism in postcolonial; anti-Semitism; criminal terrorism; embassy bombings; hijackings, aircraft; hostages; Ku Klux Klan; Montoneros; Munich Olympics crisis

Vietcong, the

The name "Vietcong" was coined by the United States during the Vietnam War to

Ho Chi Minh founded the Vietminh in 1941, a group who fought for an independent Vietnam and used suicide bombers to assassinate enemies. AP IMAGES

refer to Communist insurgents in South Vietnam. Part of a Communist guerrilla movement in the region, these insurgents fought with the North Vietnamese army against U.S. and South Vietnamese forces and engaged in terrorism against their enemies, assassinating and kidnapping thousands of people. Consequently the Vietcong were targeted by a joint U.S.-South Vietnam campaign that sought to kill or imprison as many Vietcong as possible. As a result, over twenty thousand Vietcong were killed during the war and more than twenty thousand were imprisoned. However, in the process many innocent people were killed as well, largely because many of the South Vietnamese officials involved in the campaign were corrupt. They accepted bribes to release guilty prisoners or arrest innocents and treated prisoners so

badly that many died in prison. Some of the officials also engaged in terrorist attacks on the guerrillas and their sympathizers, displaying the same level of violence as those they sought to destroy.

SEE ALSO: wartime terrorism

Vietminh, the

Founded by Communist nationalist Ho Chi Minh in 1941, the Vietminh (Vietnam Doc-Lap Dong-Minh), or League for the Independence of Vietnam, fought for an independent Vietnam during the 1940s and routinely used suicide bombers to assassinate its enemies. It engaged in other forms of terrorism as well, against both the Japanese who occupied parts of the country during World War II and the French who had established a colonial government in Vietnam in the 1880s. Aided by a peasant militia, the group attacked French forces until 1953, when France decided to pull out of the region.

SEE ALSO: bombers, suicide

vigilante terrorism

There are two types of vigilante terrorism: vigilante state terrorism and vigilante communal terrorism. The latter occurs when ordinary members of a community publicly torture or kill someone. In some cases, vigilantes act out of a belief that they must take justice into their own hands—that is, that the victim deserves punishment for some crime but might not get it because of a flawed justice system. In other cases, vigilante community terrorism arises from racist beliefs, as occurs when all-white lynch mobs hang African Americans simply because these victims are black. Vigilante state terrorism is state terrorism whereby government personnel or security forces attack individuals or groups without official authorization or sanction, typically out of a desire to protect the political status quo. Victims of vigilante state terrorism might be people whom the state considers dangerous or they might be members of a group, race, or religion that the state considers to be "undesirable." But again, those engaging in vigilante state terrorism, such as members of death squads, are acting without state sanction.

SEE ALSO: death camps; lynching

Waco incident

"The Waco incident" refers to an event that many right-wing extremists in the United States believe justifies their anti-government stance, which is based largely on the notion that the U.S. government abuses its power. On February 28, 1993, seventy-six federal agents from the U.S. Bureau of Alcohol, Tobacco, and Firearms (ATF) approached the seventy-acre compound of a religious group called the Branch Davidians near Waco, Texas, with a warrant authorizing them to search for illegal weapons. (They had heard that the group's leader, David Koresh, had been stockpiling weapons and training his followers in military tactics in preparation for an apocalypse he believed would soon occur.) As they tried to enter the compound, which was known as Mount Carmel, Branch Davidians shot at them, and in the resulting gunfight four ATF agents

The devastating fire that took place in Waco, Texas, in 1993 was the result of a standoff between the FBI and religious group, the Branch Davidians, at their compound. RON HEFLIN. © AP IMAGES

and at least six Branch Davidians were killed. The ATF agents then surrounded the compound and began a fifty-one-day siege that was soon conducted by the Federal Bureau of Investigation (FBI). FBI negotiators worked to secure the release of sixteen adults and twenty-one children, one of whom carried a note saying that those who remained in the compound were willing to die. Nonetheless the FBI agents continued to try to force them to come out, using a variety of tactics that included shutting off their electricity and water, shining bright lights at the compound all through the night, and blaring loud music at it twenty-four hours a day. Finally the FBI decided to flush the Branch Davidians out with tear gas, and to this end they brought in army tanks to ram the walls and fire the tear gas canisters inside. During this assault, however, a fire broke out, which the government later said was set by the Davidians but right-wing extremists insisted was started by the FBI attack. In either case, stored ammunition in the compound soon began exploding, and the fire became a conflagration. Seventy-five people died in the blaze, leaving only nine survivors, and afterward a public outcry against these deaths led to changes in FBI policies regarding standoffs. This was not enough, though, to satisfy right-wing extremists, many of whom used Waco as a rallying cry for terrorist attacks against the federal government. Because of this cry for vengeance, federal authorities are particularly vigilant every April 19, the date of the final assault on the compound, fearing that a major terrorist attack will take place on that anniversary.

SEE ALSO: Branch Davidians; terrorist anniversaries

Waffen SS, the

As the elite fighting unit of the Schutzstaffel (SS) of Nazi Germany, the Waffen SS accompanied the German army as it marched across Europe in 1939–1941, and it was responsible for many of the atrocities committed then and later during World War II. The first such atrocity to be documented was the execution of fifty innocent Jews during the Polish military campaign of 1939. The Waffen SS then worked with the guards of a concentration camp, the Totenkopf (Death's Head), to round up Polish Jews, Gypsies, and others that the German regime considered "undesirable" elements of society. When the Jews in Warsaw, Poland, tried to resist being transported to concentration camps, the Waffen SS quelled their revolt, killing approximately twenty thousand Jews. The Waffen SS went on to commit many other atrocities, including the slaughter of eighty-five British prisoners in a French barn in 1940, and participated in a Russian operation in 1941 that resulted in the death of over a half million innocent Russians. By this time the Waffen SS routinely shot prisoners and hostages to save themselves the trouble of guarding and transporting them, and it massacred Jews by the hundreds. (Because most Waffen SS members were volunteers who were extremely passionate about the Nazi cause, they typically felt no remorse about slaughtering Jews and obeyed their leader, Adolf Hitler, without question.) After the Allies invaded Nazi-occupied France in 1944, the Waffen SS engaged in terrorist attacks against Allied forces, and in 1944 it slaughtered eighty-three American prisoners in Belgium. In 1945, the Waffen SS killed thousands of German soldiers for refusing to fight or trying to flee battlegrounds. As a result of all of these atrocities, after the war the International Military Tribunal at Nuremberg, Germany, in 1946 found hundreds of Waffen SS members guilty of war crimes and sentenced them to various prison terms.

SEE ALSO: Hitler, Adolf; Schutzstaffel (SS), the; war-crimes trials

Wailing Wall incident, the

In 1929, violence broke out at the Wailing Wall, a wall in Jerusalem sacred to both Jews and Muslims. In August of that year, a Jewish boy accidentally kicked a ball onto the property of an Arab. A fight broke out between the two, during which the boy died of a stab wound. In protest, a group of Jews held a demonstration at the Wailing Wall. This angered Arabs, who attacked and killed several demonstrators. Similar attacks continued for days, not only in Jerusalem but elsewhere in Palestine, and by the time British authorities there could quell the violence, over 130 Jews had been killed and over 300 seriously hurt.

SEE ALSO: Palestine

war-crimes trials

War crimes are attacks on people who are not actively involved in a war's hostilities, whether because they are innocent civilians or because they have been taken captive as prisoners of war. Consequently when a combatant harms a noncombatant, the attacker can be put on trial once the war is over. For example, after World War II, a series of trials against war criminals took place in Nuremberg, Germany. Beginning in 1945, these trials resulted in the prosecution of several hundred Nazis, many formerly of the Waffen SS (a paramilitary force of the Nazi Party), for slaughtering innocent civilians and prisoners of war and sending Jews and others to death camps. Some of those convicted were sentenced to prison, others executed; twenty-two of the defendants were military or political leaders, and of these, twelve were hanged, seven imprisoned, and three acquitted. Another trial held in Tokyo, Japan, from June 1946 to November 1948, addressed war crimes by the Japanese. Twenty-five people were convicted at the Tokyo Tribunal, with eighteen being sentenced to prison and seven to death by hanging. Both the Nuremberg and the Tokyo war-crimes trials were overseen by the United Nations (UN) International War Crimes Tribunal.

SEE ALSO: United Nations; Waffen SS, the; wartime terrorism

War on Terror

"The War on Terror" is the phrase coined by U.S. president George W. Bush and his administration to refer to the U.S. response to the September 11, 2001, terrorist attacks on American soil. This response included the enactment of the Patriot Act and other changes in U.S. laws and policies related to antiterrorism and counterterrorism measures and the way that local, state, and federal agencies work together to combat terrorism. It also includes activities abroad that are intended to fight terrorism, such as the attacks on Afghanistan and Iraq in the aftermath of September 11. The War on Terror is ongoing, which means that any country that supports terrorism in the future risks attack, at least while Bush is president. However, when Bush's political party (the Republicans) lost control of the U.S. Congress in November 2006, the media began to speculate on whether some aspects of Bush's War on Terror, including infringements on citizens' rights in the name of searching for and spying on terrorists, would remain in place.

See Also: antiterrorism; Bush, U.S. president George W.; counterterrorism; Patriot Act, the U.S.; September 11 attacks on America

wartime terrorism

Terrorism against civilians during wartime has been common throughout history, particularly during civil wars, but in modern times this violence has been on a larger scale, with deliberate terror campaigns involving mass bombings, shootings, and executions designed to eliminate entire ethnic, religious, or ideological groups. Such was the case, for example, with genocidal attacks between the Hutus and Tutsis in Rwanda and with ethnic cleansing in Bosnia and other parts of the former Yugoslavia, both during civil wars in the 1990s, and with the Nazis' attempts to exterminate the Jews during World War II. Also in World War II, a Nazi fighting unit called the Waffen SS committed a number of wartime atrocities against innocent people, slaughtering not only Jews but prisoners of war (POWs) in great number. Attacks on POWs have occurred in many wars, despite the fact that captors who mistreat POWs are subject to being tried postwar for their actions. But wartime terrorism is not committed just against people perceived as enemies or undesirables. It is also employed to dissuade civilians from siding with the enemy or otherwise interfering with the war effort or to confine civilians to certain regions. As an example of the latter, during the Vietnam War the United States created "free fire zones" where anyone who ventured into these regions was considered a fair target and subject to immediate death. Sometimes, however, wartime terrorism stems not from calculated attempts to slaughter or influence civilians but from unintentional violence arising from the heat of passion or fear. For example, heightened emotions probably led to the Vietnam War massacre of South Vietnamese villagers by U.S. soldiers at My Lai in 1968.

See Also: Africa, terrorism in postcolonial; anti-Semitism; Bosnian genocide; ethnic cleansing; genocide; Holocaust, the; Waffen SS, the; war-crimes trials

weapons of mass destruction (WMD)

Weapons of mass destruction, or WMD, are weapons with the ability to kill extremely large numbers of people at one time. Specifically, these weapons are nuclear, chemical, or biological in nature. Nuclear weapons are the most desired by terrorists and the most feared by world leaders, because such weapons can devastate entire cities and leave them uninhabitable for years. However, nuclear weapons are dangerous to transport, expensive to obtain, and both expensive and dangerous to manufacture, which is why no terrorist has yet employed them. A more feasible alternative to a nuclear bomb is the dirty bomb, which combines small amounts of radioactive materials with conventional explosives; such bombs contaminate cities enough to make evacuation necessary in order to keep citizens from getting sick, but they do not necessarily kill in large numbers. Chemical weapons also tend to kill in small rather than large numbers, because they are difficult to distribute among the populace. For example, when the Japanese terrorist group Aum Shinrikyō tried to inflict mass casualties by releasing a nerve gas, sarin, in the Tokyo, Japan, subway system, only twelve people died, though thousands fell ill, because the chemical did not disperse as widely as the group anticipated. However, terrorists with money and military expertise at their disposal—which provides them with vehicles, airplanes, or other delivery systems specially designed to carry chemical agents—have had more success with using chemical agents as WMD; for example, in the late 1980s the dictator of Iraq, Saddam Hussein, bombed Kurdish villages with deadly toxic gasses that killed thousands. The inability to affect widespread areas and therefore large numbers of people is a disadvantage of biological weapons as well. Terrorism experts fear that this problem may cause terrorists to try other means of delivery in the near future, such as contaminating food sources. Consequently governments have been stockpiling vaccines and medicines that will combat biological agents such as anthrax, smallpox, and food-borne illnesses should the need arise.

SEE ALSO: Aum Shinrikyō bioterrorism; chemical weapons; Hussein, Saddam; Kurds, the; nuclear weapons; sarin gas

weapons, types of terrorist

Terrorists use a variety of weapons. The most common are firearms, which include guns, rifles, submachine guns, assault rifles, and rocket-propelled grenades. They also use surface-to-air missiles, a shoulder-fired weapon with a targeting system that enables it to hit low-flying aircraft, and rocket launchers. Explosives are another mainstay of terrorism; they include plastic explosives, fuel oil, and fertilizer. Bomb types include gasoline bombs, pipe bombs, and car and truck bombs. To a much lesser extent, terrorists have used chemical and biological weapons, but most have not been successful in causing a large loss of life with these, even though such chemical

and biological agents are considered weapons of mass destruction (WMD). Terrorists have also been unable to acquire nuclear bombs, though terrorism experts fear that they will someday succeed in doing so.

SEE ALSO: bombs, types of; chemical weapons; missiles, rockets, and mortars; nuclear weapons; weapons of mass destruction

Weatherman

An American left-wing revolutionary group, Weatherman arose out of the antiwar movement of the 1960s as a faction of the Third World Marxists, which in turn was a faction of the Students for a Democratic Society (SDS). With approximately four hundred members dedicated to destroying the U.S. government—which they believed was both oppressive and racist—Weatherman began its activism in 1969 in the northeastern United States, where it attacked high-school, college, and university teachers in their classrooms before delivering antigovernment speeches to shocked students. The group then engaged in violent public protests and anti-war demonstrations during which members attacked police. In March 1970, after three of its founders—Ted Gold, Terry Robbins, and Diana Oughton—were accidentally killed in New York City while making bombs, the federal government realized that the group was planning a series of bombing attacks and put out arrest warrants for several Weatherman members. Nonetheless a string of Weatherman bombings took place that year; the targets included a California army base, a New York courthouse, and a Boston, Massachusetts, bank. In 1971 the group bombed the Capitol building in Washington, D.C., but did little damage there, and in 1972 it bombed the Pentagon with similar effect. Occasional bombings continued for a few more years, but in the late 1970s Weatherman began to fracture, with many members going their separate ways. Some surrendered to authorities, others were arrested, and today the group is inactive and probably dissolved.

SEE ALSO: bombs, types of; left-wing terrorism, U.S.

West Bank and Gaza Strip, the

The West Bank is an area west of the Jordan River that includes Hebron, Bethlehem, and Jericho, while the Gaza Strip is a strip of land along the southeastern Mediterranean Sea. Both areas have been the site of a great many terrorist attacks, as Jews and Arabs struggle for control. The Gaza Strip was under British mandate from 1917 to 1948, controlled by Egypt from 1948 to 1967 (though Israel occupied it from November 1956 to March 1957), and by Israel beginning in 1967. In 1987 and 1988 there were Arab uprisings in the strip, and afterward the violence and unrest continued. In May 1994, an accord between the Palestine Liberation Organization (PLO) and Israel gave self-rule to the Gaza Strip and Jericho, and this was followed by a withdrawal of Israeli troops from these two places. Meanwhile the West Bank was to become permanently Palestinian under a 1947 agreement that also created the state of Israel; however, after Arabs objecting to the formation of Israel attacked the Israelis, Israel responded by occupying a substantial part of the West Bank. A new peace agreement led to the annexation of the West Bank by Jordan in 1950, but Israel again occupied part of it in 1967, and in the 1970s and '80s established numerous Jewish settlements there, further angering Arabs. In 1987, the Arab uprisings in the Gaza Strip spread to the West Bank, and in 1988 Jordan abandoned all claims on it. In 1991, amid ongoing Arab attacks on Jews in the West Bank, peace negotiations began in earnest, and finally Israel agreed to return large parts of the West Bank to Palestine, with the idea that Palestine would be allowed to rule itself. Nonetheless, Israelis and Palestinians continue to attack one another in the region, and it is unclear whether all aspects of the peace agreement will hold, particularly since a recent Palestinian election gave a great deal of power to members of an anti-Israeli terrorist group, Hamas. In the election, Hamas received seventy-six seats in Parliament and its rival, al Fatah, received forty-three. Despite years of fighting between the two factions and in an attempt to work together and share power of the provisional government, both sides agreed to a cease-fire in February 2007. Just days later, however, fighting broke out again in the West Bank and Gaza Strip between the two factions. Dozens of people were killed and property was destroyed.

SEE ALSO: Hamas; Israel; Palestine

white supremacists

White supremacists are right-wing extremists who believe that people of the white, or as they sometimes call it the Aryan, race are superior to all others. In the United States, many white supremacists further believe that there will one day be a war between the races, perhaps triggered by white supremacists, and that they must arm and train themselves so that whites will be victorious in this battle. The first American white supremacists were slave owners and slave traders who considered blacks to be less than human. After the Civil War freed the slaves, this attitude per-

A group of white supremacists rally during a parade to spread their radical extremist ideas that white people are the superior race. ELAINE THOMPSON. © AP IMAGES

sisted in the South, where several white-supremacist groups, most notably the Ku Klux Klan, sprung up to prevent blacks from exercising their new rights. For example, some white supremacists in the post–Civil War era known as Reconstruction used threats of violence to keep black voters from the polls on election day. After World War II, many American white-supremacist groups idolized Adolf Hitler, who as dictator of Germany just before and during the war had sought to exterminate non-Aryans so that a white "master race" would reign supreme. Because of Hitler, neo-Nazi groups, many of whose members are known as skinheads, are also white-supremacist groups. Other white supremacists are right-wing extremist Chris-

tian groups whose members believe that God intended whites to rule the earth. These include groups allied with the Christian Identity movement, such as Aryan Nations (which is also allied with neo-Nazism and the Ku Klux Klan) and the White Patriot Party (WPP), a paramilitary group whose members attacked blacks in Florida in the 1980s and which plotted unsuccessfully in the 1990s to create a white, Christian stronghold in North Carolina. White supremacists have been involved in several terrorist attacks in the United States in recent decades, most notably the bombing of the Alfred P. Murrah Federal Building in Oklahoma City, Oklahoma, in 1995. The bomber in this case, Timothy McVeigh, was influenced by a 1978 novel, *The Turner*

Diaries, that was written by a white supremacist and neo-Nazi named William L. Pierce under the pseudonym Andrew Macdonald. Its story concerns a future time when American society has been taken over by nonwhites, particularly Jews and blacks, and Aryan revolutionaries employ terrorism to return control to whites. The novel advocates indiscriminate violence, saying that it is often necessary for innocent civilians to die for the greater good; portrays blacks as violent cannibals; lauds whites for hanging blacks, Jews, and other minorities and their supporters; and expresses great vitriol for whites who have married outside their race.

SEE ALSO: Aryan Nations; Christian Identity movement; Ku Klux Klan; McVeigh, Timothy; neo-Nazis; Oklahoma City bombing; racism; skinheads; *Turner Diaries, The*

Wilmington massacre

The Wilmington massacre of 1898 is an example of the violence against African Americans that occurred in the South in the aftermath of the Civil War. After the war, white supremacists in the Southern states engaged in widespread terrorism against blacks, lynching and assassinating African Americans in an attempt to keep them from exercising their new rights. (Between 1893 and 1915, at least seventeen hundred African Americans were lynched.) Black voters were especially targeted, as whites sought to scare them away from polling places. At the same time, in North Carolina white politicians enacted laws that made it extremely difficult for blacks to register to vote; for example, blacks had to pass a literacy test in order to register, even though at the time few blacks could read. Nonetheless in the city of Wilmington, North Carolina, blacks were able to make substantial gains. By 1898, many owned businesses, and the city boasted the only daily African American newspaper in the country (the *Daily Record*). Angered by such prosperity, white politicians throughout the state gave speeches calling for the elimination of all blacks from American society, and their words began to inspire antiblack riots in various cities. In Wilmington just prior to the November 1898 elections, the then racist Democratic Party held rallies encouraging whites to keep blacks away from the polls by any means necessary, and when blacks tried to arm themselves for protection, white merchants refused to sell them guns. Consequently few blacks voted, and the Democrats won control of the Wilmington government. However, they were unwilling to wait to take office, and right after the election they seized power. Among their first acts was an order that the *Daily Record* be immediately shut down, and an angry mob of whites descended on the newspaper office to set it on fire, then began shooting blacks at random in the streets. No one knows how many African Americans were killed during this massacre, because bodies were dumped in secret, but by some estimates it was as many as several hundred. Historians do know, though, that while similar antiblack riots subsequently took place in Illinois in the cities of Springfield in 1908, East St. Louis in 1917, and Chicago in 1919, the loss of life was nowhere near that of the Wilmington massacre.

SEE ALSO: lynching; racism

Wobblies, the

"The Wobblies" was the nickname given to the Industrial Workers of the World (IWW), a radical labor organization established in Chicago, Illinois, in 1905. Its members were representatives of forty-three groups opposed to the decision of another labor organization—the American Federation of Labor (AFL)—not to allow unskilled workers in certain unions. At first the Wobblies tried to effect change through politics, engaging in protests, boycotts, and other forms of demonstration in order to express its opposition to various companies and organizations and to the capitalist system as a whole. Gradually, however, the group came to embrace violence instead, sabotaging the equipment of companies that would not give more power to its workers. During World War I, the Wobblies also sabotaged copper production in an attempt to prevent this material from being contributed to the war effort, because the group was opposed to U.S. participation in the conflict. In response, the government arrested many members for these activities, convicting some under the Sabotage and Espionage Acts, and by 1925 it had lost most of its members.

SEE ALSO: left-wing terrorism, U.S.

women terrorists

Most terrorists throughout history have been men. In 1969, however, a woman terrorist came to worldwide attention with her participation in the hijacking of TWA Flight 840: twenty-five-year-old Leila Ali Khaled, a Palestinian guerrilla who belonged to a group called the Popular Front for the Liberation of Palestine (PFLP) and was a passionate revolutionary. (She boarded the plane with a copy of a book about Latin American revolutionary Che Guevara, *My Friend Che.*) After her photograph subsequently appeared in newspapers, she underwent plastic surgery to regain her anonymity and continue her terrorist attacks. Khaled became famous because the modern world had never before heard of a "girl terrorist," as the press called her. But soon the public was made aware of other women terrorists as well. The first were, like Khaled, Palestinians who fought against Israel alongside their men. Others were with secular nationalist groups involved in similar conflicts, such as the Tamil Tigers of Sri Lanka who sought to create an independent state for the Tamils, a Hindu people long at odds with the Buddhists in their country. Most of these women, though, did not choose to fight with men, but instead supported terrorism in ways considered in their cultures to be more suitable for a female—that is, they did not engage in armed combat, but did help maintain armed units. Gradually, however, women terrorists began to participate in suicide bombings. In 2002, for example, Palestinian terrorist groups finally began to employ women suicide bombers after long arguments over whether or not women were allowed to die for Islam. (The most persuasive of these arguments noted that the history of Arabs in the Middle East included several notable women warriors, such as an Afghan woman named Malalai who fought against the British in the nineteenth century.) The most extreme Islamic groups were even more reluctant to accept women suicide bombers, but in September 2005 al Qaeda used its first woman, who blew herself up in Iraq near the Syrian border. Terrorist experts believe that al Qaeda set aside its gender bias because foreigners, especially Americans, are less likely to search Arab women out of a fear that this physical violation would anger Muslims, who have strict rules regarding who can touch women and where. Another reason for the acceptance of women terrorists among Islamic extremists might be a shortage of male terrorists. As for the women's motivations, some are passionate about a cause, as Khaled was, but more are motivated by revenge, wanting to destroy those who killed their loved ones. This is the case, for example, with thirty-five-year-old Sajida Mubarak al-Rishawi, who unsuccessfully tried to blow up American soldiers in Jordan, along with herself, because her three brothers and her brother-in-law had been killed by U.S. troops. It is also the case with a type of terrorist in Chechnya that the press has dubbed "the black widows." These women target Russians because Russians killed their husbands or sons; in one suicide bombing alone, in the summer of 2000, a "black widow" killed twenty-seven members of Russian Special Forces, and during four months in 2003, black-widow suicide bombers killed 165 Russians. Terrorism experts believe that in the coming years, more women in the Middle East will turn to terrorism as a form of revenge—and perhaps also as a form of empowerment, as often occurs with women terrorists in Western nations like the United States. There, it is not unusual to find women holding as much power in terrorist groups as men, but typically this occurs in left-wing organizations such as those dedicated to environmentalism. Many right-wing extremists, on the other hand, consider women to be inferior to men, just as many Islamic extremists do, and relegate them to lesser roles in their terrorist groups.

SEE ALSO: Chechen separatists; Guevara, Che; left-wing terrorists, U.S.; Popular Front for the Liberation of Palestine (PFLP); right-wing terrorists, U.S.; bombers, suicide

World Trade Center bombings

Eight years before the World Trade Center was destroyed in the September 11, 2001, terrorist attacks, the complex was bombed by Middle Eastern terrorists who saw the twin towers as symbols of American capitalism. The blast occurred at approximately 12:18 PM on February 26, 1993, on the second level of the parking garage beneath Tower One. The bombing left a crater roughly 150 feet (46m) in diameter and five stories deep and destroyed sewer, water, and electrical lines. Experts later determined that the explosives—approximately sixty-eight hundred tons of material, most of it fertilizer (urea nitrate), and three cylinders of compressed hydrogen gas—had been inside a Ford Econoline van rented from the Ryder rental agency in Jersey City, New Jersey. Fragments of this vehicle provided federal investigators with enough information for them to identify the van as one that had been reported stolen the day before the bombing. The Federal Bureau of Investigation (FBI) arrested the renter, Mohammed Salameh, and soon linked him to Nidel Ayyad, a chemist who had rented an apartment in which bomb-making materials were discovered. Investigators also connected Salameh to a storage facility containing urea nitrate, and where witnesses had reported seeing three tanks of hydrogen gas being delivered. Another link between the crime and Salameh and Ayyad was on the envelope of a letter sent to the New York Times on March 3, 1993, claiming responsibility for the bombing in the name of Allah; the two men's saliva was on the sealed flap, along with that of a third terrorist, Mahmud Abouhalima. Other associates of Salameh and Ayyad were eventually identified as well, including Ramzi Ahmed Yousef, who was believed to have planned the attack and helped make the bomb, and Eyad Ismoil, believed to have driven, parked, and detonated the bomb. Yousef and Ismoil fled the United States after the bombing, but in 1995 Ismoil was arrested in Jordan and in 1997, Yousef in Pakistan. The two were convicted of murder and conspiracy in November 1997, while Salameh, Ayyad, Abuhalima, and another man, Ahmad Ajaj, who had provided the terrorists with bomb-making instructions, were convicted in 1994.

SEE ALSO: bombs, types of; September 11 attacks on America

Yakuza, the

A Japanese criminal-terrorist organization, the Yakuza sprung up after World War II as a brotherhood of criminals that functioned much like the Mafia crime family originating in Sicily. By the 1960s, according to Japanese authorities, there were approximately 70,000 Yakuza members in Japan, and by the 1970s approximately 250,000, making it one of the fastest-growing criminal-terrorist organizations. Its members, many of them bearing tattoos, are organized into hundreds of individual gangs controlled by crime bosses. They engage in drug trafficking, gambling, prostitution, extortion, and other illegal activities, not only in Japan but also in other parts of the Asian Pacific, in Hawaii, and along the West Coast of the United States, where its influence remains strong today.

SEE ALSO: criminal terrorism; Mafia, the

Yugoslavia

During the 1990s, the former Yugoslavia experienced a great deal of violence arising from its transition from a Communist to a democratic nation. At that time, the country had six separate republics (Serbia, Croatia, Bosnia-Herzegovina, Macedonia, Slovenia, and Montenegro) and six distinct ethnic groups (Serbs, Croats, Albanians, Macedonians, Slovenes, and Slav Muslims) with different religious beliefs and practices. During the 1980s, these ethnic groups began attacking one another, and as ethnic tensions escalated, national-

ist sentiments grew as well, until one republic after another demanded independence. By the summer of 1991, the country was involved in a civil war. From 1991 to 1995, hundreds of thousands of people were killed in the conflict, many as part of an ethnic cleansing, or genocide, campaign designed at ridding particular regions of certain ethno-religious groups. The violence was especially bloody in Bosnia-Herzegovina, where Orthodox Christian Serbs, Muslim Bosnians, and Roman Catholic Croats all sought to exterminate one another; in some parts of the republic, Serbs established concentration camps where civilians were raped, tortured, and murdered. Croatians and Muslim Bosnians soon established their own camps as well, where they too committed atrocities against prisoners (though not nearly to the degree of the Serbs). Eventually the situation in the former Yugoslavia became so bad that the international community stepped in to stop the violence. The United Nations (UN) sent a peacekeeping force and humanitarian aid into the region, established economic and political sanctions against Serbia, and created a tribunal to try individuals for committing war crimes. As the violence continued, more and more international troops went to the former Yugoslavia to restore order, and in 1995 these peacekeeping forces engaged in air strikes against Bosnian Serbs in an attempt to destroy their bases and end their terrorism. The Serbs responded with even more violence, kidnapping UN soldiers and massacring Bosnian Muslims by the thousands.

These massacres caused international outrage and threats of massive bombings against Serbian targets; these threats finally convinced the Serbs to agree, in December 1995, to end the conflict in Bosnia-Herzegovina, and the rest of the violence in the region soon de-escalated as well.

SEE ALSO: Bosnian genocide; ethnic cleansing

Zimbabwe African National Liberation Army (ZANLA)

The Zimbabwe African National Liberation Army (ZANLA) arose out of a political struggle in Rhodesia (now Zimbabwe) in 1965. At that time, the country was a British colony controlled locally by its white colonists, even though 95 percent of the population was black African. This situation led to unrest among black Rhodesians, and in response the British government decided to transfer power to them. The white colonists not only objected to this but illegally declared Rhodesia independent from Britain in November 1965, thereby inspiring the creation of two terrorist groups dedicated to driving out the white colonists. ZANLA was one of these groups; it was based in the territory of Mozambique, was comprised primarily of members of the Shona tribe, and received arms and training from China. (The other group was the Zimbabwe People's Revolutionary Army, or ZIPRA, based in the territory of Zambia, comprised primarily of members of the Ndebele tribe, and supported by the Soviet Union.)

Both groups brutally attacked white colonists, including women and children, as well as members of each other's tribe, anyone who expressed support for the white government, and blacks who used cosmetics to make their skin appear lighter. Sometimes the terrorists would beat their victims to death; other times they would shoot or stab someone while forcing the victim's loved ones to watch. They also burned people to death, blew them up, cut off their limbs before executing them. Thousands were killed (the police had evidence of nearly three thousand murders by 1979, but many more were committed), and thousands more people were abducted and forced to serve the terrorist groups, by destroying bridges and roads, burning white colonists' crops, or committing similar acts.

Meanwhile the white government tried in various ways to end the violence. For example, in 1973 it established minefields in order to contain the terrorists to certain areas, evacuating villagers from these areas, and in 1974 it used helicopters to strike at terrorists from the air. The governing body also used undercover agents to encourage violence between the two terrorist groups, hoping the terrorists would destroy each other. In 1977, however, the white government gave up and turned control of Rhodesia over to black Africans—but because these newly appointed blacks did not support either terrorist group, the terrorists refused to accept their leadership and the violence continued. Consequently it was not until 1980, after Britain stepped in to force an election, that the terrorists laid down their weapons and agreed to abide by the results of a majority vote. The leader of ZANLA, Robert Mugabe, won the election and assumed the presidency of the country.

SEE ALSO: Zimbabwe People's Revolutionary Army

Zimbabwe People's Revolutionary Army (ZIPRA)

The Zimbabwe People's Revolutionary Army (ZIPRA) was a terrorist group that arose out of a political struggle in Rhodesia (now Zimbabwe) in 1965. At that time, Rhodesia was a British colony controlled by its white colonists, even though 95 percent of the population was black African. Black Rhodesians protested against the unfairness, and in response the British government decided to transfer power to them. The white colonists objected to this and without authority, declared Rhodesia independent from Britain in November 1965. This inspired black Rhodesians to retaliate, creating two terrorist groups dedicated to driving out the white colonists. ZIPRA was one of these groups; it was based in the territory of Zambia, comprised primarily of members of the Ndebele tribe, and received arms and training from the Soviet Union. (The other group was the Zimbabwe African National Liberation Army, or ZANLA, which was based in the territory of Mozambique, comprised primarily of members of the Shona tribe, and supported by China.)

Both groups brutally attacked white colonists of both sexes and of all ages, as well as members of each other's tribe. Also targeted was anyone who expressed support for the white government, and blacks who used cosmetics to lighten their complexions. Sometimes the terrorists fatally beat their victims; other times they would shoot or stab them in front of loved ones. They also burned people to death, blew them up, or cut off their limbs before executing them. At least three thousand people were murdered by 1979, and thousands more were abducted and forced to serve the terrorist groups in their cause, either by destroying bridges and roads, burning white colonists' crops, or by similar means.

The white government tried in various ways to end the violence. For example, in 1973 it established minefields in order to contain the terrorists to certain areas, and in 1974 the government used helicopter air strikes against the terrorists. Undercover agents were also employed to infiltrate the two terrorist groups and encourage violence in an attempt at getting the terrorists to destroy each other. All attempts by the white government were defeated, and in 1977 the whites gave up and turned control of Rhodesia over to black Africans. However, because the blacks who were appointed did not support either terrorist group, the terrorists refused to accept their leadership and the violence continued. Consequently not until the British stepped in to force an election in 1980 did the terrorists lay down their weapons and agreed to abide by the results of a majority vote, giving the leader of ZANLA, Robert Mugabe, the presidency of the country.

SEE ALSO: Zimbabwe African National Liberation Army

Zionism

A political movement, Zionism arose during World War I among European Jews committed to creating a Jewish state in Palestine, where their people had lived prior to their expulsion by the Romans in the second century. In 1917, in response to persecution of Jews in Germany, Zionist supporters in the British government convinced Britain to issue the Balfour Declaration, which stated that Britain would support the creation of such a state. However, one year later the British government also declared that it would support Arabs' right to govern their own lands. These differing positions fueled conflict in the

Middle East, with Jews feeling they had the right to establish their own nation in Palestine and Arabs feeling they had the right to keep Jews out of Palestine. After World War I, as Jews began moving to Palestine with the expectation of establishing a homeland there, acts of terrorism became common on both sides of the dispute; adding to the tension was the fact that whereas among Arabs it was the custom to allow peasants to continue to live on any land that changed ownership, Zionist settlers in Palestine expelled Arab peasants from any land they bought.

But despite numerous acts of violence throughout the 1920s, '30s, and '40s, in 1948 an independent Jewish state—Israel—was created. To many Jews, this meant that Zionism had succeeded. Others, however, argued that because Israel did not include all of the Jews' ancestral land, Zionism had not yet reached its goal. In either case, the day after Israel was formally established, the Arab League—comprised of Lebanon, Egypt, Jordan, and Syria—declared war on Israel. Even after Israel won this war, Arabs and Jews continued to fight over who had the right to occupy certain lands, particularly the West Bank and Gaza Strip, thereby continuing the violence in the Middle East.

SEE ALSO: Jewish Defense League; Palestine; West Bank and Gaza Strip, the

Chronology

The following are representative of the many significant acts of terrorism that have occurred throughout history:

60–61 In response to an attempted revolt by Britons in the British Isles, the occupying Romans engage in terrorism against the populace both out of revenge and to keep another revolt from occurring.

July 1099 In Jerusalem, Christians of the Western Church massacre thousands of Muslims and Orthodox Christians as part of the First Crusade.

11th–13th centuries The Assassins Sect commits numerous terrorist acts in the Middle East.

13th–15th centuries Christians massacre thousands of Jews in Central Europe.

15th–17th centuries In Spain, the Inquisition—a Roman Catholic tribunal designed to identify heretics—results in the torture or execution of thousands.

March 5, 1770 British soldiers in Boston, Massachusetts, kill five Americans during a riot that helped trigger the American Revolution; this event is known as the Boston Massacre.

June 1793–July 1794 In France, the Reign of Terror leads to the execution of as many as forty thousand people, most by guillotine.

19th century The U.S. government forces Native Americans from their lands, killing thousands in the process.

1811–1816 After English craftsmen calling themselves Luddites destroy textile machinery and weaving looms at mills, the British government decrees that "machine breaking" is a crime punishable by death; several Luddites are then killed by mill guards or executed in public hangings.

1848 Revolutions occur in many parts of Europe but are quelled.

1870s Irish coal miners in Pennsylvania belonging to a terrorist group called the Molly Maguires target mine owners with bombings and assassinations.

1882 The beginning of decades of lynchings of African Americans by white supremacists in the United States.

1882–1892 In France, anarchists plant bombs at various locations, including a Lyon music hall and a Paris café, and fire into a crowd at the Paris stock exchange.

May 3, 1886 During a labor strike against the McCormick Harvesting Machine Company in Chicago, Illinois, known as the Haymarket Riot, unionists and anarchists trigger a confrontation between demonstrators and police that results in several deaths on both sides.

1894–1912 Anarchists are responsible for the assassination of several world leaders: France's president Said Carnot in 1894, Austria's empress Elizabeth in 1898, Italy's king Umberto in 1900, America's president William McKinley in 1901, and Spain's prime minister Canalejas y Mendez in 1912.

January 9, 1905 Russian police kill hundreds of demonstrators in a massacre later known as Bloody Sunday.

October 1, 1910 Twenty workers at the *Los Angeles Times* newspaper offices in California are killed by a bomb planted by members of a labor union opposed to the paper's antiunion editorials.

June 28, 1914 Serbian national terrorists assassinate Franz Ferdinand, the archduke of Austria.

1915 In Ottoman, Turkey, the Turks commit genocide against Armenians, killing hundreds of thousands.

April 24–29, 1916 In what became known as the Easter Rebellion, Irish rebels try to drive British occupying forces from Dublin, Ireland, but fail.

April 13, 1919 British soldiers in colonial India commit a massacre in the city of Amritsar, firing into a peaceful assembly of men, women, and children for nearly ten minutes; 380 Indians are killed and 1,200 seriously wounded.

September 16, 1920 Anarchists bomb Wall Street, the site of the New York Stock Exchange, in New York City, killing thirty-five and injuring nearly three hundred.

1934–1945 German dictator Adolf Hitler employs a special police force, the Gestapo, to kill or imprison socialists, Communists, Jews, homosexuals, Gypsies, and others he considers to be undesirable members of society. After invading Poland in 1939, he establishes death camps there and in Germany dedicated to exterminating as many Jews as possible, a genocide known as the Holocaust that continues until his death in 1945.

1940–1956 The "Mad Bomber," George Metesky, terrorizes residents of New York City, planting thirty-seven bombs at various locations in the Manhattan area.

July 22, 1946 The Jewish terrorist organization Irgun Zvai Leumi bombs the King David Hotel in Jerusalem, killing ninety-one people.

April 9, 1948 Jewish terrorists kill over two hundred Arab men, women, and children in the Palestinian village of Deir Yasin.

November 1, 1950 Puerto Rican nationalists attempt to assassinate U.S. president Harry S. Truman.

July 20, 1951 A Palestinian terrorist assassinates Jordan's king Abdullah I.

March 1, 1954 Four Puerto Rican nationalists attempt to assassinate members of the U.S. House of Representatives, opening fire in the visitors' gallery of the House Chamber; five Congressmen are injured but none is killed.

1954–1964 Muslim nationalists in Algeria engage in a war of independence against the French colonial government controlling the country; both sides engage in terrorism.

1955–1956 In Algeria, nationalists of the National Liberation Front (FLN) begin engaging in terrorism against European settlers, often savaging victims before killing them; attacks include the Philippeville Massacre, during which thirty-seven men, women, and children are slaughtered, the assassination of French political leader Amédée Froger, and a two-day murder spree during which forty-nine innocent people die.

March 20, 1960 In South Africa, white policemen murder sixty-nine black protestorrs in a racially motivated slaughter later called the Sharpeville Massacre.

1961–1996 State-sponsored terrorism during a civil war in Guatemala results in the death or disappearance of over two hundred thousand people.

September 15, 1963 Members of the Ku Klux Klan bomb the Sixteenth Street Baptist Church in Birmingham, Alabama, killing four children and injuring over twenty adults, in a racially motivated attack.

1964–1965 The Tupamaros terrorist group becomes active in Uruguay, bombing the homes and offices of foreign diplomats and businessmen.

July 1968 Members of the Popular Front for the Liberation of Palestine (PFLP) hijack a Boeing 707 of Israel's El Al airline shortly after it leaves Rome, Italy, en route to Tel Aviv, Israel; the hostages are eventually released unharmed in Algiers, and afterward El Al stations armed guards on its planes.

1969 Popular Front for the Liberation of Palestine (PFLP) members continue to hijack airplanes from various airlines, typically exchanging hostages for terrorists held in Europeans prisons; however, the group avoids El Al flights after an attempted hijacking of such a plane results in a hijacker's being shot by airplane guards.

1970 In Beirut, Lebanon, members of the Popular Front for the Liberation of Palestine (PFLP) fire rockets at four targets associated with the United States: the U.S. embassy, the Bank of America, the John F. Kennedy Library, and the American Insurance Company.

March 1971 Members of the American terrorist group Weatherman bomb the U.S. Capitol building, damaging seven rooms.

July 27, 1971 In Paris, France, Palestinian terrorists bomb the Jordanian embassy.

November 28, 1971 Palestinian terrorists assassinate the Jordanian prime minister in Cairo, Egypt.

December 1971 Palestinian terrorists try unsuccessfully to assassinate Jordanian ambassadors in England and Switzerland.

January 30, 1972 British forces shoot at Irish Catholic demonstrators in Northern Ireland, a massacre later dubbed Bloody Sunday.

May 31, 1972 Members of the Japanese Red Army terrorist group attack passengers waiting to board planes at the Airport near Tel Aviv, Israel, killing twenty-six and injuring seventy-six.

July 1972 The Provisional Irish Republican Army (IRA) is responsible for more than twenty bombings in Belfast, Northern Ireland.

September 5, 1972 Eight terrorists storm into the rooms of Israeli athletes at the Olympic Village in Munich, Germany, where the 1972 Olympic Games are being held, wounding a coach, killing one athlete, and taking nine others hostage; these hostages, along with five terrorists and a policeman, are later killed during a rescue attempt at a nearby military airport, where the terrorists expected to board a plane to safety.

March 1973 Palestinian terrorists attack the Saudi Arabian embassy in Khartoum, Sudan, during a party; the U.S. ambassador and two other people are killed.

July 1973 Popular Front for the Liberation of Palestine (PFLP) terrorists work with Japanese Red Army terrorists to hijack a Japan Airlines 747 airplane en route to Tokyo, Japan; the hostages are released and the plane is destroyed after landing in Libya.

August 5, 1973 Palestinian terrorists throw grenades and shoot at civilians at a Tel Aviv, Israel, airport, killing five and injuring over fifty.

December 1973 In London, England, the Irish Republican Army (IRA) kills or injures dozens of people using car bombs and mail bombs; two months later, the same group kills eleven bus passengers by planting a bomb in luggage.

February 5, 1974 Heiress Patty Hearst is kidnapped in Berkeley, California, by members of the Symbionese Liberation Army and later joins in their terrorist activities, possibly because of a condition of psychological duress known as the Stockholm syndrome.

Fall 1974 The Provisional Irish Republican Army (IRA) is responsible for dozens of bombing attacks at sites throughout England, including pubs, stores, and tourist attractions.

April–August 1975 The Japanese Red Army attacks American and Swedish embassies in Malaysia, and the Baader-Meinhof Gang (also called the Red Army Faction) attacks the West German embassy in Stockholm, Sweden; the latter attack results in the arrest of the terrorists, but the Japanese Red Army terrorists escape via a flight to Libya.

October 1975 Two Turkish ambassadors, one in Austria and one in France, are assassinated by unknown terrorists.

1975–1979 The Communist government of Cambodia known as the Khmer Rouge executes, tortures, and mistreats millions of its citizens, leading to the death of approximately 2 million.

July 4, 1976 Palestinian and West German terrorists hijack an Air France Airbus, taking 103 passengers hostage, but are subsequently killed or captured by Israeli forces at an airport in Entebbe, Uganda.

October 1977 Three Palestinian terrorists hijack a West German airliner, taking eighty-seven people hostage, but are killed by German forces after landing in Mogadishu, Somalia; all of the hostages are rescued safely.

August 1978 Islamic extremists firebomb a theater in Abadan, Iran, killing over 430 people.

1978–1995 Someone calling himself the Unabomber—later identified as Theodore Kaczynski—sends bombs through the mail, killing three people and injuring twenty-two.

1979 Islamic fundamentalists declare a *jihad*, or holy war, against the Soviets after their invasion of Afghanistan, and Muslim fighters from throughout the Middle East enter the region to attack Soviet forces there.

November 1979 Islamic revolutionaries seize the U.S. embassy in Tehran, Iran, taking 66 Americans hostage; 53 of them are held for 444 days, until January 1981. Meanwhile, in Saudi Arabia, over 300 Islamic extremists seize the Grand Mosque in Mecca, holding it until December 4 when government forces kill 161; during this period, Islamic extremists in Islamabad, Pakistan, set fire to the U.S. embassy under the belief that U.S. forces were involved in the ultimately successful attempt to retake the mosque.

1980 Bombings by unknown assailants occur in public places in West Germany, France, Italy, and Kenya.

July 1980 The former Turkish prime minister, Nihat Erin, is assassinated in Istanbul, Turkey, while the former prime minister of Syria, Salah al-Din Bitar, is assassinated in Paris, France.

1982 Members of the Armed Forces of National Liberation (FALN), a Puerto Rican nationalist group, bomb several targets in New York, including the headquarters of Merrill Lynch, the New York Stock Exchange, the American Stock Exchange, Chase Manhattan Bank, the IBM building, and federal buildings; no one is injured in these attacks, and the buildings suffer only minor damage. Meanwhile, Puerto Rico experiences several bombings and attacks on police officers.

April 18, 1983 In Beirut, Lebanon, the group Hezbollah detonates a car bomb in front of the American embassy; sixty-three people are killed and more than a hundred injured.

1983–1984 An American neo-Nazi group called the Order engages in various acts of racially motivated violence, including the murder of a Jewish radio personality.

1984 Unknown bombers strike in India, Iran, Lebanon, and Italy, killing dozens.

1984–1985 Members of the Animal Liberation Front commit various acts of violence in the United States in an attempt to destroy businesses and medical-research facilities that use animals to test products and medicines.

May 8, 1985 Skinheads attack nonwhites during a riot in Brussels, Belgium, killing thirty-eight people and injuring over two hundred.

June 23, 1985 Air India Flight 182, en route from Toronto, Canada, to London, England, explodes at an altitude of 31,000 feet (9400m) over the Atlantic Ocean; terrorism experts generally believe members of a Sikh extremist group known as the Babbar Khalsa Society is responsible, and that the bombings were in response to an attack on a Sikh shrine in Amritsar, India, by the Indian government in 1984.

October 7, 1985 Four terrorists from the Palestine Liberation Front (PLF) take over the Italian cruise ship *Achille Lauro* en route from Genoa, Italy, to Ashod, Israel, holding its 427 passengers and 80 crew members hostage for two days. During the ordeal the four men kill a wheelchair-bound Jewish American, sixty-nine-year-old Leon Klinghoffer, and throw him overboard.

November 6, 1985 Members of the Colombian guerrilla group M-19 storm the Palace of Justice in Bogota, Colombia, and take everyone there hostage; when Colombian forces attack the building two days later, all of the guerrillas and eleven supreme court justices are killed.

November 23, 1985 Members of the Abu Nidal Organization (ANO) hijacks Egypt Air Flight 648 and kill two Israeli and three American passengers; during the rescue operation at a Malta airport, an Egyptian counterterrorism group, Force 777, kills fifty-seven passengers.

December 27, 1985 Members of the Abu Nidal Organization (ANO) kill seventeen people and injure over one hundred at airport terminals in Rome, Italy, and Vienna, Austria.

September 6, 1986 Members of the Abu Nidal Organization (ANO) kill twenty-one people and wound over one hundred while attempting to hijack a Pan Am Boeing 747 jet at a Pakistani airport.

April 1987 Tamil extremists in Sri Lanka kill over one hundred Sinhalese men, women, and children after forcing them off public buses.

February 1989 Ayatollah Ruhollah Khomeini of Iran calls for the assassination of author Salman Rushdie, who then goes into hiding; many Muslims consider Rushdie's novel, *The Satanic Verses*, to be an insult to their faith.

June 1989 Chinese forces attack demonstrators in Tiananmen Square in Beijing, killing or injuring thousands.

1991 A Radisson hotel in Amman, Jordan, is bombed; al Qaeda operatives are believed to be responsible.

1992–1995 Genocide deemed "ethnic cleansing" occurs in Bosnia, Srebenica, and Herzegovina as three ethnic groups, the Serbs (who are of the Orthodox Christian faith), the Muslims (members of the Islamic faith), and the Croatians (Roman

Catholics) engage in terrorist acts against one another; most of the genocidal violence is perpetrated by Serbs against Muslims, thousands of whom are massacred.

1992–1998 In Algeria, Islamic extremists engage in terrorism against the government, which retaliates with violence; approximately seventy-five thousand Algerians are killed and roughly twenty thousand disappear.

February 26, 1993 Middle Eastern terrorists detonate a bomb on the second level of the parking garage beneath Tower One of the World Trade Center in New York, leaving a crater roughly 150 feet (45m) in diameter and five stories deep and destroying some sewer, water, and electrical lines.

November 1993 Members of the Animal Liberation Front (ALF) firebomb several department stores in Chicago, Illinois.

1994 Hutus and Tutsis in Rwanda commit genocide against one another; by some estimates, more than half a million people die during this violence.

March 1995 Members of Aum Shinrikyō release sarin nerve gas in the Tokyo, Japan, subway system, killing twelve and injuring thousands.

April 19, 1995 Timothy McVeigh bombs the Alfred P. Murrah Federal Building in Oklahoma City, Oklahoma, killing 168 and injuring hundreds more.

June 1995 Approximately fifty Chechen separatists take at least fifteen hundred people hostage at a hospital in Budyonnovsk, Russia, holding them for fifteen days. Russian forces then storm the building; over one hundred hostages are killed and hundreds more wounded before a cease-fire is declared and the terrorists are allowed to leave, only to be tracked down later and either killed or arrested.

June 25, 1996 Members of Hezbollah detonate a truck bomb beside the Khobar Towers, which houses military personnel near the King Abdul Aziz Air Base in Saudi Arabia; 19 U.S. military personnel are killed and 515 injured.

July 27, 1996 In Atlanta, Georgia, three pipe bombs hidden inside a backpack explode in Centennial Park, one of the sites of the 1996 Olympic Games; over a hundred people are injured, two of whom die (one from injuries sustained in the blast and the other from a heart attack). After an extensive investigation, authorities determine that the bomber was antiabortion activist Eric Robert Rudolph.

December 1996 In Lima, Peru, members of the Tupac Amaru Revolutionary Movement seize the Japanese embassy (the ambassador's residence), holding hundreds captive until a military action frees the hostages in April 1997.

January 1997 An abortion clinic in Sandy Springs, Georgia, is bombed, probably by the antiabortion group Army of God, while antiabortion activist Eric Rudolph, who is affiliated with the Army of God, bombs an abortion clinic and a nightclub for gays and lesbians in Atlanta, Georgia, and an abortion clinic in Birmingham, Alabama.

August 7, 1998 Over 250 are killed and approximately 5,000 wounded in car bombings at U.S. embassies in Nairobi, Kenya, and Dar es Salaam, Tanzania, a coordinated attack believed to have been orchestrated by members of al Qaeda.

August 1998 The Real IRA explodes two car bombs in Northern Ireland, killing or injuring hundreds and damaging over two hundred homes and other buildings.

August 1998 After American ships in the Arabian Sea and the Red Sea fire missiles at six suspected terrorist bases in Afghanistan near its border with Pakistan and destroy a pharmaceutical factory in Sudan that U.S. officials believed was supplying chemical weapons to al Qaeda operatives, a terrorist group calling itself Muslims Against Global Oppression (MAGO) retaliates by bombing a Planet Hollywood restaurant in Capetown, South Africa, killing one person and injuring twenty-five others.

October 23, 1998 Antiabortion activist James Charles Kopp murders abortion provider Dr. Barnett Slepian in Amherst, New York.

December 1998 Islamic terrorists in Yemen kidnap over a dozen tourists; during a rescue attempt, four of the hostages are killed.

February 1999 Several Kurds seize the Greek embassy in Vienna, Austria, taking seven people, including the Greek ambassador, hostage but soon release them unharmed.

March 1999 Hutu terrorists kidnap sixteen foreign tourists at a gorilla park in Uganda, killing eight before releasing the rest.

April 2000 Abu Sayyaf terrorist group kidnaps twenty-three people, including foreign tourists and journalists, from a resort on the Malaysian island of Sipidan, holding them for ransom for months while negotiating their release.

2000–2002 Palestinian terrorist group al Aqsa Martyrs Brigade commits dozens of suicide bombings, car bombings, and sniper attacks against Israeli civilians in the West Bank.

October 12, 2000 Islamic terrorists ram an explosives-laden boat into the USS *Cole* in Aden Harbor, Yemen, killing seventeen sailors and injuring more than thirty.

September 11, 2001 Roughly three thousand Americans are killed after nineteen members of the al Qaeda terrorist network hijack four large passenger jets, flying two of them into the World Trade Center towers in New York and one of them into the Pentagon building in Washington, D.C.; the fourth plane, probably intended to strike the White House, crashed in a Pennsylvania field after passengers retaliated against the hijackers. The following month, the United States responds by bombing Afghanistan and sending ground troops into the country, ultimately capturing the cities of Kabul and Kandahar and replacing the religious regime running Afghanistan, the Taliban, with a new, interim government supported by the United States.

Fall 2001 Several people in New York and Washington, D.C., are exposed to anthrax, some fatally, after coming into contact with contaminated letters intended for prominent politicians or members of the media.

December 2001 Members of Hamas kill or injure dozens of Jews in the West Bank in an aggressive attempt to drive out Israeli occupying forces.

December 22, 2001 Richard Reid, commonly known as "the Shoe Bomber," smuggles explosives onto an American Airlines flight in his shoes, but is subdued before he can ignite them.

2001–2002 Sixty-nine suicide bombings during a twenty-one-month period kill 547 Israelis and 1,712 Palestinians, including women and children, during a Palestinian uprising against Israel.

2001–2007 In Iraq, insurgents attack occupying U.S. forces on a daily basis, killing thousands.

January 2002 American journalist Daniel Pearl is kidnapped in Pakistan, and a videotape of his execution by terrorists is later sent to the media.

February 2002 Hundreds are killed in India after mob violence breaks out between Islamic and Hindu extremists.

May 8, 2002 An Islamic suicide bomber kills fourteen people in Karachi, Pakistan, after detonating a car bomb near a hotel shuttle bus.

October 2002 Two nightclubs are bombed in Indonesia on the island of Bali, killing hundreds; terrorism experts believe the Islamic terrorist group Jemaah Islamiyah is responsible.

October 23, 2002 Chechen separatists take roughly 900 hostages at a theater in Moscow, Russia, and hold them for two and a half days before Russian forces raid the theater and gas its occupants, killing 129 hostages and 42 terrorists.

August 2003 The United Nations (UN) headquarters in Iraq is bombed, an attack probably masterminded by prominent al Qaeda member Abu Musab al Zarqawi.

May 2004 A videotape surfaces showing the execution of an American hostage, Nicholas Berg, taken in Iraq; terrorism experts believe the voice on the tape is that of al Qaeda member Abu Musab al Zarqawi.

September 1, 2004 Chechen separatists take over twelve hundred people hostage at a school in Beslan, Russia, then wire the school with explosives; after a three-day standoff, Russian troops unintentionally trigger an explosion, followed by a shoot-out in which over three hundred people, including several of the terrorists, die and over seven hundred are wounded.

September 2005 The first-known female al Qaeda suicide bomber blows herself up in Iraq near the Syrian border.

October 13, 2005 The Islamic terrorist group Yarmuk takes over one hundred hostages in Nalchik, Russia, as part of an attack on the town in protest of anti-Muslim sentiments in the region; the terrorists are killed in a shoot-out by hostage-rescue forces.

June 2006 An Israeli soldier is captured by Palestinian militants; Israel blames Hamas and bombs targets connected to the group over a five-month period, killing more than three hundred Palestinians; after Israelis wipe out a family of nineteen civilians during one attack, an immediate international outcry results in a tenuous cease-fire.

July 2006 Hezbollah ambushes two Israeli army Humvees near the border between Lebanon and Israel, capturing two Israeli soldiers; Hezbollah intends to exchange the captured soldiers for certain Muslims who were imprisoned in Israel after Hezbollah kidnapped three Israeli soldiers in October 2000. However, because eight Israeli soldiers were killed during the 2000 kidnapping, Israel responds this time by bombing targets in Lebanon that were either connected to Hezbollah or might benefit the group (such as an airport and seaports). Hezbollah counters by lobbing rocket missiles over the border at Israel until Israel calls off its attacks.

December 2006 In this one month alone, 112 U.S. soldiers are killed by insurgents in Iraq in an attempt to drive occupying forces from the country. This is the highest monthly total of U.S. casualties for 2006 and the bloodiest month since November 2004.

2006–2007 A civil war develops in Iraq, during which members of two Muslim sects, the Shiites and the Sunnis, engage in politically and religiously motivated violence against one another, slaying dozens of innocent civilians.

February 2007 Members of two Palestinian factions, Hamas and al Fatah, using rocket-propelled grenade launchers, rockets, and assault rifles, battle in the Gaza Strip over control of the Palestinian provisional government; dozens are killed or injured, two universities are damaged by fire, and a radio station is blown up despite an announced cease-fire by the leaders of both sides just days before.

For Further Research

Sean Anderson and Stephen Sloan, *Historical Dictionary of Terrorism*. 2nd ed. Lanham, MD: Scarecrow, 2002.

Patricia Baird-Windle and Eleanor J. Bader, *Targets of Hatred: Anti-Abortion Terrorism*. New York: Palgrave, 2001.

Dirk J. Barreveld, *Can America Win the War on Terrorism?: A Look into the Root Causes of World Terrorism*. New York: Writer's Club, 2002.

Tore Bjorgo, ed., *Terror from the Extreme Right*. Portland, OR: Frank Cass, 1995.

Caleb Carr, *The Lessons of Terror: A History of Warfare Against Civilians*. New York: Random House, 2002.

Richard Clutterbuck, *Terrorism in an Unstable World*. New York: Routledge, 1994.

Morris Dees, with James Corcoran, *Gathering Storm: America's Militia Threat*. New York: HarperCollins, 1996.

Steven Emerson, *American Jihad: The Terrorists Living Among Us*. New York: Simon & Schuster, 2002.

Jonathan Harris, *The New Terrorism: Politics of Violence*. New York: Julian Messner, 1983.

Christopher Hewitt, *The Effectiveness of Antiterrorist Policies*. New York: University Press of America, 1984.

John Kelsay and James Turner Johnson, eds., *Just War and Jihad: Historical and Theoretical Perspectives on War and Peace in Western and Islamic Traditions*. New York: Greenwood, 1991.

Harvey W. Kushner, ed., *Essential Readings on Political Terrorism: Analyses of Problems and Prospects for the 21st Century (Of Special Interest)*. Lincoln: University of Nebraska Press, 2002.

Harvey W. Kushner, ed., *The Future of Terrorism: Violence in the New Millennium*. Thousand Oaks, CA: Sage, 1997.

Walter Laqueur, *The Age of Terrorism*. Boston: Little, Brown, 1987.

Walter Laqueur, ed., *Voices of Terror: Manifestos, Writings and Manuals of al Qaeda, Hamas, and Other Terrorists from Around the World and Throughout the Ages*. New York: Reed, 2004.

Lorenz Otto Lutherer and Margaret Sheffield Simon, *Targeted: The Anatomy of an Animal Rights Attack*. Norman: University of Oklahoma Press, 1992.

Gerald McKnight, *The Terrorist Mind: Why They Hijack, Kidnap, Bomb and Kill*. New York: Bobbs-Merrill, 1974.

Mohammad Mohaddessin, *Islamic Fundamentalism: The New Global Threat*. Washington, DC: Seven Locks, 1989.

Edward Moxon-Browne, ed., *European Terrorism*. New York: G.K. Hall, 1994.

Brigitte Nacos, *Terrorism and the Media: From the Iran Hostages to the World Trade Center Bombing*. New York: Columbia University Press, 1994.

Loretta Napoleoni, *Terror Incorporated: Tracing the Dollars Behind the Terror Networks*. New York: Seven Stories, 2005.

Benjamin Netanyahu, *The Terrorism Reader*. New York: Meridian, 1986.

David C. Rapoport, and Yohah Alexander, eds., *The Morality of Terrorism: Religious xand Secular Justifications*. New York: Pergamon, 1982.

Walter Reich, ed., *Origins of Terrorism: Psychologies, Ideologies, Theologies, and States of Mind*. Washington, DC: Woodrow Wilson Center, 1998.

Simon Reeve, *One Day in September: The Full Story of the 1972 Munich Olympics Massacre and the Israeli Revenge Operation "Wrath of God."* New York: Arcade, 2000.

Gideon Rose and James F. Hoge, *How Did This Happen? Terrorism and the New War*. New York: Public Affairs, 2001.

Richard E. Rubenstein, *Alchemists of Revolution: Terrorism in the Modern World*. New York: Basic, 1987.

Claire Sterling, *The Terror Network: The Secret War of International Terrorism*. New York: Holt, Rinehart & Winston, 1981.

Leonard B. Weinberg and Paul B. Davis, *Introduction to Political Terrorism*. New York: McGraw-Hill, 1989.

Jonathan R. White, *Terrorism: An Introduction*. 3rd ed. Belmont, CA: Wadsworth, 2001.

David J. Whittaker, ed., *The Terrorism Reader*. 2nd ed. New York: Routledge, 2003.

Works Consulted

James Adams, *The Financing of Terror*. New York: Simon & Schuster, 1986.

Yonah Alexander and Alan O'Day, eds., *Terrorism in Ireland*. London: Croom Helm, 1984.

Yonah Alexander and Allan S. Nanes, eds., *Legislative Responses to Terrorism*. Boston: Martinus Nijhoff, 1986.

Yonah Alexander and Michael S. Swetnam, eds., *Cyber Terrorism and Information Warfare: Threats and Responses*. Ardsley, NY: Transnational, 2001.

Yonah Alexander and Milton M. Hoenig, eds., *Super Terrorism: Biological, Chemical, and Nuclear*. New York: Transnational, 2001.

Zigad Abu Amr, *Islamic Fundamentalism in the West Bank and Gaza: Muslim Brotherhood and Islamic Jihad*. Bloomington: Indiana University Press, 1994.

Paul Avrich, *Anarchist Portraits*. Princeton, NJ: Princeton University Press, 1990.

Charlie A. Beckwith, *Delta Force: The Army's Elite Counterterrorism Unit*. San Diego: Harcourt, Brace, Jovanovich, 1983.

Dallas A. Blanchard, *The Anti-Abortion Movement and the Rise of the Religious Right: From Polite to Fiery Protest*. New York: Twayne, 1994.

Frank Bolz, Kenneth J. Dudonis, and David P. Schulz, *The Counterterrorism Handbook: Tactics, Procedures, and Techniques*. 2nd ed. Boca Raton, FL: CRC, 2002.

Jim Bradbury, *The Medieval Siege*. Rochester, NY: Boydell & Brewer, 1992.

Anthony Burton, *Urban Terrorism: Theory, Practice, Response*. London: Cooper, 1975.

Howard L. Bushart, John R. Craig, and Myra Barnes, *Soldiers of God: White Supremacists and Their Holy War for America*. New York: Kensington, 1998.

Raimondo Catanzaro, *The Red Brigades and Left-Wing Terrorism in Italy*. New York: St. Martin's, 1991.

Gerald Chailand, *Terrorism: From Popular Struggle to Media Spectacle*. Atlantic Highlands, NJ: Saqi, 1987.

Paul Chevigny, *Edge of the Knife: Police Violence in the Americas*. New York: New Press, 1995.

Noam Chomsky, *Pirates and Emperors: International Terrorism in the Real World*. New York: Black Rose Books, 2000.

William L. Cleveland, *A History of the Modern Middle East*. Boulder, CO: Westview 1994.

Richard Clutterbuck, *Guerrillas and Terrorists*. Chicago: Ohio University Press, 1980.

James Coates, *Armed and Dangerous: The Rise of the Survivalist Right*. New York: Hill & Wang, 1987.

Cindy C. Combs, *Terrorism in the Twenty-First Century*. 2nd ed. Upper Saddle River, NJ: Prentice-Hall, 2000.

Juan E. Corradi, Patricia Weiss Fagen, and Manuel Antonio Garretón, eds., *Fear at the Edge: State Terror and Resistance in Latin America*. Berkeley: University of California Press, 1992.

Martha Crenshaw, *Terrorism, Legitimacy, and Power*. Middletown, CT: Wesleyan University Press, 1983.

Martha Crenshaw, ed., *Terrorism in Africa*. New York: G.K. Hall, 1994.

Martha Crenshaw and John Pimlott, eds., *Encyclopedia of World Terrorism*. Vols. 1, 2, and 3. Armonk, NY: M.E. Sharpe, Inc., 1997.

Paul Dixon, *Northern Ireland: The Politics of War and Peace*. New York: Palgrave, 2001.

William Doyle, *The Oxford History of the French Revolution*. New York: Oxford University Press, 1989.

John Ellis, *From the Barrel of a Gun: A History of Guerrilla, Revolutionary and Counter-Insurgency Warfare, from the Romans to the Present*. Mechanicsburg, PA: Stackpole Books, 1995.

Richard A. Falk, Gabriel Kolko, and Robert Lifton, *Crimes of War*. New York: Vintage, 1971.

Jay P. Farrington, *Domestic Terrorism*. Philadelphia: Xlibris, 2001.

M.I. Finley, *Politics in the Ancient World*. New York: Cambridge University Press, 1983.

Lawrence Zelic Freedman and Yonah Alexander, eds., *Perspectives on Terrorism*. Wilmington, DE: Scholarly Resources, 1983.

Kathleen Gay, *Encyclopedia of Political Anarchy*. Santa Barbara, CA: ABC-CLIO, 1999.

John George and Laird Wilcox, *American Extremists: Militias, Supremacists, Klansmen, Communists, & Others*. Amherst, NY: Prometheus, 1996.

Paul Gilbert, *Terrorism, Security, and Nationality*. New York: Routledge, 1994.

Adrian Guelke, *The Age of Terrorism and the International Political System*. New York: St. Martin's Press, 1995.

Ernesto Ché Guevara, *Guerrilla Warfare*. Trans. J.P. Morray. New York: Monthly Review, 1961.

Harold D. Guither, *Animal Rights: History and Scope of a Radical Social Move-*

ment. Carbondale: Southern Illinois University Press, 1998.

Ted Robert Gurr, *Handbook of Political Conflict: Theory and Research.* New York: Free Press, 1980.

William Gutteridge, ed., *Contemporary Terrorism.* New York: Facts On File, 1986.

Frederick J. Hacker, *Criminals, Crusaders, Crazies: Terror and Terrorism in Our Time.* New York: W.W. Norton, 1976.

Donald Hanle, *Terrorism: The Newest Face of Warfare.* Washington, DC: Pergamon-Brassey's, 1989.

Christopher C. Harmon, *Terrorism Today.* London: Frank Cass, 2000.

Bruce Hoffman, *Inside Terrorism.* New York: Columbia University Press, 1998.

Mark Juergensmeyer, *Terror in the Mind of God: The Global Rise of Religious Violence.* Berkeley: University of California Press, 2001.

Charles W. Kegley, ed., *International Terrorism: Characteristics, Causes, Controls.* New York: St. Martin's, 1990.

Harvey W. Kushner, *Encyclopedia of Terrorism.* Thousand Oaks, CA: Sage, 2003.

Harvey W. Kushner, *Terrorism in America: A Structured Approach to Understanding the Terrorist Threat.* Springfield, IL: Charles C. Thomas, 1998.

Saul Landau, *The Guerrilla Wars of Central America: Nicaragua, El Salvador, and Guatemala.* New York: St. Martin's, 1993.

Walter Laqueur, *History of Terrorism.* New York: Transaction, 2001.

Walter Laqueur, *The New Terrorism: Fanaticism and the Arms of Mass Destruction.* New York: Transaction, 1999.

Sidney Lens, *The Labor Wars: From the Molly Maguires to the Sitdowns.* Garden City, NY: Anchor, 1974.

Seymour Martin Lipset and Earl Raab, *The Politics of Unreason: Right-Wing Extremism in America, 1790–1977.* 2nd ed. Chicago: University of Chicago Press, 1978.

Peter Mansfield, *The Arab World: A Comprehensive History.* New York: Pelican, 1977.

Carlos Marighella, *Minimanual of the Urban Guerrilla.* Chapel Hill, NC: Documentary, 1985.

Gus Martin, *Understanding Terrorism: Challenges, Perspectives, and Issues.* Thousand Oaks, CA: Sage, 2003.

Peter H. Merkl, ed., *Political Violence and Terror: Motifs and Motivations.* Berkeley: University of California Press, 1986.

Wayman C. Mullins, *A Sourcebook on Domestic and International Terrorism: An Analysis of Issues, Organizations, Tactics, and Responses.* 2nd ed. Springfield, IL: Charles C. Thomas, 1997.

Loretta Napoleoni, *Terror Incorporated: Tracing the Dollars Behind the Terror Networks.* New York: Seven Stories, 1995.

Jay Robert Nash, *Terrorism in the 20th Century: A Narrative Encyclopedia From the Anarchists, Through the Weatherman, to the Unabomber.* New York: M. Evans, 1998.

Patricia Netzley, *Environmental Literature: An Encyclopedia of Works, Authors, and Themes.* Santa Barbara, CA: ABC-CLIO, 1999.

Frank M. Ochberg and David A. Soskis, eds., *Victims of Terrorism*. Boulder, CO: Westview, 1982.

Albert Parry, *Terrorism from Robespierre to Arafat*. New York: Vanguard, 1976.

J. Roland Pennock and John W. Chapman, eds., *Anarchism*. New York: New York University Press, 1978.

Tina Rosenberg, *Children of Cain: Violence and the Violent in Latin America*. New York: Penguin, 1992.

George Rosie, *The Directory of International Terrorism*. New York: Paragon House, 1987.

Rik Scarce, *Eco-warriors: Understanding the Radical Environmental Movement*. Chicago: Noble, 1990.

Glenn E. Schweitzer, with Carole C. Dorsch, *Superterrorism: Assassins, Mobsters, and Weapons of Mass Destruction*. New York: Plenum, 1998.

Brent L. Smith, *Terrorism in America: Pipe Bombs and Pipe Dreams*. Albany: State University of New York Press, 1994.

Woodruff D. Smith, *European Imperialism in the Nineteenth and Twentieth Centuries*. Chicago: Nelson-Hall, 1982.

Richard D. Sonn, *Anarchism*. New York: Twayne, 1992.

Edward M. Spiers, *Chemical and Biological Weapons: A Study of Proliferation*. New York: St. Martin's, 1994.

Peter St. John, *Air Piracy, Airport Security, and International Terrorism: Winning the War Against Hijackers*. New York: Quorum, 1991.

Maxwell Taylor and Ethel Quayle, *Terrorist Lives*. Washington, DC: Macmillan, 1994.

Jonathan B. Tucker, *Toxic Terror: Assessing Terrorist Use of Chemical and Biological Weapons*. Cambridge, MA: MIT Press, 2000.

M. Walzer, *Just and Unjust Wars*. 3rd ed. New York: Basic Books, 1992.

Eugen Weber, *Apocalypses: Prophesies, Cults, and Millennial Beliefs Through the Ages*. Cambridge, MA: Harvard University Press, 1999.

Meyer Weinberg, *Racism in Contemporary America*. Westport, CT: Greenwood, 1996.

Thomas George Weiss David P. Forsythe, and Roger A. Coate, *The United Nations and Changing World Politics*. 3rd ed. Boulder, CO: Westview, 2001.

Paul Wilkinson, *Political Terrorism*. Cambridge, MA: Harvard University Press, 1974.

John B. Wolf, *Fear of Fear: A Survey of Terrorist Operations and Controls in Open Societies*. New York: Plenum, 1981.

Howard Zinn, *Terrorism and War*. New York: Seven Stories, 2002.

Periodicals

Jeff Barnard, "Four Plead Guilty in Ecoterrorism Firebombings," *Ventura County (CA) Star*, November 10, 2006.

Jeff Barnard, "Three More Plead Guilty to Being Members of Ecoterrorist Cell," *Ventura County (CA) Star*, July 22, 2006.

William J. Broad and David E. Sanger, "Fraying of Restraints Risks a Second Nuclear Age: Expert Says 49 Nations Have Skills, Materials to Build Bombs," *Ventura County (CA) Star*, October 15, 2006.

Hussein Dakroub, "Leader of Hezbollah Says It Won't Surrender Weapons," *Ventura County (CA) Star*, September 23, 2006.

Christopher Dickey, "Women of al Qaeda," *Newsweek*, December 12, 2005, p. 27.

Sarah El Deeb, "Hamas, Fatah Fighting Kills 17 Before Another Bid at Truce," *Ventura County (CA) Star*, February 3, 2007.

Jim Garamone American Forces Press Service, "Myers Discusses Haiti, Terrorism, Brazil's Shoot-Down Policy," March 11, 2004. United States Department of Defense Web site, American Forces Information Service News Articles, www.defenselink.mil/news/Mar2004/n03112004-200403112.html.

Anne Gearan, "Syria, Iran, Hezbollah Hope to Topple Lebanon, U.S. Says," *Ventura County (CA) Star*, November 2, 2006.

Charles Hanley, "'Decapitation' of Terror Leadership Rarely Deals Mortal Blow, Experts Say," *Ventura County (CA) Star* January 22, 2006.

Charles Hanley, "Report: Fewer Wars, More Conflicts," *Ventura County (CA) Star*, June 29, 2006 "Irish Republican Army Has Ceased Terrorism," *Ventura County (CA) Star*, October 5, 2006.

Charles Hanley, "Irish Republican Army Has Ceased Terrorism," *Ventura County (CA) Star*, October 5, 2006, October 5, 2006.

Elizabeth A. Kennedy, "Ethiopian Forces Are Attacked in Somalia's Capital, Witnesses Say," *Ventura County (CA) Star* January 8, 2007.

Walter Laqueur, "World of Terror," *National Geographic*, November 2004, pp. 72–81.

Karin Laub, "Weary of War, Israelis Seem to Want Normalcy." *Ventura County (CA) Star*, January 27, 2006.

Pat Milton, "FBI Worries Terrorists, Mob May Team Up," *Ventura County (CA) Star*. October 2, 2006.

Office of the Coordinator for Counterterrorism, "Latin America Terror Regions Activity: Patterns of Global Terrorism, 2000." April 2001. Reprinted by the United States Action Group at www.unitedstatesaction.com/latin-america-terror.htm.

David T. Pyne, "The New Second Front in the War Against Terrorism: Incoming President of Brazil Supports Terrorism and Will Implement Anti-American Policies," *American Partisan*, December 19, 2002. www.american-partisan.com/cols/2002/pyne/qtr4/1219.htm.

Tom Raum, "Facism New Buzz Word Among Republicans," August 30, 2006. http://news.aol.com/elections/story/_a/fascism-new-buzz-word-among-republicans/200608

Matthew Robinson, "Chasing Shadows: What We Know and Do Not Know About the USA Patriot Act & Civil Liberties in the Era of Terror," www.justiceblind.com/usapatriotactseries.html.

Nancy San Martin, "Contra, Sandinista Back in Race to Lead Nicaragua," *The Ventura County (CA) Star*, November 5, 2006.

Amy Teibel and Ibrahim Barzak, "Cease-Fire Reached in Mideast," *Ventura County (CA) Star*, November 26, 2006.

Evan Thomas, "So What Now, Mr. President?" *Newsweek*, December 11, 2006, p. 30.

Evan Thomas and Rod Nordland, "Death of a Terrorist," *Newsweek*, June 19, 2006, p. 22.

"Two Plead Guilty to University Ecoterrorism Firebomb Attack," *Ventura County (CA) Star*, October 5, 2006.

"Unabomber Ted Kaczynski," www.rotten.com/library/bio/crime/serial-killers/unabomber.

Web sites

Answers.com, www.answers.com. An online encyclopedia that offers information on terrorist attacks as well as biographical information on terrorists and world leaders.

CNN.com www.cnn.com/world. Includes news stories about terrorists and terrorist events.

Federal Bureau of Investigation, www.fbi.gov. Site of the U.S. Federal Bureau of Investigation, with information about terrorist and counterterrorist activities.

GlobalSecurity, www.globalsecurity.org. A reliable source of background information and news stories on defense, intelligence, and homeland security.

Moreorless, www.moreorless.au.com. This site lists short biographies of the world's heroes and villains of the twentieth century.

Terrorism Research Center, www.terrorism.com. Provides information on terrorism and counterterrorism research and activities, profiles of terrorists and terrorist groups, and a list of links to sites with related information; however, articles can be accessed only by paying subscribers.

Index

The Greenhaven Encyclopedia of Terrorism

N

Nagasaki (Japan) bombing, 74
Namangani, Juma, 174
Namibia, 108, 282
Narco-terrorism, 101, 113, 198, 283, 284
    See also Drug trade
Narodnaya Volya (The People's Will), 36, 225, 228
Nasjonal Samling Party (National Union), 255–256
Nasrallah, Hassan, 200
Nasser, Gamal Abdel, 256
National Alliance, 51, 303
National Infrastructure Protection Center, 102–103
National Liberation Army (Ejército de Liberación Nacional, or ELN), 93, 101, 225
National Liberation Army (NLA), 205
National Liberation Front (FLN), 29–30, 31, 106
National Liberation Front of Corsica (FLNC), 132, 226
National Movement for the Restoration of Pakistani Sovereignty, 246
National Organization of Cypriot fighters (EOKA), 69, 110, 143, 226–227
National Right to Life Committee (NRLC), 40
National Union for the Total Independence of Angola (UNITA), 19, 36
Nationalism/nationalists, 94, 106–110, 227
    African, 210
    Arab-Muslim, 30–31, 45–46, 106–107, 147, 215
    Asian, 52–54
    Irish, 116
    U.S., 70, 307
    See also Ethno-nationalist terrorism; Fascism; Nazism
Native Americans, extermination of, 31–32, 64, 138
NATO. *See* North Atlantic Treaty Organization (NATO)
Nazi Germany
    extermination of Jews, 122, 129–130, 138–139, 261, 286
    terrorist activities, 176, 202, 268–269, 309
    See also Gestapo; Hitler, Adolf; Nuremberg trials; Schutzstaffel (SS); Waffen SS
Nazism, 128, 157, 228

Ndebele tribe, 327, 328
Neave, Airey, 171
Nechayev, Sergey, 59, 228
Neocolonialism, 228–229
Neo-Confederates, 193
Neo-Nazis, 128, 193, 236, 279, 295, 319–320
    See also Jews, violence against; Racism; Skinheads
Nepal, 52
Nerve gas, 163, 169
Netherlands, 108, 120, 160
Neutron bombs, 73, 233
New People's Army (NPA), 230, 249
New Woman All Woman Health Center bombing, 67
Newton, Huey, 69
Nicaragua, 96, 230–231
Nicaraguan Democratic Force (FDN), 96
Nicholas II (czar), assassination of, 271, 272
Nichols, James, 92
Nichols, Terry Lynn, 92, 212, 231, 236
Nidal, Abu. *See* Banna, Sabri al-
Nigeria, 19–20, 227
Nizaris Ismailis, 55–56
North Atlantic Treaty Organization (NATO), 18, 131, 166, 190–191, 302
North Korea, nuclear weapons, 74, 82, 189
North Vietnam, 96, 109
Northern Alliance, 290
Northern Ireland, 76, 171–173, 231–232, 261, 279, 305
Northern Ireland Act of 1993, 98
Norway, German occupation, 255–256
Nosair, El Sayyid, 183, 260
Nuclear weapons, 73–74, 77, 163, 232–233, 298, 316–317
    North Korea and, 74, 82, 189
    See also Atomic bombs; Hiroshima (Japan) bombing
Nuremberg trials, 233, 315

O

Ocalan, Abdullah, 193
Occidental Petroleum pipeline, attack on, 93
October Revolution (1917), 41, 301
    See also Russian Revolution, 1905 and 1917
Odeh, Abdul Aziz, 118
Official Irish Republican Army

(Official IRA), 171
Ogaden region, 20, 281
Ohnesorg, Benno, death of, 139
Oil companies, violence against, 20, 93–94
Oklahoma City bombing, 98, 235–236, 280, 291, 296, 303, 307, 319–320
    perpetrators, 29, 76, 92, 101, 167, 211–212, 231, 269
Olympic Games as terrorist targets, 236
    See also Atlanta's Centennial Park bombing; Munich Olympic crisis
Omar, Mohammed, 289–290
Omega 7, 236–237, 253
Operation Backfire, 237–238
Operation Desert Shield, 63, 247
Operation Desert Storm, 162, 169, 247
Operation Eagle Claw, 111, 120, 160, 238
Operation Enduring Freedom, 64, 98, 238
Operation Iraqi Freedom, 163, 169–170
Operation Peace for Galilee, 175
Operation Rescue, 40
Opium. *See* Drug trade
ORDEN, 119
Order, the, 51, 239, 303
Organization for the Oppressed of the Earth, 154, 239–240
Organization for the Protection of the People's Struggle (OPLA), 141, 142
Organization of Petroleum Exporting Countries (OPEC), attack on, 86
Organization of the Islamic Revolution, 216
Organization of Volunteers for the Puerto Rican Revolution, 253
Ortega, Daniel, 231
Orthodox Christians, 45, 77–78, 138, 190, 227, 275, 325–326
    See also Christian-Muslim conflicts
Otis, Harrison Gray, 202–203
Ottoman Turkish Empire, 49, 166, 189, 303
Oughton, Diana, 317
Our Father's House, 143

P

Pace, Charles, 79
Packable bombs, 297
Pahlavi, Mohammad Reza (shah),

The Greenhaven Encyclopedia of Terrorism

U

V

About the Author

Patricia D. Netzley has written over forty-five nonfiction books on a wide range of topics. Her works include *The Greenhaven Encyclopedia of Paranormal Phenomena*, *The Greenhaven Encyclopedia of the Civil War*, *The Encyclopedia of Movie Special Effects*, *The Encyclopedia of Women's Travel and Exploration*, *Environmental Literature*, and *Social Protest Literature*. Netzley also writes novels for children, young adults, and adults. She is a member of the Society of Children's Writers and Illustrators and the Romance Writers of America, and teaches writing courses for the Institute of Children's Literature.

About the Consulting Editor

Moataz A. Fattah is an assistant professor of political science at Cairo University in Egypt and Central Michigan University. He is currently a visiting scholar at the American University in Cairo, the research manager of the Program for Dialogue of Civilizations at Cairo University, and senior consultant to the director of the Arab League's Arab Women's Organization. He has published extensively on Middle Eastern politics, including the books *Democratic Values in the Muslim World* and *The Economic Function of the State in the Middle East.*